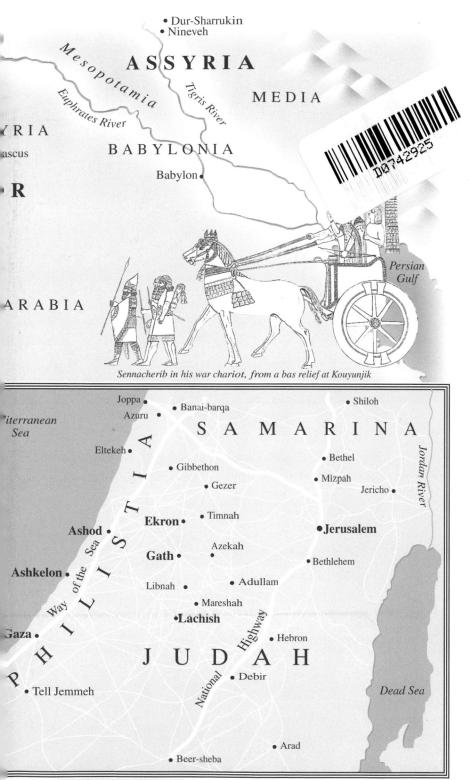

Dur-Sharrukin
Nineveh

ASSYRIA

Mesopotamia

MEDIA

Tigris River

Euphrates River

BABYLONIA

YRIA
ascus

Babylon

R

ARABIA

Persian Gulf

Sennacherib in his war chariot, from a bas relief at Kouyunjik

Joppa
Azuru
Banai-barqa
Shiloh

iterranean Sea

S A M A R I N A

Eltekeh

Bethel

Jordan River

Gibbethon

Mizpah

Gezer

Jericho

Timnah

Ekron

Ashod

Jerusalem

Azekah

Gath

Bethlehem

Ashkelon

Libnah

Adullam

Mareshah

Lachish

Way of the Sea

Gaza

Hebron

P H I L I S T I A

J U D A H

Debir

National Highway

Dead Sea

Tell Jemmeh

Arad

Beer-sheba

THE RESCUE OF JERUSALEM

HENRY TROCMÉ AUBIN

THE
RESCUE
of
JERUSALEM

THE ALLIANCE BETWEEN
HEBREWS AND AFRICANS IN 701 BC

DOUBLEDAY CANADA

Doubleday Canada and colophon are trademarks.

National Library of Canada Cataloguing in Publication Data
Aubin, Henry T., 1942-
    The rescue of Jerusalem : the alliance between Hebrews and Africans in 701 BC

Includes bibliographical references and index.
ISBN 0-385-65912-1

1. Jerusalem—History—Siege, 701 B.C. 2. Egypt—History—To 332 B.C.
3. Nubia—History. 4. Assyria—History. 5. Middle East—History—To 622.
6. Bible. O.T. History of Biblical events. I. Title.

DS62.23.A93 2002a   933'.03   C2001-904056-3

Jacket image: Jürgen LIEPE/ ©IMA
Jacket design: CS Richardson
Printed and bound in the USA

Published in Canada by
Doubleday Canada, a division of
Random House of Canada Limited

Visit Random House of Canada Limited's website:
www.randomhouse.ca

10   9   8   7   6   5   4   3   2   1

To the memory of my uncle
DANIEL TROCMÉ
1912–1944

Arrested by the Gestapo in Le Chambon-sur-Lignon, France,
he died at the Maidanek concentration camp in Poland.
He is honored at the Yad Vashem Holocaust Memorial
in Jerusalem as a "righteous gentile."

And to
PENNY
joy of my life,
without whom this book would not exist.

and
NICOLAS, NISHI, RAPHAËLLE and SETH,
for whose generation, and the next,
it's meant.

CONTENTS

ACKNOWLEDGMENTS

IT'S BECAUSE OF happenstance that, long after leaving university, I became interested in ancient history. When I had children in Sunday school in the mid-1980s, Julie Dawson, an active member of St. Andrew's-Dominion-Douglas United Church, Montreal, tried to recruit me to become a teacher. She chuckled at my excuse that I knew nothing about biblical stories, said it would be fun to discover them and, by amiably dragooning me, exposed me to the intellectual challenge of the "great code," as Northrop Frye called the Old Testament. That opened the door for me to the ancient world in general. I'm grateful to the persistent Ms. Dawson.

During the years of preparing this book, greatly appreciated encouragement has come from numerous friends and kin, including Catherine Aubin, Janet Cheasley, Steve Cheasley, William Edgar, Josey Grossman Fisher, David McLauchlin, Antoine Maloney, Geneviève Martin-Trocmé, Edmund Sears Morgan, Marie Morgan and Robin Palin. I thank them all. For his wizardry in averting a computer disaster, I am indebted to Jean-Claude Lachapelle. Newspaper colleagues have been generous with their talent—Justin Stahlman in devising the map, Jeff Heinrich in translating a German text and Rob Ramsey, Andrea Shepherd and Tim Simpson with computer know-how. I am also thankful for help from McGill University library staff including Maria De Souza,

Elizabeth Dunkley, Klaus Fiedler, Elizabeth Gibson, Marc Richard, Janice Simpkins, and Francisco Uribe. At the Jewish Public Library in Montreal, librarian Ronald Finegold also provided superb help. I owe much to the kindness of academic specialists. Donna Runnalls and Barry Levy, past and present deans of McGill's Faculty of Religious Studies, looked at an embryonic draft of the book in 1993 and assured me that the subject was worth pursuing. Sheila McDonough, professor emeritus of religion at Concordia University, read an intermediate draft and made splendid suggestions. Professor Eugene Orenstein, a specialist at McGill on the Zionist movement, kindly reviewed Chapter 20.

I am particularly grateful to three scholars whose works were among the most astute and insightful encountered during my research. Despite not knowing who I was, and despite my lack of academic credentials, Ronald E. Clements, William H. McNeill and Bruce G. Trigger each showed extraordinary generosity of spirit in reading my manuscript in its entirety and offered useful suggestions and encouragement. Any errors in the book are, of course, my own doing.

In the publishing world, certain individuals have provided the manuscript with the caring professionalism that I thought only existed in authors' fantasies. For the dedication of my literary agent, Beverley Slopen, for the belief in the book shown by publisher and editor Juri Jurjevics and associate publisher Laura M. C. Hruska at Soho, and for the meticulous care of editor Meg Taylor at Doubleday Canada, I am profoundly thankful.

This book has been a real *projet de famille*. In addition to providing the inspiration for it, our children—Nick, Nishi, Raphaëlle and Seth—have been an ongoing source of strong support. To my wife, Penelope, my gratitude is boundless. She, too, has become fascinated with Kushite civilization, and in doing separate research on its linguistic aspects. She has pointed me to many pertinent books, helped me with various texts in Egyptian, Hebrew and Greek and acted as a sounding board and tireless editor. We have spent hundreds of pleasant weekends sharing the dining-room table, with sleeping cats establishing the boundary between our respective stacks of papers and index cards. A more companionable sort of research is hard to imagine.

BC

734 Assyria (under Tiglath-pileser III) invades Philistia and advances as far as the Egyptian border.

c. 734 Israel and Syria fail in their attempt to conquer Judah.

733-2 Assyria (under Tiglath-pileser) campaigns in Philistia and appoints an Arab tribe as guardian of the Egyptian border area. It also conquers Damascus and Israel.

c. 728 Kush (under Piye) conquers Lower Egypt, then withdraws.

726-5 Israel (under Hoshea) rebels against Assyria and appeals in vain to "So, king of Egypt" for military aid.

723-2 Assyria (under Shalmaneser V) conquers Israel's capital, Samaria.

720 Assyria (under Sargon II) destroys what remains of Israel and starts deporting its leadership class. Assyria also advances to Gaza and to the border of Egypt.

716   Assyria (under Sargon) campaigns at least as far as the
        Egyptian border and possibly into Egypt's territory.

712   Assyria (under Sargon) crushes rebellion by the Philis-
        tine city of Ashdod.

c. 712 Kush (under Shabako) reconquers all of Egypt.

701   **Assyria (under Sennacherib) invades rebellious
        Phoenicia, Philistia and Judah. Kushite Egypt
        (probably under joint rule of pharaohs Shabako
        and Shebitku) confronts the Assyrians before they
        can seize Jerusalem.**

679   Assyria (under Esarhaddon) campaigns in Philistia and
        Judah for the first time in 22 years. It advances to
        Egypt's border.

677   Assyria (under Esarhaddon) again invades Philistia.

674   Assyria (under Esarhaddon) tries to invade Egypt and is
        defeated by Kushite- Egyptian forces under Taharqa.

671   Assyria (under Esarhaddon) invades Egypt, routs
        Taharqa without capturing him and deports his family to
        Nineveh.

667   Assyria (under Assurbanipal) responds to Taharqa's re-
        establishment of his rule over Egypt by invading the
        country. It conquers Thebes and drives Taharqa south.

664   Taharqa dies and is succeeded as pharaoh of the 25th
        Dynasty by his kinsman Tanwetamani. Meanwhile,
        Assyria establishes the rival 26th Dynasty.

663   Assyria (under Assurbanipal) pillages Thebes and drives the Kushites from Egypt permanently.

622   Scroll of Deuteronomy is said to be discovered in Jerusalem during reign of Josiah.

612   Fall of Nineveh. Assyrian Empire collapses several years later.

609   Egyptian army (under 26th Dynasty) defeats Judah in battle and kills Josiah.

597   Babylon (under Nebuchadrezzar) conquers Jerusalem.

586   Babylon (under Nebuchadrezzar) reconquers rebellious Jerusalem. It destroys the city and forces Judah's leadership classes into exile.

B ECAUSE THIS BOOK contests many experts' views on important historical events, and because I want to persuade these
scholarly skeptics, the presentation of supporting evidence meets
exacting research standards. For the purpose of streamlining, however, much of the elaboration appears in endnotes. Also, to be as
clear as possible for general readers, the book departs from scholarly stylistic conventions in several minor ways:

■ To avoid confusion, quotations employ uniform spellings. For
example, "Ramesses" appears as "Ramses," "Amun" as "Amon" and
"Cush" as "Kush." (When name variations involve more than trivial spelling differences, however, the variations remain intact, as
when a writer uses "Tirhakah" rather than "Taharqa.")

■ While many scholarly works rely primarily on a single translation of the Bible, this book will use many different biblical translations. When choosing a translation of a given biblical passage,
my criterion is clarity of expression. (On the few occasions in
which I select a translation because of its distinctive interpretation,
I will indicate that.) When no translation has a clear advantage, I
will use the New Revised Standard Version.

■ In giving dates, this book will use BC and AD. While BCE
and CE may have the advantage of being religiously neutral, BC
and AD are more widely understood.

■ The endnotes use a minimal number of abbreviations:

ANET	*Ancient Near Eastern Texts Relating to the Old Testament*
ARAB	*Ancient Records of Assyria and Babylon*
AT	American Translation
JPS	Jewish Publication Society (1985)
KJ	King James translation
NEB	New English Bible
NIV	New International Version
NRSV	New Revised Standard Version
RSV	Revised Standard Version
TEV	Today's English Version

■ To help readers get a rough idea of the background of the many experts cited, I will give brief descriptions of scholars when this information is readily available. Often this tag may amount to no more than a university affiliation. *This background is not intended to reflect a scholar's current status.* In very many cases these descriptions will be outdated: a scholar may have changed universities, retired or died.

I completed the book's main draft in mid-1997. Pending publication, I have monitored the flow of pertinent books and major journals and feel reasonably confident I have incorporated those research findings that are most significant.

Unless otherwise indicated, the translations of French-language articles and books will be my own.

I ORIGINALLY UNDERTOOK this research not as a historian but as a parent. My adopted son happens to be of African descent. In reading him the stories of Hercules, King Arthur, Charlemagne and Daniel Boone that I had loved as a child, and that his older brother had also greatly enjoyed, I saw that these did not resonate with him the same way. Stories that had implicitly affirmed the value of my own and my other son's background, which is white European, meant less to Nick. A subsequent search for tales of heroes from African history turned up disappointingly little material, either historical or legendary, to fire a nine-year-old's imagination. With my wife's encouragement, I looked at books on African history for adults to see if they contained raw material that could be adapted. That's how I came across some dry descriptions of a civilization I had barely heard of before, that of the Kushites, or Nubians, who lived in what is now northern Sudan and southernmost Egypt.

Their history gripped me immediately. In the late eighth century BC a king of Kush took control of all of Egypt, right up to the Mediterranean, and formed its 25th Dynasty. For two generations Kush was among the most powerful nations anywhere in the Mediterranean world. There is much debate today about the color of many of ancient Egypt's dynasties.[1] Of the total of 31 dynasties,

however, there is one which all historians—Afro-centric, Euro-
centric and straight-up scholars—agree was black, as that term
is commonly used in North America. That dynasty is the 25th.[2]
This was a rich period. From the few surviving records of this
kingdom emerges a monarch, Piye, whose chivalrous adventures
make him every bit the valorous equivalent of David, Arthur or
Charlemagne.

In this roundabout way I stumbled across an odd detail.

One of the history books made fleeting mention of a military
expedition that a Kushite pharaoh in 701 BC had dispatched to the
Near East. Its destination corresponds to today's Israel. Its aim: to
prevent an Assyrian conquest of Jerusalem. The pharaoh's enterprise
riveted me. Never had I heard of black-African forces in ancient
times journeying outside the continent. Also, never had I seen evidence that seemed to refute so strongly certain extremists' anti-
Semitic claim, which was then attracting considerable publicity, that
blacks and Hebrews had been adversaries throughout history. The
Kushites' long-distance attempt to save the Hebrew capital, Jerusalem, implied a strong alliance between these two peoples.

Curious, I went to the primary sources to learn more. With a
gentle tug at this loose end, an astonishing story with vast ramifications began to unravel.

This book is about that Kushite expedition's fate and unrecog-
nized impact on our world. Although no one could have foreseen
it at the time, the outcome of the African mission to Jerusalem set
off a series of events that have helped define religion in the West
and have determined the course of history. The Kushites' intervention enabled the fragile, war-torn Hebrew kingdom to survive
and nurse itself back to economic and demographic health, thereby
allowing the Hebrew religion, Yahwism, to evolve within the next
several centuries into Judaism. From Judaism's monotheistic trunk
grew, of course, the two great offshoots, Christianity and Islam.
Without the Kushites' role in 701 BC, then, the world would have
become inconceivably different.

The events at Jerusalem that year also go a long way toward
answering an intriguing question that, somehow, no one ever
seems to ask: How did the Holy City become holy in the first

place? That holiness predates Jesus and even Judaism. This book investigates the origins of this extraordinary religious status and sheds new light on the murky historical circumstances that set Jerusalem on course to be, thousands of years later, the world's tinderbox.

If what happened at Jerusalem in 701 BC was so pivotal in shaping history, why is it not already widely known? The question was so absorbing that I undertook a separate investigation to find the answer. In fact, until a little more than a century ago the story was common knowledge in the West. Up to that time many eminent Christian and Jewish scholars freely acknowledged the Kushites' role. How and why over the last century historians deprived this largely African army of due credit is part of the story. Although today's experts do not generally appear racist themselves, they have incautiously accepted the anti-African conclusions of colonial-era scholars—scholars whose writings are often quite explicitly racist. To demonstrate History's unprofessional treatment of Kushite civilization as an ongoing trend, I have documented many of the more recent examples.

The Kushites' audacious contestation of Assyrian power in 701 BC represents, I am convinced, one of history's more heroic exploits. In doing this research, I was stunned by the extent to which Western scholarship, consciously or not, has unjustly ignored a momentous African contribution to history. Setting the record straight requires confronting deeply entrenched skepticism. Like me, many people have been brought up with the idea that sub-Saharan Africa was incapable or disinclined to do the sort of things that in this case it plainly did. Only by discussing and supporting every point can I convince them—scholars and the general public alike.

TO UNDERSTAND THE Kushite expedition's objective, as well its effect on history, it is essential to gain a firm grasp of the state of Hebrew society in the late eighth century BC, particularly the period from about 720 to 701 BC. This was a time when Greek civilization was still at an awkward stage: the Athenian golden age of Pericles, the

Parthenon and the flowering of democracy were still three centuries away. The Persian empire under Cyrus would emerge only a century and a half later. And Rome at the time was but a village.

Naively, at the outset, I had assumed that the rudimentary background on ancient Hebrew society that I had learned at Sunday school would be useful. In fact, it's not. Popular conceptions can hinder an understanding of ancient Hebrew society's true political and social conditions.

University libraries devote entire shelves to books that deal with the period, the so-called "Era of the Hebrew Monarchy"— the time from the late eleventh century to the early sixth century BC (1020-586 BC). Yet scholars are now calling many if not most of those tomes' most basic assumptions into question, and the debate over these conditions is vigorous, sometimes acrimonious, all the more so because of many protagonists' religious sentiments. As Amélie Kuhrt, of University College London, puts it in her recent and masterful study of the period, "The powerful manner in which the historical experience of the Israelites has been structured in the Old Testament has imposed a framework from which it is hard for modern historians to free themselves."[3]

The spectrum of scholarly opinion roughly splits into three camps: the traditional, the conventional and the minimalist.

THE *TRADITIONAL* VIEW subscribes to the main outline of history as the Bible presents it. This view enjoys wide currency in popular culture: North American news magazines and Hollywood, through movies like *The Ten Commandments* and *Prince of Egypt*, tend to reflect the traditional view's premises. According to this perspective, Moses would have led the Hebrew people out of Egypt, where they had been held in servitude, and put them on the path to nationhood. Most traditional historians confidently date this epic journey to the 13th century BC.

Traditionalists include many non-fundamentalists who doubt that the waters of the Red Sea actually parted to let Moses and his followers pass and who also question whether these refugees wandered about the Sinai Peninsula for a full 40 years. But all traditionalists accept the main thrust of the Bible's account that, after an arduous but spiritually uplifting journey, Moses died within sight of the Promised Land, then known as Canaan. His followers would then have entered that territory, destroyed many cities (such as Jericho) held by indigenous Canaanites and taken possession of this land today known as Israel.

Traditionalists also accept that 12 Hebrew tribes—often disputatious—settled the land. Towards 1020 BC, Saul would have become the first Hebrew king. In *c.* 1000 BC, his successor, David, would have forged the 12 tribes into a single nation, Israel; after conquering Jerusalem, one of the last Canaanite strongholds, he would have made it his capital. Under David's son and successor, Solomon, the Hebrew state would have grown into a gloriously sophisticated and wealthy center of an empire stretching from as far as the eastern Sinai to what is now central Syria. David and Solomon's reigns are known as the period of the United Monarchy; it shines as Hebrew history's great golden age.

The Bible says that after Solomon's death, an internal power struggle caused the kingdom to split in two. In this new period of the Divided Monarchy, ten of the 12 tribes remained together to form a northern kingdom which retained the name "Israel" and whose capital was Samaria; the other two tribes made up the more modest kingdom of Judah, whose capital was Jerusalem.

Although the people of the two kingdoms were "kin," or "fellow countrymen," in the Bible's words,[4] they often sought to weaken each other and sometimes even went to war. For example, the Bible says that during the reign of Israel's King Jehoash (798-782 BC) the northern kingdom invaded Judah, tore down much of Jerusalem's wall and plundered the city.[5]

Yet the Bible suggests that Judah was more solid than Israel in one crucial way: political stability. Between the death of Solomon and the late eighth century BC, it describes members of no fewer than seven different families[6] as succeeding each other on Israel's throne in a train of intrigue and assassination. Meanwhile the smaller kingdom was a model of stability, gliding along under a single dynasty—that which David had founded. King Hezekiah would have been the Davidic line's 14th ruler.

CONVENTIONAL, OR STANDARD, historians form the mainstream of biblical scholarship. Because these historians are so numerous, readers may assume that, unless otherwise noted, experts to whom this book refers fit into this conventional, or centrist, range of opinion.

These historians are more reliant than traditional scholars on archaeological evidence, and this has led them to question, for example, whether Moses' followers conquered Canaan by force. No physical vestiges have been found, they say, to suggest that any cities were destroyed in or around the appropriate time period of the 13th century BC.[7] Some believe, rather, that the Hebrews may have arrived in Canaan through peaceful infiltration; others say the Hebrews may themselves have been mostly indigenous Canaanites all along who achieved a distinct identity by means of social rebellion. Mark S. Smith, a specialist on the period who teaches at St. Joseph's University in Philadelphia and at the University of Pennsylvania, confidently states: "The record would suggest that the Israelite culture largely overlapped with, and derived from, Canaanite culture. In short, Israelite culture was largely Canaanite in nature."[8]

So far as the period of the monarchy goes, however, conventional historians tend to accept the basic framework of political history as the Bible presents it, although they bring more skepticism than do traditionalists to secondary aspects. They accept the idea of Solomon's empire, for example, but they shrink its size. They also doubt whether that ruler had the grandeur and wisdom that the Bible ascribes to him.

MINIMALIST HISTORIANS ARE still only a minority, but they have gained significant ground since the early 1990s. They consider much of the Bible's presentation of history, including the political side, to contain only a very minimum of solid fact. Their opinions are even more dependent on archaeological data than those of conventional historians.

Some minimalists contend that David and Solomon had no empire at all—not even a small one. Israel and Judah may have existed in ancient times, they say, but always as separate entities. Indeed, some of these historians go so far as to assert that in the 10th century BC both Israel and Judah were in such an elementary form of social and political evolution that they cannot rightly be called *states*. They would only have been *chiefdoms*.

David W. Jamieson-Drake, of Duke University, defines a "state" as a society that possesses a critical mass of upwards of 100,000 people, that includes a class of professional artisans, that carries on considerable trade with other regions and that establishes actual institutions rather than mere kinship as the "primary basis of social organization."[9] The northern kingdom of Israel would have been the first to possess the sedentary population necessary to reach such a point, says Thomas L. Thompson, of the University of Copenhagen. He places that evolutionary benchmark in the ninth century BC.[10] But Judah would have lagged well behind. Jamieson-Drake categorizes Judah as a "small state in the eighth-seventh centuries, but not before."[11]

Some minimalists even cast doubt on whether David ever lived, either as a king or a chief.[12] As Thompson and his colleague at the University of Copenhagen, Niels Peter Lemche, put it,

> there is no room for a historical United Monarchy, or for such kings as those presented in the biblical stories of Saul, David or Solomon. The early period in which the traditions have set their narratives is an imaginary world of long ago that never existed as such. In the real world of that time, for instance, only a few dozen villagers lived as farmers in all the Judaean highlands. Timber, grazing and steppe were all marginal possibilities. There could not have been a kingdom for any Saul or David to be a king of simply because there were not enough people.[13]

The Bible's version deserves to be challenged, say Lemche and Thompson, "not because the Bible is 'wrong,' but because the

Bible is not history, and only very recently has anyone ever wanted it to be." To try to construct ancient Hebrew society from the Bible, they argue, is as futile an exercise as trying to reconstruct early medieval England on the basis of King Arthur stories or feudal Germany from Wagner's *Siegfried*.[14] The reality of the people whom the Bible depicts as the Hebrews' great enemy has even come into question; for Herbert Niehr, of Germany's University of Tübingen, "'Canaan' is an ideological term coined by biblical writers in order to create an 'anti-people' in comparison to 'Israel.'"[15]

While the minimalist viewpoint denies that political unity between Israel and Judah ever existed, it does not rule out the possibility of a special affinity between the two. This would explain why in the Bible the Judahites see themselves included in the broad term "Israelites."[16]

THE THESIS THAT important bonds existed between Hebrew and Kushite monarchs depends on none of these three perspectives on Hebrew history. This thesis is perfectly adaptable to any one of these views.

My principal source is the Hebrew Bible, also known as the Old Testament. The weight I give it may make some readers wonder if my thesis itself relies on the same kind of factual ambiguity that characterizes the Bible's account of the Hebrews' arrival in the Promised Land and the reigns of such early monarchs as David and Solomon. The answer is no.

By good fortune, the mists of history dissipate sharply in the decades just before the forging of the Hebrew-Kushite alliance. The reason is this: for Hebrew affairs in the period prior to the mid-eighth century BC, biblical texts are almost the only accounts we have. Starting with the eighth century BC, however, contemporary records from other cultures have survived that mention Hebrew affairs. These texts, from Assyria and Greece, provide independent corroboration. For example, because the Bible and an Assyrian text of the late eighth century BC both speak of a Judahite monarch named Hezekiah, we know that this king is not simply mythic. Biblical, Assyrian and Greek texts all give different insights into the Hebrew-Kushite alliance that existed during this time.[17]

There is irony in this. Many biblical stories for which little if any verification exists have become renowned. Billions of people today have learned at least some of these factually uncertain stories as children. Yet the world has lost sight of the great Hebrew-Kushite alliance even though solid evidence abounds that it truly existed—and even though the evidence strongly suggests, as we will see, that the alliance produced a military feat that deserves recognition as one of world history's most influential events.

PART ONE

A People
On the Brink

[Assyria] established the most efficient military,

financial, and administrative system the world had

yet seen. The army was its heart. . . . The principal

business of the nation became war. . . . This was

the first truly military society in history.

R. Ernest Dupuy and Trevor N. Dupuy

The Encyclopedia of Military History

CHAPTER ONE

An Obscure Event
that Changed the World

IN THE SUMMER of 701 BC, in an out-of-the-way corner of the Near East, the inhabitants of a modest hilltop city feared for their lives. They knew that it was just hours before the invader arrived—not just any invader, but the Assyrian army, the mightiest fighting force their world had known. Defense against a siege was futile. Those whom the invader did not massacre, he would march into exile.

From the flat roofs of their homes, the people could peer northward over the fortifications. Behind the yellow limestone hills rose a column of smoke. They could guess that it came from the town of Ramah, seven miles away. Then another column ascended, this one from Anathoth, five miles distant. A stream of refugees advanced toward the city.

Suddenly, the people heard shouts and clatter from within their own walls—the anger of soldiers. From the city gate, knocking out of their way anyone who would stop them, poured many of the city's own troops. From the roofs, the people could see infantry running down the road southward. Close behind them came chariots; the senior officers aboard them lashed their steeds. Anyone who had thought the commanders would stop the deserters was disappointed. The charioteers barreled past the troops and out of sight, fleeing for their lives.

The Assyrians had left this capital city of 20,000, which they called Ursalimmu, for the very end of their rampage through the kingdom. In recent days, refugees from afar had reported on the invaders' easy advance. They had besieged and destroyed more than 40 of the kingdom's cities, towns and forts. With horror, the new arrivals could relate the fate of stout-walled Lachish, the city second in size after Ursalimmu. Despite a furious defense, it had fallen. Then, in full view of surviving citizens, the young Assyrian king had the city's leaders stripped naked, staked to the ground and skinned alive.

A resident of Ursalimmu left an eye-witness account of what he described as the approaching doomsday. The man, whose name was Yesha'yahu, did not blame the Assyrians for the kingdom's devastation. Rather, he reproached Ursalimmu's royal court and its landowning class. Yesha'yahu assailed this elite for oppressing the poor and letting bribery pervade the justice system. "Your princes" he said, "are . . . companions of thieves." In part because of the leaders' abuse of power, Yesha'yahu declared that the national deity—one of many locally-honored gods—felt the kingdom had betrayed him. This god, said Yesha'yahu, was now using the Assyrians as an instrument with which to punish this "people loaded with iniquity."

It is from Yesha'yahu that we know the route of the Assyrian advance. The third and last column of smoke came from barely a mile away, emanating from a village named Nob that lay just behind the ridge, two miles off.

The enemy poured over the ridge and into sight. "The fertile valleys were filled with chariots," describes Yesha'yahu with awe, "soldiers on horseback stood in front of the city's gates."

After the army made camp, according to another account, three Assyrian envoys strode up the hill to the city wall. Ursalimmu's king dispatched three of his officials to meet them. If Ursalimmu surrendered, the envoys declared, all the ordinary people would be deported and scattered among the empire's farflung provinces. Everyone knew what would happen if their king were to stand fast: they had only to think of Lachish. Yet Ursalimmu's king refused to capitulate.

The envoys quickly guessed that the beleaguered monarch was gambling on last-minute help from a foreign ally, Egypt. They mocked him for his naiveté, saying the pharaoh's army was unreliable and impotent. Ursalimmu would have a better chance of surviving, the envoys said sarcastically, if its king sent out his few remaining soldiers to meet the Assyrians on the battlefield. But such taunts failed to sway the king.

The enemy responded by commencing its siege. It surrounded the city with an earthwork, an imposing barrier of soil and rock. The Assyrian emperor would later haughtily write that this made Ursalimmu's king as vulnerable as a "bird in a cage."

To his fellow citizens, Yesha'yahu predicted "a day of tumult and trampling," of "battering down of walls and a cry for help to the mountains." The Assyrians, he said, would smash the city as easily as someone hurling a clay pot against a wall. Needing no convincing, the people could only await their fate.

▣

THE ASSAULT NEVER came.

Instead, the astounded people of Ursalimmu witnessed their enemy's sudden departure—before it had a chance even to place a ladder or a siege tower against the walls.

From their housetops, said Yesha'yahu, the people made the city "full of shoutings." Ursalimmu erupted into an uproarious time of "festivity, [of] killing oxen and slaughtering sheep, eating meat and drinking wine."

We know where the invaders went. They made their way back to their capital, Nineveh, located in present-day Iraq. But the reason for the Assyrian evacuation is one of history's great puzzles. The withdrawal is not a minor anecdote of history. More than any other event, Ursalimmu's survival that day has led to its eventual status as Western civilization's most sacred city.

The inhabitants of the city did not call it Ursalimmu. They pronounced it Yerushalayim. The name in English is Jerusalem.

▣

FOR HEBREWS AT the time of the Assyrian invasion, the aura of great holiness that now envelops Jerusalem simply did not exist. More than two centuries would have passed since the days when the Bible says that King David and his son King Solomon had made Jerusalem the urbane seat of a glorious realm. At the time of the invasion that grandeur, if it had ever existed, had dissolved. In 701, Jerusalem was little more than the dusty capital of a rustic kingdom. Some historians say that at this time most Hebrews would have seen the city as no more religiously special than several other localities in their territory.[1] Indeed, as the Assyrians were approaching, Yesha'yahu went so far as to suggest, scathingly, that the capital of this "godless" and "sinful" people resembled Sodom and Gomorrah. Only after the failed siege did the city's religious character take on important changes.

Three notable figures emerge from the invasion.

One is Yesha'yahu, that rueful social critic. He is best known today as Isaiah,[2] one of the foremost prophets of the Hebrew Bible/Old Testament.

Isaiah's commentaries are not the only biblical texts that depict the invasion; other later accounts take a different view of another figure, the leader of the kingdom that Isaiah saw as so wayward—Judah's King Hezekiah. It is these writings that have determined this monarch's elevated reputation in history. According to this view, the kingdom owed its survival to Hezekiah's faith in the national deity. To explain why he found divine favor, these later biblical accounts present him as the most righteous and worshipful monarch in Judah's entire four-century existence.[3]

The third historical personage is the Assyrian king, Sennacherib. Later in his lengthy career he would go on to achieve so many battlefield triumphs that, without even a hint of irony, he would call himself the "king of the universe."[4] The only military setback that we know of is the one he suffered at Jerusalem.

THE CITY'S SURVIVAL in 701 BC is often called the Deliverance. It is not just another of ancient history's sidelights but one of its pivotal events. This is for several reasons.

First, Jerusalem's rescue is responsible for the very survival of the Hebrew people and their culture. Had Jerusalem perished then, this society—small and fragile—would have disappeared. Because Judaism had not yet evolved, the destruction of Hebrew culture at that point would have meant that this faith could not have emerged several centuries later. As mentioned earlier, neither of Judaism's two principal offshoots, Christianity and Islam, could have arisen.

Secondly, the Deliverance not only gave Hebrew culture the time in which to develop a new and enduring concept of the god-head but it also helped shape that concept's actual content. Prior to Sennacherib's invasion, the Jerusalemites' god was a national deity with no special powers beyond the immediate region in which he was located. His name was Yahweh—or, in written Hebrew (which has no vowels), YHWH. (Some Christians use instead a variation that came into use in the Middle Ages, Jehovah.) Every small kingdom in the region had its own favored deity, and the grandeur of each of these gods was roughly commensurate with the might and prosperity of that god's people. Compared with the Assyrians' main deity, whose name was Ashur, Yahweh was weak.

The outcome of the crisis outside Jerusalem's walls revolution-ized all this. While Assyria's defeat of several nearby coastal king-doms earlier in that same campaign would have demonstrated to Jerusalemites that Ashur was mightier than those states' gods, when Assyria failed to take Jerusalem this meant that Yahweh had bested Ashur and possessed more power than he and those other kingdoms' gods. It would take several generations to develop this interpretation fully.[5]

Over the next several centuries, the Hebrews' evolving view of their national deity's essential character would alter much of humanity's theological landscape. Largely because of his success against Assyria's aggression, Yahweh's power was understood to be boundless and his dominion universal—so that there could be no room for any other gods at all. In the development of Western humanity's view of the godhead, the Deliverance marks a major step: it helped change the perception of Yahweh from a parochial to universal deity, from god to God.

A third effect of the Deliverance is its great influence in making Jerusalem sacred soil for each of the three great monotheisms. Later generations of Hebrews would see the city's survival as a miracle. In their eyes, that miracle served as incontestable and spectacular evidence that, despite his anger at its sins, Yahweh loved this city—his city.

As the University of London's Ronald Clements, a leading specialist on this period's theological currents, observes, it is in the Deliverance that one finds much of the origin of the enduring "Zion tradition"—the belief that Jerusalem is the city of God.[6] For Jews it is the holiest of all places: it was atop Mount Zion, the hill on which the city first grew, that the Bible says Solomon built the original Temple. Jews and Christians call this summit the Temple Mount; Muslims know it as Haram al-Sharif, or the Noble Sanctuary. For Christians, Jesus's aura confirms the city's uniquely exalted status: it was in Jerusalem that Jesus would spend his last days, die and rise again in glory, and there that he is to return on the Day of Judgment. For Muslims, the city is one of the three most holy places: it is from Haram al-Sharif, now the home of the glittering shrine of the Dome of the Rock, that Muhammad would ascend the ladder to Allah's throne.

Finally, some experts believe that the rescue of Jerusalem in the face of almost impossible odds contributed significantly to the Hebrews' self-identity. One such expert is Bernard J. Bamberger, a Liberal Reform rabbi and a former president of the Synagogue Council of America. In his 1957 book, *The Story of Judaism*, he says that "the effects of this unexpected and miraculous deliverance upon the mind of the people of Judah [*i.e.*, the Hebrews] were enormous. A sense of national greatness, a conviction of high destiny was born."[7]

Given this belief in Jerusalem as God's city, then, we can appreciate a decision made several centuries after the siege by those anonymous ancients who edited and added new material to texts that were to become part of the Hebrew Bible. Because it was via Jerusalem's survival of that siege that Yahweh revealed the city's importance to him, they gave the story of that experience an extraordinary prominence: they presented the story not only in the Book of Second Kings but also in two other books of scripture. This makes the Deliverance one of the most emphasized events of the entire Hebrew Bible.[8] It is not unheard of for an event to receive more than one telling in the Hebrew Bible; Moses' acquisition of the Ten Commandments, for example, is told twice.[9] But three extended narratives devoted to the same event is unique.

Repetition is not a strict measure of importance, of course. For the Bible's original editors, no event was more important than the Exodus—Moses' liberation of the Hebrew people from both servitude and worship of pagan gods in Egypt. Nonetheless, in terms of theological significance, the Deliverance did *approach* the Exodus. Cecil Roth, an authority on Jewish history and editor-in-chief from 1966 to 1970 of *Encyclopaedia Judaica*, says this about the Hebrews' response to Assyria's withdrawal in subsequent centuries: "Later generations could ascribe this deliverance to nothing less than a supernatural intervention, *second only* to that which had secured the freedom of the Israelites from the Egyptian captivity" [emphasis added].[10]

If people today have never heard of this story, however, they should not be in the least embarrassed. Curiously, in modern times it has lost its prominence. Many respected books on ancient history or biblical history gloss over the failed siege in a few rapid sentences, if they even mention it at all. Karen Armstrong's 1996 best-selling history of Jerusalem, for example, devotes only one of its more than 400 pages to the crisis.[11] Still, that's better than Andrew Sinclair's 1995 book, *Jerusalem*, which—though the publisher promises the complete history of the "Struggle for the Holy City"—overlooks it entirely. So does Rabbi Joseph Telushkin in a 1997 book with the sweeping title *Biblical Literacy: The Most Important People, Events, and Ideas in the Hebrew Bible*. While the scholarly press *does* churn out a constant and voluminous flow of articles and books touching on the crisis of 701 BC, these tend to deal with secondary aspects—for example, which of the three biblical accounts of the siege is the oldest, whether Hezekiah was as keen on religious reform as the Bible says and what the latest archaeological digs show about Jerusalem's fortifications at the time. The modern scholars whom I have quoted—Clements, Bamberger and Roth—are unusual in that they are among the few who have paused to consider the larger historical ramifications of the events of 701 BC.[12] Most of their peers do not dispute these implications so much as ignore them.

Yet only one or two centuries ago, the Deliverance was among the better known stories in the Hebrew Bible. In 1815, for example, when Lord Byron wrote about the crisis in a popular poem, "The Destruction of Sennacherib," he did not have to bother explaining who Sennacherib was, nor did he even have to mention Jerusalem explicitly.

Why is the story so little known today, even within circles that are relatively familiar with biblical history? One reason may be that the story ends on a note that is, for modern audiences in particular, quite disappointing. The Book of Second Kings depicts the siege's tension-filled early stages in a fairly factual and straightforward manner, yet in describing the story's climax, the Assyrian withdrawal, the text's tone abruptly changes. It ascribes the city's salvation to a cause that is wholly supernatural.

The Assyrians were on the point of conquering the city, says the Bible, when one night

> the angel of the Lord went out and put to death 185,000 men in the Assyrian camp. When the people got up the next morning—there were all the dead bodies! So Sennacherib king of Assyria broke camp and withdrew. He returned to Nineveh and stayed there.[13]

In other words, what saved Jerusalem was divine intervention. For non-fundamentalists, this *deus ex machina* ending is hard to accept.

Even if we were to give credence to a supernatural conclusion to a story that is essentially historical, as distinct from mythical or fictitious, it is unsatisfying to have no idea of how the angel destroyed the enemy. The angel arrives and, poof, the enemy perishes. In the story of the Exodus, the same special angel—"the

angel of the Lord"—accompanies Moses and his Hebrew followers as they flee from servitude in Egypt. But, in terms of storytelling, the Exodus story is as thrilling as the Deliverance's climax
is flat. The Exodus narrative allows us to visualize every element
of the successful flight, including of course the wonderfully vivid
crossing of the Red Sea.[14]

The common assumption is that in the Deliverance story the
angel stands in the place of some factual cause—that the role of the
angel obscures the real circumstances of this great event.

One of the more common theories is that an epidemic leveled
Sennacherib's army. Neither that theory nor any other, however,
has rallied a consensus. No one in the last century has focused on
the question in any depth: the most attention the mystery ever gets
is a few pages, and even that is exceptional. In academic circles,
there is widespread resignation that a cogent solution will never be
found. As Robert R. Wilson, professor of the Old Testament at
Yale, recently put it, "In spite of many ingenious attempts from
antiquity to the present day, there is no good way to rationalize the
miraculous salvation of Jerusalem."[15]

This book represents a fresh attempt. It will focus on an agent
to which modern scholarship has given little attention: the foreign
army on which Hezekiah pinned his hopes. It may not have been
so impotent as the Assyrians wanted him to think.

FROM ANCIENT RECORDS, the following incomplete story
emerges:

In 701 BC, Egypt's pharaoh sent his army on a foreign mission.
Marching eastward, the soldiers crossed the Sinai's rocky, sun-
scorched desert, then entered the territory that today corresponds to Israel.

Some of the pharaoh's troops were native to Egypt itself, but
most were dark-skinned soldiers from Kush. The pharaoh, who
remained in Egypt after dispatching the army, was himself a
Kushite, a member of Egypt's 25th Dynasty.

The expedition consisted of archers and other infantry, cavalry

and the elite of the military class, charioteers.[16] Their mission
was to confront the Assyrian army.

We know that the pharaoh's army marched northward past
Gaza and encountered the Assyrians on the plain at a place called
Eltekeh, southeast of what is now called Tel Aviv. At the time,
this would have been Philistine territory.

We also know that Sennacherib claimed to have won this battle decisively.

Finally, we know that the Assyrians then climbed into the
hills behind the coast and conquered almost everything until
only one significant site remained untaken: Jerusalem.

But it is precisely at this point—specifically, between the time
of the delivery of the Assyrian terms of surrender and the time
of the angel-caused withdrawal—that the facts become murky.
We have three different sources—ancient texts. None of them is
clear.

Of these sources, the one that sheds the most light is the
Bible. It says that the Assyrians were threatening to destroy
Jerusalem when suddenly Sennacherib received a report that a
Kushite-led army was advancing.[17] It seems likely that this would
have been a second expeditionary force that the pharaoh had
mustered after sending off the one that fought at Eltekeh. A
month or more may have separated the arrival in Israel of these
two stages of the pharaoh's campaign, possibly because this second army would have had to travel all the way from Kush.[18]

The Bible adds one intriguing detail. It says that the commander of this advancing army was a certain "Tirhakah." This is
a variation of the name Taharqa, whose name occurs in Egyptian records. From independent sources, we know that Taharqa
was then a Kushite prince,[19] a younger brother of the pharaoh.
Some historians believe Taharqa would have been commander in
title only and have left much of the work to more experienced
generals, because at the time he would probably have been about
20 or 21 years old.[20]

Unfortunately, that is all the Bible says about this new contingent from Egypt. It makes no mention of a battle or any other
kind of encounter between the Assyrians and Prince Taharqa's

force. Indeed, the biblical text never alludes again to Kushite-Egyptian involvement. Taharqa's approaching army simply vanishes from history.

MOST SCHOLARS WOULD say that the disappearance of this Kushite-Egyptian army was well-deserved.

Early in the 20th century, one of the most celebrated of all archaeologists and historians on Egypt, the American James Henry Breasted, deemed the Kushites to have been unreliable allies for the besieged Hebrews: "Sennacherib," he concluded, "disposed of Taharqa's army without difficulty. . . ."[21]

In a landmark book by William Y. Adams, of the University of Kentucky, Taharqa emerges as almost pathetic. It states that Taharqa, who eventually became pharaoh and ruled Egypt for 26 years, ranks as "one of the most unsuccessful military commanders in history."[22] Although it was published in 1977, Adams' book is still the most widely cited study to date of Kushite civilization.

Harsh judgments remain the norm. For example, in an assessment published in 1995, Kenneth Kitchen, a University of Liverpool expert known for his generally meticulous research in this period of Egyptian history, calls Taharqa's venture of 701 a flat-out "dire defeat."[23] Yet if you look more closely at all these and other scholars' harsh assessments, you will notice that these experts have more in common than negative conclusions: they offer no hard evidence on which to base their judgments.[24]

Something else is peculiar. Most scholars give little consideration to a radically different assessment by a Greek geographer and historian of the first century AD. That writer, Strabo, comments that Taharqa is undeservedly little known by his Greek contemporaries: he includes the Kushite in a list of seven ancient military leaders who, he says, headed important but under-publicized "expeditions . . . to lands far remote."[25] This places Taharqa in illustrious company: among the other figures on Strabo's list, for example, is the Persian Empire's founder, Cyrus the Great.

Who, then, is closer to the truth? Most modern historians who tend to see Taharqa as a military pushover? Or this ancient Greek historian who regards Taharqa as having compiled a military record that merits a permanent place in history?

CHAPTER TWO

Vulnerable Judah

For the Hebrews, the devastation that Assyria inflicted in 701 BC was no isolated ordeal. Four other times in the previous third of a century the imperial army had stormed into the territory of either Israel or Judah. Hebrew history over the millennia abounds with times of disaster, and among the most harrowing was this period of Assyrian hegemony.

The empire's reasons for wanting to bring Israel and Judah to heel had little to do with religion or ethnicity and everything to do with the happenstance of geography. The two kingdoms were located in what was at the time among the world's most intensely coveted regions—that end of the Fertile Crescent that abuts the eastern Mediterranean.

Assyria wanted control of this territory. Some of the world's most lucrative overland trade routes passed through Israel and its immediate coastal neighbors, Philistia and Phoenicia; Judah, stuck up in the highlands to the south, was less strategically located but was within easy striking distance of some of the most important routes. Three Philistine cities on the coast or near it—Gaza, Ashdod and Ashkelon—were the major outlets for the thriving trade with Arabia. Tyre, Sidon and Byblos, to the north, were the great ports of Phoenicia, the seafaring power whose ships fanned out across the entire Mediterranean. Possessing only meager natural resources, Assyria relied on international trade to sustain its economy. Hayim Tadmor, an expert on the empire, hypothesizes that Assyria's initial interest in the region was "largely motivated by the . . . aim of dominating the Mediterranean seaports and gaining control over their commerce."[1]

The region also served as a land bridge for armies marching between Mesopotamia and Egypt.[2] If Assyria was to invade the Nile Valley, its forces would have no choice but to pass through this general area, lying as it did between desert and sea.

Because this book will refer constantly to this region, the theater of war in 701, a precise name for it would be useful. The familiar names, however, don't fit: Canaan, for example, covers too small a territory and Middle East, Near East and Levant apply to too large an area. Let us, then, use the ancient Egyptian name for the region, *Khor*. As used here, Khor will include the western end of the Fertile Crescent, the territory encompassing the ancient kingdoms of Judah and Israel, Philistine lands, Phoenician lands, Syria and, for good measure, the less strategic area near the Dead Sea occupied by the minor kingdoms of Ammon, Moab and Edom. This territory corresponds roughly to the modern states of Israel, Palestine, western Jordan, Lebanon and western Syria.[3] It excludes the Sinai.

A generation before Sennacherib's invasion, the two Hebrew kingdoms were of unequal weight—economically, culturally and demographically. Israel was considerably more prosperous, encompassing as it did most of the best cropland. In educational and artistic matters, the northern kingdom was also the more advanced.[4] Conventional historians say that Israel, with its 10 tribes, could claim a population at that time of about 800,000 and that Judah, with two tribes, may have had 200,000 to 250,000 people.[5] A relatively rigorous estimate based on recent archaeological findings, however, suggests that Judah may have had a population of only about 120,000.[6] What is plain is that even by the most generous measure neither kingdom would have had a population base from which to draw an army capable of standing up to Assyria's.[7]

Of all the earlier hostilities between Hebrews and Assyrians, two in particular bore on the events of 701 BC. Because Assyrian records corroborate much of the biblical version, minimalist historians do not question this version's general reliability.

The first episode took place in c. 734 BC. The two kingdoms had never been close friends, and at this time Assyria's imperial ambitions in Khor had the effect of turning the adjoining states into combative enemies.

To resist Assyrian encroachment, Israel and Syria became allies and then tried to enlist Judah in their coalition. Judah's King Ahaz refused, and to demonstrate his loyalty to Assyria's King Tiglath-pileser III, he sent him a substantial tribute of gold and silver.[8] Israel and Syria then sought forcibly to replace Ahaz with a monarch who would rally Judah to the coalition.[9] In a conflict known as the Syro-Ephraimite war, Israel invaded Judah and besieged Jerusalem, where Ahaz was holding out. Ahaz defended the city successfully.

Judah's subservience to the empire paid off. In 733-732 BC the Assyrians stormed into Syria and Israel and conquered them, but they spared Ahaz's neutral kingdom (or chiefdom).

The invaders chopped Israel's territory into four parts: three of these segments became provinces of the Assyrian empire and the fourth endured as the semi-independent state of Samaria. This rump kingdom, whose capital was also called Samaria, may have measured a scant 45 miles or so in length and 35 miles in breadth,[10] making it about one-third the size of the former Israel. The Assyrian king personally chose an Israelite named Hoshea to be monarch of this tribute-paying mini-state.

Israel and Syria's struggle against Judah shows how the Assyrian threat generated intense political pressures within Hebrew society, deepening the divisions not only between Israel and Judah but within Judah itself. While perhaps the majority of Jerusalem's people, including Isaiah, may have supported Ahaz's dovish policy towards Assyria, a significant portion of Judah's overall population may have favored joining Israel's coalition.[11] A generation later, during the several years that immediately preceded 701, a similar split in public opinion—on whether to submit to or rebel against Assyria—would resurface in Judah.

The second and far more serious sequence of events occurred in the years immediately after the Assyrian king's death in 727. The heretofore docile Hoshea tried to distance Samaria from the great empire. Hoshea gambled that under a new king, Shalmaneser V, Assyria would no longer seek to keep this farflung domain intact.[12] Hoshea ceased paying tribute and sent messengers to Egypt to appeal for military support.[13] Hoshea's timing was poor: still recovering from a recent internal war, Egypt was in no position to venture abroad to confront mighty Assyria. Shalmaneser did invade the state of Samaria and, after subduing it, he imprisoned Hoshea. When rebellious elements continued to fester, the Assyrians encircled the capital, Samaria, and in *c.* 723 BC, after a siege of two or possibly three years, captured it.[14] In 720, after Shalmaneser's death and the return home of the siege forces, Samaria may have found other allies in the area and tried again to free itself.[15]

For vassal states that dared rebel, the empire reserved the ultimate penalty—annihilation of the state.[16] This would involve the wholesale deportation of members of the ruling and upper classes—priests, government officials, large landowners, soldiers, skilled tradesmen and other leadership groups. These would be forcibly sent with their families to distant parts of the empire. Replacing them would be conquered people from other regions. The empire would appoint an Assyrian governor. The strategy was to fill the formerly restive territory's leadership vacuum with disoriented foreigners preoccupied with making a fresh start in life—not with fomenting further trouble.

That is what now happened to Samaria. The new Assyrian king, Sargon II, quelled whatever coals of revolt remained and then applied the obliteration solution. He did so by deporting, by his own count, 27,290 inhabitants of the Samarian territory.[17] This uprooting would have started in 720 and continued to perhaps 715.[18] The Assyrians marched their captives off to remote exile in various corners of present-day northern Syria, Iraq and Iran. They were never heard from again. Together with the untold thousands of Israelites whom Tiglath-pileser had deported from other parts of Israel in *c.* 732, this mass disappearance gave rise to the legend of the "10 lost tribes of Israel." Conventional historians say that the "lost tribes" simply dissolved into the cultures of their new lands.[19]

The effect of the deportations that got underway in 720 BC was decisive. Samaria became a pliant Assyrian province called Samarina. Never again would what was left of the northern kingdom make even a soupçon of trouble for the empire.

The Israelite state's final years provide insights into the events of 701. Hoshea's search for foreign military assistance shows that as early as the 720's Hebrews had expectations of Egyptian help against Assyria. Even if it appears that the specific southern monarch to whom Hoshea appealed was not forthcoming, calls to Egypt for help would be made at least twice more in next quarter century. The very idea of Egyptian intervention is itself quite extraordinary. For one thing, Egypt had not been militarily involved in Khor in more than 200 years, when a pharaoh whom the Bible calls "Shishak" had raided Judah and Israel.[20] For another, the Bible customarily casts Egypt as the Hebrews' adversary. Yet, here in the late eighth century BC, Egypt suddenly surfaces as a friendly neighbor and prospective ally. So far as I am aware, no historians have called attention to this pattern of Hebrew reliance on Egypt, but it is very curious.

Hoshea's unsuccessful quest for military aid from the Nile Valley also helps explain later opposition within Judah toward Hezekiah's attempts to seek help from that source. The most notable critic was Isaiah. To rely on Egypt for help, the prophet would warn Judahites after the fall of Israel, was self-destructive folly.

In addition to these assaults on the northern kingdom, the Assyrians in *c.* 712 threatened Judah. The Philistine state of Ashdod had urged Judah, its fellow vassal, to join its revolt against the empire. The imminent prospect of an Assyrian invasion in the end induced Judah to back off and remain loyal to Sargon. Having cowed the kingdom without having to resort to force, Sargon calls himself Judah's "subduer."[21]

Ashdod did not escape Assyria's wrath. Archaeological evidence at the site shows traces of massive destruction. This was one of at least three separate military campaigns to Khor that did not include Hebrew territory in their itineraries. One can say, then, that the invasion of 701 marked the eighth Assyrian onslaught on

Khor within the lifetime of adult Jerusalemites. All of these offensives, including the last one as it rolled relentlessly through Phoenicia, Philistia and most of Judah prior to arriving at the walls of Jerusalem, had wreaked a degree of terror and destruction that was exceptional even for those brutal times. We easily understand, then, the flight of many of Jerusalem's defenders and the profound despair of those people who remained within its walls.

From the experience of these other states of Khor, we can conclude what would have happened to Hebrew society if the Assyrians had conquered Jerusalem.

Judah was the only surviving part of Hebrew society that was still viable,[22] and Jerusalem was Judah's last remaining city. The Assyrian besiegers had explicitly announced their intention to deport the vanquished Judahites en masse to faraway lands,[23] and such action against the sibling kingdom of Israel had caused the disappearance of everything having to do with its people's national identity, religion and culture. It is not much of a jump to assume, then, that if Jerusalem had perished so would everything having to do with Hebrew identity.

This assumption is so logical that virtually every historian accepts it. It is an interpretation with a long and distinguished pedigree. One of most prominent traditionalist historians of the 19th century, Heinrich Graetz, reaches this conclusion in his landmark work, *The History of the Jews*.[24] As recently as 1998, another well-known specialist on the period, Mordechai Cogan of the Hebrew University, gave this unqualified testimonial to the importance of Sennacherib's withdrawal:

> Later generations, looking back on the attack on Judah . . . , viewed it as perhaps the most fateful event in that kingdom's three-hundred-year history to that point. Had Jerusalem fallen, Judah would have gone the way of the northern kingdom of Israel and especially its capital, Samaria—to exile and extinction.[25]

Historians have recently started to give respectability to an intellectual exercise they used to shy away from: the what-if game. This is an effort to assess the historical importance of an event by projecting what the effect on the world would have been if that event had had a different outcome—if, for example, a battle had turned out the other way. In 1998, *The Quarterly Journal of Military History* asked 37 historians to identify what they deemed to be the most important might-have-been in military annals. Not surprisingly, one of them named the Greek navy's famous upset victory over Persia at Salamis in 480 BC, while another cited England's surprise defeat of the Spanish Armada in 1588. But in its presentation of these great events, this respected journal gave the last word—and the implicit place of honor—to the nomination of Sennacherib's invasion.

The scholar who made this case is William H. McNeill, professor of history at the University of Chicago and author of *The Rise of the West*, a sweeping work that won the National Book Award for history. McNeill, who subscribed to the idea that an epidemic leveled Sennacherib's force, wrote:

> Had the Assyrian army remained healthy in 701, Jerusalem would probably have been captured and its people dispersed, as had happened to Samaria only 20 years before. Think of what that would mean! For without Judaism, both Christianity and Islam become inconceivable. And without these faiths, the world as we know it becomes unrecognizable: profoundly, utterly different.[26]

He concluded: "Surely, there is no greater might have-been-in all recorded history."

If one has reason to doubt the disease theory, such an assessment makes the search for the party responsible for Sennacherib's departure all the more intriguing. What is responsible for this watershed in the history of humanity?

CHAPTER THREE

Judah's Primitive Pre-Invasion Religion

IN A RECENT paper in the scholarly journal *Judaism*, Sara Japhet, the Yehezkel Kaufmann professor of the Bible at the Hebrew University, makes this penetrating observation:

> The deliverance of Jerusalem from the Assyrian threat in the days of Hezekiah, and the contrast between its survival and the destruction of the kingdom of Israel, may be seen as the seed which would grow and flourish in later generations into a *new theology of election* [emphasis added].[1]

"Election" is the belief that a deity has elected, or chosen, individuals or a collectivity as its own. It is the idea that enabled Hebrews to see themselves as the Chosen People. The Hebrew Bible does not smugly present this idea as an expression of divine favoritism. Rather, it shows it as including a dimension of responsibility—of having a sense of mission in the world. In the Hebrew Bible, Yahweh says that his people will serve as "a light to the nations—so that all the world may be saved."[2] As H.H. Rowley, professor of Hebrew language and literature at the University of Manchester in England, puts it, "That Israel was the Chosen People, and that she was chosen for service, is the clear teaching of the Old Testament as a whole."[3]

Election is one of the most influential ideas in religious history. Christianity and Islam have also adopted the concept. In the Christian tradition, Jesus' birth is the fulfillment of the history of the Chosen People.[4] Rowley comments: "Throughout the New Testament the term 'elect' is found many times for the Church, testifying to the belief that the Church was the elect of God. . . . Yet never is this election thought of as a rival to that of Israel, but as the continuation of that election, to which the Church had become heir."[5] This concept was particularly strong with 16th-century reformer John Calvin and with English and American Puritans. They saw themselves as the elect: God's choice of them had nothing to do with human worth and everything to do with God's mercy. The few members of the elect would be saved, but the majority of humanity would face eternal damnation. Among Muslims, some Sufis also have a comparable sense of election.

To use Japhet's imagery, Jerusalem's miraculous rescue was the "seed" that would transform the Hebrew identity. To appreciate the Deliverance's profound effect on the Judeo-Christian tradition, we need to understand the religious and intellectual soil into which it fell.

According to the traditional view of biblical history, Moses set in motion the idea of monotheism—the belief that there is only one deity. In the course of the journey that brought the Israelites from Egypt to the Promised Land, the prophet climbed Mount Sinai, where he received from Yahweh the Covenant. This, of course, is the great pact through which the Hebrews became the Chosen People: Yahweh instructed Moses to pass this message on to his followers: "[I]f you obey my voice and keep my covenant, you shall be my treasured possession out of all the peoples."[6] A crucial word here is "if." So long as the people are faithful to Yahweh, then he will treasure them so that they will know only prosperity and success; when they are disobedient, calamity will strike them. Three days later, Yahweh made clear what obedience entailed. He decreed the Ten Commandments[7] and many other laws.

In presenting the story of the Hebrew people, the Bible describes the ups and downs of Israel and Judah in a way that reflects their respect, or disrespect, for this pact: David and the young Solomon are both pious, and under them the Hebrew state accordingly attains greatness. When later in his reign Solomon slides into the worship of other gods, the kingdom's fortunes plunge. Because most subsequent monarchs of both Israel and Judah also stray from loyalty, Yahweh brings adversity to their people. When, two centuries after Solomon's time, Hezekiah arrives on the Judahite throne this decline ends abruptly. That is because, suggests the Bible, Hezekiah "held fast to the Lord; he did not depart from following him but kept the commandments that the Lord commanded Moses."[8] Well before Sennacherib's invasion, according to the Bible, the young king would have ordered the destruction of the places where his subjects worshipped other gods and allowed only one place of worship in his entire realm—that of Yahweh at Jerusalem. It is because of Hezekiah's prior loyalty to him that Yahweh protects Jerusalem from the Assyrians.

It goes almost without saying that this traditionalist view considers the faith of Moses, David and Hezekiah to have been monotheistic.[9] The Bible ascribes to David, the poet-warrior, the authorship of many of the psalms, including the famous 23rd Psalm that begins, "The Lord is my shepherd. . . ." These psalms are, of course, commonly used for monotheistic devotion. As well, the Bible says that David's son, King Solomon, had built the Temple—Jerusalem's first great place for worship of Yahweh—atop Jerusalem's hill, Zion.

Yet in approaching this period, it is better to set aside this familiar version of Judahite religion.

In recent decades, all but the most inflexibly traditionalist scholars have come to reject the idea that the faith would have been so developed by Hezekiah's reign. Even those conventional scholars who consider Moses and David to be authentic historical figures are part of this consensus. Most would say that Moses himself would not have been monotheistic. The first commandment does not say, "I am the one and only deity." Rather, its peculiar wording—"You shall have no other gods before me"—assumes that other gods exist.[10] Some scholars who believe David was a real king of the 10th century BC would acknowledge that he has no connection with the 23rd Psalm, that the psalm dates from well after the events of 701 BC.[11]

Far more agreement exists between the conventional and minimalist perspectives in regard to the religious currents of around 701 BC (and of the late eighth century BC generally) than to the several centuries that followed it. Politically weak as we have seen Judahite society to have been in the years immediately prior to the invasion, scholars of both schools would concur that the status of Yahweh as the one God would have been weaker still.

IF PIOUS YAHWISTS from Jerusalem several centuries after Sennacherib's invasion[12] could have travelled back in time and visited their city in the months leading up to that crisis, they would have found the local religion almost unrecognizable.

Many concepts and practices with which the visitors would have been familiar would not yet have emerged. They would have found, for example, no synagogues,[13] no observance of the Sabbath for the purpose of worship[14] and no circumcision.[15] The visitors would also have encountered little (possibly no) worship of Yahweh to the exclusion of other gods.

Most scholars now say that belief in a single universal deity would have crystallized only sometime during the Exile in the sixth century BC.[16] Some minimalist historians push the date further forward, saying it would have emerged gradually in the course of the fifth to second centuries BC.[17]

A specialist on the period, Morton Smith of Columbia University, sums up the prevailing view of Judah's religious climate of the eighth century BC this way: "[A]lthough the cult of Yahweh is the principal concern of the Old Testament, it may not have been the principal religious concern of the Israelites."[18] (Following common practice, he employs the term "Israelites" for the people of Israel and Judah alike.) Smith stresses that the "general attitude of the population" was to worship Yahweh in addition to other gods, notably those of the Canaanites and Philistines such as Baal and Asherah. Starting in the early ninth century BC, a movement may

have grown for the exclusive worship of Yahweh,[19] but this current—which Smith calls the "Yahweh-alone movement"—would
not have emerged from its minority status until long after the
events of 701 BC.[20] Because the movement acknowledged the existence of other deities (even if it only worshipped one), it was not
really monotheistic. For minimalists, this Yahweh-alone movement
would not have existed even as a minority faith for still some time.[21]

This distinction, however, is but a nuance. Whether a few
Judahites or none at all worshipped Yahweh as the sole deity, what
is clear is that the vast majority of Judahites in 701 would have
been polytheists.[22]

Indeed, compared to its neighbors in Khor, the Hebrew nation
in religion and culture was hardly very unusual. Smith suggests
that Judah in this period was "about as distinct an entity as 'Aus-
tria' is today" within Europe. Of the Hebrew nation, he says:

> [T]here was a nucleus of persons united by common interest, com-
> mon language, common traditions, common religious feeling (loy-
> alty to local shrines and to the national god), and such ethnic
> uniformity as can be produced by the amalgamation of many ele-
> ments, but on every side this nucleus blended into surrounding
> populations.[23]

Minimalists would emphatically agree.[24]

Monotheistic Hebrews from several centuries later would also
have been surprised at the *manner* in which the Judahites of 701
worshipped Yahweh.

In Jerusalem, the sacrifice of animals and grain would have
dominated the act of worship. The poor brought grain, and those
who could offered sheep, goats and bulls. Under Hezekiah, this
practice would have flourished. The quantity of beasts slaughtered
was seen as a measure of devotion.[25] People believed they could
earn the favor of Yahweh the same way they could win that of other
gods—by saying the right words in the holy places and presenting
the right gifts for sacrificial burning.[26] Isaiah was particularly
incensed by what he saw as a moral void among the governing
class, a depravity that was evident to him in the exploitative way

that class treated the poor. Micah, the only other biblical prophet preaching in Judah at this time, was just as severe in his criticism of the religious establishment, saying its "priests give direction in return for a bribe."[27] Yet Isaiah and Micah's insistence that religion demanded good works and righteousness in the adherent's heart was a strictly minority view.

If, chagrined by immoral behavior, the Yahwist visitors from later centuries invoked Moses' laws to reprove Judahites of Hezekiah's day, they would have probably received puzzled looks. While a figure called Moses may have been well known in Hebrew tradition in Hezekiah's time,[28] many reputable scholars believe it unlikely that "his" laws had yet revolutionized mainstream Hebrew thought.[29] The Ten Commandments in particular, they say, may date from no earlier than the seventh century BC.[30] Minimalists put the date later still.

Indeed, if the visitors sought to invoke the authority of some other sacred writings, they would have been hard-pressed to put their hands on any, either ancient or recent. No Bible existed at this time. Nor was there any other form of canon, or text believed to be the word of Yahweh.[31] Referring to the texts of Isaiah, among many others, Robert Pfeiffer, an Old Testament scholar at Harvard University, observes, "Some of these ancient writings are literary masterpieces, but none of their authors expected to have his book canonized as scripture. . . ."[32] In later centuries individuals whose identities are unknown edited the old, existing scrolls or composed new ones.[33]

Eventually, circumcision would be widely seen as a symbol of the Covenant.[34] But circumcision could not have carried this symbolic dimension during Hezekiah's reign for the simple reason that the Covenant (as we now know it) did not yet exist.

Contrary to widespread understanding, Moses's doctrine of the Covenant did not originate with a thirteenth-century BC figure named Moses. As Hanoch Reviv notes, Yahwism was only able "to add the instructive novelty of the Covenant" in the late seventh century BC.[35] Pfeiffer declares unequivocally that every mention in ancient scripture of Yahweh's Covenant with Israel is later than the late seventh century BC.[36]

We can understand, then, why the self-identity of Hebrews as God's Chosen People had not yet emerged by 701. Sheldon Blank, professor of the Bible at Hebrew Union College, in Cincinnati, points out that the writings of the original prophet Isaiah show that he "knew nothing of a chosen people."[37]

Some scholars, like Japhet, date the full emergence of this sense of election to the late seventh century, during the reign of Josiah prior to the Exile; others place it in the sixth century BC during the Exile, and still others—the minimalists—maintain that it would have come after that national ordeal.

It is in this fundamental matter of religious vocation that these visitors might have felt themselves to be most different from their ancestors in Hezekiah's time. The visitors would have been Jews, the people of Judah in 701 BC were not. The term "Jew" came into being to describe the followers of Judaism, and conventional historians think that Judaism only took form about a century and a half (the process was gradual) after Hezekiah's reign,[38] reaching a recognizable identity during the Exile with the emergence of monotheism. To minimalists, the date might have followed the Exile by three or even four centuries.[39]

SEVERAL CLOSELY RELATED developments, then, occurred in the several centuries after the Deliverance: the understanding of the Covenant, the sense of divine election and the belief in the primacy of Moses' law. To these we must add another building block in the development of western thought: the composition of the history of the ancient Hebrews from the time of Moses onward to the Exile. Six books of the Bible recount that history. They are the books of Joshua, Judges, First and Second Samuel and First and Second Kings. Their version of events shows how Yahweh controls history. All six reflect the just-desserts philosophy. That is, when the leaders of the Hebrew people turn their backs to Yahweh and his laws, disasters occur, and when they are loyal to him only good things happen. The failure of Sennacherib's invasion, for example, demonstrates that when Hebrew society, starting with its monarch, honors Yahweh, society and monarch alike are immune to misfortune.

To try to discover what really happened in 701 and to grasp its effect on later religious thinking, we have to understand how this philosophy of history influenced our principal biblical source for the Assyrian invasion. That source is the last of these six books, the Book of Second Kings.[40] The authors-editors of Second Kings transform the story of the Assyrian invasion from a grave political misadventure to a theological event of the first magnitude, from a close call to the Deliverance. Ronald Clements says that the invasion "forms a kind of high-point in the whole story of the monarchy" which spans the last four of those six books.[41]

Scholars call the six books the Deuteronomistic History. Their term for its viewpoint is Deuteronomic philosophy. These terms come from the Book of Deuteronomy, the biblical text that immediately precedes the six books of Deuteronomistic History, and that inspires all of them.

The Deuteronomistic History tells of the dramatic discovery of the Book of Deuteronomy.[42] In the eighteenth year of Josiah's reign—which would be 622 BC—workmen were repairing the Temple of Solomon, says Second Kings, when the high priest came across a scroll that apparently had been concealed inside the edifice. The scroll was ostensibly centuries old. Its text contained Moses' farewell speech to his followers just prior to his death. In it, Yahweh, speaking through Moses, describes the laws to which he wanted his followers to adhere. Among these are the Ten Commandments. The Bible presents these sacred imperatives in two places, here and in the Book of Exodus, but many scholars agree that this lesser-known Deuteronomy version is the older of the two. The Deuteronomistic History presents this fortuitous find as a turning point in Hebrew history: it says that Josiah, upon learning the content of the scroll, was so appalled at how his kingdom had departed from Moses' instructions that he at once purged his realm of paganism.[43] He put the kingdom back on the Yahwist path from which, according to the Bible, it had strayed after the end of Hezekiah's reign.

Conventional historians say the scroll was, in fact, written relatively soon before its "discovery" in 622. (Some suggest the core of the text dates from immediately prior to 622; others say it was written a few decades before, and still others speculate that thinkers in Israel might have composed it before that kingdom's collapse in 720.)

While conventional scholars recognize the theological coloration of these Deuteronomistic accounts of Hebrew history, they tend to accept much of the factual information that these texts contain. Minimalists are doubtful. Some of them suggest that King Josiah was no great religious reformer and that whatever innovations he did bring in would have been mostly administrative.[44] Although the Book of Second Kings extols Josiah for promoting the scroll's lofty ideals, a skeptical Philip Davies of the University of Sheffield, in England, dates the composition itself of the Book of Deuteronomy to the sixth or even the fifth century BC[45]—long after the lifetime of this supposed great royal patron. If this late origin is correct, it would further suggest the value of exercising caution when trying to reconstruct the events of 701 on the basis of the main biblical source, the Deuteronomistic History.[46]

⊡

ON THE EVE of the Assyrian crisis, then, Judah's religious soil had little to distinguish it from other nearby peoples'. The only surviving texts from contemporary intellectuals are the declarations of Isaiah and his fellow prophet Micah, who preached in the hill country near Lachish. Both men saw their society as squalid and richly meriting the devastation that Sennacherib was about to inflict upon it. When, despite the success with which the Assyrians had exterminated Israel in 720 and had overcome neighboring kingdoms in 701, Sennacherib failed completely at Jerusalem, one can appreciate why successive generations of amazed Judahites would ask themselves, "Why us?"

It is in this searching intellectual climate that the seed of chosenness would germinate.

CHAPTER FOUR

Three Adversaries: Leftist Preacher, Reckless King, Pitiless Emperor

O F THE IMPORTANT historical figures in the Hebrew Bible, Isaiah, who preached from at least 736 to 701,[1] is one of the most shadowy. His ideas and character are both difficult to understand.

Upon first venturing into the early section of the Book of Isaiah, readers may wonder at the prophet's outlandish traits. Witness his overwrought pessimism in predicting doom. Witness, too, his description of himself walking about Jerusalem "naked and barefoot" for three years,[2] an image that has inspired generations of New Yorker cartoonists to spoof modern would-be prophets as wild-eyed, underdressed folk wandering about with placards saying "Repent!" This was his way, Isaiah says, of warning against Judah's joining the anti-Assyrian rebellion of 713 that was led by the Philistine city of Ashdod. The prophet said he intended his nakedness to serve as a preview of how the Assyrians would strip the vanquished rebels of their clothing and march them off as prisoners of war.

Especially perplexing are some statements by Isaiah on Sennacherib's invasion that are glaringly contradictory. In the period leading up to the aggression, Isaiah had insisted that Yahweh would use Assyria as an instrument of his own anger to punish Judah for its faithlessness. Then, at the last minute, the prophet appears to change his mind, predicting that Jerusalem would emerge unscathed. In Isaiah 31, this change is particularly jarring; that text insists that Jerusalem's defenders "will all perish together," yet the very *next sentence* trumpets that Yahweh himself will help them and will "fight upon Mount Zion." Yahweh, the text goes on to say, "will protect and deliver" Zion, and the Assyrians "shall flee."[3] (Had Isaiah based his prediction of the Assyrian invasion's failure purely on political and military analysis, one might understand how changing circumstances could have made him reconsider his prediction; but this was not a political pundit's change of mind, this was a prophet's U-turn on a deeply-rooted religious conviction.) Nowhere does the Book of Isaiah offer an explanation for this dizzying reversal, and it is easy for readers to assume that the prophet was theologically flighty, perhaps even mentally erratic.

Anyone seeking to understand the historical or the religious content of the Book of Isaiah runs into two obstacles. The first is the problem of chronology. The prophet has much to say about three different crises involving Assyria. Unfortunately, the passages in question do not disclose explicitly to which of these crises they refer. The prophet's formal utterances, known as oracles, are usually at least a half dozen verses in length and often much more, and the ancient editors of the Bible have simply spliced these oracles together without regard for date or obvious logic. Thus an Assyria-related oracle that one scholar says is probably based on events in the months leading up to the siege of 701 BC may appear in the text just ahead of an oracle that the scholar says refers to Assyria's attack on Ashdod *c.* 713; as well, a passage that deals with events immediately after the lifting of the siege of 701 bobs up *before* either of the others.

There is, moreover, little unanimity on these identifications. Countering one scholar's confident insistence that a passage refers to Sennacherib's invasion will be another scholar's equally assured declaration that the oracle alludes to an earlier threat. Adding to readers' frustration is that many of these biblical experts give no adequate reasons for disagreeing with each other. (As a rule of thumb, I try to adopt the consensus position on questions of dating and authorship; when departing from that, I will explain why.)

The second obstacle is the matter of authenticity. The prophet Isaiah is clearly not the author of many passages in the Book of Isaiah. Almost all scholars agree that the Book of Isaiah is the work of several different authors living at different times (although overarching themes give their work coherence). Most of chapters 1-39 are generally attributed to "First Isaiah"—that is, the prophet of the eighth century BC, and the only one who is pertinent to this book. Chapters 40-55 belong to "Second Isaiah" (sometimes also called "Deutero-Isaiah," after the Greek word for second), who is commonly supposed to have lived during the Exile of the sixth century BC. Many scholars say that a "Third Isaiah" (or "Trito-Isaiah") composed Chapters 56-66; this section deals mostly with the post-Exilic period of the late sixth century. Within this triptych further divisions occur. Thus in First Isaiah, chapters 36-39, which deal with Hezekiah's reign, appear to be lifted almost holus-bolus from 2 Kings 18-20,[4] while the so-called "apocalyptic" section, consisting of chapters 24-27, may be the latest part of the entire book.[5] As well, the author of Second Isaiah is sometimes deemed to have composed chapter 35—an uplifting poem, full of religious hope—that has, for unknown reasons, found its way into the so-called First Isaiah segment.[6] One can appreciate why the University of London's Ronald Clements, whose Isaianic research is exceptionally penetrating, describes the Book of Isaiah in its entirety as "one of the most complex literary structures of the entire Old Testament."[7]

This is the simple part of the authenticity puzzle. What is hard is detecting which of the many *remaining* portions of Chapters 1-39 either belong to the "real" First Isaiah or were composed after his lifetime by the prophet's disciples or by later biblical "redactors," as the canon's editors are often called. Scholars agree that these later anonymous contributors tried to add to the original prophet's religious insights by updating them or amplifying them in ways they saw appropriate, but scholars often disagree in determining which verses are insertions.

The portion of the Book of Isaiah called First Isaiah is, in other words, a jumble of ambiguities. A curious person cannot even begin to understand it without referring to recondite books and articles in scholarly journals. And even when one does this, the experts' contradictory decipherments can still make for confusion.

Having gone through this exercise, my take on Isaiah is now very different from the slightly mad scourge whom I perceived in my first reading. Once one grasps the catastrophic reprisals that Assyria was capable of inflicting upon rebellious vassals, Isaiah's warnings of doom seem less shrilly alarmist than soberly realistic. As for his "naked" portrayal of POWs, Assyrian bas-reliefs un-earthed in the last 150 years show that indeed these invaders dis-robed captive soldiers to humilate them, and Isaiah's attempt to dramatize Judahite combatants' similar fate may have been an unabashed example of what today is known as street theater—an effort to make his message vivid and accessible to everyone, not just the royal court. (Isaiah's nakedness, some historians conjecture, not unreasonably, would not have been total.[8])

Here's another enigma about Isaiah: no one knows how his statements (as well as those of most other biblical prophets) came to be written down. The common premise is that prophets were not writers but preachers. Many scholars assume that the prophets' own disciples wrote down these utterances,[9] but how this process would have worked is unclear. Were the disciples scribbling down statements as they were delivered? Were they writing down the statements sometime after they were made, relying on memory? In those pre-bullhorn days, it may have been hard for a public speaker to be nuanced, and even if he were, the scribes may not have jot-ted down every word: they retained the essence. Whatever the process for transcribing Isaiah's thoughts, it was imprecise, and this is another reason for being wary of certain peculiar statements ascribed to him.

But how about the most important puzzle of all? What expla-nation can there possibly be for the prophet's apparent flip-flop on his predicted outcome of Assyria's descent upon Jerusalem? The answer, according to analyses by Clements and some other experts, is that the "real" Isaiah was always consistent. He *did* say Sen-nacherib would smash Judah and punish her for her people's faith-lessness; he appears *not* to have later changed his mind and said that the emperor's invasion would fail. Isaiah is widely assumed to have died shortly after the Assyrian retreat (at any rate, he left no oracles after the celebrations marking that event) and editors probably inserted the latter view posthumously, perhaps a century or more later.[10] The real Isaiah was wrong in predicting that Sennacherib would triumph at Jerusalem, and he was consistently wrong.[11] Although traditionalist scholars would disagree, his prophecies were far from infallible. (Isaiah was right, however, in predicting the devastation that the kingdom of Judah *as a whole* would suffer.)

The real Isaiah describes himself as married and as having two sons.[12] So far as his personal life goes, that is about all of which we can be certain. His social and occupational background, as well as the respect (or, in some quarters, lack of it) that he received in Jerusalem, can only be inferred from his pronouncements. From his remarks concerning Ahaz's reign, we gather that Isaiah at that time enjoyed some influence at the royal court; many historians assume that his access to the palace stemmed from his origins in the landowning nobility and from his early career, possibly as a government official. His rich use of language and metaphor also suggest a superior education. "No other figure of the Old Testament," says Clements, "shows so commanding a control of the use of irony and word-play."[13] In order to have attracted the following that he did, Isaiah could not have been as I first imagined him— an excited misanthropist, a wearying person. Rather, he would have had to possess charisma and a bearing that added weight to his articulate, uncompromising criticism of many of mainstream society's premises.

Despite his possibly patrician origins, Isaiah became the champion of the underdog. His morality was socially rooted. Yahweh requires his followers, he declared, to "stop doing evil and learn to do right. See that justice is done—help those who are oppressed, give orphans their rights and defend widows."[14] The message that Yahweh wanted people to live righteously, rather than simply go through the motions of ritualistic worship, including the offering of sacrifices, is perhaps the most enduring contribution of Isaiah and, as well, of Micah, Judah's other prophet of that period.[15] Micah says Yahweh wants people "to do justice and to love kindness, and to walk humbly with your God."[16] Twenty-seven centuries later, few Jewish, Christian or Muslim thinkers would be able improve on the simple and succinct expression of that ideal, which remains central to the three faiths.

As regards government policy, Isaiah believed that social justice—and not aggrandizement of territory or military prowess—should be Judah's chief priority. For him, Judah's failure to care for its disadvantaged members and to live righteously was what had caused Yahweh to use Assyria as an instrument of punishment. The 19th-century French historian Ernest Renan shrewdly asks:

> Does one not seem to be reading the words of a rabid socialist of our own day, declaiming against the army, making mock at patriotism, predicting with a kind of savage joy future disaster, and summing up his views much as follows: "Justice for the people, that is the true vengeance; reform society, and you will be victorious over your enemies; wherever the poor are victimized, wherever the rich enjoy privileges, there can be no country." Isaiah, it is fair to add, gives these dangerous truths a brilliancy which they have never possessed since.[17]

The Book of Isaiah's most celebrated line among modern advocates of peace and social justice is about how, in an ideal future, people will "beat their swords into plowshares."[18] In fact, a respectable body of experts believe the verse may not be authentic to the eighth-century prophet.[19] Yet those who cherish the high-minded line have this consolation: it is thoroughly consistent with his thinking in 701. For him, Hezekiah's struggle against Sennacherib was madness.

HEZEKIAH WAS A generation younger than Isaiah. Of his personal life, we know only a little. From his name, we see that he would have been raised as a Yahwist: in Hebrew, his name means "Yahweh has strengthened" or "Yahweh strengthens." He married a woman called Hephzibah. He had at least one son, Manasseh, and more than one daughter. As was normal for the monarchs of many countries in that day, he had concubines.[20] He continued to rule until his death some years after Sennacherib's retreat.

The Book of Second Kings presents Hezekiah as the ideal, unblemished monarch: "He trusted in the Lord God of Israel; so that there was no one like him among all the kings of Judah after him, or among those who were before him. For he held fast to the Lord; he did not depart from the commandments that the Lord commanded Moses."[21] As well, the Book of Second Chronicles extols Hezekiah's zeal in transforming Judah into a profoundly Yahwist society.[22] The Book of Isaiah, however, strikes a most discordant note. The passages that may be attributed to the original prophet are never so rash as to mention the king explicitly, but they nonetheless cast a consistently harsh light on his reign.[23] Isaiah castigates the ruling class as a whole: "Ah, you who make iniquitous decrees, who write oppressive statutes, to turn aside the needy from justice. . . ."[24] He calls the "rulers" of Jersualem "companions of thieves."[25] Micah's take on the power structure is also scathing. City officials and priests alike, he declares, make decisions on the basis of graft.[26] Going even further than Isaiah, he affirms that the "rulers" of Judah "hate good and love evil" and also "despise justice and distort all that is right." These rulers, he says, "build Zion with bloodshed, and Jerusalem with wickedness."[27] Hard words.

There are other reasons for supposing that Hezekiah was hardly an ideal leader. His assumption that Judah could break away from Assyria with impunity was a miscalculation whose consequences for the kingdom were nearly catastrophic. As well, in the face of the Assyrians he commanded little loyalty from his those around him. Many of Jerusalem's senior army leaders deserted him when Sennacherib first threatened Jerusalem.[28]

It is also worth noting that archaeological evidence suggests that those workers on a major pre-siege construction project regarded the king with something short of adulation. This astonishingly ambitious project is what is today called Hezekiah's Tunnel (or the Siloam Tunnel). This is a 1,750-foot long shaft hacked through Jerusalem's limestone base that, according to the conventional view among scholars,[29] served to deprive the Assyrian besiegers of water from a spring outside Jerusalem's walls by diverting that water to a reservoir within the walls. Pertinent is an inscription carved into the tunnel's wall by the diggers upon the completion of their labors. The six-line inscription details the workers' sense of triumph, but there is not a word of reference to the king. In a detailed study of this inscription, one scholar observes that the absence of the king's name is "rather extraordinary when the inscription is compared with commemorative royal inscriptions of a similar nature from elsewhere in the contemporary Near East."[30] Omission of any mention of the sponsor of so successfully audacious a project seems consistent with the lack of loyalty that the civic leaders evinced when they deserted their king.[31]

A final reason for doubting Hezekiah's leadership is that the Bible indicates that at some point during the Assyrian invasion, Hezekiah became "sick and almost died."[32] The text does not give us enough information to judge whether this illness was psychosomatic or an unfortunate coincidence. In either case, when his kingdom was on the brink of catastrophe, he appears—for good reason or bad—to have provided his people with something less than exemplary helmsmanship.

Hezekiah's arrival on Judah's throne came at roughly the same period as Israel's collapse in 720 BC, perhaps preceding it by several years. The year of accession is in dispute: a likely date is *c.* 727 BC, but it is possible that the new king came to power only several years after Israel's disintegration.[33]

That northern neighbor's downfall had several effects on Judah. While it eliminated an occasional invader, it also isolated Judah— no longer did it have a senior partner with which, for all the political strains between them, it shared a sense of kinship. And, of course, Israel's demise produced a flow of refugees to the southern kingdom.

Archaeological remains tell of Jerusalem's dramatic transformation during this period from a sleepy town into a bustling center. Before Israel's collapse, Jerusalem had a population of only 6,000-8,000 people.[34] By the time of the invasion of 701, it may have had two or three times that number. For lack of space inside the walls, many people had no choice but to build homes beyond them.

For Isaiah and Micah, the most important outcome of Israel's obliteration was the religious lesson that it held. Both prophets used the larger kingdom's downfall to bolster their message about the dangers of impiety. Yahweh, they preached, had punished Israel because of its evil ways. They warned that Judah was just a step behind Israel along this disastrous path and that, unless it changed its ways, Yahweh would also destroy the southern kingdom.

Composed after the dust had settled from the Assyrian strife, the Book of Second Kings develops this theme. Its back-to-back accounts of the invasions of Israel in 722-720 and Judah in 701 reflect the Deuteronomic view that sinners suffer but the pious prosper: Second Kings describes how, prior to the Assyrian onslaught, the people of Israel "built themselves high places," that is, hilltop altars for the worship of gods other than Yahweh. They also "set up pillars and sacred poles" of the fertility cult, "did evil things, angering YHWH" and "abandoned all the commands" of the deity, so that the god deployed Assyria to bring punitive ruination to their kingdom.[35] In describing Hezekiah only some 20 verses later, Second Kings employs the same elements to dramatize the differences in the two kingdoms' theological performances; this literary device might be called the contrasting parallel. The text says that Judah's monarch

> abolished the high places, and broke the sacred pillars, and cut down the pole of Asherah. . . . In YHWH God of Israel he put his trust; there was no one like him among all the kings of Judah following him, or among those before him. He was loyal to YHWH; he did not turn away from him, but kept the commands which YHWH had given Moses. And so YHWH was with him; in all that he undertook, he was successful [emphasis added].[36]

The Bible indicates that this religious reform would have taken place before, not after the invasion, so that the Deliverance was in response to it.[37]

Second Kings alludes to another aspect of the king's religious reform. It says that Hezekiah ordered the demolition of altars and shrines *to Yahweh* scattered around the kingdom—with the sole exception of Jerusalem's Temple. The king "told the people of Judah and Jerusalem to worship only at the altar in Jerusalem."[38] Elsewhere, the Bible presents Hezekiah's centralization of the Yahwist cult at the Temple, and his successful exhortation to all Judahites and people of the former territories of Israel to worship there, as one of his defining acts of greatness.[39] The measure gave Mount Zion unprecedented religious importance.

Most conventional historians accept the idea that Hezekiah carried out a religious reform that was significant but less thorough than the Bible presents it. If they are right in saying that at least *some* historical foundation exists for the Bible's assertions that Hezekiah centralized the worship of Yahweh at the Temple,[40] they are probably also right in suggesting that this would have carried unmistakable political ramifications. The Temple was within a few yards of the royal palace. Tadmor suggests confidently that Hezekiah's "elevation of the Temple as the sole legitimate place" could in part have been a "calculated move to consolidate his control over the cult and priesthood."[41] For Hezekiah, all this would have meant increased wealth. Carl D. Evans, of the University of South Carolina, says that the centralization of worship would have "had the effect of placing additional resources under the king's control, enhancing the royal treasury and providing the occasion for creating an administrative system to handle the increased contributions."[42]

Yet it is not easy to embrace the idea of Hezekiah's Yahwist-alone piety. For one thing, Isaiah makes no mention of it. For another, the Bible elsewhere makes a statement that is hard to square with the notion that Hezekiah was exclusively devoted to Yahweh. Shortly after hailing Hezekiah for tearing down pagan constructions, Second Kings tells us that it was King Josiah, Hezekiah's great-grandson, who dared take the decisive step of destroying those pagan altars that Solomon had built for his foreign wives.[43] If Hezekiah had crusaded against polytheism, it is astonishing that he could have missed these: the altars to foreign deities would have been located just outside the city's walls on the Mount of Olives,[44] within view of the royal palace.

Archaeology also raises questions about Hezekiah's religious reform. In an article published in 1995, Nadav Na'aman, of Tel Aviv University's department of Jewish history, says

> archaeological evidence shows that a cultic shrine in Lachish apparently remained intact until the town's conquest by Sennacherib. This is an indication of the non-reliability of the text [*i.e.*, 2 Kings 18:4,22], according to which Hezekiah removed the cult places from all the towns of Judah.[45]

Na'aman also sees an absence of "clear archaeological evidence for any cultic reform mentioned in the Bible" and concludes that the "execution of a wide-ranging reform by Hezekiah is doubtful."[46] Biblical writers of later generations, he suggests, credited Hezekiah with a sweeping religious reform as a means of explaining why Yahweh spared Jerusalem from sharing the same disastrous destiny as Israel.[47]

Even though the archaeological record is too spotty to demolish totally the notion of Hezekiah as a comprehensive religious reformer,[48] Na'aman's view is eminently plausible.

Still more doubtful than the idea of Hezekiah as a great ecclesiastical centralizer is the supposition that his so-called religious reform would have stressed good works. Isaiah and Micah alike excoriate the religious establishment for its emphasis on sacrifice and ritual[49] and bemoan its total inattention to righteous behavior. It is nonsense to contend, as do some historians, that Hezekiah was a social reformer.[50] Not even the most idealizing passages on Hezekiah in Second Kings or Second Chronicles make mention of *any* social reforms.

One thing that would certainly have improved under Hezekiah, however, is the level of Judahite society's dynamism. Israel had been, of course, the more prosperous and sophisticated of the Hebrew kingdoms, and while war would have impoverished many of its post-720 refugees to Judah, other emigrés would have brought considerable wealth with them. Property prices in Judah would have risen accordingly. During Hezekiah's reign, artists, writers and other talented Israelites among these refugees might well have contributed to an unusually high standard of culture.

This new spirit of confidence would also show itself in assertive nationalism. Under Ahaz, the state had been able to cap the widespread public sentiment favoring greater independence from Assyria. Now, under Hezekiah, that would change.

EARLY IN HIS reign, Hezekiah—like his father before him—treated Assyria with great deference.

Thus in 716 when the imperial army swept through Philistia as far as the Egyptian border, Sargon paid Judah no attention. The little kingdom was well-behaved.

In 713, however, when some of the nearby Philistines rebelled, Judah showed signs of restiveness. In that year, the leader of the coastal Philistine city of Ashdod, Iamani, formed a coalition of coastal states that rebelled against Assyrian rule. An inscription by Sargon tells of how Ashdod also looked inland for help, sending to Judah, Edom and Moab "numberless inflammatory and disdainful messages to set them at enmity with me" and join the revolt.[51] That Judah was tempted to join is clear from Isaiah's desperate and prolonged "nakedness" campaign to rally public opinion against the rebellion. As we saw earlier, however, Hezekiah in the end did not participate and Sargon spared Judah the lash. The empire quickly crushed the coastal rebellion, forcing Iamani to flee to Egypt. Again, the Assyrian army advanced as far as the Egyptian border.

Yet Hezekiah's dream of enlarging his kingdom did not abate. When his son was born in 710, it may be significant that the king named him Manasseh. The name of one of the more prominent northern tribes was also Manasseh, and one scholar plausibly suggests that for Hezekiah to name his son (and successor, as it turned out) after it, could have implied the hope of making political inroads among the people of that tribe's traditional territory.[52]

At roughly this time, perhaps a few years after his son's birth, Hezekiah employed military force to expand his territory. Second

Kings says of Hezekiah, "He rebelled against the king of Assyria and would not serve him. He attacked the Philistines as far as Gaza and its territory, from watchtower to fortified city."[53] Another source, an Assyrian document, indicates that among these seizures by Hezekiah was the large, fortified Philistine city of Gath,[54] best remembered today as the hometown of the David's foe, the biblical giant Goliath. Judah's annexation of the Gaza territory may not have reflected a policy of territorial aggrandizement for its own sake but, rather, a strategy of trying to neutralize bastions of Assyrian support within Khor.

Why did Hezekiah show such bold confidence and defy mighty Assyria?

In 705, the dreaded Sargon had died. His son Sennacherib, crowned the following year, was an unknown quantity. (After the death of the two previous Assyrian kings, Tiglath-pileser in 727 and Shalmaneser in 722, many territories under the imperial yoke—including Israel on both occasions—had similarly sensed weakness and rebelled. If the unsuccessful outcome of those revolts offered a cautionary lesson for Judah, it was ignored.) The circumstances of Sargon's death may help shed light on Hezekiah's motivation to rebel. The emperor was killed in a battle far from Assyria and his body never recovered. That the ancients often saw such an event as a dire omen for the deceased leader's side may have helped embolden Judah.[55] Another important factor in Judah's action was an abundance of allies, something that had not been the case in the earlier Ashdodite rebellion.

After Sargon's death, one militarily powerful ally may have been Babylonia. Its king, Merodach-baladan, may have sent diplomatic envoys to Jerusalem at about this time.[56] Many historians plausibly argue that Babylonia, Assyria's strongest enemy, was encouraging revolts at different points in the empire to overload Nineveh's military capabilities.

In addition, Judah found allies within Khor itself.

Two peoples lived along Khor's coast. To the south, in what is today western Israel, were the Philistines. The latest theory is that they came to Khor from the Aegean world in perhaps the thirteenth century BC. The Philistines quickly became acculturated and within several generations appear to have adopted much of the native Canaanites' language and religion.[57] Philistia never became a unified state; rather, it was organized on the basis of five distinct city-states, each with rural territory. Historians call the five-city league the Philistine "pentapolis." In the context of the crisis of 701, what is pertinent is that the Philistines had a tradition of military competence and that four out of the league's five members now became part of the anti-Assyrian coalition. Ekron and Ashkelon were willing partners, while Hezekiah's annexation of Gaza and Gath had brought those cities into the rebellion. Only the fifth, the freshly humbled Ashdod, remained submissive to Assyria.

The other people on Khor's coast were the Phoenicians, who lived in what is today, roughly speaking, Lebanon. Racially and culturally, they were Canaanites.[58] Their cities, like those of the Philistines, were not united. Phoenicia's principal cities enjoyed spectacular success in commerce, strategically located as they were where major trade routes from Mesopotamia, Egypt, Arabia and the Mediterranean converged. The rebellion offered the king of Tyre,[59] one of the principal city-states, the opportunity to shake himself free of Assyrian control. This king, named Luli, also controlled nearby Sidon, a second major Phoenician maritime center, and would have been a leading figure in the eastern Mediterranean world.

The Judahites were evidently torn between joining the coalition and steering clear of it. Renan, writing more than a century ago on the basis of clues from the Book of Isaiah, has laid out a vivid, plausible scenario for that political clash that no other scholar, to my knowledge, has either challenged or improved upon. He sees a polarization consisting of two informal groupings, or parties:

> In Jerusalem, the military and patriotic party urged that an opportunity which they regarded as excellent should not be lost for crushing the standing danger of the freedom of the East. This military party appears to have been almost indifferent to matters of religion; they were not, at all events, Yahwists of the reformed school. . . .; they were hard, perhaps unjust, towards the people, as aristocrats so often are.

In striking contrast to them, like white upon black, stood out the party of democratic theocracy and of religious puritanism, opposed to the lay state and to military precautions, being intent solely upon religious and social reforms.[60]

According to this hawk-dove scenario, the military party, rebuffed during Ahaz's reign, would likely have seen its numbers and influence soar with the arrival of refugees—including wealthy and patrician ones—from the northern kingdom, where a muscular stance towards Assyria had long prevailed. (A modern analogy might be the truculence of some Cuban emigrés who fled to southern Florida after Fidel Castro's communist takeover of their homeland in 1960; resentful of being dispossessed of their property, they sought to enlist the help of the country they had fled to, in this case the United States, to regain their homeland.) Israelite refugees may have found support in their host society since many wealthy Judahites would have rankled under the tribute that Assyria demanded of them.

Isaiah would have been close to the dove party, but not all doves would have agreed with his theological reasoning. For Isaiah, Judah's priority should be internal reform, namely the creation of a righteous society. If the kingdom could be so, Yahweh would bless it and keep it safe and prosperous. If Judah continued to do too little to reform itself internally, Yahweh's punishment—which the Assyrian juggernaut was prepared to inflict—would descend upon it. Some doves would doubtless have been against rebellion for largely pragmatic reasons: as Israel's experience had attested, provoking Assyria could be counterproductive to the extreme.

The anti-rebellion party also might have been concerned by Judah's complicity in an event that Nineveh would have seen as particularly outrageous. Assyria had earlier appointed a man named Padi as ruler of Ekron. In *c.* 702 BC, the people of that city deposed the puppet. Instead of executing him, however, they had him taken to Jerusalem for imprisonment.[61] The ruler who replaced Padi became one of the coalition's leaders. Padi's arrival in Jerusalem for incarceration must have further inflamed the debate.

What was Hezekiah's role in all this? The consensus among historians is that Hezekiah was the rebellion's leader.[62] Yet no one, to my knowledge, has presented supporting evidence. The idea of Hezekiah as ringleader reflects an inflated idea of Judah's standing in Khor; it appears to be one of those views that, repeated often enough, takes on a life of its own.[63]

To mount a credible case that Hezekiah was the leader, one would have to explain why King Luli of Tyre, in particular, was not.[64] Luli was the head of a major commercial centre whose farflung trade was evidently suffering from Assyria's interference. It is hard to imagine the worldly Phoenician city-states playing second fiddle to what they would have considered to be the rustic, relatively underdeveloped, militarily modest kingdom of Judah. It is safer to consider Judah to have been a fairly important member of the coalition, or at best possibly *a* leader, but almost certainly not the leader. This is also more in keeping with Hezekiah's lack of a commanding personality.

My assumption is that a vigorous hawk party, its strength augmented by immigrants from the former northern kingdom who had lost their property to Assyria, urged Judah to join breakaway movements in other vassal states. Hezekiah, weak monarch that he was, did not lead this current within his own country, much less in Khor as a whole. Rather, the current carried him.

THE COALITION'S JUDGMENT of their new Assyrian lord's character and abilities was grossly off the mark.

Before taking power, Sennacherib already had considerable military and administrative experience,[65] and he was able to get off to a strong start.

We have far more reliable information about Sennacherib's career than about Hezekiah's. Like all Assyrian kings, he described his reign in his annals, the monarch's yearly accounts of his principal achievements. The annals make it clear that, upon his coming to power in 704 BC, Sennacherib aimed to show that he would run the empire in his father's iron-fisted style, and then some. In his first military campaign, which took place in 703 and early 702, he defeated the combined forces of the Babylonians and their Elamite ally. He claimed to have conquered and looted "75 of his strong, walled cities, of Chaldea, and 420 small cities of their environs."[66] It is noteworthy that in this his maiden campaign Sennacherib applied his predecessors' policy of deporting recalcitrant inhabitants of conquered territories—and on a large scale.[67]

In his second campaign, which took place in 702 BC, Sennacherib appears to have hit cruising speed. He quelled the defiant Kassites, hunting them down in the rugged Zagros Mountains of present-day western Iran and, again, deporting many of the survivors and replacing them with settlers from elsewhere.[68] Were the restive vassals of Khor paying attention? Even if they were, their revolt had probably already passed the point of no return. By 702, Hezekiah's grab of territory held by loyal Assyrian vassals and the Ekronites' overthrow of Padi, Assyria's man, would likely already have taken place.

What kind of overlord was it that Judah and its allies were provoking? What was his character?

The annals are revealing.[69] They present Sennacherib as someone with, to put it mildly, an exalted sense of self. In addition to calling himself "king of the universe," his other favorite names included "perfect hero," "first among all princes," the "flame that consumes the insubmissive," he "who strikes the wicked with the thunderbolt" and "favorite of the great gods."[70] His flair for architecture reflects this self-image. A year after his withdrawal from Jerusalem, he started to build his new capital city, Nineveh, and strove to make it even more impressive than his father's capital, Dur-Sharrukin ("Sargonsburg"). Nineveh's centerpiece was the "Palace without Rival," a 70-room edifice that was the Versailles of the ancient world. With such features as human-headed stone bulls 18 feet high guarding doors, and with a throne room 55 yards in length, the scale and magnificence of the building was in part designed, as one expert puts it, to reinforce visiting foreign leaders' "inclination to submit."[71]

Despite his taste for luxury, Sennnacherib was no softie, no royal stay-at-home who let his generals earn his glory for him. The emperor accompanied his armies everywhere. In his 702 campaign against the Kassites, for example, he was forced to abandon the royal chariot and travel by horse. In those days, when saddles lacked stirrups and consisted of little more than padding, this required excellent riding skills, particularly on steep inclines. He writes: "In the midst of the high mountains I rode on horseback, where the terrain was difficult, and had my chariot drawn up on ropes [up the mountainsides]; where it became too steep, I clambered up on foot like the wild ox."[72]

In some campaigns, the land was far too rugged for chariots to be of any use at all. In such cases Sennacherib would use the sedan chair, a covered seat borne on poles by muscular men, the ancient counterpart of the general's Jeep. Here, several years after the 701 conflict, he gives this swaggering but poignant account of his campaign against hill tribes east of the Tigris River:

> I had my camp pitched at the foot of Mount Nipur and with my picked bodyguard and my relentless warriors, I, like a strong wild-ox, . . . led the way. Gullies, mountain torrents and waterfalls, dangerous cliffs, I surmounted in my sedan chair. Where it was too steep for my chair, I advanced on foot. Like a young gazelle I mounted the highest peaks in pursuit of them. Whenever my knees gave out, I sat down on some mountain boulder and drank the cold water from the water skin to quench my thirst. To the summits of the mountains I pursued them and brought about their overthrow.[73]

This is not an emperor who presents himself as a superman but as a human, hard-working commander who leads his men through the strains and frustrations of military operations.

The contrast between Sennacherib and Hezekiah is sharp. The Bible frequently describes other kings of Judah or Israel in battlefield situations, often giving unstinting praise to their martial leadership. Yet while the Bible tells how during Hezekiah's reign Judah enlarged its territory by military means, never does it show the king himself as remotely near a battle. King versus king, the conflict of 701 BC was no contest.

Sennacherib not only welcomes combat, he positively gloats on the horrors his men inflict on the enemy. In a disturbing description of a battle against Elam, several years after his withdrawal from Khor, he cherishes a grisly series of scenes that escalates into bloodlust:

> Humbanundasha, the field-marshal of the king of Elam, a trustworthy man, commander of his armies, his chief support, together with his nobles . . . , speedily I cut them down and established their defeat. I cut their throats like lambs. I cut off their precious lives as one cuts a string. Like the many waters of a storm, I made the contents of their gullets and entrails run down upon the wide earth. My prancing steeds harnessed for my riding, plunged into the streams of their blood as into a river. The wheels of my war chariot, which brings low the wicked and the evil, were besplattered with blood and filth. With the bodies of their warriors I filled the plain, like grass. Their testicles I cut off, and tore out their privates like the seeds of cucumbers of June. Their hands I cut off.[74]

Julius Caesar's most famous line, used as he recounted his military exploits in Gaul, is, "I came, I saw, I conquered." Six centuries before, Sennacherib wrote down this line about his campaign against the Kassites in the Zagros Mountains: "I destroyed, I devastated, I turned into ruins."[75]

Such was the mentality of the young emperor who would next turn his attention to Khor.

CHAPTER FIVE

"Like the Wolf on the Fold"

AFTER THE LAST winter rains,[1] Sennacherib's army would have journeyed across the Euphrates and toward those troublesome subjects at the empire's western extremity.

As it marched along the arc of the Fertile Crescent toward Khor that spring of 701 BC, the army must have made an imposing spectacle. Just how big this force was is uncertain, but in major campaigns Assyria may sometimes have fielded armies approaching 100,000 men,[2] and this campaign would have qualified as major. The army would have stretched for miles. In his powerful poem, "The Destruction of Sennacherib," Lord Byron imagines the force as it surged westward across the plains:

> The Assyrian came down like the wolf on the fold,
> And his cohorts were gleaming in purple and gold;
> And the sheen of their spears was like the stars on the sea,
> When the blue wave rolls nightly on deep Galilee.

Byron is inventing the uniforms' colors. But his energetic verse captures the invader's aura of unstoppable might.

To someone watching this army pass, one of its most striking features would have been its disciplined regimentation. This was no ragtag bunch. Unlike the various kingdoms of Khor, Assyria had an army composed largely of professionals. It was also a standing army, on duty year round. While Judah and its neighboring countries had largely to make do with farmers, shepherds and shopkeepers conscripted for emergencies,[3] augmented by mercenaries and professionals, Assyria possessed a veritable war machine. To justify its costly existence and to keep the troops content with plunder, Assyrian kings had to involve the army in military campaigns every year or two, whether or not there was a true crisis that needed attention. Military historian Trevor N. Dupuy observes that the nation's "wealth and prosperity were sustained by booty and by what seems to have been the first truly military society in history."[4] A.K. Grayson, an expert on Assyria at the University of Toronto, underscores the point: "The chief occupation of the Assyrian king and state was warfare."[5]

What did the army look like? Most of Sennacherib's soldiers wore similar cone-shaped helmets and, in battle, chain mail over their torsos and legs. All would have worn their hair long but neatly cut at their shoulders; all would have boasted full beards two to three inches long, trimmed in a squarish manner. That the many bas-reliefs depict all soldiers, without exception, with such beards suggests that they were as *de rigueur* as crewcuts among recruits today.

Anyone observing Sennacherib's troops would have remarked on another trait—their strikingly different ethnicities. Assyrian kings would commonly press the elite forces of conquered nations into their service.[6] Of the many foreign components, the one we happen to know most about was a unit from Samaria, part of the late kingdom of Israel. Military records unearthed from the remains of Sargon's military buildings in the Assyrian city of Nimrud show that 13 officers headed this sizable Hebrew chariot corps.[7] Such officers, suggests historian Stephanie Dalley, would have been "among the wealthiest and most prestigious members of the royal court." She adds: "The Samarians who served as a national unit in Sargon's royal army must have been so professional as to be utterly reliable, even though they were serving in the army of their conqueror."[8] Whether this crack unit accompanied Sennacherib on his campaign of 701 is uncertain. Still, it is fair to note that Israel's troops were not known for having a soft spot for their Judahite neighbors. Earlier in these same officers' lifetimes, during the Syro-Ephraimite War, Israel's forces had poured into Judah and unsuccessfully besieged Jerusalem.[9]

The Assyrian army had three main formations: infantry, cavalry and chariot corps. Each of those broke down into specialized categories.[10]

Thus the infantry consisted of spearmen, archers and slingmen; in addition to those weapons, most of these footmen carried straight swords for hand-to-hand fighting. The spearmen did not hurl their missiles; rather, they hung onto them and used them for stabbing. These soldiers clutched small, circular shields generally made of wicker and covered with leather. The wicker could take the form of plaited reeds or willow twigs; its main advantage was that it was light and could easily absorb arrows and blows.

The archers' shields were far bigger, extending from head to toe. Indeed, sometimes these shields even curved backward over the archer's helmet, especially useful against enemy archers shooting from an elevated position, such as a city's battlements. So unwieldy was this screen that each Assyrian archer required an attendant to hold it. This helper would vigilantly adjust the shield to the line of incoming fire, while the marksman concentrated on his aim. The archers' bows were generally "composite"—made of narrow layers of soft and hard wood, animal sinew and horn all glued together. The horn, often from water buffalo, went on the side of the bow that was away from the archer.[11] The glue might take more than a year to dry.[12] The adhesive was made of the boiled-down skin and tendon of cattle plus the skin and bones of fish. So strong was the weapon made of all these layers that it would take two men to bend and string it. The effort was worthwhile: an arrow from a composite bow could kill a person at 300 to 400 yards; at close to twice that distance it could at the least inflict injury.[13]

The third kind of foot-soldiers, the slingmen, operated in teams of two behind the archers. They would share a sack of stones. The sling consisted of a small rectangular piece of leather to which two rawhide cords were attached. When the soldier placed a stone in the leather, it became enclosed and would not drop while the soldier, grasping the cords in one hand, whirled it repeatedly above his head. At the right moment he would release one of the cords, sending the missile on its potentially lethal way.

Saddles with stirrups having not yet been invented,[14] horsemen's feet simply dangled or clutched the horses' sides. The riders thus lacked the steadfast base needed for slashing downward forcefully with swords. The Assyrian cavalry relied instead on two other weapons, the spear and the bow. Horsemen specialized in one or the other.

Horseborne spearmen would be grouped together as a unit. Their job—to charge into an enemy's ranks on the battlefield. Behind them followed footmen with spears.

Mounted archers, composing the other group, often had assistants who, riding alongside, held protective shields for their mutual protection. A duo might ride to an advantageous position and remain there for a while, picking off the enemy.

When traveling, chariots frequently used three horses: two to pull and one, roped behind the chariot, to be used as a spare in the event of injury to one of the others. Yigael Yadin, head of the Hebrew University's Institute of Archaeology in Jerusalem and one of the foremost authorities on ancient combat techniques, deems the chariotry to have "represented the principal strength and power of the Assyrian army in open battle."[15] Chariots were swift-moving platforms: they provided firm footing for archers as they sped from one part of the battle zone to another. To allow for maximum mobility, they often hovered at the periphery of the action. Under Sargon and Sennacherib, chariots commonly had three-man crews: one man would shoot, one would drive and one would hold shields for the others. Spears would be kept on board in the event the chariots should enter the fray itself. As with the cavalry, one of the chariotry's tactics was to smash into the enemy ranks and wreak confusion.

Included in this long procession of military units were innumerable supply wagons. These were filled with more than simply food and spare weapons. Some would be loaded with hundreds, perhaps even thousands, of shovels and picks for building earthworks around besieged cities. Others carried huge beams that, when assembled, became deadly catapults and siege towers.

Finally, oxen pulled oddly-shaped skeletal structures with six wheels, structures that, when covered with specially tailored hides, resembled squat, lumbering animals larger than elephants. When the people of a besieged city would see these great machines approaching, some of them six yards long and two or three yards high, they would feel terror, and with reason.

Some historians call these mechanisms "battering rams," but that is a misnomer. Their purpose was seldom to bash down a door or wall. From bas-reliefs, we know their operation was more agile. Inside each of them, slung like a horizontal pendulum, was a huge metal bar. Its forward edge was a bit like an ax-blade. The crew inside would stick the blade between two stones in a city's wall and then wiggle the bar from side to side until the stones fell out and a hole was made big enough for troops to rush in. All the while, of course, defenders atop the wall would rain down missiles and burning oil. For this reason, the machine would often boast a turret that rose like a giant head. Inside the turret, a spotter would look for huge rocks about to descend on the machine and move the machine out of harm's way; he might also have vessels of water with which to douse any flames. For added protection, the besiegers would roll tall towers near the machine. From them, archers could rake the ramparts with arrows. One bas-relief shows several of the machines at work next to each other, attacking like wolves in a pack.

JUDAH'S ARMY DID not seek to challenge the Assyrians on any battlefield. Instead, Judah took elaborate steps to prepare its cities for sieges. It is likely that Judah was aware of Sennacherib's intentions well before his army set out.[16]

The archaeological evidence at Lachish, Jerusalem and numerous smaller fortified sites suggests that authorities equipped them with clay storage jars in anticipation of sieges; about two feet high, these vessels would likely have been filled with oil, wine and other foodstocks.[17] Most adults had already faced invasions earlier in their lives and were old hands at taking elaborate defensive measures. But the Jerusalemites knew that the coming Assyrian invasion called for extraordinarily ambitious steps. Says the Bible:

> When Hezekiah saw that Sennacherib intended to attack Jerusalem also, he and his officials decided to cut off the supply of water outside the city in order to keep the Assyrians from having any water when they got near Jerusalem. The officials led a large number of people out and stopped up all the springs, so that no more water flowed out of them. The king strengthened the city's defenses by repairing the wall, building towers on it, and building an outer wall. In addition, he repaired the defenses built on the land that was filled in on the east side of the old part of Jerusalem. He also had a large number of spears and shields made.[18]

The matter-of-fact tone belies the exceptional nature of the engineering projects.

The reference to the water supply is of particular interest. The modest springs in nearby hills could be blocked with rocks and other material. Eventually, because water flows where it meets least resistance, the backed-up subterranean water would find fissures elsewhere in the limestone terrain, perhaps at some distance. These new sources, however, might spring up in either in hard-to-spot locations and/or in rugged terrain that might be difficult for water-hauling vehicles to reach.

Yet this operation in the outlying hills would have represented only a sidelight to the centerpiece of the defenders' water-denial strategy. A little later, the same biblical passage goes on to say that the Jerusalemites were able to divert their city's own water supply: "It was King Hezekiah who blocked the outlet for Gihon Spring and channeled the water to flow through a tunnel to a point inside the walls of Jerusalem."[19] This was Hezekiah's Tunnel. Archaeologists' discovery of the 500-yard-long passage has shown it to be a most impressive feat of hydraulic engineering. The water that otherwise would have overflowed from the Gihon Spring and cave and streamed down the Kidron Valley now took this sinuous course below the city and arrived at a reservoir just beyond the centuries-old wall at the southern end of the city.

To prevent Assyrian access to this reservoir, the Jerusalemites had to achieve another major engineering project: they built a previously mentioned "outer wall," in places a stout 23 feet thick and 16 feet high, to enclose the reservoir, or Siloam Pool as they called it. The vital Gihon Spring was also inside this wall and, to make it doubly difficult for attackers to take possession of this site and unblock the water source, Hezekiah built at the spring a bulky tower 30 feet high. This wall, which gave much of the city a second ring of defense, also sheltered neighborhoods that had formerly sprawled outside the original wall. It is likely refugees from Israel after 720 accounted for much of this extra-mural population. As well, the Jerusalemites reinforced the old, inner wall; to do so, they tore down houses to use their limestone blocks.[20]

In addition to all this, the anti-Assyrian coalition urgently deliberated playing its ultimate card—sending envoys to Egypt to seek military assistance.[21]

Isaiah was opposed to this, and strenuously so.

Earlier in his career, the prophet had been contemptuous of Egypt as a potential ally for practical (as well as theological) reasons. Little wonder: over the course of the ninth and most of the eighth centuries BC, Egypt had declined into a collection of petty warring states, none of them sufficiently powerful to be able to confront Assyria. Egypt's military deficiency was one of Isaiah's key arguments when appealing to Judah to stay out of Ashdod's rebellion against Assyria in 713. Scorning his king's diplomatic feelers to determine possible Egyptian assistance for such a revolt, he described Egypt as a land in which "Rival cities will fight each other, and rival kings will struggle for power."[22] He concluded: "No one in Egypt, rich or poor, important or unknown, can offer help."[23] This analysis was, as we will see, accurate in 713, and Egypt's military impotence may help explain why Hezekiah refrained from joining Ashdod's revolt.

But now, in the period immediately prior to Sennacherib's invasion, Egypt's internal politics were very different. In *c.* 712, a new ruler had moved to take effective control of all Egypt, save perhaps parts of the Delta. His name was Shabako, and he was a Kushite.

Under him and his successors, Egypt attained a level of military strength that it had not seen in centuries.

Despite Egypt's revitalization, Isaiah remained opposed to Judah looking to Egypt for help, even during the frantic period when Sennacherib's assault was imminent. Now, however, with this new dynasty in power he dropped his former argument that Egypt was militarily incompetent. Instead, he acknowledged that Egypt might offer help but argued that this would still not suffice for military success. Isaiah's reasoning had become largely theological. Referring to those leaders of the military or patriotic party to which Hezekiah was now firmly allied, he preached:

> Those who go to Egypt for help are doomed! They are relying on Egypt's vast military strength—horses, chariots, and soldiers. But they do not rely on the Lord, the holy God of Israel, or ask him for help. He knows what he is doing! He sends disaster. He carries out his threats to punish evil men and those who protect them. The Egyptians are not gods—they are only human. Their horses are not supernatural. When the Lord acts, the strong nation will crumble, and the weak nation it helped will fall. Both of them will be destroyed.[24]

As we have already seen, for Isaiah the Assyrians were like a club that the Lord would use to punish the "godless nation" with which he was angry.[25] No one, Hebrews or Kushites or anyone else, could thwart Yahweh's will. If Judah were now to drag Kushite Egypt into the war, the prophet argued, it would effectively be bringing its ally to slaughter.

The only way for Judah to avert its divinely ordained ruination, Isaiah insisted, was to make Yahweh change his will, and that, of course, could be done only through Judah's adoption of more religious reform, social justice and righteous behavior.

But with Sennacherib about to invade, Hezekiah must have dismissed Isaiah's theological approach as hopelessly lacking in *realpolitik*. Desperately, the coalition[26] dispatched envoys to appeal for military help from Egypt's new masters.

The Kushites were the rebel alliance's last hope.

CHAPTER SIX

The Kushites' Self-Interest

W HO WERE THE Kushites? And why did they accept the coalition's appeal to send forces abroad for the high-risk mission of confronting so formidable a foe?

The Egyptians called the land directly to the south of them "Kush." The modern term is "Nubia." Ancient Greek texts refer to Kush as "Ethiopia" (which in Greek means "land of burnt faces"). The ancient term "Ethiopia" is not to be confused with the existing country of that name. Ethnically and geographically, the ancient sub-Saharan kingdom of Kush[1] is distinct from the modern state of Ethiopia, which lies southeast of it.

Egypt's 18th Dynasty conquered Kush in the 16th century BC, according to the standard dating that this book will utilize.[2] Kush was a large prize, about equal in area to the Egypt of the pharaohs—that is, Upper Egypt and Lower Egypt combined, or the so-called "Two Lands." Kush's prime arable land, however, would have been substantially less: the Nile's flood-plain, with its rich black soil, was far narrower in Kush, with its tighter river valley, than in the relatively flat expanses of much of Egypt. Kush's population was also far smaller, perhaps below half a million people.[3] Estimates of Egypt's population in the late eighth century BC range from 2.5 million to more than double that.[4]

Egypt's domination of these southern highlands was lucrative. Gold was the major resource and may largely explain Egypt's presence in Kush.[5] Numerous goldmines pocked the arid hills of northern Kush between the Nile and the Red Sea.[6] The Egyptians also developed a plantation economy in Kush. Farmers worked on large estates owned by the pharaoh, by the local nobility or by temples that were established throughout the territory.[7]

Egypt often appointed Kushites as high officials to help run the system, and the pharaoh eventually ran Kush not as a foreign colony but as an appendage of the Egyptian state's administrative structure,[8] something that would help explain why in the eighth century BC the Kushites would see Egypt as a kindred land, not a foreign one. Indeed, as far back as the 14th century, says Stuart Tyson Smith, an archaeologist at the University of California at Los Angeles, the Kushites tended to see the Egyptians "more as neighbors and collaborators than as oppressors or competitors."[9]

In addition to gold, this prosperous economy produced abundant cattle, dates, honey and wine for export. From Kush itself or from lands to the south came incense, gums, elephant tusks, leopard skins, exotic animals such as giraffes and elephants, ebony and other precious woods, not to mention slaves.[10]

In the view of today's historians, the Egyptians encouraged the spread of their own religious and cultural practices, in effect "Egyptianizing" much of the population without smothering many of the existing mores. In time, the Kushites embraced wholeheartedly the variety of worship practiced in neighboring Upper Egypt: the most important god was Amon, the center of whose worship was at Thebes, the capital of Upper Egypt. It is unlikely that Egypt imposed willy-nilly the worship of Amon; rather, that god may have blended in with an earlier ramlike deity of the Kushites so that, as one writer speculates, these southerners may have "considered him as their own."[11] The Kushites had less interest in the gods of Lower Egypt, such as Ptah, though they still did respect them.

As they had proved in resisting earlier Egyptian advances, the Kushites were redoubtable warriors. They adopted the latest developments in military technology and tactics, such as the use of chariots, and sent many soldiers into the service of the pharaoh.

In about the 11th century BC, beset by its own domestic problems, Egypt left Kush. No one knows how, but the now-independent Kushites seem to have gathered great political and cultural strength. By the eighth century BC, they had become militarily superior to Egypt.[12]

The kingdom's temporal and spiritual capital was Napata, a city just above the Nile's fourth cataract. Napata's most unusual natural feature was a mesa rising 300 feet from the plain almost like a giant altar. This dramatic landmark, called the Pure Mountain— or today, Gebel Barkal—was seen as Amon's dwelling place. Even after Kush eventually gained its independence, this state cult of Amon would continue as the kingdom's ideological foundation.

The political structure built upon it would show remarkable longevity. The Kushite kingdom, which was known in its later phases by the name of Meroë, existed at least 1,100 years. That is longer than the span of such other better-known states as ancient Assyria, Israel, Greece, Rome or the Hittite empire. Even more astonishing is Kush's political and social stability during those centuries. While scholars do not know whether there was a turnover of dynasties, William Adams observes that the "unbroken continuity of the monarchy seems beyond dispute."[13] True, the Egypt of the pharaohs enjoyed a much longer reign (about 3,000 years) than Kush. But bear in mind that during that time Egypt frequently fell into political disunity, splitting into two or more states and sometimes being taken over, and ruled for a century or more, by groups from outside the Nile Valley, such as the Hyksos and the Libyans. Indeed, in Egypt of the late eighth century BC no fewer than three different pharaonic dynasties were co-existing uneasily. For the kingdom of Kush, no evidence exists of similar rupture or discontinuity.[14] When in the fourth century AD the kingdom finally did wither, this may have been due less to internal problems than to disruptions originating from the outside world.[15]

Bruce Trigger, a noted McGill University anthropologist who has excavated in the Sudan and Egypt and written extensively on ancient societies on several continents, departs from his normal low-key, matter-of-fact tone when discussing Kush's long life. He calls the kingdom a "spectacular success."[16] Expressing puzzlement as to how Kush could have thrived for more than a millennium, Trigger suggests that this "may reflect a knowledge of statecraft" derived from "Nubian prototypes" of which almost nothing is known. Trigger speculates that home-grown influence in forming these political skills may have been greater than the influence of centuries of exposure to the values of Egyptian occupiers. This is one sign of a value system built around the concept of harmony that will help us later to grasp the unusual reasons for Kush's decision to confront Assyria. It will also help explain its particular strategy in doing so.

In *c.* 759 BC, under King Kashta, Kush intervened in some unknown manner in Upper Egypt and exercised leverage, if not sovereignty,[17] over the affairs of Thebes, the capital, and Upper Egypt generally. While the nature of this influence is uncertain, there is no sign that Upper Egypt saw Kush as a hostile occupying force or even as an unwelcome intruder. Indeed, motivated by self-protection, traditional Theban circles may even have sought the intervention of Kush as a means of stabilizing Egypt's fractious political landscape.[18]

As the site of the great temple of Amon, Thebes was far more than a spiritual center. The best picture we have of its material role in Upper Egypt dates from the time of Ramses III in the 12th century BC. Donald Redford's description evokes awe:

> The extent and wealth of the temple of Amon in the twilight of the New Kingdom is staggering. On the death of Rameses III it owned 600,000 acres [more than 930 square miles] of land, 421,362 head of cattle, 433 gardens, 65 towns (nine in Canaan), 46 carpenters' shops, and a fleet of 83 cargo boats. Over 85,000 chattels and farmers labored on the god's estate, exclusive of the priests. The bequests of a single pharaoh (Ramses III) to Amon included nearly 1.5 tons of gold and silver, 2.5 tons of copper, over 1,000 jars of incense, over 25,000 jars of wine, 310,000 measures of grain, besides substantial amounts of flax, vegetables, and fowl. In the 21st Dynasty Amon's "estate" is coextensive with Upper Egypt.[19]

After that time, the status of Thebes deteriorated substantially. It lost much of its population, wealth and political power. That is the context for the Kushite entry into the region.

It is under Kashta's son and successor, Piye, that a clearer picture of the new Kush emerges. In the last third of the eighth century BC, its army strode out of the African interior and into the Mediterranean world.

This was a time in which all of Egypt, not just Thebes, was in cultural and political decline. Disunity was acute. Fragmenting that part of Egypt lying north of Theban-controlled territory were 11 separate political units, each claiming independence. Running this hodgepodge were five separate kings, as well as assorted princes and chiefs.[20] The kings included Osorkon IV, a descendant of the 22nd Dynasty who still used the title of pharaoh although he was, in Kenneth Kitchen's expression, but a "powerless shadow-pharaoh."[21] Osorkon's capital was the monument-filled city of Tanis in the eastern Delta. The 23rd Dynasty also still had a pulse, though barely; heading it was one Iuput II, a "pharaoh" whose authority was confined to the district of Leontopolis, in the central Delta.

It was here in northern Egypt, and particularly the Delta, that jockeying for power among rival fiefdoms was most intense. The Delta warlords were mostly descended from Berbers who, possibly because of climate change and famine,[22] had come to the Egyptian Delta from Libya starting in the 12th century BC. Militarily adept, these Libyans—some blue-eyed and fair-skinned, others more swarthy, their soldiers often wearing a long braid dangling from one side of their heads—had worked as mercenaries for pharaohs and adopted Egyptian mores. In the tenth century BC, one of their number, the commander of all the armed forces and an in-law of the royal family, eased himself into power as pharaoh. Named Sheshonk, most scholars say he corresponds to an infamous biblical personage, one Shishak.[23] According to the First Book of Kings, shortly after Solomon's death, "King Shishak of Egypt came up against Jerusalem; he took away the treasures of the house of the Lord and the treasures of the king's house; he took away everything."[24] In addition to Sheshonk's 22nd Dynasty,

Libyans also composed the 23rd Dynasty, which got under way in the ninth century.

In the late eighth century BC, the most vigorous of the Libyans' descendants was Prince Tefnakht, of the western-Delta city of Sais. He exploited the disarray by forging alliances with several other rulers, including Osorkon IV. With these allies, Tefnakht invaded the Nile valley south of the Delta: his goal appears to have been to make himself the effective pharaoh of Lower Egypt. He may have threatened to invade as far south as Thebes itself.[25] Politically, that would have constituted an invasion of the Kushites' sphere. Also, this would have represented a grave setback to the institutionalized worship of Amon. At this point the Kushites were already exercising substantial control in Upper Egypt, perhaps almost by default. As supporters of Amon, these southerners reinforced the pervasive influence of Amon's Thebes-based priesthood against de-stabilizing forces in Upper Egypt.

Tefnakht advanced beyond Memphis and took control of almost all of Lower Egypt and even the northern portion of Upper Egypt. Theban authorities may have appealed to Napata for help.[26] Leaving his seat of power in Napata, Piye (or Py or Piankhi, as he is also known) swept down the Nile to confront him around 728.[27] Piye's own account of it is a detailed, exciting and chivalric narrative that is a little-known masterpiece of ancient literature.[28] In a series of encounters that included a naval battle on the Nile and assaults on cities climaxing with the capture of Lower Egypt's principal city, Memphis, Piye defeated the rebels and had himself crowned as pharaoh of both Lower and Upper Egypt.[29]

Yet Piye did not remain in Egypt or otherwise seek to exercise real power there. In what for us may seem like a perplexing climax to the conflict, Piye pardoned those rebels who expressed contrition and who paid him copious tribute, including Osorkon and Teknakht himself. Then, instead of consolidating his position and leaving occupying forces in place to exercise control, the "conqueror" almost immediately sailed back to Napata, apparently taking with him most of his forces. There he remained, pharaoh of all Egypt in name only. His permanent absence from Lower Egypt left the field open for a comeback by Tefnakht, who set himself up as pharaoh of the new 24th Dynasty, and for the continued reign of the 22nd Dynasty's Osorkon IV. Meanwhile, the 23rd Dynasty was tapering out, its authority limited to the area immediately surrounding the city of Leontopolis in the east-central Delta. That three pharaonic dynasties could coexist in the Delta attests to the region's enduring division. Osorkon and his 23rd-Dynasty counterpart, Iuput II, were essentially spent forces—in Kitchen's words, "local petty chiefs."[30] They were the last of their respective lines, and were subordinate to the strongman Tefnakht.

Adams gives a well-balanced summation of Piye's campaign:

> Although he assumed the titles of the pharaoh, [Piye] was neither a conqueror nor a despot of the ordinary sort. His intervention in Egypt was prompted by direct and repeated pleas from the north, and his chief interest from beginning to end seems to have been to relieve the threat to Thebes, and thus protect the domains of Amon. The vigorous pursuit of that policy led him to subdue every rival prince in Egypt, but having obtained their nominal submission he was content to return homeward and leave Egypt to its own devices. Not surprisingly, his enemies rewarded his humane and lenient treatment by repudiating their oaths and resuming their dynastic ambitions the moment his back was turned.[31]

Some historians have expressed puzzlement over Piye's decision to disengage from the politics of Lower Egypt,[32] others scorn.[33] Yet the policy proved to be far from disastrous. In making his comeback, Tefnakht kept to the north, never seeking to extend his authority south of Memphis[34] or otherwise acting to provoke Piye. Indeed, one can ask if imposing themselves on the north was really an option for the Kushites. Controlling Lower Egypt—and in particular the Delta, whose swamplands were a paradise for fugitives and rebels—would have been beyond the resources of Kush, whose population was far smaller than that of Lower Egypt.

Rather than subjugate and exploit Egypt, Piye gave it an unusually long leash. I.E.S. Edwards of the British Museum reaches the reasonable conclusion that Piye was content to "establish a protectorate over the country while leaving its administration largely in the hands of those who were already in authority."[35] From their actions, it is clear the Kushites' aim was not to dominate but rather to restore order to a land that they held in esteem and with which they shared a common heritage (particularly a religious one), a land with which for centuries they had enjoyed a close, non-adversarial relationship.

THE KUSHITE WITHDRAWAL from Lower Egypt would have taken place about a year after their arrival. The Napatans' absence would continue until about 712, several years after Piye's death. This is the most likely date of their second conquest of Egypt,[36] which would have been carried out by Piye's brother and successor Shabako. Historians usually date the start of the 25th Dynasty to Shabako's conquest rather than that of Piye, since Piye did not establish continuous rule in Egypt.

The 16 years or so between the two conquests represents an unsettled interlude in the affairs of Lower Egypt. It appears to be this tumultuous period that Isaiah is describing when, speaking for Yahweh, he declares, "I will stir up Egyptians against Egyptians, and they will fight, one against the other, neighbor against neighbor, city against city, kingdom against kingdom."[37]

In this period between Piye's conquest of Lower Egypt in 728 and Shabako's reconquest in 712, Hebrews, Assyrians, Egyptians and Kushites interacted significantly.

Around 726-725, King Hoshea of Israel stopped paying tribute to Assyria and appealed to Egypt for help against Assyrian reprisals. In trying to grasp Judahite-Egyptian relations in this period, it is important to know to *whom* among Egypt's many rulers, real and nominal, Hoshea appealed. Second Kings says only that Hoshea sent his envoys to one "So, king of Egypt."[38] Among the swarm of kings, princes and chiefs in Egypt, none had a name resembling that. A lively debate therefore exists among scholars over precisely which potential ally the biblical writer may have had in mind. Scholars have proposed three separate candidates for "So": Osorkon IV, Tefnakht and Piye.[39] Each theory contains at least one fatal flaw. Osorkon was too weak to offer real help, Tefnakht had more sympathy for Assyria than Israel and Piye was too remote geographically.

A combination of two of these, however, would make most sense. King So would have been Osorkon but only in that Delta king's capacity as a middleman to Piye. The Kushite king was in Napata, hard to reach for Samarian messengers unfamiliar with the long, difficult route. Osorkon, on the other hand, ruled over Tanis in the northeastern Delta, the first kingdom the messengers would have come to as they entered Egypt. The former ally of Tefnakht now recognized Piye as his overlord, and his family and that of Piye had a close, almost in-law relationship. Indeed, Piye would probably have had ambassadors at Osorkon's court. In any event, Osorkon's couriers could have swiftly relayed all communications to Napata. For these reasons, the Delta king would have been the appropriate conduit through which to appeal to Piye.[40]

Whoever the real addressee was, Hoshea was unable to obtain help from him. Because the Israelite king had withheld tribute, Assyria's King Shalmaneser had Hoshea thrown into prison. Hoshea's rebellious stance must have received broad public support, because Shalmaneser then invaded Israel and besieged the capital, Samaria.[41]

In 720, on the same foray into Khor in which they stepped up their deportation of the soon-to-be '10 lost tribes of Israel,' the Assyrians under Sargon conquered Gaza and then, about a day's march southwest of that city, seized Raphia, on the doorstep of Egypt in the eastern Sinai. An Egyptian leader, who may have been Osorkon IV,[42] dispatched an army commander to join forces with the disenfranchised king of Gaza, Hanno, to turn back the Assyrians at Raphia. Our only source is Sargon. He dismissively writes that this commander "became frightened at the clangor of my weapons and fled, to be seen no more."[43] In another of his writings, Sargon expresses even more contempt for the Egyptian commander, saying he "ran off like a shepherd whose sheep have been carried off."[44]

Whether the Egyptian defense performed so lamentably is open to question. Assyrian royal texts served as propaganda for home consumption. In his description of this clash, Sargon says that

only Hanno was captured. He does not mention taking any Egyptian prisoners. Often, Assyrian kings do allude in their records to
captures they may have made, so the omission here could have significance. Two things, however, are incontestable: Sargon did create by his own account "havoc" just inside Egyptian territory[45]
and he did not advance farther.

Around 716, Sargon again invaded Philistia. He advanced
beyond Raphia, probably to at least as far as the "Brook of Egypt,"
or Wadi el Arish, the traditional Egyptian border in the eastern
Sinai.[46] This modest stream ran into the Mediterranean perhaps 50
miles southwest of Gaza. The change in topography made it a
natural location for a frontier: east of the Brook of Egypt lay cultivated fields and pasture, but west of it there was only scrub and
desert wastes.[47]

This time, rather than fight, an Egyptian leader, whom most
scholars identify as Osorkon,[48] sent tribute to Sargon: "The terror-
inspiring glamor of Ashur, my lord, overwhelmed him," writes
Sargon, using one of his favorite expressions, "and he brought as
a present 12 big horses from [Egypt] which have not their equal in
this country [Assyria]."[49] Intended for breeding purposes, this gift
was a handsome one; the tribute would likely have had military
value, since the bloodline lent itself to war horses. This present
therefore would have conveyed a greater sense of appeasement
than chests of jewels or some other conventional tribute that
Osorkon had probably already bestowed upon him.[50] The point
here is that anyone concerned about Assyria's designs would not
have been reassured by the fact Sargon had halted at the border:
Assyria had demonstrated its capability of invading Egypt.

This campaign must have alarmed both Egypt and vigilant
Kush for a second reason. Sargon established a military garrison at
the border.[51] This must have represented a constant reminder of
Assyria's military threat. What's more, it could have served as a vexing filter for Egypt's overland trade with Khor. The garrison may
have functioned as a tollgate or as a point for transferring shipments from Egyptian caravans to Assyrian-controlled ones.

In 712, Sargon sent a force to put down Ashdod's rebellion,
which had started the year before. In a vain attempt to summon

military help, the Philistine rebels sent what Sargon describes as "bribes" to an unnamed Egyptian king, presumably one of the Delta monarchs (perhaps Osorkon).[52] Sargon writes that the leader of that rebellion, Iamani, fled deep into Egypt, apparently to an area under Kushite control.[53] It is significant that even at this time, more than a decade before 701, a second anti-Assyrian rebel in Khor—Israel's Hoshea having been the first—should have seen the Kushites as a potential recourse against the empire.

It was shortly after this, perhaps in this same year, that Shabako followed Piye's example and invaded Lower Egypt. He conquered the entire territory, overcoming the army of Bakenranef of Sais, who was Tefnakht's son and his successor as the pharaoh of the 24th Dynasty.

Why did Piye's brother take over Egypt? The aggression has puzzled some historians[54] and prompted others to make trivializing hypotheses. T.G.H. James, for example, speculates that what inspired Shabako was crass power politics or petty sibling competition—an attempt to equal Piye's achievement.[55] But this ignores the Assyrian dimension. Shabako's likely motive was to unify Egypt and strengthen it so as to better defend against invasion.[56]

Three times in the previous eight years, Assyrians had advanced to the gates of Egypt. Just why they had not invaded the Nile Valley is unclear. Perhaps it was that their armies had suffered too many casualties in earlier combat in Khor. Perhaps they lacked supplies for a large army's arduous trek across the Sinai desert. Perhaps the tribute from the frightened rulers of northern Egypt made it easier to turn back.

Or maybe—an intriguing possibility—the Assyrians had not halted at Egypt's traditional border in the eastern Sinai in 716 but had actually entered Egypt proper. Hayim Tadmor, of the Hebrew University in Jerusalem, cites a text by Sargon on that campaign that includes these two sentences: "I opened the sealed harbor of Egypt. The Assyrians and Egyptians I mingled together and I made them trade with each other."[57] Sargon does not identify this "sealed harbor." But Tadmor speculates that he may be referring to Pelusium or Sile, the easternmost of ancient Egypt's ports. These two cities are near where the Suez Canal now pierces the isthmus, roughly 130 miles west of Lower Egypt's customary border at the Brook of Egypt.

If Tadmor's suggestion is correct, it means that the Assyrians had not simply knocked at Egypt's door but had penetrated well beyond it. From Shabako's viewpoint, Assyria would have been in an excellent position to summon a large army to this city and to use it as a staging area for a full-scale invasion of the Nile Valley.

Quite aside from the hard-to-resolve question of which side of the border the "sealed harbor" was on,[58] we should not overlook something else in Sargon's statement: "I made [Assyrians and Egyptians] trade with each other." Tadmor's assessment of the Assyrian king's rationale seems valid: "This passage of great importance elucidates the economic motives behind the military campaigns on the Egyptian border. . . ."[59] Sargon plainly succeeded in imposing on Egypt a trade arrangement congenial to Assyria.

Regardless of whether the Assyrians had advanced to Pelusium/Sile or simply the eastern Sinai, Egypt would have seen their presence as a grave threat to its national interest in terms of both defense and international commerce. The Kushites would not have wanted simply to view this passively from afar.

Unlike Piye's conquest of Egypt 16 years before, no stela has been found that would indicate just how Shabako's campaign fared or what resistance it encountered. What is clear, however, is that the new pharaoh, unlike his late older brother, became, loosely speaking, overlord of the entire country. He even moved to establish some degree of authority in Sais, the stronghold of Tefnakht and Bakenranef. He appointed as Sais's governor a man called Ammeris, perhaps a Kushite.[60] This is not to say that all Egypt was docile under Kushite rule, but it is to say that Shabako and his two successors of the 25th Dynasty, Shebitku and Taharqa, restored a degree of unity to Egypt that it had not seen in 300 years.[61]

␣

IN SUMMING UP pharaonic Egypt's 3,000 years, James makes this acute observation: "Perhaps the first and most important quality that typified this civilization was continuity. In every aspect of

Egyptian life, in every manifestation of of its culture, a deep conservatism can be observed."[62] This was particularly true under the 25th Dynasty. In reviving an Egypt that was unified and strong, the Kushite pharaohs looked back to shining periods of centralized rule, to the New Kingdom (16th to 13th centuries BC) and even the Old Kingdom (27th to 22nd centuries BC). As Adams notes, their "aim was nothing less than the restoration of Egyptian culture and religion to their original 'purity'. . . ."[63] The 25th Dynasty's conservatism manifests itself in the way Piye and other pharaohs had themselves buried in Kush inside pyramids, a pharaonic tradition that had lapsed many centuries before.[64] Just as the Kushite pharaohs' religious rites returned to ancient forms,[65] so did their art, spectacularly. With its ambitious renovation of great monuments and construction of new ones, this dynasty may have done more to enhance the glory of Thebes than any Egyptian rulers since Ramses IV some 400 years before.[66]

One scholar, Karl-Heinz Priese, suggests that political considerations may have played a role in this harking back to ancient monarchs' ways. He says that "as a result of the [Kushite] sovereign's need to appear as a 'genuine' pharaoh, an exaggerated form of orthodoxy was flaunted."[67] Historian Steffen Wenig, an expert on Kushite art, agrees, saying the Napatan pharaohs sought to help "legitimize" their rule through use of titles, crowns and jewelry that resembled those of Egyptian monarchs.[68] Yet Wenig also notes that they played up their distinctive origins. Wall paintings at a temple built by Taharqa at Qasr Ibrim, for example, depict this pharaoh "not with a red-brown skin, as was customary in Egypt, but with the dark brown flesh tone characteristic of Kushites. This suggests that Kushite rulers were proud of their southern origin and, however Egyptianized they became, they remained so throughout their history."[69]

What about the quality of the art, including the architecture, under the 25th Dynasty? Although modern scholarship tends to be dismissive of the dynasty's political and foreign-policy aspects, art experts as a rule are generous. John H. Taylor, a curator in the British Museum's department of Egyptian antiquities, notes that while the Kushites borrowed from archaic Egyptian models "they brought to sculpture and relief a 'southern' element all their own, which shows in the vigor and unprecedented realism of their works, together with an emphasis on the ethnic features of the Nubians."[70] Indeed, says German scholar Dietrich Wildung, the Kushites had "extraordinary" artistic impact in their injection of "vigorous new originality" into Egypt's traditional forms of architecture and sculpture.[71] W. Stevenson Smith, curator of Egyptian art at the Boston Museum of Fine Arts, further observes that, "The revival of Egyptian art which began in Dynasty XXV was . . . part of the resurgence of the Egyptian spirit which, without any real modification from abroad, was stimulated by vigorous Kushite rulers who had close religious ties with Thebes and a long tradition of Egyptian civilization."[72] Three art experts, three users of the word "vigor." One understands why Jean Leclant, an eminent authority on Kushite art and a professor at the Institut de France, sums up the 25th Dynasty's impact on Egyptian art in this laudatory manner: "Under . . . Shabako, Shebitku and Taharqa, Egypt underwent a veritable renaissance."[73]

REGARDING THE FIRST Kushite conquest of Lower Egypt, it is curious that historians have made no serious attempt to explain why a people from Africa's interior embarked on this extraordinary campaign c. 728 that reached the shores of the Mediterranean, the first initiative of this kind in recorded history.

Just as Assyria's menacing shadow affected Shabako's reign, so that Mesopotamian power might well have helped impel his predecessor Piye's military campaign. I believe Piye's sweep into Lower Egypt was motivated to a significant extent by a desire to demonstrate to Assyria that an invasion of the country would be met with force.[74]

Assyria had been on Egypt's doorstep before. In 734 BC, during his invasion of Khor, the Assyrian king Tiglath-pileser had sacked Gaza and gone as far as the Egyptian border. There, he erected a statue of himself, an unmistakable way of marking his territory.[75] Two years later, after putting down a rebellion elsewhere in Khor, Tiglath-pileser had returned to the Egyptian border in order to exercise control over the main trade route through the Sinai to the Nile valley. He named an Arab sheikh to a new position as "overseer on the Egyptian frontier"[76] and there erected a another statue of "my royal self" as a token, he said, of the "power and might which . . . I established over the lands."[77] These actions demonstrate a serious intent to wield some degree of control over Egypt's commerce with Khor.

In conquering Egypt, therefore, Piye would have prevented Tefnakht's expansion into central Egypt and perhaps even to Thebes, while cooling the turmoil in Lower Egypt. Second, he would have signalled to Assyria the Kushites' military ability to defend the territorial and commercial interests of both Egypt and Kush.[78] Therefore, it would have been in Piye's interests for Tefnakht and Osorkon to command substantial forces, so long as these were not used to expand again into Egypt's heartland. Without this military presence, Assyria might easily invade.

This second rationale—sending a message to Assyria—was probably the clinching reason for Piye's invasion. Otherwise, he could simply have made a defensive stand somewhere north of Thebes, preventing further territorial gains by Tefnakht and letting Lower Egypt go its own way. By advancing to the Delta, Piye demonstrated to Assyria that Kush had the will and the ability to defend all of Egypt. Better for the Kushites to face a tired and strained invader near the Sinai than to confront the same army in middle Egypt, after that army had rested well and reinvigorated itelf with the abundant provisions at hand.

By reducing (though not ending) Lower Egypt's internal divisiveness and turmoil, Piye also strengthened Egypt for a possible showdown with Assyria.[79] We may surmise that among the 11 separate political entities in Egypt at the time, at least several may have been in friendly contact with Assyria in the expectation that they could benefit from Assyrian intervention in Egypt. Seen in this light, Piye's granting of a pardon to Tefnakht and Osorkon, and his tolerance for their return to power once they had pledged loyalty to him, seems less like altruistic naiveté than a recognition that their continued presence (without unbridled expansionism) could prevent the sort of power vacuum that might lead to more internal disorder. These former rebels presented the first indigenous line of defense against invaders from the Sinai. Piye saw himself as guardian of Egypt's interests. The last thing he wanted was for Egypt to become easier prey for Assyria.

Indeed, his stela contains a line that suggests he was sending a message beyond Kush and Egypt. As the stela describes Piye sailing northward up the Nile to engage the enemy, along the way worshipping at Thebes to seek strength from Amon, it states: "the grandeur of his majesty attained the Asiatics and every heart trembled before him."[80] For "Asiatics," read all people east of Sinai.[81] It is hard to think of why Piye would be proud of impressing foreigners unless it was to deter their aggression.

Tiglath-pileser died in 727, removing some of the immediate Assyrian threat and permitting Piye to return to Napata, probably that same year. He could do so because he had made his point.

This could explain why Sargon did not penetrate Lower Egypt's threshold in 720. Egypt's defenders, who might have included Osorkon, appear to have been successful, since Sargon did not enter. It would be logical that, as part of a peace accord after his conquest, Piye had insisted that in the event of a future Assyrian threat Lower Egyptian statelets such as Osorkon's Tanis help defend the Sinai (instead of accommodating themselves to Assyrian invaders and serving as their appointed stand-ins, as Sais was to do several generations later). Piye would have been sure to leave some of his own forces behind in the north to stabilize this uneasy coalition.

Fortifying this hypothesis that the Napatan king adopted a strategy of defending Egypt are two separate collections of reliefs from Sargon's palace in Assyria and the temple of Amon at Napata. Adorning the palace at Dur-Sharrukin is a wall relief depicting a battle in which Assyrian horsemen confront infantrymen. The facial features of the latter allow their identification as Kushites, says one scholar who deduces that the conflict would have had to be against Sargon in his Sinai/Gaza campaign of 720.[82] Another relief shows soldiers with similar features serving as defenders in an unidentified siege; this, too, has also been given a date of 720.[83] Both sculptures, then, appear to give Kushite soldiers a leading role in the defense against an Assyrian campaign.

At Napata, a military scene carved into the temple wall has faintly survived. Anthony Spalinger, of New Zealand's University of Auckland, dates it to Piye's reign.[84] The scene shows four Kushites soldiers on foot, and one on horseback, defeating enemy troops. From their helmets, Spalinger concludes the foe must be Assyrian: the precise style of helmet, which resembles an inverted funnel with a knob at the top, was in use during the rule of Tiglath-pileser and Sargon (but not during Sennacherib's reign). Spalinger does not attempt to give a date or location for the battle, but 720 in the Sinai would seem a logical context.

Both the Assyrian and the Kushite artists portray their own sides as having the upper hand. Although no historians have attempted to put these scenes into an adequate political context, these sculptures are important as they attest to a Kushite effort to defend Egypt from Assyria as early as Piye's time.

This coherent rationale for Kush's double conquest of Egypt, in *c.* 728 and *c.* 712 provides a logic for the sudden emergence of this north-central African kingdom as a guiding force in Egypt in the last third of the eighth century BC. In the absence of such a rationale, one might have to assume that it was *sheer luck* that the dynasty that was in power in 701 just happened to possess one of the strongest—probably *the* strongest—army in Egypt in many centuries.[85]

That the Kushites were in the right place at the right time in 701 was no accident of history. And that they responded positively to Hezekiah's appeal for military help was also no fluke.

AT TIMES OF serious crisis in earlier centuries, aging pharaohs had occasionally elevated younger kinsmen to share the throne with them. The two pharaohs would be equal in theory, both holding the same divine status, though each would have his own areas of specialization. While the younger monarch would generally be responsible for military affairs, the senior pharaoh would continue to deal with other nations' leaders.[86]

Around 706, Shabako appears to have created such a co-regency, elevating his son, Shebitku, to share power with him.[87]

Establishing this co-regency would have made good sense. Because of the huge amount of territory involved and the need for rapid decisions during the crisis years, one pharaoh may have been primarily responsible for Lower Egypt, scene of most of the military build-up, and the other for the rest of Egypt and Kush. Shebitku would probably have been in charge of defending the frontier[88] while his father would have overseen the south, retaining ultimate authority over foreign policy and diplomacy.[89]

Because few contemporary writings that deal with Shebitku have survived, we know even less about him than Shabako. One of the few things that is certain is that he extradited Iamani, the refugee rebel, to Assyria around 705. Sargon ascribes this to his own pressure on Shebitku: "the terrifying splendor of my royalty overpowered him and fright overcame him. . . ."[90] The Kushites, he says, placed Iamani in "fetters, shackles and bonds of iron . . . and they brought him before me into Assyria, after a most difficult journey." Some historians see this Kushite response as spineless; John Bright goes so far as to call it "craven."[91]

Yet appeasement may well have been Egypt and Kush's only sensible option. Sargon appears to imply that he had threatened Shebitku with an invasion,[92] and the last thing the pharaoh needed was to bring down the fury of Assyria on Egypt before he was ready to make his own bold move.

ALLOWING EVENTS TO speak for themselves, we can see the reasons behind the 25th Dynasty's incursion into Khor.

The first, of course, is self-defense. Assyria had cut a destructive swath through Khor and then advanced to the threshold of Egypt, treasurehouse of the ancient world, in an increasingly menacing manner a total of five times in the previous 33 years (in 734, 733-732, 720, 716 and 712). On one of those occasions, 716, it had perhaps barged through the door. Assyria eventually did invade Egypt—unsuccessfully in 674 and victoriously in 671. The empire represented a mortal threat to it. Did Egypt have intelligence that Sennacherib planned to invade Egypt in 701, after bringing Khor to heel? Or that he planned to do so in the next several years, after consolidating his control of the region? We do not know. But the 25th Dynasty would have deemed it madness to sit back and wait. The new Assyrian king's appetite for war, as displayed in his swift response to the rebellion in Khor and in the conquests he had already undertaken east of Nineveh during the first three years of his reign, showed him to be ruthlessly ambitious.[93]

For Egypt, northern Philistia and the Phoenician cities of Sidon and Tyre were of little defensive significance (though very important for trade). But southern Philistia, including Ekron, Ashkelon and Gaza, were crucial. Southernmost Khor represented a land bridge between the Assyrian empire and Egypt. Assyria, which had no navy, needed an advance position to serve as a logistical base for any invasion across the Sinai and into Africa.[94]

The 25th Dynasty, in short, felt it needed to preserve southern Khor as a relatively neutral zone, or buffer, in order to protect the Nile Valley, including not only Lower and Upper Egypt, but Kush as well. Despite its remoteness, Kush was not invulnerable to attack. Far from it. In 591 BC, under Psamtik II of the 26th Dynasty, an Egyptian army employing Ionian, Carian and Rhodian mercenaries would sack the Nile city of Napata. Later that same century, Persia's King Cambyses would also try to conquer Kush, apparently turning back when he ran out of supplies. And in the first century BC, the Romans succeeded in reaching Napata and plundering it.

The dynasty's second reason was trade. Kush and Egypt had important commercial ties to maintain with the region. Egypt's major overland trade road, the "Way of the Sea," traversed the Sinai and continued along the coast of Philistia until Phoenicia, the trading centre of the Mediterranean and the Near and Middle East. Sea trade was extensive as well; Byblos, located in present-day Lebanon, traditionally ranked as Egypt's favored port in Khor.[95] By sea came timber, particularly cedar, from Phoenicia's coniferous forests. Egypt, with little wood of its own, needed the timber for shipbuilding and construction of buildings. Other products from

Khor that found markets in Egypt included olive oil, wine and spices, as well as salves and alum, both used in medicine,[96] and resin, a timber by-product used in mummification.

Keeping these land and sea routes open and free of hostile interference would have been a central economic concern for Egypt and Kush alike. It is unclear to what extent, if any, the Assyrian Empire was hindering trade at this time. The pharaoh might have feared, however, that if Sennacherib were to succeed in consolidating his hold on the region, Egyptian and Kushite commercial interests could only suffer, just as rolling back the Assyrian presence could only help. Trade, then, may not have been a primary reason for the Kushite Dynasty's intervention, but it would have represented a handsome fringe benefit.

It was in Kushite Egypt's compelling self-interest, then, to commit itself totally to the task of keeping southern Khor out of Assyrian hands. After sending an initial army, composed of forces that were already in northern Egypt, to confront the Assyrian army, the government would have felt the stakes sufficiently high to mobilize and dispatch additional troops from elsewhere in Egypt or Kush.

WHEN DECIDING TO launch themselves militarily in the Middle East, would the Kushite planners have felt out of their element there or on unfamiliar ground?

Contrary to the popular understanding, sub-Saharan soldiers were no strangers to that part of the world. Records indicate their involvement in Khor for at least 1,500 years prior to Sennacherib's invasion. Indeed, some six centuries before that conflict, Kushite soldiers serving under the ultimate authority of Egypt were actually posted in Jerusalem as defenders of that town. Prior to 701, the most recent involvement of black Africans in Khor would have probably been *c.* 712, when some served as mercenaries in the Ashdodite rebellion against Assyria.[97] For Kushite strategists in 701, an expedition across the Sinai and into the coastal plain and hills of Khor would not have been seen necessarily as a geographically exotic adventure. It would have been within the Kushite military's traditional area of deployment.

Yet military activity was not the only means by which Kushites had become familiar with Khor and even regions beyond. Commerce was another. Kushite trade missions would have journeyed as far as Assyria. The Kushites bred an unusually large horse in the dry highlands of the Dongola Reach, on the west bank of the Nile just below Kawa and downstream from Napata.[98] In an article on Assyrian forces, Stephanie Dalley describes a document from 732 BC that has been found at Nimrud, Assyria's capital at the time. The document mentions Kushites in such a manner as to suggest that Kushite "horse experts were at the court of Tiglath-pileser, and that the business of importing Nubian horses into Assyria began in earnest during his reign."[99]

The Assyrians deemed the large "Kush" horse to be the most desirable of all breeds for the chariotry (as distinct from the cavalry).[100] So coveted was it as a battle horse that, Dalley speculates, the unstated main objective of both Tiglath-pileser and Sargon in establishing trading posts at (or inside) the Egyptian border was to improve their pipeline to the horses.[101] Various states in Khor also appear to have prized these matchless chariot-pullers.[102] The point is that prior to its ascendancy in Egypt, Kush was not so isolated from markets in Khor and Mesopotamia as one might imagine. (Indeed, it is reasonable to ask whether a mission to Assyria's capital by Kushite horse experts did not also serve as an opportunity for intelligence gathering.)

How much of an underdog would Kushite Egypt have been in a matchup between its total forces and Assyria's total forces?

Spalinger's even-handed study of the available evidence of Kushite field tactics, weaponry and protective gear in Piye's reign concludes that these were "backward" compared with Assyria's.[103] Still, Kush would have taken pains over the next generation to narrow the military gap between itself and Assyria. An allusion by Isaiah to Kushite Egypt testifies to the impressiveness of its forces just prior to the showdown of 701. The prophet says Jerusalem seeks help from the 25th Dynasty's forces because of its "trust in the multitude of their chariots and in the great strength of their horsemen."[104]

Kushite Egypt probably also had the element of surprise in its favor. After all, no pharaoh since the marauding Shishak, 200 years before, had sent an army to Khor, and that had been in an offensive, not defensive capacity. Sennacherib may have anticipated that the 25th Dynasty would follow the familiar pattern of waiting for the Assyrian army to reach the Sinai before trying to block it.

Finally, we do not know what portion of Assyria's total armed forces was on that campaign in Khor. Anticipating an easy sweep, Sennacherib may not have campaigned at maximum strength. We can confidently assume, however, that the 25th Dynasty was ready to throw everything it had at Sennacherib. For Shebitku, sending his troops into Khor would have been the penultimate gamble. If, having drained Egypt and Kush of all available manpower for this desperate attempt to head the enemy off, the 25th Dynasty should lose in Khor, the Nile Valley would be virtually defenseless.

If in the late summer of 701 BC Judah's survival was hanging in the balance, so, too, was the security of Egypt and, ultimately, of Kush.

PART II

The Solution

"Perhaps the mystery is a little too plain,"

said Dupin.

Edgar Allan Poe

"The Purloined Letter"

CHAPTER SEVEN

The Three Sources

IN HIS HIGHLY regarded 1967 volume, *Isaiah and the Assyrian Crisis*, Brevard Childs, professor of the Old Testament at Yale Divinity School, laments that it will never be possible to detect the reason for Sennacherib's withdrawal without the discovery of "fresh extra-biblical evidence."[1] The complaint has become widely cited. Other investigators of the crisis use the eminent expert's cry of despair as kind of ritual alibi for their own lack of success. "Only by digging up a new inscription somewhere," they seem to be saying, "will anyone ever be able to do more than guess at the solution to this important mystery."

Yet the evidence already exists. The three familiar primary sources are chock full of telling but overlooked clues. The trick is this: to find them, it helps to be free of preconceptions that the Kushites were incapable.

In Sennacherib's own accounts, the king presented his version of the campaign of 701 BC in several different genres. The principal one is the annal, a record that Assyrian rulers customarily wrote for each year of their reign. Written in cuneiform on a surface of baked clay and first translated into English in 1878, the principal annal that describes the campaign is about 700 words long.[2] The text is highly self-serving. Like all annals, it emphasizes the aspects of the campaign that the ruler perceives as positive and covers up setbacks. In this text for 701, the "king of the universe" makes no explicit mention that he failed to conquer Jerusalem.

In addition, part of a brief Assyrian text (of a more religious nature) has survived.[3] It contributes modestly to our knowledge of the campaign: it states that Sennacherib conquered one Judahite town, Azekah, which is north of both Lachish and Libnah, and also one city, whose name has been lost but which could be Gath,[4] the Philistine stronghold south of Ekron that Hezekiah had annexed during his expansionist phase.

The most vivid account of Sennacherib's atrocities is a wordless one. It is the bas-relief of the siege of Lachish in 701. The king mounted this finely detailed sculpture on his palace walls at Nineveh. It depicts the tactics and awesome weaponry that he used to conquer Judah's second largest city as well as the punishments that he inflicted on its inhabitants, including the execution of recalcitrants by means of torture. The tableau presents Sennacherib on a hilltop receiving tribute from Hebrew captives; the resplendent king sits on his throne in front of the royal tent, while two attendants, standing on either side of him, wave fans made of plumes.

The cuneiform inscription above the king's head states matter-of-factly: "Sennacherib, the mighty king, king of the country of Assyria, sitting on the throne of judgment, at the entrance of the city of Lachish. I give permission for its slaughter."[5]

In addition to providing vainglorious decor, the relief had a didactic function. In the most blunt and colorful terms, it made clear to envoys or other visitors from subject societies the risks inherent in rebellion.[6] For any visitor to miss that point would have been difficult: the sculpture was more than eight and a half feet in height and measured 88 feet in length.[7] Imagine 17 Ping-Pong tables placed on their ends, vertically, one next to the other—a veritable stone IMAX.

The relief, now at the British Museum, also had an ulterior political function. By calling attention so spectacularly to Sennacherib's triumph at one Judahite city, the artwork served to divert attention from his vexing failure to capture the same country's capital. Like the annal that described the same campaign, it was part of the cover-up.

Here is the main annal. The text is a modified version of the standard translation by Daniel David Luckenbill.[8]

In my third campaign I marched against Hatti. Luli, king of Sidon, whom the terror-inspiring glamor of my lordship had overwhelmed, fled far overseas and perished. The awe-inspiring splendor of the "Weapon" of Ashur, my lord, overwhelmed his strong cities such as Great Sidon, Little Sidon, Bit-Zitti, Zaribtu, Mahalliba, Ushu, Akzib and Akko, all his fortress cities, walled and well-provided with feed and water for his garrisons, and they bowed in submission to my feet. I installed Ethba'al [Tuba'lu] upon the throne to be their king and imposed upon him tribute due to me as his overlord to be paid annually without interruption.

As to all the kings of Amurru—Menahem from Samsimuruna, Tuba'lu from Sidon, Abdili'ti from Arvad, Urumilki from Byblos, Mitinti from Ashdod, Buduili from Beth-Ammon, Kammusunadbi from Moab and Aiarammu from Edom—they brought sumptuous gifts and—fourfold—their heavy presents to me and kissed my feet. Sidqia, however, king of Ashkelon, who did not bow to my yoke, I deported and sent to Assyria, his family-gods, himself, his wife, his children, his brothers, all the male descendants of his family. I set Sharruludari, son of Rukibtu, their former king, over the inhabitants of Ashkelon and imposed upon him the payment of tribute and of presents due to me as overlord—and he now pulls the straps of my yoke!

In the continuation of my campaign I besieged Beth-dagon, Joppa, Banai-barqa, Azuru, cities belonging to Sidqia who did not bow to my feet quickly enough; I conquered them and carried their spoils away. The officials, the patricians and the common people of Ekron—who had thrown Padi, their king, into fetters because he was loyal to his solemn oath sworn by the god Ashur, and had handed him over to Hezekiah, the Judahite—and he [Hezekiah] held him in prison, unlawfully, as if he [Padi] be an enemy—had become afraid and had called for help upon the kings of Egypt and the bowmen, the chariot corps and the cavalry of the king of Kush, an army beyond counting—and they actually had come to their assistance. In the plain of Eltekeh, their battle lines were drawn up against me and they sharpened their weapons. Upon a trust-inspiring oracle given by Ashur, my lord, I fought with them and inflicted a defeat upon them. In the melee of the battle, I personally captured alive the Egyptian charioteers with their princes and also the charioteers of the king of Kush. I besieged Eltekeh and Timnah, conquered them and carried their spoils away. I assaulted Ekron and killed the officials and patricians who had committed the crime and hung their bodies on poles surrounding the city. The common citizens who were guilty of minor crimes, I considered prisoners of war. The rest of them, those who were not accused of crimes and misbehavior, I released. I made Padi, their king, come from Jerusalem and set him as their lord on the throne, imposing upon him the tribute due to me as overlord.

As to Hezekiah, the Judahite, he did not submit to my yoke. I laid siege to 46 of his strong cities, walled forts and to the countless small villages in their vicinity, and conquered them by means of well-stamped earth-ramps and battering-rams brought thus near to the walls combined with the attack by foot soldiers, using mines, breeches as well as sapper work. I drove out of them 200,150 people, young and old, male and female, horses, mules, donkeys, camels, big and small cattle beyond counting, and considered them booty. Himself I made a prisoner in Jerusalem, his royal residence, like a bird in a cage. I surrounded him with earthwork in order to molest those who were leaving his city's gate. His towns which I had plundered, I took away from his country and gave them over to Mitinti, king of Ashdod, Padi, king of Ekron, and Sillibel, king of Gaza. Thus I reduced his country, but I still increased the tribute and the presents due to me as his overlord which I imposed later upon him beyond the former tribute, to be delivered annually. Hezekiah himself, whom the terror-inspiring splendor of my lordship had overwhelmed, sent me after my departure to Nineveh, my royal city, his elite troops and best soldiers, which he had brought into Jerusalem as reinforcements, with 30 talents of gold, 800 talents of silver, precious stones, antimony, large cuts of red stone, couches inlaid with ivory, chairs inlaid with ivory, elephant hides, ebony wood, boxwood and all kinds of valuable treasures, his own daughters, concubines, male and female musicians. In order to deliver the tribute and to do obeisance as a slave, he sent his personal messenger.

The Hebrew Bible/Old Testament's three accounts of the events of 701 BC are roughly similar. Of these, the two earliest are the Second Book of Kings 18:13-19:37 and the Book of Isaiah, chapters 36 and 37. The other version, compiled well after the others, is the Second Book of Chronicles, chapter 32.

The Second Kings and the Isaianic texts are almost, but not quite, identical. A resounding majority of scholars[9] maintain that the Isaiah version was copied from the Second Kings text, rather than the other way around. The Second Kings narrative is also very slightly longer.[10] This book will reflect that general view and use Second Kings as the preferred text. Conventional scholars say that the Second Kings account was mostly written in the period of the seventh-sixth centuries BC.

For our purposes, the Book of Second Chronicles is of relatively little significance. Conventional scholars say it appears to have been written in the latter part of the fifth century BC or perhaps the early fourth century.[11] Almost all scholars agree that whoever wrote Chronicles borrowed heavily from the Second Kings/Isaiah prototype. It provides little new information that is reliable.[12] (Chronicles retells the siege story from a different perspective. While the Second Kings account emphasizes the role of the prophet Isaiah during the siege, for example, Chronicles plays up Hezekiah's performance and elaborates on his prior religious reforms. It also makes no mention of Taharqa's advance.)

The main version, in Second Kings, is more than just an account of an important event. Its *context* within the Bible is also significant. Four of the Hebrew Bible's books—First and Second Samuel and First and Second Kings—describe sequentially the rule of David's royal dynasty over its entire four-century span. In this official history, Second Kings' account of the Deliverance of Jerusalem occupies a literary function that, as noted, Ronald Clements describes as "a kind of high-point in the whole story of the monarchy which begins in 1 Samuel 8 and does not conclude until 2 Kings 25."[13] Why so lofty a function? Earlier, when describing Solomon's reign in First Kings, this biblical history had told of how Yahweh at that time chose Jerusalem as his city—"My name shall be there," Yahweh had declared, referring to the Temple.[14] Yahweh's choice, Clements observes, now "comes to its fullest justification in the story of the city's rescue out of the very grip of Sennacherib."[15] The story represents a key element in what he calls "the belief that this city [Jerusalem] was the subject of a special destiny in the election and historical fortunes of Israel."[16]

In the three books that recount the Deliverance—Second Kings, Isaiah and Second Chronicles—some passages are historically reliable but many others are not, providing false information that has thrown many experts off the trail. We will review the passages' credibility later.

First and Second Books of Kings were originally a single book of the Bible that has been divided. As the University of Chicago's Steven W. Holloway has pointed out, the book "is a theological history; it does not attempt to offer an objective or dispassionate reportage of 'facts.' Its authors were primarily concerned with the didactic possibilities of the reigns of their kings for illustrating the interplay of the divine and human wills in light of the present."[17] Still, the books of Kings are far more reliable than the books of Chronicles. As Holloway points out, "the Chronicler" took many more liberties with his sources "according to the exigencies of his theological program." He adds that the "historical value of Chronicles is slender, and should be used with great caution for the purposes of historical reconstruction."[18]

In addition to these three narrative versions of the siege, the Bible also contains fleeting passages that refer to the events of 701. The most useful are scattered in early chapters of the Book of Isaiah. Unlike chapters 36 and 37 of the same book, these passages do not repeat what is already in Second Kings. Many experts agree that either the prophet himself composed these oracles at the time of the events or else that others wrote them after his death while they were under the impress of those events.

The Hebrew Bible contains allusions to the crisis elsewhere, for example Micah 1:8-16. But these shed only a little additional light.

Below is the pertinent text from Second Kings. This rigorous translation, very slightly modified here,[19] is by Mordechai Cogan and Hayim Tadmor in the Anchor Bible series.

Here are two points on style:

■ True to the original Hebrew, the following translation renders "YHWH" instead of "Yahweh" or, as in most English translations, "Lord."

■ This text is presented here in three different typefaces. This is to distinguish between different segments of the narrative that will be discussed later.

CHAPTER 18

13 In the fourteenth year of King Hezekiah, Sennacherib, king of Assyria, attacked all of Judah's fortified cities and seized them. 14 Whereupon Hezekiah, King of Judah, sent a message to the king of Assyria at Lachish:"I admit my guilt.Withdraw from me and whatever you will impose upon me, I shall bear." The king of Assyria then imposed [a payment of] 300 talents of silver and 30 talents of gold upon Hezekiah, king of Judah. 15 And so Hezekiah turned over all the silver stored in the House ofYHWH and in the palace treasury. 16 At that time Hezekiah stripped the doors of the Temple Hall and the posts, which he himself had plated, and delivered them to the king of Assyria.

17 The king of Assyria dispatched the Tartan, the Rab-saris and the Rab-shakeh from Lachish to King Hezekiah in Jerusalem, together with a large force. They marched up to Jerusalem and took up positions by the conduit of the Upper Pool on the Fuller's Field Road; 18 and they called for the king. Eliakim, son of Hilkiah, the royal steward, Shebna the scribe, and Joah, son of Asaph, the recorder, came out to them.

19 The Rab-shakeh spoke to them, "Tell Hezekiah, thus said the Great King, the king of Assyria, 'What is this confidence of yours? 20 Do you think that plans and arming for war can emerge from empty talk? Now, in whom have you put your trust that you rebelled against me? 21 Here now, you put your trust in this splintered reed staff, in Egypt; that if someone leans upon it, it pierces his palm and punctures it. That is

Pharaoh, king of Egypt, to all who put their trust in him!'

22 And if you tell me, 'It is in YHWH our God that we put our trust!' Is he not the one whose high places and altars Hezekiah removed, and then ordered throughout Judah and Jerusalem, 'You must worship before this altar in Jerusalem?'

23 Now, come make a wager with my master, the king of Assyria: I will give you 2,000 horses, if you will be able to supply riders for them. 24 And so, how could you turn down one of my master's minor servants and trust in Egypt for chariots and horsemen? 25 Now was it without YHWH that I marched against this place to destroy it? YHWH said to me, 'Attack this country and destroy it!'"

26 Eliakim, son of Hilkiah, Shebna and Joah then said to the Rab-shakeh, "Please speak Aramaic with your servants; we understand it. Do not speak Judean with us within earshot of the people on the wall." 27 But the Rab-shakeh answered them, "Was it to your master and to you that my master has sent me to speak these words? Was it not rather to the men sitting on the wall, who, together with you, will have to eat their own excrement and drink their own urine?"

28 Then the Rab-shakeh stepped forward and called out loudly in Judean, "Hear the message of the Great King, the king of Assyria. 29 Thus said the king, 'Do not let Hezekiah deceive you, for he cannot save you from me.' 30 And do not let Hezekiah have you put your trust in YHWH by saying, 'YHWH will surely save us; and this city will not be handed over to the king of Assyria.' 31 Do not listen to Hezekiah; for thus said the king of Assyria, 'Send me a gift and surrender to me! Then each one of you will eat of his own vine and of his own fig tree and will drink the water of his own cistern; 32 until I come to transfer you to a land like your own land, a land of grain and new wine, a land of bread and vineyards, a land of olive oil and honey. Stay alive and don't die.' Do not listen to Hezekiah when he incites you by saying, 'YHWH will save us!' 33 Did any of the gods of these nations ever save his land from the king of Assyria? 34 Where are the gods of Hamath and Arpad? Where are the gods of Sepharvaim?

Where are the gods of Samaria? Did they save Samaria from me? 35 Who of all the gods of the countries was able to save his land from me, that YHWH should be able to save Jerusalem from me?"

36 They remained silent and did not answer a word, for it was the king's order, "Do not answer him!"

37 Thereupon Eliakin, son of Hilkiah, the royal steward, Shebna the scribe, Joah, son of Asaph, the recorder, came to Hezekiah with their garments rent, and reported the Rab-shakeh's message to him.

CHAPTER 19

1 When King Hezekiah heard this, he rent his garments and put on sackcloth and entered the House of YHWH. 2 He sent Eliakim, the royal steward, Shebna the scribe and the elder priests, dressed in sackcloth, to Isaiah, son of Amoz, the prophet. 3 They told him, "Thus said Hezekiah, 'This day is a day of distress, of rebuke and of contempt. Children have come to the breach, but there is no strength for the birth. 4 Perhaps YHWH your God will listen to all the words of the Rab-shakeh, whom his master the king of Assyria sent to taunt the living God and will punish him for the words which YHWH your God has heard. So do offer a prayer for this last remnant!'"

5 Now when the servants of King Hezekiah came to Isaiah, 6 Isaiah said to them, "Speak thus to your master: Thus said YHWH, 'Do not be frightened by the words you have heard by which these attendants of the king of Assyria reviled me. 7 Behold, I will put a spirit in him, so that he will hear a report and return to his own country, and I will strike him down by the sword in his own country.'"

8 Now the Rab-shakeh withdrew, and since he heard that the camp had moved from Lachish, he found the king of Assyria engaged in battle at Libnah. 9 He [the king of Assyria] received a report about Tirhakah, king of Kush: He has set out to do battle with you. *So again he sent messengers to Hezekiah: 10 "Speak thus to Hezekiah, king of Judah, 'Do not let your God deceive, the one in whom you put your trust, by thinking that Jerusalem will not be*

*given over to the king of Assyria. 11 Now surely you have heard what
the kings of Assyria did to all the lands—destroying them! And you—
will you be saved? 12 Did the gods of the nations save them whom my
ancestors destroyed, Gozan and Haran and Reseph and the Edenites
of Telassar? 13 Where is the king of Hamath and the king of Arpad
and the king of Lair, Sepharvaim, Hena and Iwwah?'"*

*14 Hezekiah received the letter from the messengers and read it.
He then went up to the House of YHWH; Hezekiah spread it out
before YHWH, 15 and Hezekiah prayed before YHWH, "O YHWH,
God of Israel, enthroned upon the cherubim, You, alone, are God of
all the kingdoms of the earth. It was You who made heaven and earth.
16 Turn your ear, O YHWH, and listen; open your eyes, O YHWH,
and look. Listen to the message that Sennacherib has sent to taunt the
living God. 17 It is true, O YHWH, that the kings of Assyria have laid
waste the nations and their lands, 18 and put their gods to fire—for
they are not gods, but only man's handicraft, mere wood and stone;
thus they were able to destroy them. 19 But now, O YHWH, our God,
save us from his hand, so that all the kingdoms of the earth may know
that You, YHWH, alone, are God."*

*20 Then Isaiah son of Amoz sent a message to Hezekiah: "Thus
said YHWH, God of Israel, 'I have heard your prayer to me concerning Sennacherib, king of Assyria. This is what YHWH has spoken concerning him:*

*21 "Maiden Daughter Zion
despises you, scorns you.
Daughter Jerusalem
shakes her head after you.
22 Whom have you taunted and reviled?
Against whom have you raised your voice?
And raised your eyes heavenward?
Against the Holy One of Israel!
23 Through your messengers you taunted YHWH by saying,
With my many chariots, [. . .]
I ascended mountain peaks, the far reaches of the Lebanon.
I felled its tallest cedars, its choicest firs.
I entered its remotest lodge, its rich woodlands.*

24 It was I who dug and drank strange waters,
And with the soles of my feet I dried up the Niles of Egypt.
25 Have you not heard? From of old, I did it.
In ancient days, I fashioned it. Now I have brought it about—
And it is: Fortified cities crashing into ruined heaps,
Their inhabitants powerless, dismayed and confounded.
They were like grass in the field, and fresh pasture;
Like straw on rooftops, blasted by the east wind.
27 Your every action and your every pursuit, I know.
28 Because you have raged against me, and your uproar rings in
my ears,
I will put my hook in your nose and my bridle through your lips,
and turn you back on the very road by which you came.
29 This shall be the sign for you:
This year you shall eat from the aftergrowth,
next year from the self-sown;
but in the third year, sow and reap,
plant vineyards and enjoy their fruit.
30 The remaining survivors of the house of Judah shall add on
roots below and produce fruit above.
31 For a remnant shall emerge out of Jerusalem,
And a survivor from Mount Zion. The zeal of YHWH shall
effect this.
32 Therefore, thus said YHWH concerning the king of Assyria:
He shall not enter this city, nor shall he shoot an arrow there.
He shall not move up defenses before it,
nor throw up a siege mound against it.
33 He shall go back by the same road he came; but into this
city,
he shall not enter. The word of YHWH.
34 For I will defend this city and save it for my own sake
and for the sake of David, my servant."
35 That night, YHWH's angel went out and struck the Assyrian
camp—185,000 men! At daybreak there were dead bodies all about.
36 So Sennacherib, king of Assyria, broke camp and left.
He returned to Nineveh, where he resided. *37 Once, as he was*

worshipping in the House of Nisroch, his god, Adrammelech and Sharezer, his sons, struck him down with the sword and then fled to the land of Ararat. Esarhaddon, his son, became king.

◎

THE GREEK AUTHOR of the first important narrative history of the world, Herodotus, visited Egypt approximately 250 years after Sennacherib's invasion. His brief account of the hostilities of 701,[20] just over 300 words in length, reflects a point of view that is not so much Greek as Lower Egyptian—since it was Lower Egyptians who were Herodotus' sources.

In the following text, translated by Aubrey de Sélincourt:
- Hephaestus corresponds to the Memphite god Ptah.[21]
- Sethos was Shebitku.[22]

Next on the throne after Anysis was Sethos, the high priest of Hephaestus. He is said to have neglected the warrior class of the Egyptians and to have treated them with contempt, as if he had been unlikely to need their services. He offended them in various ways, not least by depriving them of the 12 acres of land which each of them had held by special privilege under previous kings.

As a result, when Egypt was invaded by Sennacherib, the king of Arabia and Assyria, with a great army, not one of them was willing to fight. The situation was grave; not knowing what else to do, the priest-king entered the shrine and, before the image of the god, complained bitterly of the peril which threatened him. In the midst of his lamentations he fell asleep, and dreamt that the god stood by him and urged him not to lose heart; for if he marched boldly out to meet the Arabian army, he would come to no harm, as the god himself would send him helpers.

By this dream the king's confidence was restored; and with such men as were willing to follow him—not a single one of the warrior class, but a mixed company of shopkeepers, artisans and market-people—he marched to Pelusium, which guards the approaches to Egypt, and there took up his position.

As he lay here facing the Assyrians, thousands of field-mice swarmed over them during the night, and ate their quivers, their bowstrings and the leather handles of their shields, so that on the following day, having no arms to fight with, they abandoned their position and suffered severe losses during their retreat.

There is still a stone statue of Sethos in the temple of Hephaestus; the figure is represented with a mouse in its hand, and the inscription: "Look upon me and learn reverence."

Herodotus labored under a huge handicap: this traveller of the fifth century BC gleaned his information from interviews with people who had only a spotty understanding of the facts. It is as though an amateur historian today were to reconstruct the U.S. Revolutionary War on the basis of Americans' folk memory: the dumping of a cargo of tea into Boston harbor by feisty dissidents and the apocryphal story of young George Washington admitting he chopped down his father's prized cherry tree might well loom larger than any discussion of the economics of colonialism or of General Washington's military strategy. Yet folk memory often contains grains of truth. Just as the Boston tea party evokes oppressive taxation and the cherry-tree yarn illustrates Washington's widely perceived integrity in the course of his presidency, so a factual base probably underlies Herodotus' version. The trick is to identify this base.

The most spectacular of the account's inaccuracies, of course, is the peculiar assertion that it was mice that drove away the invaders; later we will examine that statement.

Other oddities also leap out. One is the identification of Sennacherib as the "king of Arabia and Assyria" and of leading the "Arabian army." This would reflect the imperial forces' high foreign content. Another error is the Greek writer's statement that the Assyrians marched as far as "Pelusium," which is inside Egypt, not far from where the Suez Canal now joins the Mediterranan: in fact, Sennacherib never entered Egypt and probably did not get within 100 miles of Pelusium. What that geographical detail suggests is that the people of northern Egypt remembered

Sennacherib's campaign as a real threat to their country's security.[23] In addition, it is possible that, with blurred hindsight, in describing Sennacherib's invasion of 701 they may have borrowed elements from other Assyrian aggressions of the tumultuous 716-674 period. (As seen in Chapter 6, Hayim Tadmor suggests that in 716 the Assyrian army under Sargon may have reached Pelusium. Another possible element: in 674, the 25th Dynasty defeated at an unknown location inside Egypt an army led by Sennacherib's son and successor, Esarhaddon.)

Of the three ancient accounts of the events of 701, Herodotus' tale is the most problematic. But we would do well not to follow the example of some historians[24] and dismiss his account out of hand.

Of the ancient sources, there is no question as to which yields the most clues as to why Sennacherib turned tail. Biblical experts like Yale's Childs may minimize its informational value in regard to that question, but the Bible is truly useful. Like Edgar Allan Poe's purloined letter that lies in so obvious a place that the searchers do not find it, the Bible's evidence lies in full view.

CHAPTER EIGHT

The Kushites See "Chaos" Approaching

IN RESPONDING TO the entreaty from Judah and other members of the coalition to help stave off the invader, Shabako and Shebitku faced two daunting challenges. The pharaohs would confront the strongest military power ever to appear in the Mediterranean basin. And, in doing so, they would have to cope with a great handicap: their own forces were out of position and in disarray. That the pharaohs had to send their forces in two contingents, probably many weeks apart, suggests that the strategy of countering Assyria by means of a large-scale pre-emptive strike had not been planned long in advance. The contrast to Sennacherib's assiduously organized campaign is dramatic.

So, too, is the difference in equipment. The Kushites were more lightly armed than the Assyrians. Although they carried round shields, like Sennacherib's men, they wore relatively little protective gear like helmets and armor.[1] Most of the ordinary soldiers were probably barechested. Their kilts were slightly shorter than those of the Assyrians; unlike those of the Assyrians, which were wrapped around the hips more like a bath-towel, these kilts were joined in front. Some soldiers of standing wore kilts of leopard skins.

Like the Assyrians, the Kushites' elite forces would have been the cavalry and chariotry. Their skill in horsebreeding was renowned in the ancient world; their war chariots would also perhaps have been of the same large size, capable of holding three men, as their enemy's.[2] Still, it is doubtful that the Kushite chariotry and cavalry were the equal of their Assyrian counterparts for the simple reason that they lacked the same battle-hardening experience. The Assyrian equestrian corps engaged in combat almost annually. The Kushites' fighting had been sporadic and usually against relatively easy competition. Assyria had tested itself against the Babylonians, Elamites and other formidable adversaries.

But the most striking difference between the Kushite and Assyrian armies could not have been seen with the eye. It was the difference in what was going through their leaders' hearts and minds—in their belief systems. For the Assyrian kings, the religious justification for conquest was the aggrandizement of the god Ashur's domain and glory.[3] But the principal god of Kush and Upper Egypt, Amon, was no imperialistic deity. It was not through conquest *per se* that his worshippers honored him. Nonetheless, it was their Amon-based faith that impelled the Kushites to intervene in Khor.

The name Amon means "hidden one." His worshippers considered him to be invisible and often likened this invisibility to breath. He was the animating spirit of the universe. Some scholars see worship of Amon as closely anticipating monotheism. A Belgian specialist, Johannes de Moor, notes that in the course of the second millennium BC Amon more or less absorbed many other deities in Egypt's pantheon, including the sun-god Re, so that "all gods were in reality but manifestations of one god, Amon-Re"[4]—or, to put it more simply, Amon. Of the 10 or so dynasties that ruled in the course of the first millennium BC, the 25th Dynasty certainly promoted the worship of Amon the most vigorously.

One served Amon by living according to *ma'at*. This is a venerable concept, going back to the Old Kingdom, that underlies that Egyptian civilization's world-view. Lionel Casson, a classics professor at New York University, lucidly describes this crucial notion:

> The word is almost impossible to translate precisely, but it involved a combination of such ideas as "order," "truth," "justice," and

"righteousness." *Ma'at* was considered a quality not of men but of the world, built into it by the gods at the moment of Creation. As such, it represented the gods' will. A person endeavored to act in accordance with the divine will because that was the only way to place himself in harmony with the gods. For the Egyptian peasant *ma'at* meant working hard and honestly; for the official it meant dealing justly.[5]

Symbolizing the concept in ritual was a goddess, herself called Ma'at. But *ma'at's* real place was outside the temple. Ideally, the principle was supposed to pervade not just everyday life but even relations between states. Amon appointed the pharaoh to uphold *ma'at*. Egypt's turmoil leading up to the Kushite conquest of 728 BC—the discord involving 11 political entities, including the 22nd, 23rd and 24th pharaonic dynasties—was for the Kushites an "extraordinary offence to the earlier concept of *ma'at*," observes David O'Connor.[6] What Piye and his successors sought to do was restore that form of peace. The Kushites were "genuinely devoted to *ma'at*," says O'Connor, of the University of Pennsylvania. He adds: "Their devotion, they argued, generated supernatural aid and demonstrated the legitimacy of the Kushite accession."

It also helped shape Kushite foreign policy. *Ma'at* did not exist in isolation. It stood in opposition to what the Egyptians called *isfet*, which meant chaos or injustice, and which was always threatening *ma'at*-ordered culture. The traditional view, dating back eons, was that the pharaoh was divinely appointed to reinforce and safeguard *ma'at*. Faced with Sargon and Sennacherib's threatening advances toward Egypt in the late eighth century, the Kushites would have seen those emperors as agents of chaos and regarded themselves as sustainers of *ma'at*. While defense of the Nile Valley and trade considerations were the immediate reasons for the Kushites' pre-emptive strike into Khor, the overarching reason was the need to maintain *ma'at*.[7] Egypt's indigenous dynasties had showed themselves incapable or unwilling to acquit themselves of their pharaonic responsibility as Amon's representatives to repel chaos from Egypt. That explains why, starting with Piye, the Kushites felt themselves religiously called upon to fill the leadership void.

⌖

HERODOTUS SHEDS VALUABLE light on Kushite Egypt's internal politics in 701. Relying on Lower Egyptian sources, he says that the priest-like Kushite pharaoh was unable to bring in members of the "warrior class of the Egyptians," having previously "neglected" these soldiers and "treated them with contempt." Herodotus adds: "He offended them in various ways, not least by depriving them of the 12 acres of land which each of them had held by special privilege under previous kings. As a result, . . . not one of them was willing to fight."[8] In saying that *no* Egyptians took part in the conflict, Herodotus' version obviously exaggerates. When in his annal Sennacherib describes the battle of Eltekeh, the king observes that Egyptian charioteers and princes are fighting alongside Kushite bowmen, cavalry and charioteers.[9] But there are reasons to think Herodotus' version contains some truth: among the forces that marched to face the Assyrians, Egyptians were *under*-represented.

As we have seen, Egypt was anything but monolithic. While the 25th Dynasty had succeeded in bringing a measure of unity to the Two Lands after reconquering Lower Egypt in 712, not all enmities would have been extinguished. If Assyria intended to conquer Egypt, it would have made sense for it to nurture good relations with native elements within the targeted country, elements that would not stand in the way of the conquerors, that might even assist it with the conquest and that would, after a victory, help administer the country. Such is the *modus operandi* of many empires.

With which of Lower Egypt's factions would Sennacherib have cultivated warm ties in the lead-up to the crisis of 701? Although the record is silent, the logical party would be Sais, seat of Tefnakht's short-lived 24th Dynasty. The record speaks loudly about hostilities between Kushites and Saites during the periods both shortly before and shortly after Sennacherib's reign. In the decades before Sennacherib took power, the Kushites had twice overthrown the Saite rulers, first when Tefnakht was leader in *c.* 728 and then when his son Bakenranef held the throne about 16 years later. Afterwards, in the mid-seventh century BC when Assyria drove the Kushites from Egypt, Sennacherib's grandson installed the Saites as vassal rulers of the 26th Dynasty. Such was the bad blood between the two groups that the Saite pharaohs sought to expunge all traces of their Kushite predecessors from temples and other buildings.[10] Indeed, in the early sixth century BC the 26th Dynasty invaded Kush itself and laid waste to much of it.

When Herodotus speaks of very poor relations between the 25th Dynasty and a Lower Egyptian "warrior class," then, he is probably alluding to the embittered members of the Saite military that Kush had defeated in 712. One can understand why Shabako, and later Shebitku, would not have eradicated this army. *Ma'at* is one reason: the concept involved important ethical and political dimensions aimed at de-escalating animosity. In 728, showing *ma'at*, Piye had forgiven his adversaries after they had sworn fealty to him, even going so far as to pardon a former vassal named Namlot who had betrayed him to join Tefnakht's rebellion. And later, in a policy move not directly related to the Saite officers, Shabako abolished all capital punishment for criminals, a truly astonishing action in the ancient world where executions were a justice-system staple.[11] Shabako instead put criminals to work building dikes against flood waters. (The action moved Diodorus, the Greek historian of the first century BC, to comment approvingly, "His motive was to mitigate the rigor of punishment for those under sentence, while providing substantial benefits to the towns in place of useless penalties."[12]) So now, with the Saite officers on his hands, Shabako showed mercy rather than trying to execute, imprison or enslave them.[13] This propensity for forgiveness by Kushite monarchs is a departure from the behavior of most of their Egyptian counterparts. It may reflect an interpretation of *ma'at* distinctive to their culture.[14]

Shabako's treatment of the Saite officers might have had a practical advantage: it could have reduced resentment in the Delta against the Napatans and thus enabled them to focus on the external threat. By stripping the officers of generous land holdings, the pharaoh might also have loosened the military class's dominance in the Delta. In redistributing this property among civilians, he may have hoped to win popular support for the Kushite dynasty and weaken whatever pro-Assyrian sentiment existed.

In retrospect, it's hard to say that this Kushite policy toward the Saite military class was a blunder. True, the Saite officers still felt sufficiently resentful against the 25th Dynasty as to refuse to join its war effort against Sennacherib. The boycott suggests that even at this early date the Saite military was assuming that it had something to gain from an Assyrian conquest of Egypt. Still, the Saites did not actively make trouble for the Shabako-Shebitku tandem during the campaign against Sennacherib. Had they they mounted a fifth-column insurrection while Kushite forces were in Khor, the events of 701 might have turned out very differently. What *is* clear, however, is that the Kushite regime's inability to rally all of the Delta forces to its cause aggravated the military disparity between itself and Assyria.

Little wonder, then, that Herodotus describes Pharaoh Shebitku as lacking confidence until, in a dream, the pharaoh's god "stood by him and urged him not to lose heart." Herodotus says that Shebitku, compensating for the warriors' refusal to march with him, assembled a "mixed company of shopkeepers, artisans and marketpeople" to wage the military campaign. This is not as bizarre as it may sound. Years before, ever wary of a possible conflict with Assyria, the Kushites would probably have prepared for such an emergency by forming a militia in Egypt. Composing such a body would have been ordinary people from a variety of civilian walks of life. This militia's purpose would have been to complement the backbone of the military, a professional standing army that would have been stationed in northern Egypt and made up not only of Kushites but also of regular Egyptian troops from Tanis and other locales more friendly to the Kushite Dynasty than Sais.

Herodotus' underlying point, of course, needs no adjusting. Struggling to scrape together the manpower with which to confront Sennacherib, Shebitku entered the conflict as a desperate underdog.

THE BEGINNING OF the conflict belonged to the Assyrians.

According to Sennacherib, after following the curve of the Fertile Crescent to reach Khor, the imperial army came to the rebel Phoenician city of Sidon. It was a pushover. Sidon's overlord, Luli, the king of Tyre, fled to Cyprus. "The terror-inspiring glamour of my lordship," Sennacherib explains, "had overwhelmed [him]." Bombastic though Sennacherib's self-praise may be, his ability to strike profound fear in his foe is undeniable: Sidon and other cities in the region under Luli's control—the annal names six—quickly capitulated. Sennacherib placed his own man as king of Sidon.

Still, despite the annal's depiction of unalloyed triumph, there may have been one hitch: Tyre. That very major port, about 40 miles down the coast from Sidon, was located on an island several hundred yards from a town on the mainland. (Four centuries later, Alexander the Great would build a causeway to join Tyre to the mainland, and sand deposits would in time turn the island into a peninsula.) Sennacherib reports that he seized this mainland town, Ushu, but he is curiously silent about the fate of Tyre itself. Why? He may not have taken it. In his *History of Tyre*, H. Jacob Katzenstein surmises that the Assyrians lacked the ships with which to capture the island. His reasonable conclusion: "Sennacherib did not succeed in conquering Tyre, and therefore he speaks of Eloulaios [Luli] only as 'king of Sidon.' He hides his failure to conquer Tyre by not mentioning the city, which at this period was the most important in Phoenicia."[15]

Moving southward along the Mediterranean coast, Sennacherib next defeated the rebel Sidqia, king of the Philistine city of Ashkelon. It is not clear if Sennacherib advanced as far down the coast as Ashkelon, but he did vanquish four cities north of it that belonged to King Sidqia. One of these cities was the port city of Joppa, or Jaffa, which corresponds to the modern city of Tel Aviv. Sennacherib deported Sidqia and his family to Assyria.

Up to this point, the only serious action that Assyrian troops appear to have encountered was siege warfare. Now this changed. Having crossed the Sinai desert and marched northward up Philistia's coast, the army of combined Kushite and Egyptian forces confronted the Assyrians roughly a dozen miles south of Tel Aviv on the low hills near Eltekeh.

The only record that we have of this battle is Sennacherib's annal. Although it is brief, it helps us visualize the scene.[16] In addition to archers, the 25th Dynasty's army contained "Egyptian charioteers" as well as "charioteers of the king of Kush"—the elite royal squadrons. The Kushite royal cavalry was also present, and "an army beyond counting."

One thing is curious about Sennacherib's description of his foe: he makes no mention of infantry other than bowmen. Anthony Spalinger speculates that this is not a simple oversight. The omission may mean, he suggests, that the Kushite-Egyptian force "was not composed of hard-line infantry but rather of quickly moving units better able to harass and geared to a swift victory rather than to a prolonged battle wherein a large deployment of troops was required."[17] This reinforces the idea that the plodding militia would not have been part of this strike force. Spalinger makes an additional plausible deduction: in the absence of much infantry, he concludes that the 25th Dynasty's army "was outnumbered in both men and in material."[18]

In his annal, Sennacherib of course asserts that he "inflicted a defeat" upon these forces. But in questioning that, Spalinger[19] and many other scholars make a strong case. Hayim Tadmor infers from omissions in Sennacherib's account "that the 'victory' was rather exaggerated."[20] The Assyriologist points out that "no cogent details of the [opponent's] defeat are given (except the statement about prisoners taken 'in the midst of battle'), no numbers are mentioned, no booty is listed."

Kenneth Kitchen agrees, deducing that the Assyrians "merely repulsed, not routed" the Kushite-Egyptian forces, thereby permitting them to regroup.[21] It is worth noting that Sennacherib claims only to have captured an unstated number of Egyptian and Kushite charioteers and Egyptian princes; he says nothing about slaying or capturing Kushite commanders, whether they be royalty or not. In Assyrian annals, it is a convention to describe victories with emphasis on the ignominious fate of defeated enemies, often with statistical precision on the number of prisoners taken. Here, such detail is conspicuously absent.

After encountering this Kushite-Egyptian obstacle, Sennacherib continued on his sweep, advancing through the olive-growing countryside to Ekron. Archaeologists say a mudbrick wall surrounded the city, and that at the city's highest point a citadel tower had been constructed out of stones the size of boulders.[22] Ekron did not withstand the attack. Sennacherib asserts, "I . . . killed the officials and patricians who had committed the crime [of rebellion] and hung their bodies on poles surrounding the city."

He then moved into Judah itself where, by his own count, he captured "46 of [Judah's] strong cities [and] walled forts and . . . countless small villages in their vicinity."[23] The vanquished cities may have included the former Philistine city of Gath, which Hezekiah had annexed.[24] He may have begun to deport some Judahites, though probably not many.[25]

Sennacherib captured these walled enclosures by means of siege. More specifically, he says he "conquered them by means of well-stamped earth-ramps, and battering-rams brought thus near to the walls combined with the attack by foot soldiers, using mines, breeches as well as sapper work." Although the king's wording appears to say that all 46 sites required this drastic treatment, it seems likely that some of them might have capitulated more readily.

The famous relief in Sennacherib's palace tells the story of Lachish's fall in pictorial detail. The assault on Judah's second largest city demonstrated the kind of treatment that the Assyrians were capable of inflicting on Jerusalem. This attack undoubtedly had impact on Jerusalemites: as astute practitioners of psychological warfare, the Assyrians would have seen to it that eyewitness descriptions by Judahites of Lachish's collapse reached the capital, their next major target.

Here is the superb blow-by-blow "translation" of that sculpture by Sir Austen Henry Layard, the celebrated British excavator who in the late 19th century unearthed the relief along with the rest of Sennacherib's palace.[26] Lachish, he says, was evidently of great extent and importance. It appears to have been defended by double walls, with battlements and towers, and by fortified outworks.

The country around it was hilly and wooded, producing the fig and the vine.

The whole power of the great king seems to have been called forth to take this stronghold. In no other [Assyrian] sculptures were so many armed warriors seen drawn up in array before a besieged city.

In the first rank were the kneeling archers, those in the second were bending forward, whilst those in the third discharged their arrows standing upright, and were mingled with spearmen and slingers; the whole forming a compact and organized phalanx. The reserve consisted of large bodies of horsemen and charioteers.

Against the fortifications had been thrown up as many as 10 banks or mounts, compactly built of stones, bricks, earth and branches of trees, and seven battering-rams had already been rolled up to the walls.

The besieged defended themselves with great determination. Spearmen, archers and slingers thronged the battlements and towers, showering arrows, javelins, stones and blazing torches upon the assailants. On the battering-rams were bowmen discharging their arrows, and men with large ladles pouring water upon the flaming brands, which, hurled from above, threatened to destroy the [rams]. Ladders, probably used for escalade, were falling from the walls upon the soldiers who mounted the inclined ways to the assault.

The events in the bas-relief do not occur simultaneously but sequentially. Other scenes show events after the city's fall.

Beneath its walls were seen Assyrian warriors impaling their prisoners, and from the gateway of an advanced tower, or fort, issued a procession of captives, reaching to the presence of the king, who, gorgeously arrayed, received them seated on his throne.

Amongst the spoil were furniture, arms, shields, chariots, vases of metal of various forms, camels, carts drawn by oxen and laden with women and children. . . .

Several prisoners were already in the hands of the torturers. Two were stretched naked on the ground to be flayed alive, others were being slain by the sword before the throne of the king. The haughty monarch was receiving the chiefs of the conquered nation, who crouched and knelt humbly before him. They were brought into the royal presence by the Tartan of the Assyrian forces . . . , followed by his principal officers.

This "Tartan" is the same high official whom Second Kings describes as later coming to the walls of Jerusalem to demand surrender.

The archaeological evidence in recent decades confirms much of what the bas-relief has to say about the attack itself. Those vestiges that have been unearthed indeed suggest a heroically desperate defense. After the Lachishites had repelled the Assyrians' initial assaults, the besiegers constructed a ramp of stones that, say excavators, rose to the very top of the city's wall.[27] A horizontal platform would have rested on the summit of this steep incline; from the platform, siege machines and soldiers could attack the defenders from an equal height. Traces remain of the Lachishites' response: they built a counter-ramp out of debris. This construction rose even higher than the attackers' ramp.

Excavators have found an iron chain and large stones with perforations through which ropes would have been attached. The defenders would have used these to try to topple the siege machines.

By constructing this counter-ramp, the Lachishites would have bought themselves time with which to build a *new* line of defense to fall back upon once the Assyrians had finally overrun the city wall. That may be the second wall that Layard refers to.

Archaeologists also made a gruesome discovery at Lachish: four caves used as mass graves. They counted bones of some 1,500 people, presumably victims of the siege. Some of these bones were burnt, leading archaeologists to speculate that if these people had not actually burned to death, they died, in one expert's careful words, in "a catastrophe in which fires were involved," and the corpses were then placed in these caves.[28] An examination of 695 of the skulls has led another expert to conclude that almost half belonged to adult females and to so-called "immature" individuals, which would mean that these were civilians rather than regular soldiers.[29]

When the Assyrians soon gathered under the walls of Jerusalem, the people of that city would have had reason to expect the enemy to show the same kind of determination against them.

[◦]

ISAIAH, OBSERVING THE condition of Judah from the vantage point of Jerusalem, declares, "Your country is desolate, your cities lie in ashes."[30] Of the entire country, he says, only Jerusalem is left, "as defenseless as a watchman's hut in a vineyard or a shed in a cucumber field."[31]

The prophet also says that many—indeed, he claims "all"—of Jerusalem's top leaders (presumably military) ran away and were captured without resistance.[32] But we know that Hezekiah was not totally abandoned: Second Kings says that at least three senior court officials, none of them military, did remain with Hezekiah throughout the siege.[33]

According to a reconstruction of the campaign based on Isaiah, the Assyrians would have advanced on Jerusalem in two groups.[34] While the main force remained with Sennacherib in the general region of Lachish, a smaller group would have descended on Jerusalem from the Assyrian province of Samarina (formerly, Samaria) to the north. This smaller group would presumably have reached Jerusalem first and initiated the siege.

The Book of Second Kings says that while Sennacherib was engaged at Lachish, he sent from there to Jerusalem a "large army." It was commanded by the Tartan—or viceroy—who in the Assyrian army was second only to the king.[35] Two other senior royal attendants accompanied him: the Rab-saris, literally the chief eunuch, and the Rab-shakeh, or literally the chief cupbearer or butler.[36] These two officials' actual functions, however, would have greatly transcended their rather menial titles. They would have been among high-ranking members of the imperial elite. The Rab-shakeh's duties, while hard to pin down, would have included military and civil responsibilities, perhaps even the administration of a province.[37]

The Lachish relief depicts the senior of these three august Assyrians. Layard's description of the king's main general standing outside Lachish's walls suggests how grandly imposing he must have looked to Jerusalemites a few days or weeks later when he confronted them with terms of their surrrender. The Tartan, his squared beard reaching his chest, was "clothed in embroidered robes, and wore on his head a fillet adorned with rosettes and long tassled bands."[38] His rich robes also had tassles and reached his ankles. No contemporary source describes the physical appearance of the Tartan's two companions at Jerusalem, the Rab-shakeh and the Rab-saris, but they must have been comparably elegant. As emissaries of the world's greatest empire, part of their job in encountering the Jerusalemites would have been to inspire them with awe and a sense of abject inferiority.

The three walked up to the city's walls. There, within full hearing of Jerusalemites crowding the rampart, they parleyed with three ranking officials of Hezekiah's court. The Assyrian speaker was the Rab-shakeh. While he was not the trio's highest-ranking member, he was evidently fluent in the language of Judah, which he used in addressing Hezekiah's representatives.[39] (Cogan & Tadmor speculate the official may even have been of Hebrew origin, his family having been deported from Israel to Assyria.[40]) From the content of his remarks, it is clear that he switched from reading aloud a letter from Sennacherib to speaking spontaneously on his own authority.[41]

The biblical text presents the envoy as skillfully weaving a series of arguments in favor of surrender.

Jerusalem bases its self-confidence, says the Rab-shakeh, on empty talk, instead of on military skill. In relying on the pharaoh for help, he says, Jerusalem is like a person who seeks support by leaning on a reed and whose hand will be punctured when that reed inevitably splinters. He is employing adroit, incisive wordplay: the reed was a symbol that Egyptians commonly used to denote Upper Egypt.[42]

Hezekiah, he goes on, has already undermined Yahweh's authority. The king "destroyed" that god's altars and shrines in the countryside, centralizing the cult in Jerusalem. Yahweh therefore owes Hezekiah no favors. Yahweh himself "told" Sennacherib to destroy all of Judah, the Rab-shakeh claims, an argument that seems to seize on Isaiah's declarations that Sennacherib's army is but an instrument of divine punishment.

The official added a taunt. If Jerusalem would rather resist than give up, Assyria will then even lend the city 2,000 horses—"if you can find that many men to ride them"—a way of underscoring the desertions and the futility of Hezekiah's resistance.

With colorful imagery, the Assyrian then lays before the Jerusalemites the alternative. If Hezekiah rejects the terms of surrender, they will needlessly starve, having to "eat their own excrement and drink their own urine." If the city yields, Assyria will deport the people to an unnamed land of "olive oil and honey."

Finally, the Rab-shakeh says, no national gods have ever successfully stood up to Ashur, even the national gods of more powerful people than the Judahites. The list of conquered nations includes Samaria—a painful reminder to Jerusalem's Yahwists of their co-religionists' tragic fate just two decades before.

It is important to understand that this scene owes much to Second Kings writers' theological embellishments. It is rather unlikely, for example, that the Rab-shakeh could have been familiar with Isaiah's argument that Yahweh was using Assyria to destroy Jerusalem. Still, the core of the encounter rings with authenticity. Had the parley never in fact occurred, it would have made for more fluid story-telling for Sennacherib himself to call for surrender at the city's gates. As well, even though only one imperial envoy is necessary to speak to the Jerusalemites, the story presents three, a pointless clutter, and it carefully identifies each by an exotic title that actually existed. Another element that rings true is the Rab-shakeh's insistence on pitching his oration as much to the crowd on the rampart as to royal officials: when Hezekiah's anxious representatives ask the Rab-shakeh to switch from Hebrew to Aramaic, the language of the western Assyrian Empire that the townspeople will not understand, he shows his skill at intimidation by insisting on continuing in Hebrew, the language of Jerusalemites. He also insinuates that, by requesting a parley in a language the citizens do not know, the royal court is trying to pull a fast one on ordinary folks.[43] Indeed, he even hints that if Hezekiah does not capitulate, the people should overthrow him. These are not the sort of details and subtleties that one would expect a narrator to invent. Indeed, we know that in a parallel situation involving a siege of Babylon, the Assyrians also used this same ploy of addressing ordinary citizens in hopes of undermining their loyalty.[44]

However, the authenticity of the next scene, which accents the importance of Yahwist piety, is less clear. When his officials return to the palace and report to Hezekiah on the Assyrian's speech, the despairing king humbles himself, ripping his clothes and donning sackcloth, and visits Yahweh's temple. He then sends a message to Isaiah, even though the prophet is a vehement critic of the royal court, and tells him, "May the Lord your God hear these insults [from the Assyrians] and punish those who spoke them."[45]

Sennacherib's annal speaks of surrounding the city with an earthwork, and it is probably at this point—after Hezekiah has refused to yield—that this barrier goes up. This wall of soil and rocks would have kept anyone from fleeing the city, thus preventing any diminution in the number of mouths to feed and, hence, effectively hastening the siege's end. It would also have prevented Hezekiah himself from escaping or sending troops out to launch a surprise attack on the Assyrian camp.

Second Kings gives Isaiah a role more prominent than one would expect. Responding to Hezekiah's message on the need for Yahweh to punish Assyria for having insulted the deity, the prophet tells his king (via messenger) not to worry. Isaiah says reassuringly that Yahweh had this to say about Sennacherib: "Behold, I will put a spirit in him, so that he will hear a report and return to his own country, and I will strike him down by the sword in his own country."[46] Isaiah's stated confidence in the city's invulnerability is a tip-off that this particular scene is not historical.

Sennacherib, having conquered Lachish, is busy besieging a smaller city, Libnah, just north of Lachish. While there, he receives a report that an Egyptian army is approaching under the command of Kush's "King Tirhakah"—Taharqa. The young Napatan is, in fact, only a prince at this moment and will not become pharaoh until 690 BC. (When the Book of Second Kings was written much later, Taharqa was famous as a pharaoh, not as a prince.

Kitchen has a useful analogy: today, people might say that Queen Elizabeth II of England was born in 1926. He notes, "Only a fool and a pedant would seek to 'correct' the . . . statement" by pointing out that she was a princess, not a queen, at her birth.[47]) Many scholars assume that Shebitku would have placed Taharqa, then aged 20 or 21, in nominal command of this force, with generals acting as important advisors.[48]

Several scholars challenge Taharqa's involvement. In a minority view, Donald Redford calculates that Taharqa would have been in his teens in 701. Only a biblical writers' gaffe, he says, can explain the reference to Taharqa: "Quite simply, Taharqa's was the only Pharaonic name known to the author of 2 Kings 19 for the period . . . ."[49] Dutch scholar Klaas Smelik also insists that the "biblical author did not know the name of the Egyptian commander and therefore opted for Tirhakah" because he was well-known.[50] Paul Dion and Spalinger also focus on the biblical writer's faulty memory. While Dion, of the University of Toronto's Department of Near Eastern Studies, does not question Taharqa's presence on grounds of age, he deduces that the biblical author simply "threw in Taharqa because of this pharaoh's well-known resistance to Assyria in the second quarter of the seventh century."[51] For his part, Spalinger declares that the name of Egypt's Shebitku "was soon forgotten" after his death and for the writer of Second Kings the "well-known" Taharqa therefore became the obvious choice.[52] In short, the Bible simply plucked Taharqa's name out of thin air.

To this barrage of skepticism about the Napatan prince's participation, I offer several observations.

■ A tender age is no barrier where nominal rank is concerned. The New Kingdom was the great inspirational model for the 25th Dynasty, and the greatest of the New Kingdom's pharaohs was Ramses II. When that ruler was a 10-year-old prince, he received the titular position of commander-in-chief of the army. The child remained at home during foreign wars, but at the age of 14 or 15 he accompanied the army to the western Delta in a campaign against the Libyans.[53]

■ In the ancient world, a more-than-token leadership role in military affairs was quite within the grasp of males of high station who were in the 18-21 age range. The most obvious example is Alexander the Great. The ancient sources report that the Macedonian prince was 18 years old when he led a unit of 2,000 cavalry, part of a larger army, into full-pitched battle against the Greeks—and performed brilliantly. Those sources say that when Alexander was 20 his father died, that the Macedonian army acclaimed him king, that he led an expeditionary force northward beyond the Danube to subdue hostile peoples, and that he destroyed the rebellious Greek city of Thebes. The ancient texts also say that when he was 21 he debarked with his army on a Turkish beach, hurled his spear into the sand and declared that Asia was his—and that he then went on to trounce the mighty Persians. If historians accept the veracity of this performance, and also that of young Ramses, resistance to accepting Taharqa's participation in the Judah campaign seems curious.

■ Taharqa demonstrated remarkable leadership qualities in the course of his long career. If he possessed such qualities as an adult, it follows that even as a young man these may well have manifested themselves.

Although Taharqa was young, it is a matter of record that Shebitku showed marked preference for Taharqa over other, older male members of the royal family, members who might ordinarily expect precedence over him. In an inscription at Kawa, composed after he had himself become pharaoh, Taharqa writes about how Shebitku "had preferred him to his other brothers" during the period that appears to have led up to the conflict of 701.[54]

■ Also, at the time of this important meeting with Shebitku, Taharqa may have already possessed a military background. The translators of the Kawa text suggest that the Egyptian term Taharqa uses to describe himself at the time of that meeting, "young man," may contain the nuance of meaning "young warrior." The term is *hwn nfr*; the translators say this may well refer to the "ancient designation for elite troops."[55] Such a status would strengthen the idea that Taharqa possessed respectable army credentials.

■ Years later, the choice of Taharqa as pharaoh would represent a departure from what William Adams calls the Kushites' "preferred order of succession" whereby the crown would revert to the deceased king's surviving oldest brother and then to younger brothers. If there were no more brothers, the crown would go to the original king's oldest son.[56] Adams' attempt to explain this break with tradition seems reasonable: if others with better family-tree credentials than Taharqa were passed over, he says, it was "perhaps because he had shown exceptional ability at an early age."[57] If the pharaoh overlooked such credentials in selecting Taharqa as his successor, it is easy to imagine him earlier disregarding them in choosing an expedition commander.

■ The claim that biblical writers forgot all about Shebitku, as well as his co-regent Shabako, and therefore omitted their names from the account of the Deliverance, is highly questionable. In a 1965 article, Michael C. Astour examines the reference to one "Sabteca" in Genesis 10:6-7. On the basis of a linguistic analysis, he concludes that "this name is obviously identical with that of the pharaoh Sabataka"[58]—which is itself a variant form of Shebitku. Astour's brief, four-page article makes no attempt to examine the historical ramifications of his research. But if the Southern Illinois University scholar is correct in his interpretation of "Sabteca," this would demolish Spalinger, Dion and Redford's weakly argued supposition that biblical writers knew nothing of Shebitku and that they simply slapped Taharqa's name into the Deliverance story because he was the only Kushite pharaoh they had heard of.

■ If the Kushite-Egyptian army had indeed played only an irrelevant or peripheral role in the Assyrian withdrawal, as most scholars maintain, it is easy to understand why the biblical writers might not have greatly cared whose name they attached to the leadership of that army. If the army had been irrelevant, in other words, so might its leadership.[59] If, however, the army had played a decisive role, the biblical writers' attitude would be much more serious. It is unlikely they would have treated lightly the identity of the leader of the military force that had saved the kingdom.

■ Finally, there is this. In the first century BC, the Greek writer Strabo referred to Taharqa as an illustrious leader of a military expedition. Although Strabo does not identify that expedition, his characterization of Taharqa as a great military figure adds credibility to Second Kings' assertion.

It seems very probable, then, that Prince Taharqa was deeply involved in the leadership of an army that Shebitku dispatched to Khor—not necessarily the army that fought at Eltekeh but the one that subsequently arrived in Khor. Taharqa's specific role is more difficult to nail down. Taharqa could have been the effective leader, or the titular leader with few real responsibilities, or one of several members of royalty sharing in the leadership (and because he eventually became pharaoh, the one who later became most closely identified with that campaign). Or, he could have held the title of leader *and* at the same time shared the effective leadership with generals.

Whatever the case, because this Kushite prince is the only person whom any ancient sources identify as belonging to the expedition's leadership, it is entirely proper to call this second force "Taharqa's army."

If I had to choose the likeliest of the four plausible scenarios for Taharqa's role, I would select the last—that Shebitku gave his promising young cousin the ultimate authority over this second army while surrounding him with experienced military professionals.

IT IS JUST after Sennacherib hears word of Taharqa's approach, that the logic of the Second Kings account becomes bewildering. The narrative appears to repeat some of the story's main elements:

In an apparent response to the report of Taharqa's approach, Sennacherib sends Hezekiah a letter that essentially repeats the message that the Rab-shakeh had already delivered: that the god Ashur can crush Hezekiah just as he did the kings of cities that the Rab-shakeh has previously listed. Hezekiah reacts to this second message in much the same way as he did to the first one: He goes to the Temple of Solomon, complains of Assyria's insults of Yahweh and calls on Yahweh to deliver Jerusalem from Assyria.

Isaiah enters the story a second time, saying once again that Assyria will fail to destroy Jerusalem—let alone even shoot an arrow at it.

If the story line becomes perplexing in this section of the biblical account, so does the quality of the writing. The rigorous narrative that makes the Rab-shakeh's insidious speech a treat to analyze, and the pithiness that characterizes Hezekiah and Isaiah's statements, give way to windy, didactic declarations by all three speakers.

It is now that the story's double climax arrives. In the night following Isaiah's declaration that Yahweh will save the city because of his attachment to David's dynasty, "YHWH's angel went out and struck the Assyrian camp—185,000 men! At daybreak there were dead bodies all about."[60] There is no explanation of what means the angel employed for this mass slaughter. Sennacherib, who before had been belittling Yahweh, lifts the siege of Jerusalem and returns to Nineveh.

In the second climax, two of Sennacherib's sons kill their father. A third son, Esarhaddon, succeeds him. The narrative makes this patricide sound as though it took place on the heels of Sennacherib's return to Nineveh, an expression of Yahweh's swift justice.

This two-fold climax, laden with religious import, is a two-fold disappointment. The first climax relies on a miraculous solution that will strain the credulity of most modern readers. The other climax relies on the cheap trick of telescoping events. The historical fact is that the king went on to enjoy another 20 years of conquest before his sons assassinated him. (*All* historians who deal with Sennacherib's invasion agree on this 20-year interval.)

Scholars consider the literary device of the angel to be like an opaque screen that conceals the real cause for Assyria's withdrawal. Let us now consider their favorite theories on this cause.

CHAPTER NINE

Four Current Explanations for the Deliverance

Frustrated by the avenging-angel finale to the story of the Deliverance, experts have come up with several theories to explain Sennacherib's exit. Here are four leading ones.[1]

Some scholars and popular historians alike focus on the fact that, in Second Kings 19:7, the prophet Isaiah cites Yahweh as declaring that he, Yahweh, will cause King Sennacherib to hear a report and, as a result, return to his own land. These writers propose that the report stated that tensions had erupted somewhere in the empire. Because Assyrians and Babylonians were enemies, the common suggestion is that it was the Babylonians who were fomenting the trouble. Records show that conflict broke out between them in 703 BC and again in 700. Although no evidence exists of hostilities in 701, these writers say, usually with no argumentation, that Babylonian disruption that year could have warranted Sennacherib's urgent attention and forced him to leave Judah.[2]

This troubles-elsewhere theory, however, does not explain why Sennacherib would have left Khor *permanently*. After 701, he reigned another two decades. Yet he never came back to Khor to finish what he had started. (Despite his boast in his annal of being Hezekiah's overlord, his hegemony over Judah in the years after

701 is to be questioned.) After quelling any problems elsewhere in his empire, then, why would he not return to Judah?

He did not lack opportunity. As one of the top experts on the Assyrian empire, Daniel David Luckenbill, observes in his account of Sennacherib's reign, in 699 a "period of comparative quiet now set in."[3] If his hands were free, why would Sennacherib not have used this hiatus to reaffirm himself in Khor? It was clearly not because he grew weary of war. Later in his reign, Sennacherib fought in many lands with the same gusto as ever.

Why, too, would Sennacherib have had to withdraw all his forces from Judah in order to respond to an emergency elsewhere? Indeed, why could he not have left a modest contingent in place at Jerusalem in order to maintain the siege? With an earthwork already in place to thwart Hezekiah's escape and to prevent any open battle, such a contingent could have kept the siege going indefinitely. These troops would hardly have been stranded far from supplies: the Assyrian province of Samarina lay just 10 miles north of Jerusalem. In the event of a future threat to themselves, the city's besiegers could have obtained military reinforcements from the same source.

Sennacherib had already subdued almost all of Judah except for the capital. Jerusalem was located far from the center of Judah and was not itself of primary strategic importance. Why did Sennacherib make no effort to turn the rest of the country into an integral part of the Assyrian Empire (similar to Samarina) while Jerusalem was holding out?[4] Most of Judah was in ruins and incapable of further resistance, so such a step would also have required few if any of his first-string combat soldiers. Garrisoned troops and imperial administrators could have done the job.

The accounts of Herodotus and the Bible on Sennacherib's withdrawal are, of course, very different, the one crediting mice with forcing the withdrawal, the other an angel. But they do have at least two things in common. Given the huge disparity between the versions, recognition of common denominators is important in trying to discover what might really have happened.

In both accounts, the Assyrians retreat because of adverse conditions in the immediate vicinity. That is, the mice and the angel both descend on the Assyrian camp. In other words, in both ancient texts the Assyrians' problem is close by and occurs inside the theater of war. That differs fundamentally from the troubles-elsewhere theory which posits that the cause of Sennacherib's departure was distant and external to the campaign in Khor.

One question, then, is this: if this theory is true, why did the Lower Egyptian folk memory (the basis of Herodotus' account) and the biblical writers not reflect this matter of distance? Both these sources could have attributed Sennacherib's departure to some event—supernatural or not—that took place outside of Judah and that did not require the Assyrians to retreat for their own safety.[5]

The second common denominator is that both Herodotus and the biblical narratives depict Sennacherib's withdrawal as involving duress and compulsion. In Herodotus' account, once the Assyrians discover that the mice have nibbled through their leather equipment and their bowstrings, they flee. Pursued by Egypt's forces, the Assyrians "suffered severe losses during their retreat." In the biblical story, after thousands of Assyrians are killed during the night, the survivors abruptly withdraw. In both versions, the Assyrians depart in conditions of fear and suffering. Those conditions are inconsistent with those of the troubles-elsewhere theory. That theory would lead one to suppose that the Assyrians felt something quite different—frustration, for having to quit a campaign before it was over.

ALL THREE BIBLICAL narratives on the invasion state that an angel of Yahweh annihilated many of the Assyrians in their camp outside Jerusalem, forcing Sennacherib to withdraw.[6] The two earliest accounts, in Second Kings and the Book of Isaiah, go so far as to state that the angel slew exactly 185,000 men, obvious hyperbole. One writer suggests that an ambiguity in the original texts may have created the high number, and that the real meaning may be 185 "picked" men—that is to say, senior officers. Other biblical experts have likewise labored to make the number of dead seem more plausible.[7]

The epidemic theory enjoys a following that is larger than that of all other theories combined. These proponents include some of the most distinguished scholars on the Hebrew Bible and ancient Africa, as well as popular writers and standard reference works.[8] Many of these give at least some weight to the idea that the angel is a metaphor for a disease that suddenly swept through the Assyrian camp. Some adherents also find support in the aforementioned passage in Herodotus, which blames field mice. True enough, ancient literature does offer examples (the *Iliad*, I.39, and First Samuel 6:4-5) of the mouse or rat as symbol of the plague; and it is, of course, a scientific fact that rodents can be carriers of plague.

Although the epidemic theory is dominant in terms of numbers of supporters, it would be inaccurate to say that a scholarly consensus exists in favor of it. From my sampling of more than 100 scholars who deal with with the events of 701, perhaps as many as 40 per cent abstain from subscribing to any theory at all. A consensus requires a decisive majority, and the epidemic theory falls short of obtaining that from the overall scholarly ranks.

Despite this theory's popularity, no one has dealt with its many problems.

For one thing, why wouldn't the biblical storytellers have spelled out that an epidemic was the angel's instrument? Divinely-sent epidemics enjoy a perfectly honorable place in biblical tradition. Thus Moses' campaign to pressure the pharaoh into releasing the children of Israel explicitly included, among other divinely sent calamities, both the disease that felled the Egyptians' livestock and, later on, the overnight affliction that killed every Egyptian's first-born son.[9] It is inexplicable why the biblical writers should be reluctant to be similarly explicit about the role that disease played in 701, if that indeed was the angel's weapon.

Also, at the stage of the campaign at which the disease would have struck, the Assyrians had little soldiering left to do. They had all but won the Khor campaign: Jerusalem was the only city of consequence that remained to be taken, and they would not have needed their full army to maintain a siege. To be forced to abandon at this very late stage, then, the Assyrians would have had to suffer truly large-scale epidemical casualties (something that the

Second Kings account, with its massive death toll, supports). Yet the positioning of the Assyrians would have made that difficult: Second Kings makes it plain that Assyrian forces were not all clustered together at the time they suffered distress.[10] That text states that a "large army" was at Jerusalem and another important force was with Sennacherib at Libnah (at least a day's journey west of the capital). If, as Sennacherib says, the Assyrians attacked a total of 46 Judahite sites, it is likely that other military units were assigned elsewhere.[11] Assyria's multi-pronged offensive would have made it hard for disease to strike a crippling blow to the army as a whole.[12]

Here's another problem. For Herodotus' account to imply sickness, his mice would have to symbolize disease in the thinking of the Egyptians who told him the story. In some neighboring cultures, such symbolism might hold. But at least two respected Egyptologists, Frank Yurco and Alan Lloyd, have separately concluded that there is no evidence for this in Egypt. Yurco, affiliated with Chicago's Field Museum of Natural History and the University of Chicago, finds significance in Herodotus' allusion to a sculpture that shows Sethos/Shebitku holding a mouse. Yurco says the mice "probably entered the story because of the statue that Herodotus saw, which may have represented the cult of Horus of Letopolis, to whom mice were sacred."[13] Horus was the divine warrior-defender of Egypt, and Letopolis was a city in the southern Delta, just north of Memphis. Lloyd, who is at the University of Swansea, in Wales, also notes that the mouse was the sacred animal of Horus of Letopolis. If the folk story had intended to depict the Assyrian army as having been devastated by disease, he argues, it "would surely have symbolized [the disease] as an attack by the Memphite Ptah's consort Sekhmet, a goddess particularly associated with pestilence."[14] He concludes: "Herodotus' Egyptian sources either did not know or ignored the fact that Sennacherib's army had been ravaged by disease."[15]

The mouse's Horus-related symbolism does not in itself invalidate the idea that disease ravaged Sennacherib's forces. Thus Lloyd, despite everything, still says that "some such disease as typhoid or cholera would be the most probable explanation" for the Assyrians' departure.[16] Yurco, too, says that "the probable outbreak of pestilence" was at least partly responsible for the with-drawal.[17] Nonetheless, their respective analyses of the mouse/disease symbolism weaken the case for this theory.

Lloyd and Yurco's reason for clinging to the epidemic theory deserves airing. Lloyd points out that Second Chronicles 32:3-4 describes the Hebrews as "tampering" (Lloyd's word) with the water supplies.[18] To him, this means contamination. Yurco also suggests that, denied access to fresh water, the Assyrians resorted to using the disease-causing water.[19]

Yet the biblical passage in question gives no reason to suppose this. It says simply that the people *blocked up* all the springs and the stream that flowed through the land. "Why," [the people] said, "should Assyrian kings come here and find plenty of water?" (emphasis added).[20]

That indicates the strategy rested on the deprivation, not the contamination, of water. This does not preclude the possibility that the Judahites fouled the water supply; but where the Bible had the perfect opportunity to mention that, it does not.

Finally, once the health of his army had returned, what would have kept Sennacherib out of Judah and southern Philistia for the rest of his career?

THE SIMPLEST IDEA of all draws its inspiration from the opening of the Second Kings account, when Hezekiah tells the invading Sennacherib: "I admit my guilt. Withdraw from me and whatever you will impose upon me, I shall bear."[21] The idea? Jerusalem surrendered.

While this camp has far fewer backers than the disease theory, in recent years it has been gaining support rapidly. Adherents include biblical scholars of the highest quality.[22] Among them are Ronald Clements, of King's College at the University of London, and Francolino Gonçalves, of L'École Biblique et Archéologique Française, in Jerusalem, both of whom have written books on Sen-nacherib's invasion that command admiration—Clements' for its nuanced insights into the Book of Isaiah's theology, Gonçalves' for the thoroughness and fairness with which it evaluates the vast body of scholarly opinion on Sennacherib's campaign. [23]

Problems, however, abound. For example, the Rab-shakeh, voicing Sennacherib's instructions, presented Jerusalem with terms of surrender that centered on mass deportation. Why would Assyria change? Also, Hezekiah's declaration ("I admit my guilt," etc.) is not a surrender statement.[24] Such an avowal of fault and a willingness to make a generous payment could be a necessary condition for reaching an agreement with Sennacherib on an Assyrian withdrawal after he, Sennacherib, suddenly no longer held a clear military advantage. Abundant tribute would in effect be a payment to ensure that he did not return.

The theory's premise is that Sennacherib, enjoying military supremacy as much as ever, would show mercy to Jerusalem. Proponents would strengthen their case if they could point to several cases, or even one case, of an Assyrian emperor of this general period showing similar leniency. In Sennacherib's annals of his lengthy reign, certainly no such aptitude for mercy is to be found.[25]

Any pardon by Sennacherib of a late-surrendering Hezekiah would, then, have represented a stunning aberration from normal Assyrian imperial policy. No supporter of this theory musters strong arguments to show why such mercy would have been in Sennacherib's self-interest.[26] The empire could not have permitted such leniency: it would have sent the wrong message to other restive vassals.[27]

If Sennacherib did accept Hezekiah's submission, why would he not have said so in his annals? There would have been no shame it it. Hezekiah's capitulation would also flatly contradict an assessment of that king by biblical writers. Second Kings says of Hezekiah, "in all that he undertook, he was successful."[28] It is hard to imagine that even the most fawning of biographers might describe a leader who surrenders his country as having enjoyed an unqualifiedly successful career.[29]

My biggest problem with the surrender theory is that, followed to its inadvertent but logical conclusion, it necessarily implies that the Bible was breathtakingly deceitful. The theory would mean that the biblical writers would have cynically turned an abject

submission to Assyria into a miraculous intervention in which
Yahweh demonstrates his love for his people. Proponents give no
indication that they have considered this problem.

The theory also implies that Yahweh has an extremely questionable sense of justice. The Assyrians show extraordinary mercy
to the Jerusalemites, and Yahweh rewards them with mass death
and defeat?

To top it off, these early writers of the Bible would have
described Hezekiah as a hero who had faith in Yahweh to the end:
"In YHWH God of Israel he put his trust; there was no one like
him among all the kings of Judah following him, or among those
before him."[30] The Hebrew-surrender theory would seem to imply
that Hezekiah, by rejecting Isaiah's advice in the story to hold fast
and trust in the Lord, utterly lacked such faith. His elevated reputation, therefore, would rest on a foundation of fraud.

So, too, would Jerusalem's eventual extraordinarily sacred status, as the belief spread among subsequent generations that Yahweh so loved Zion that he would always defend it.

THE FINAL THEORY involves the Kushites.

Years ago, I attended an investigative-reporters' seminar at
which a well-known journalist, Seymour Hersh, was a speaker.
Hersh talked about the laborious research that had gone into his
chilling exposé of how U.S. soldiers had massacred defenseless
civilians in the Vietnamese village of Mylai—a revelation that
helped undermine American public opinion's support of the Viet-
nam war and that won for the journalist the Pulitzer Prize for
international reporting. Hersh told us how, as a then-obscure free-
lancer, he had gotten wind of the tragedy. Subsequently, he looked
up Mylai in a newspaper's library, not expecting to find anything.
To his amazement, he discovered a clipping on an alleged mass
killing at that village. This article was, if I remember correctly, a
wire-service account just one or two paragraphs long. It under-
stated the scale of the slaughter and was too incomplete to have
attracted public attention. But the gist of Hersh's eventual story

was there. Somehow, Hersh told us, the major media's correspondents had simply let the original story slide by, never following it up. It was left to him, a newcomer outside the journalistic establishment, to recognize the event's significance, to explore in detail how it occurred and then to ensure the story got out to the public.

During my research, that anecdote kept coming to mind. Long after I first thought I was the lone originator of the Kushite-rescue theory, I kept stumbling across wisps of it elsewhere—the equivalent of that wire-service clipping.

Modern scholars have now and again suggested that the Battle of Eltekeh did not knock Kushite-Egyptian forces out of the conflict. Observing that Second Kings 19:9 says that a "Tirhakah"-led force was advancing toward the Assyrians, a handful of these scholars arrive at four different views of what might have happened afterwards.

The British Egyptologist Kenneth Kitchen suggests that when the Kushite-Egyptian forces surged back a second time, Sennacherib's forces were scattered at Jerusalem and other locations. To confront the new Kushite-Egyptian threat, Sennacherib hastened to regroup his own dispersed troops. When the Kushite commander realized he would have to do battle with all of the Assyrians at once, instead of piecemeal, he "discreetly retreated" to Egypt. The true reason for the Assyrian withdrawal, Kitchen concludes, was sudden disease.[31] In short, Kitchen adheres to the epidemic theory with a sidebar of Kushite-Egyptian resilience. This comeback, however, is meek and short-lived, Kitchen insists, and it has little bearing on Sennacherib's decision to withdraw. Indeed, Kitchen goes so far as to say that Pharaoh Shebitku's foreign policy lacked "real achievement."[32]

Still, Kitchen's discussion of post-Eltekeh events is the most detailed treatment of those events that I have seen.[33] In it, he makes two valuable points.

He supports the view that two separate Kushite-Egyptian armies existed.[34] Though Sennacherib's annal and the Bible each speak of only one army, these sources, he says, are referring to different armies. After Sennacherib defeated the first army at Eltekeh, its survivors might have joined the army that later appeared in

Khor. As well, Kitchen shows that the dispersal of Sennacherib's forces provided the second army, Taharqa's, with a "sudden golden opportunity" to strike.[35] Where Kitchen errs, I believe, is in his negative assessment of Taharqa's army—turning tail when the Assyrians regrouped.

A second view proposes a dual explanation for Sennacherib's departure—that is, Taharqa's approach combined with one or more of the other theories.

Thus Yurco suggested in 1980 that disease probably played a key role in the Assyrian withdrawal but that the report of Taharqa's advance may also have had something to do with it: "It was after the receipt of this rumor, and perhaps at least in part because of it, that Sennacherib suspended operations in Judah and returned ultimately to Assyria."[36] To back his claim, Yurco provides fresh and valuable insights into the logistics of how the young prince might have brought his force from Kush to Judah. Yet Yurco's article gives only muted, halfhearted credit to the role of the 25th Dynasty's military forces in ending the conflict. The article leaves one with the impression that the outbreak of disease was as critical. Hezekiah's blockage of water sources, it says, "might well have induced an outbreak of pestilence."[37] Indeed, touching another base, the article even suggests Babylonian restiveness as an added factor.[38]

In his 1988 book, Lloyd says that while the main cause of the withdrawal was an epidemic, an incipient Babylonian rebellion and possibly a Kushite advance may have contributed. In this context, he writes but one sentence on the possibility of Taharqa's involvement.[39]

Writing in 1989, D.J. Wiseman, professor of Assyriology at the University of London, also finds traces of Kushite participation.[40] He suggests Taharqa's intervention in combination with the outbreak of a disease, perhaps bacillary dysentery, turned Assyria back. He gives two sentences to this.

In a 1991 book, William Hamilton Barnes, gives the same dual credit: "I suspect that some sort of renewed Egyptian activity may well have had something to do with this remarkable deliverance. . . . Indeed, a sudden outbreak of the plague . . . , perhaps coupled with the threat (or actuality) of renewed Egyptian pressure may well have forced Sennacherib to break off the siege."[41] Barnes, of Southeastern College, in Florida, does not expand beyond these two sentences.

I think all four of these scholars are right in giving some degree of credit to the Kushites in the post-Eltekeh stage of the conflict. They do not, however, give credit enough. None of them presents a solid argument for why disease would have been so instrumental. Their views tend to be buried in obscure academic writings that general readers do not normally see. These scholars' treatment is fleeting—a sentence or two here or there. Yurco is the most expansive, devoting several paragraphs to Egypt's military revitalization under the 25th Dynasty, but disease still overshadows Kush's possible role in Sennacherib's withdrawal.[42] These scholars' treatment of the Kushites' role is so weakly presented that their argumentation, if one can call it that, will persuade few people.

A third view, which Luckenbill and Donald Redford espouse, is closer to what I feel is the truth.

In a 1924 book on Assyria, Luckenbill suggests that Kushite Egypt's force could be solely responsible for ousting Sennacherib. In a four-sentence passage (the longest sustained discussion that I have encountered on actual Kushite success against Sennacherib), Luckenbill says the Battle of Eltekeh conceivably could have occurred *not before* the siege of Jerusalem, as Sennacherib's account appears to place it, but *during* the siege. The professor of Semitic languages at the University of Chicago says "it is altogether possible" that Sennacherib "may have been fought to a standstill," and so he abandoned the siege.[43] The cautious suggestion has received scant attention; I am unaware of a single citation by other writers in the ensuing 70-odd years.

In a 1992 book, Redford goes even further than Luckenbill. The Egyptologist from the University of Toronto says the Battle of Eltekeh itself was an outright victory for the Kushite-Egyptian army. Of Eltekeh, he declares flatly, "there can be no doubt that it was an unexpected and serious reverse for Assyrian arms, and contributed significantly to Sennacherib's permanent withdrawal from the Levant."[44] He presents this startling, unequivocal hypothesis in just two sentences, however, with little argument to back it up.[45] While many other scholars say Sennacherib exaggerates the extent of any victory at Eltekeh, and Luckenbill suggests that the battle was a "possible" draw, I am aware of no one besides Redford who asserts that it was a flat-out defeat for Assyria. Indeed, three pages later in his next allusion to the crisis of 701, Redford's tone seems slightly less emphatic: whereas before he had said that the 25th Dynasty had contributed to Sennacherib's withdrawal "significantly," now it is only "partly" responsible for it.

I accept Luckenbill's and Redford's hypothesis that the Kushite-Egyptian force played a major role in turning back the Assyrians. Yet even though I think they are right, they are unconvincing.

These scholars simply declare their view, offering little supporting evidence. As with the other writers who give partial credit to the Kushites, this means their hypothesis languishes from inattention. Indeed, the passing treatment all these writers give to the denouement of the invasion conveys little appreciation of the event's historical significance. Most readers of their books and articles might assume that the event was of negligible consequence.

The larger problem with Luckenbill's and Redford's hypothesis is the reasoning behind it. They say that the decisive event in the entire conflict was the Battle of Eltekeh. If that clash was what truly forced Sennacherib to lift the siege at Jerusalem, it would, as Luckenbill says, have had to take place after the siege was under way. Second Kings says that Sennacherib was at Lachish during the siege: Sennacherib's invasion took him from Sidon south down Khor's coastal plain, and Eltekeh is located well before Lachish. After capturing Lachish, Sennacherib's army would have had to travel about 20 miles north, as the crow flies, to an area through which it had already passed. Why? What possible strategic objective could Sennacherib have attained by backtracking to this pacified area? It would take the king farther away from besieged Jerusalem, his main remaining challenge.[46]

Redford's assertion that "there can be no doubt" that Eltekeh was a "serious reverse" for Sennacherib requires an explanation of why the Assyrian king would lie so egregiously about that battle's outcome. That Sennacherib's annals are self-serving is plain: he inflated his victories and minimized or (as in the case of the Khor campaign) omitted his setbacks. But it would be quite another level of deceit for the king to claim victory if in fact he had suffered a crashing, campaign-ending defeat.[47] Propaganda though they are, Sennacherib's annals are the record, and it is hard to dismiss the record outright (especially without supporting argument).

Still, although their reasoning is untenable, I believe Luckenbill and Redford are headed in the right direction when they suggest that Kushite Egypt's forces made a strong showing in the end.

I see no reason to dispute the widespread view that Kushite-led forces at Eltekeh suffered either a modest setback or at best achieved a draw. Whatever the outcome, the battle of Eltekeh did not have a decisive impact on the larger conflict. The pivotal events would have taken place well after Eltekeh.

In my opinion, the best account for the failure of Sennacherib's campaign is in a book published in 1978 and reissued in 1997, *Battles of the Bible*. The authors of this in-depth description of ancient conflicts are Chaim Herzog and Mordechai Gichon. Several years after the book's publication, Herzog became president of Israel (1983-1993). Prior to that he had been ambassador to the United Nations, governor of the West Bank and chief of military intelligence in the Israeli Defense Forces. He has published several books on Israel's history. Herzog's co-author, Gichon, is a senior lecturer in military history and classical archaeology at Tel Aviv University. Like Herzog, he came to the study of history via a successful career in intelligence work.

After the Assyrians won at Eltekeh, say Herzog & Gichon, Sennacherib rampaged over the countryside:

> At that moment, the Egyptian Pharaoh Tirhakah culled fresh hope from the intelligence that Sennacherib was wasting his forces in Judah and decided that no better opportunity would be found to fall upon the weakened Assyrian rear and bring about Sennacherib's complete defeat.
>
> When Sennacherib became aware of this imminent danger, he had no choice but to break off contact everywhere and to beat a hasty and ignominious retreat under cover of night.[48]

Of all the books and articles I have seen, this comes closest to what I feel really happened.

In the two decades that have passed since the book's publication, I am not aware of any citations of these authors in this context. It is not hard to see why. *Battles of the Bible* devotes only those two sentences, quoted above, to the role of Taharqa's army. The book gives no argumentation for how Taharqa was able to achieve this. It gives no sources. And it casts Taharqa's role within a rather questionable war scenario.[49]

Interestingly, the two former military-intelligence officers also fail to identify Taharqa himself as Kushite (despite the fact that Second Kings 19:9 plainly describes him as such). They only call him Egyptian. Nor do they say that the army that fought at Eltekeh contained any Kushite elements. Of all the scholarly treatments of the 701 conflict, this is the only one I know of that completely skips over the advancing army's Kushite content.

But there is something still more peculiar about Herzog & Gichon's treatment. In the nine pages that the book spends on Hezekiah's conflict with Sennacherib, Taharqa's army—with its two sentences—gets far less attention than, of all people, Hezekiah's ancestor King Rehoboam, son of Solomon. Using the Book of Second Chronicles as their source, Herzog & Gichon credit Rehoboam with building Lachish and other fortified sites in Judah.[50] Because the Assyrians lost many men while taking these sites, the authors suggest, they were leery of confronting Taharqa's army. For *Battles of the Bible*, defensive emplacements—two centuries old at the time of Hezekiah—thus overshadow Taharqa's own role in the so-called miracle of 701. Displaying a transparent nationalist bias, the authors stress that these aging fortifications— not the foreign army—played the "decisive part" in Sennacherib's withdrawal.[51] This is a bit like saying that the ultimate credit for London's survival of the Blitz in World War II belongs not to the aviators and other active defenders but to bygone builders of the Underground and various deep basements that were used as public shelters.

THESE OCCASIONAL SCHOLARLY accounts that credit Taharqa's army with varying degrees of success have, then, several things in common. They tend to be extremely brief. They are unconvincing. They present a Kushite role in forcing Sennacherib's departure not as an up-front, coherent theory but rather, *sotto voce*, almost as a parenthetical aside. Indeed, in a puzzling omission, not one of the accounts that credits the Kushites with some role ever alludes even vaguely to the historical importance of the Assyrian departure. A reader would assume the conflict to have been but a trivial anecdote of history. Little wonder that these accounts have had no impact whatever on the public's understanding of Africa's role in Western history.

CHAPTER TEN

Evidence for the Kushites, I

SIX REASONS LEAD to the conclusion that troops dispatched by Egypt's Kushite Dynasty forced the Assyrian withdrawal. Singly, none of these reasons may be enough to persuade. Collectively, they are strong and coherent. Here is the first.

For excellent reasons, all scholars concur that a certain portion of the biblical material that describes the events of 701 BC was conceived for theological purposes. As factual history, that specific part of the account is worthless. Scholars generally agree on the location of this suspect material within the Second Kings' version of the Deliverance, which as we saw in Chapter 7 is the oldest and most historically valuable of the Bible's three renditions of Assyria's invasion. This suspect material consists principally of a single chunk of text, 26 and a half verses in length. It was inserted like a wedge after the rest of the story had been composed. If one simply omits this material and then reads the biblical text straight through, free of this bulky theological insertion, the vital role of the Kushite-Egyptian forces becomes instantly clear.

The Book of Second Kings as a whole is the fruit of a long process, stretching over more than one generation, of composing, editing and re-editing material derived from various sources—including, among others, oral tradition and archival texts.[1] The book is a patchwork. The specific passage in the book that describes

Sennacherib's campaign (*i.e.*, 2 Kings 18:13 to 19:37) reflects this larger trend. For a casual reader, this segment may appear to be a unified story. Yet, as we have seen, a large amount of the narrative's action appears to occur twice. In the 1880's, a German scholar, Bernhard Stade, examined this curious structure and theorized that it was the result of different people writing different parts of the Second Kings invasion narrative at different times.[2] Stade's contention that the text contains not two, but three parallel texts[3] appears not to have been seriously challenged since 1912 and is now generally accepted.[4] Although I am critical of many of these experts' other opinions, on this matter of a collagelike structure their arguments seem sturdy.

Specialists identify these three pieces of text as A, B[1] and B[2].

Account A is the shortest by far, consisting of only 18:13-16. This passage describes the tribute that Hezekiah had to give Sennacherib after his withdrawal and explains how the Hebrew king had to strip much of the gold and treasure from Jerusalem's Temple of Solomon. Notes Brevard Childs: "It is generally assumed that [this account] rests upon an archival source which preserved the material chiefly because of its concern with the temple and its treasury."[5] The archives would have been the Temple's.

Account B[1] makes up 18:17 to 19:9a (that is, up to midway in verse 9). Account B[1] suddenly resumes again at the very end of chapter 19, verse 36.[6] *Of the three accounts, B¹ is of the most interest to us.* In their book, Mordechai Cogan & Hayim Tadmor reach this reasonable conclusion: "B[1] bears the markings of authentic events, close to the time of Sennacherib's invasion; inasmuch as persons, places, situations are all vividly recalled, it would seem that B[1] was composed under the impress of the events themselves."[7] This may have been within roughly 50 years of 701.[8] Estimates by most top-tier specialists are approximately the same.[9]

Account B[2] is what interrupts B[1]. It is the wedge of text, from 19:9b through 19:35, that disrupts the flow of the story. It would have been written after B[1]. (Some experts add nuance to this view of three main divisions. They say the overall story may possibly also contain subdivisions—short, fragmentary passages that may have been added separately.[10] But even these experts agree on the narrative's basic three-piece structure; these subtleties need not distract us.)

Most specialists date B^2 several generations after B^1 to the Deuteronomistic period of the Exile.[11] If they are right, that would place B^2 in the heart of the sixth century BC, with a minor part of it perhaps later still: one expert suggests that at least one fragment of B^2 reflects thinking of the post-Exile period.[12]

Generally, the more time that elapses between an event and the account of it, the less likely is the account's accuracy. That is one reason for downgrading the credibility of B^2 relative to that of B^1. Another reason is that those who wrote B^2 did more theological tinkering with their material than did those who wrote B^1. The main point of B^2 is that Yahweh will defeat those who dishonor him and will reward those who trust in him. Says Childs of B^2: "The effort to picture Hezekiah as the type of the faithful king has emerged as a dominant concern. The understanding that there is a radical alteration of traditional material which serves a new function for the author should provide a warning against a simple-minded historical reading of the text."[13]

The B^2 account introduces a story that runs somewhat parallel to the action of B^1. It features a repeated, blasphemous threat by Sennacherib to the besieged city, Hezekiah's repeated distress upon receiving that threat, his repeated visit to the Temple, and a repeated assurance by Isaiah that Yahweh will defend the city and make the Assyrians withdraw; none of these repeated elements, however, is identical to its counterpart in B^1. In B^2, Assyria's blasphemy becomes more intense, Hezekiah's visit to the Temple more confident, the Lord's role in saving Jerusalem more direct, the setback of the Assyrian army more momentous. As Childs puts it, the B^2 version reflects the author or authors' "strong theological concern to edify."[14] Francolino Gonçalves cogently theorizes on the reason for the B^2 revision:

> As with B^1, upon which it depends, B^2 uses as its point of departure the fact that Sennacherib did not destroy Jerusalem. . . . As the B^1 account presents it, however, the outcome of the events was too modest for the purposes of the B^2 author. Wanting to highlight the

fact that Yahweh is the only God of all the earth, this author needed a much more dramatic denouement. As well, he had to change the Assyrian's challenge to Yahweh[15] into a blasphemy of the most shocking kind.[16]

Between the parallel accounts, here is by far the most important difference:

■ In B², the prophet Isaiah says Yahweh will make Sennacherib withdraw (19:32-34) and then, in the next verse, Yahweh does so as his angel slays the Assyrian soldiers.

■ In B¹, however, Isaiah says Yahweh will make Sennacherib withdraw by having him hear a report or rumor (19:7)—both terms are acceptable translations.[17] Then, two verses later, Sennacherib hears a report that "Tirhakah," king of Kush, is approaching with an army to fight him.

Once the B¹ biblical narrative speaks of Taharqa's approach in a tone of excited anticipation, what happens? An anticlimax. No sooner is Taharqa introduced than B² intrudes, changing the subject entirely. One moment Sennacherib hears the report that Taharqa is threatening him and the next moment, according to the B² insert, Sennacherib, apparently unruffled, sends the envoy to Jerusalem a second time to demand surrender. It is not until after the end of B², more than two dozen verses later, that Sennacherib withdraws from Judah. The causal relationship between the report of Taharqa's approach and the Assyrians' withdrawal becomes harder to see: in standard editions of the Bible, more than a full page of double-columned text intervenes. This makes it easy for a reader to interpret the retreat as the consequence of the angel's smiting of Assyrian forces.

Clearly, to begin to understand what happened in 701 BC one has to read Second Kings by lifting out the entire B² wedge and ignoring it. No modern scholars, to my knowledge, have explored this obvious solution in a serious, straightforward manner. This consistent failure to link the narrative flow of two parts separated by an artificial interruption is quite mystifying.

The perplexing trend starts with the "father" of the collage theory himself, Stade. In his 1886 article, Stade proposes that the story be read in the obvious manner—that Isaiah's prophesy that Sennacherib would return home after hearing a "report" (19:7) is fulfilled two verses later when the king hears of Taharqa's advance.[18] But although Stade credits the report with causing the Assyrians to leave (19:36), he also asserts that the report "misled" them.[19] The report, in other words, was false. Stade, who makes this surprising deduction without giving any reasons, thus deprives the Kushites of credit for saving Jerusalem.

Stade's hypothesis of a misinformed Sennacherib has fallen out of fashion. But among even the most eminent of the modern biblical analysts of the invasion, the tradition he founded of overlooking the Kushite role marches on.

Childs, for one, notes in passing the "close connection" between 19:7 and 19:9; he even observes that the "prophecy of Isaiah had been fulfilled in the rumor, which caused Sennacherib's return."[20] But then, instead of pausing to discuss that report/rumor, he veers away to pursue other matters. He responds to the whole question of Taharqa's involvement by abruptly ending all discussion of it.

Other specialists at least give reasons for denying the Kushites credit, although they do so only in passing. It's only fair to present these views.

Ronald Clements acknowledges the feasibility of linking the two parts of B[1]. When one makes that merger, he acknowledges, "The story requires no miraculous supernatural action on God's part, who simply causes Sennacherib to hear a report of a move by Tirhakah which compelled him to depart from Judah without pressing his attack upon Jerusalem."[21] He rejects such a reconstruction of events—not by means of critical examination of such a role by the Kushite-led army but rather, he says, because of "ample evidence" of Hezekiah's "timely surrender."[22] As discussed in the previous chapter, evidence that for Clements is ample is for me invisible.

Cogan & Tadmor devote a single sentence to discussing the report on its own merits. They assert: "That Sennacherib's retreat is explained as caused by a rumor may mean that the true nature of the 'report' (19:7) was either unknown or immaterial by the time of the storytelling."[23] Cogan & Tadmor then go on to say, very plausibly, that the core of the B[1] account "originated . . . perhaps orally at first, within the first generation of Isaiah's disciples."

The two ideas appear to be incompatible. If the B[1] narrative had been produced within a few decades (that is, "within the first generation") of the invasion, as appears likely, the actual cause of besiegers' departure could hardly have been "unknown" to its authors. If the authors themselves had not experienced the siege, plenty of survivors of the invasion would have been around to tell them what had happened.[24] It thus seems quite strange that the cause of their kingdom's survival would either have been "unknown" to them or deemed by them to be so unimportant or "immaterial" as to be not worth mentioning. The writers would either have had to be incurious in the extreme or simply obtuse.

Gonçalves's reasoning is more involved. He acknowledges candidly: "Concretely, the content of that report is Taharqa's entry into the war."[25] He even says that Second Kings presents a causal relationship between Taharqa's arrival and Sennacherib's departure. Yet Gonçalves insists that this can have no historical basis. Rather, he suggests, this business about Taharqa arriving and Sennacherib scrambling away is a literary invention. Its purpose, he proposes, is to reflect a "theological concern." By casting Taharqa, representing Egypt, as causing the Assyrians' abject departure, the Second Kings writer is trying to underscore the extent of the arrogant invaders' humiliation; after all, via the Rab-shakeh, the Assyrians had earlier mocked this same Egypt.[26] Such reasoning by so serious a scholar leaves me flabbergasted: He rejects the possibility that Taharqa would have really repelled Sennacherib for the simple reason that the Second Kings writer has drawn a theological lesson from such a deed. In other words, if an event lends itself to didactic storytelling, it cannot have taken place. Following this logic, Cyrus the Great's conquest of Babylon and his emancipation of the Hebrews never took place—for the reason that the Bible draws lessons from these events.

Other rationales for denying the Taharqa denouement are also in circulation, and they are no more reasonable.[27] Denying Taharqa's involvement in the outcome, then, takes real effort. Seeing such involvement, however, requires no strain at all. All one has to do is connect the two parts of B¹, omitting that problematic wedge.

Here, without the insertion of B², is the way the narrative would read in the New International Version, onward from 2 Kings 19:5:

> *When King Hezekiah's officials came to Isaiah* [bearing the message about the Rab-shakeh's blasphemous call for surrender], *Isaiah said to them, "Tell your master, 'This is what the Lord says: Do not be afraid of what you have heard—those words with which the underlings of the king of Assyria have blasphemed me. Listen! I am going to put such a spirit in him that when he hears a certain report, he will return to his own country, and there I will have him cut down with the sword.'"*
>
> *When the field commander* [the Rab-shakeh] *heard that the king of Assyria had left Lachish, he withdrew and found the king fighting against Libnah. Now Sennacherib received a report that Tirhakah, the Kushite king, was marching out to fight against him.* [The B² break occurs here.] *So Sennacherib, king of Assyria, broke camp and withdrew. He returned to Nineveh and stayed there.*

Did the revisionists remove some B¹ material at the break that originally explained what happened between the time of the Taharqa's reported approach and Sennacherib's exit? That is something we may never know.

What we do know from this reconstructed text is that as the Kushite-Egyptian forces advance, the Assyrians withdraw. What could be clearer?

CHAPTER ELEVEN

Evidence for the Kushites, II

THE THEORY THAT the Kushite-Egyptian army rebuffed the Assyrians requires the following premise: that after the Battle of Eltekeh this army posed a credible threat to the invaders. Otherwise, Sennacherib would have had no reason to depart.[1]

In order to demonstrate that the Kushite-Egyptian forces were fully capable of intimidating Sennacherib, the burden is on me to show that these forces were fairly close by and strong. By "close," I mean that, in order to have rescued Jerusalem, the 25th Dynasty's soldiers would have had to be actively pressing the Assyrians (though not necessarily engaging them in battle).

As we have seen, Sennacherib claims to have "inflicted defeat" on the Kushite-Egyptian troops on the plain of Eltekeh, the only recorded battle between Kushite-Egyptian forces and the Assyrians in 701. On the basis of the annal's telltale omissions, many scholars have given reasonable grounds for doubting that the imperial army thrashed the southerners.[2] The pharaonic troops may thus have had the capacity to regroup.

Yet for argument's sake let's be skeptical of that assumption. Even if one were to accept the extreme-case scenario and assume that Sennacherib had utterly whipped the Kushite-Egyptian forces present at Eltekeh, it would not follow that Kushite-Egyptian forces *everywhere* would be neutralized. Leading specialists on Egypt and Judah agree that Kushite-Egyptian forces were probably divided into two contingents.[3] They draw this conclusion from Sennacherib's peculiar wording when describing his adversary at Eltekeh. Although his annal states that the Kushite pharaoh had supplied many (if not most) of the army's elite soldiers, it does not clearly say who commanded this force. From a close reading of the document, these scholars infer that the monarchs of the Delta (those whom the annal calls "the kings of Egypt") may have been in charge;[4] if Kushite royalty really had been present, the scholars assume that Sennacherib would have said so. Combining this assumption that Taharqa was absent from Eltekeh with the Bible's statement that Taharqa was at the head of an advancing force, they deduce that Taharqa's contingent had to be different from the one at Eltekeh.

This reasoning suits my purposes nicely, but it is not compelling. Sennacherib's uncertain phraseology provides only wobbly evidence of the existence of two Kushite-Egyptian forces.[5]

Fortunately, a simple way exists to tell whether the unit that Sennacherib describes at Eltekeh was different from the Taharqa-led contingent of Second Kings.

The Rab-shakeh, according to Second Kings, mocked the besieged Jerusalemites for believing an Egyptian army (presumably the same unit that Second Kings later identifies as Taharqa's) would still rescue them.[6] To know whether one or two units existed we need to know the timing of the Rab-shakeh's speech. Did it come before or after the battle of Eltekeh? The Bible makes no mention of Eltekeh, so the answer is not immediately apparent.

If the Assyrian envoy's remarks *preceded* the Eltekeh fight, it could mean that the army the Jerusalemites so yearned for was the same one that Sennacherib would soon confront at Eltekeh and weaken, if not outright defeat. That battle's unsuccessful outcome, then, would have foiled Hezekiah's plan of continuing to wait for that unit's arrival at Jerusalem to drive off the besiegers. If, however, the speech came *after* the clash at Eltekeh, the Rab-shakeh would have to be referring to another contingent sent by the 25th Dynasty.

It is quite clear that the Rab-shakeh's call for surrender does come after the clash at Eltekeh. Sennacherib's annal offers a clue.

It describes the main Assyrian forces' line of march within Khor as going north to south, from Phoenicia into Philistia and then on into Judah. This itinerary means the Eltekeh action had to come before the Lachish siege since Eltekeh, more than 20 miles north, would have been on the way to Lachish.[7] The Bible provides another clue. Although it never alludes to Eltekeh, Second Kings states that Sennacherib dispatched the Rab-sakeh *"from Lachish* to King Hezekiah at Jerusalem"[8] (emphasis added). Hezekiah was therefore pinning his hopes on the arrival of a force from Egypt that was distinct from the one that saw action at Eltekeh. This sequence bolsters the two-contingent theory conclusively.

(Of course, if we start from a different premise and assume that the Kushite-Egyptian force actually fared quite well at Eltekeh, then the force that the Jerusalemites were hoping for could have been essentially the same as that which had fought at Eltekeh.)

A more fundamental question: What evidence exists to show that the unit advancing on Jerusalem was not impotent, a "weak reed" in the Rab-shakeh's words, and that it was both strong and close by? How can we be sure that Kenneth Kitchen, a believer in the two-unit theory, is wrong when he says the second body, under Taharqa's command, "discreetly retreated" to Egypt after realizing that the Assyrians had regrouped after Eltekeh and were too powerful.[9]

To answer these questions, Herodotus is of help. Despite its confusion on some elements, his account of Sennacherib's invasion makes clear that the Kushites were not shirking a fight and were very close indeed to the Assyrians at the invasion's decisive moment. Herodotus says the Kushite king obeyed the dream in which his god urged him to "march boldly out" to meet the Assyrians. Then, in describing the conflict's outcome, the account amplifies on this dauntlessness: "As he [the king] lay here *facing the Assyrians*, thousands of field-mice swarmed over them during the night, and ate their quivers, their bowstrings, and the leather handles of their shields, so that on the following day, having no arms to fight with, they abandoned their position and *suffered severe losses during their retreat*" (emphases added).

Let us not be distracted by the odd folk image of the rampaging rodents. For our purposes, what is important is that this historian of the fifth century BC depicts the Kushite-Egyptian forces, on the very eve of the showdown, as anticipating an all-out battle. It is also important that Herodotus states that the next day the Kushite-Egyptian army was in hot pursuit of the retreating enemy. The details—such as whether, as implied, all this took place in 24 hours—are not what matter. As in so much other secondary information in Herodotus' account, the details could be wrong. What does matter is that the account's thrust presents the Kushites as active, assertive, resolute.

THE BOOK OF Isaiah contains two vivid passages that, although widely separated, have much in common. Both refer to the events of 701. Both cite Yahweh as vowing to save Jerusalem from the Assyrians. Both deal with Sennacherib's invasion in a manner that subordinates it to theology, making it hard for us to tell where the history ends and the theology begins. Both were composed long after that invasion; Ronald Clements, for one, dates them to the sixth century BC.[10] (The two passages, then, are good examples of predictions that are made after the event, a characteristic of many of the Book of Isaiah's prophecies.)

Here in Isaiah 31:8-9, Yahweh is speaking. The pronoun "him" refers to Assyria.

> "And Assyria shall fall by a sword, not of man;
> And a sword, which is not human will devour him,
> And he will flee away before the sword, and his young men shall
>   be enslaved.
> His rock [the emperor] will slip away through terror, and his offi-
>   cers desert the [battle-] flag in panic."[11]

A few lines earlier (in v. 4), the biblical writer has said that Yahweh himself will fight Zion's attackers. In this context, it is quite clear that in saying that a "sword" not wielded by humans will defeat Assyria, the passage is indicating that only Yahweh can save Yahweh's own people. That explains why—at a time of composition probably corresponding to that of the B² segment—the writers cannot come out and say that a human army is what saved the day.[12]

This passage is pertinent to my contention that Taharqa's army was both strong and pressing. First, the passage's military motif is plain. What causes the Assyrians to leave is not disease, a distant crisis or Hezekiah's surrender but rather war, as symbolized by the sword. Second, the turning point is abrupt: soldiers drop the banner and run. Again, this idea of sudden, terrorized flight does not fit any of the rival theories. These, of course, are precisely the same elements that we encounter in Herodotus.

The other text, Isaiah 14:24-25, also pictures Yahweh as triumphant over Assyria:

> Yahweh of Hosts has sworn, saying:
> "As I have planned, so shall it be,
> And as I have purposed, so shall it happen,
> That I will break Assyria in my land
> And I will tread him down on my mountains,
> Then his yoke shall depart from them
> And his burden shall leave their shoulders."[13]

To describe the invaders' fate, this passage, too, employs a vocabulary of violence: it is the divine will to "break" the enemy and "tread him down."[14] Some translations use "trample."[15] Such words suit neither the surrender theory nor the troubles-elsewhere theory. After all, an invader who departs after accepting a victim's capitulation, or who dashes off to attend to a distant rebellion can hardly be shattered or crushed. As for the epidemic theory, the action of treading down or trampling is not imagery normally associated with devastating disease. Armies and pestilence may both ravage and destroy, but only armies stomp.

The original Hebrew vocabulary is also revealing. The verb "tread," which describes the action against the Assyrians, contains the same root *(bs)* as the word used to describe the Kushite nation in Isaiah 18:7: "a nation that is sturdy and treadeth down."[16] In Isaiah 18.2, the word also describes the Kushites.[17] The passage's vocabulary, in short, fits the Kushite-rescue theory precisely.

Both these passages are consistent with Herodotus and lend themselves far more to a military success against the Assyrians than to any other explanation for the invaders' withdrawal.[18]

⊙

WE HAVE BIBLICAL evidence, then, that the 25th Dynasty could have had reinforcements in Judah in the weeks after the Battle of Eltekeh and that these troops were in a position to pose a real, not just vaguely theoretical, threat to the Assyrians.

Indeed, the language of the Book of Isaiah evokes the flight of the Assyrians under conditions of duress. That book does not, however, actually identify these invaders' pursuers (much less acknowledge that they were human). Let us for the moment put aside the evidence in Second Kings and Herodotus and ask the question: Who could possibly be these pursuers in the Book of Isaiah?

Could they have been Jerusalemite forces? No, the original Isaiah elsewhere emphasizes the city's passivity,[19] and neither Sennacherib nor Second Kings makes any mention of Jerusalemites' combativeness.

Could they have been Judahite forces still in the countryside? No, none of the primary sources alludes to any resistance by them.[20] It is reasonable to assume that the Assyrian conquest of the 46 strongpoints had effectively crushed whatever Judahite forces might have existed outside Jerusalem.[21]

Could the pursuers be Philistines or Phoenicians? No, Sennacherib had already long since overcome them or (as in the case of Tyre's besieged forces) neutralized them. Could they be troops from the neighboring kingdoms of the Transjordan—Moab, Ammon and Edom? No, even if they had been original members of the rebellion (and there is no evidence that they had been), it is indisputable that these small kingdoms had demonstrated their loyalty to Assyria well before the siege of Jerusalem had begun.[22]

The process of elimination, then, leaves us with just one lone candidate for the role of pursuer in Isaiah's scenario: the Kushite-Egyptian army. No other force could credibly have been in the right place at the right time.

⊡

IF THE KUSHITES did turn back the Assyrian army from Judah, why don't we have in hand records of their achievement in either Egypt or Kush? The pharaohs, after all, commonly left stelae, murals or other records of their military feats. A case in point is Piye's stela that recounts his conquest of Egypt. Wouldn't it stand to reason, then, that such pictorial or textual evidence would exist for a successful campaign in Judah? Three developments could account for the absence of pictorial or textual evidence.

In the course of the seventh century BC, the Assyrians under Esarhaddon, and then Assurbanipal, repeatedly invaded Egypt, smashing much of its physical magnificence. The 25th Dynasty may well have produced inscriptions or other records. One logical place for it to have displayed these would have been the traditional capital of Lower Egypt, Memphis, where Taharqa had a royal residence after he became pharaoh, but nothing remained of the 25th Dynasty's physical legacy to that city in 671 after Sennacherib's son Esarhaddon dealt with it. "I destroyed it, tore down its walls, burnt it down," he says of Memphis.[23] Thebes, as the Kushites' spiritual home in Egypt, was another likely place to leave records of feats achieved in Amon's name, but the subsequent Assyrian sack of that city reduced many of its monuments to rubble. The Assyrians would have taken particular care to obliterate whatever evidence they found referring to their own galling setbacks at the hands of the 25th Dynasty.

As mentioned, the 26th Dynasty manifested a special animosity toward Kush. That dynasty, of course, was composed of descendants of the same Delta lords whom Piye had defeated in *c.* 728 and Shabako in 712. Descendants' resentment toward the southerners was abiding. Enmity appears to have climaxed during the reign of Psamtik II from 595 to 589 BC.[24] Says László Török:

> The year 593 BC seems to mark the beginning of tense relations. The intensity of anti-Kushite propaganda in Egypt may now be judged from the meticulously executed erasure of the names of the 25th Dynasty rulers throughout Egypt and . . . of the specifically

Kushite details of the crowns in representations of the Ethiopian kings on temple walls restored or erected by them.[25]

In other words, most of whatever remaining evidence in Egypt the Assyrians might have missed in the seventh century BC, the 26th Dynasty might well have finished off in the sixth.[26]

As for the physical evidence in Kush itself, Psamtik invaded Kush, and some scholars believe his troops went as far upriver as the capital, Napata, wrecking much of it.[27] Centuries later, a Roman army did likewise. While Piye's stela of his conquest of Egypt was discovered in relatively good condition at Napata in 1862, on the whole Kush's monuments have survived invasions and the elements far less successfully than Egypt's. Napata's remains today are barebones in the extreme. Made of a soft variety of sandstone, the only building material within hundreds of miles,[28] they continue to deteriorate in the wind-driven sand. Aside from the craggy beauty of the sacred mountain, Gebel Barkal, and several steep-sided pyramids, little remains of the Kushites' great capital: from the sandy wastes emerge the stumps of massive columns and almost nothing else. By comparison, shattered Thebes today seems positively robust.

The modern world has also been inconsiderate. Completed in 1902, the original Aswan Dam flooded what had been thriving Kushite territory on the banks of the Nile without a prior survey of monuments and other archaeological objects. A few years later the dam was raised, inundating still more Kushite vestiges.

Finally, completed in 1970, came the much larger Aswan High Dam, Egypt's pre-eminent development project of the 20th century. Stretching one and a half miles across the Nile, the dam has created a lake that extends southward 300 miles. It has submerged many of Lower Nubia's Kushite remains in the Nile Valley, both in Egypt and Sudan.

While the dam was still under construction, UNESCO sponsored an ambitious operation to rescue ancient buildings, statuary, artifacts and other remains. Archaeological teams from many countries joined in the urgent effort, which was optimistically named the International Campaign to Save the Monuments of

Nubia. The campaign's world-famous success was moving the imposing New Kingdom temples of Abu Simbel, including four colossal statues of Ramses II, to an elevation well above the level of the new lake.

But while the campaign saved almost all the high-profile glories, it was far less diligent in excavating and rescuing less dramatic vestiges. At an international conference held in 1994 to mark the 30th anniversary of that campaign, the evaluation of the work was harsh. A prominent member of the original Scandinavian team, Torgny Säve-Söderbergh, said that UNESCO gave an inferior standard of attention to ancient vestiges on Sudan's side of the border. Speaking with regret, he recalled that "a number of sites were not found, were left out of the program or only partly investigated."[29] As the waters rose, an incalculable number of cemeteries, towns and other remains were simply left in the ground.

What we can conclude is this: that the artificial lake's obstruction to further digs, the spotty nature of the excavations, particularly in Sudan, and the failure of many archaeologists to make public whatever they did find,[30] have left our knowledge of many aspects of the region's history far, far more deficient than it ought to be.[31]

CHAPTER TWELVE

Evidence for the Kushites, III-IV

IF THE 25TH Dynasty had played a central part in turning back Assyria, it logically would have obtained political and commercial advantages in much of Khor that are consistent with having been that conflict's winner. Evidence abounds that so long as Sennacherib remained on Assyria's throne, Egypt enjoyed such conditions. Indeed, these indications are so plentiful that it is hard to understand the prevailing scholarly conclusion that in these decades immediately following the invasion Egypt possessed little, if any, influence in the region while Assyria under Sennacherib continued to enjoy considerable clout, even if this was not as a heavy-handed overlord.

What sort of role in Khor would have been in the 25th Dynasty's self-interest?

Kushite Egypt would *not* have sought to exercise outright military dominance in the region. The problems would have far outweighed the benefits. For one thing, Kushite Egypt would have required a vast standing army in Khor to prevent an Assyrian return. If Kush had been unable to leave an occupying army in place in Lower Egypt after Piye's conquest of *c.* 728 BC, it is most unlikely it could have left such an army in place in a yet more distant place, Khor, a generation later. The Shabako-Shebitku coregency had its hands full simply keeping Egypt united. To have attempted such a role would have left its forces dangerously overextended.

Even if, for the sake of argument, one were to say that Kushite Egypt somehow could have mustered the manpower to stand up permanently to the Assyrian powerhouse in Khor, that effort would have been prohibitively costly. In theory perhaps, Kushite Egypt's military occupation of southwestern Khor could have helped pay for itself through the economic advantages that often accrue to a country when it dominates another. Yet in this particular case that is most doubtful. An Egyptian experience several centuries before had demonstrated that such an occupation would bring precious little net economic gain, if any.

Under the 18th and 19th dynasties, Egypt had occupied Canaan, the name often used for southwestern Khor (including Philistia and the land that would eventually become the Hebrew kingdoms). For these New Kingdom pharaohs, this overlordship proved to be no bonanza. Unlike lumber-rich Phoenicia, Canaan could provide Egypt with few products or commodities (including foodstuffs, livestock and metals) that it did not possess already. That is the surprising finding of Shemuel Ahituv, a Hebrew University scholar who investigated the economic benefits that Egypt derived from their occupation of Canaan. He concludes: "It is indeed probable that there was no economic interest in the Egyptian conquest of Canaan, and if such an interest existed it was very limited." The main advantage Egypt appears to have derived from Khor was control of trade routes.[1]

By the time of the 25th Dynasty, Egypt was in a position to know that outright political dominion over Khor would be far more trouble than it was worth. For reasons of both commerce and defense, the ideal would have been to keep southwestern Khor as a neutral zone, free of a threatening Assyrian presence.

ONE OF THE fascinating archaeological discoveries that relates to Kush is a fragment of a clay seal that bears the identifications of both the kings of Egypt and Assyria. This thin object is about the size of a postage stamp. According to its 19th-century discoverer, the celebrated British archaeologist Sir Austen Henry Layard, it would probably have been attached to a papyrus or parchment document (that has not survived) kept at Sennacherib's palace of Kouyunjik, located at Nineveh. The clay bears the impressions of two signet rings. Layard, who excavated this palace, has identified one of the rings as having belonged to Shabako (whom we now believe was the senior of the two pharaohs). Most likely, he says, the other ring was Sennacherib's.[2] Layard concludes: "It would seem that a peace having been concluded between the Egyptians and one of the Assyrian monarchs, probably Sennacherib, the royal signets of the two kings, thus found together, were attached to the treaty, which was then deposited amongst the archives of the kingdom." James Henry Breasted leans toward Layard's view that this artifact suggests a treaty: the seal, he remarks in passing, "may indicate some agreement between the two nations."[3] (Yet Breasted expresses no curiosity about any such pact; since he starts from the premise that "Sennacherib disposed of Taharqa's army without difficulty,"[4] he can rule out the need for any after-the-fact diplomacy.) Although some later scholars have sought to assign the seal to matters unrelated to 701, their attempts are weak.[5]

Let us try to deduce the sort of peace that such talks would have produced.

Negotiations would have involved not just Egypt and Assyria but the members of the rebel coalition, including Judah. At this parley, Assyria—despite having failed to beat back the 25th Dynasty's army—still held some very high cards. It had the potential of returning to Khor and finishing what it had started.

Once the armed conflict was over, Egypt could negotiate from a position of strength, but this strength was highly qualified. This is because Egypt lacked the means to hold on to Khor. It would have been unable to deter Assyria from storming back a year or several years later, once it was back to proper strength. Nor did Egypt, with its limited objectives of foreign trade and security of its own borders, need to rule Khor.

That helps explain why Sennacherib was able to exact heavy terms from Hezekiah. Judah had to give some of its territory to those Philistines who had been loyal to Assyria. Says Sennacherib of the Judahite king: "His towns which I had plundered, I took away from his country and gave them over to Mitinti, king of Ashdod, Padi, king of Ekron, and Sillibel, king of Gaza. Thus I reduced his country. . . ."[6] In addition, Judah had to pay a painfully large sum in gold and other treasure, as well as an unspecified number of elite soldiers and court hostages, including Hezekiah's "daughters and concubines." One gathers that the daughters were not princesses: Sennacherib does not refer to them as royal daughters. One assumes, too, that once the daughters had arrived in Assyria they were attached to Sennacherib's own court.

Perhaps significantly, Sennacherib says in his annal that Hezekiah "did send me, later" this treasure and these people. Why later? Why did the Assyrians not carry everything to Nineveh at once? Sennacherib's withdrawal was impromptu, so that important treaty details may have been crafted afterward with the help of diplomats who, seeking a durable peace, tried to leave all sides reasonably satisfied.

One has to assume that Hezekiah agreed to these painful terms because he understood that Sennacherib, despite his withdrawal, was not really defeated. He would have known just how easily Assyria could return to complete the devastation that the pharaoh had been able to interrupt. One can call Hezekiah's payment a bribe, tribute or indemnity. Or, because that penalty also included giving over his own concubines and offspring, one can also call it collateral, a guarantee to Sennacherib that, for the sake of the hostages, he would not again anger Nineveh by, for example, trying to regain territory the treaty had transferred to the Philistines. Finally, because Hezekiah also gave over to Sennacherib some top soldiers, one can also see the penalty as a practical limitation or handicap in the event that Jerusalem were again to feel militarily mischievous.

Still, from Hezekiah's viewpoint the pact was not—on balance— negative. Far from it. By allowing Sennacherib to save face and making it worth that foe's while never to set foot in Judah again, Hezekiah ensured two huge benefits: the survival of his war-torn kingdom and its existence as a quasi-independent state. Hurtful as would have been the loss of loved ones, treasure and territory, these represented a pittance compared to the gain.

The 25th Dynasty, of course, also gained. No evidence exists that it obtained a military "victory" in the conventional sense of the word. It achieved something better. An outright battlefield triumph, including the death or imprisonment of Sennacherib, might have invited Assyrian vengeance or, in the event that Assyria would have been so weakened that Babylon could have finished it off, the advent of another bellicose Mesopotamian superpower. (Indeed, when Babylon vanquished Assyria less than a century later, it did invade Khor repeatedly.) The negotiated settlement gave Egypt the two things it needed: security and commercial access to Khor. It also spared Egypt the need to lay down in the region an onerous military and economic infrastructure. For the pharaoh, a stalemate meant a *de facto* victory.

During several decades after the conflict period, the 25th Dynasty's political and commercial interests flourished. Without a strong negotiating position, it is hard to imagine how Egypt could have obtained such favorable terms. That, in turn, suggests it earned substantial leverage for itself through actions closely linked to Sennacherib's rushed departure from Judah.

Although Sennacherib ruled for the next 20 years, he never returned to Khor or threatened Egypt. Most certainly, this was not due to any mellowing on Sennacherib's part. To the end, this man who would soon call himself "king of the four quarters of the earth" would relish teaching the disrespectful a terrible lesson. (The most chilling example of this took place when, in 689, he finally put the Babylonians in their place by sacking Babylon, slaughtering its soldiers and razing the buildings. Then, to prevent that capital's rebirth, he destroyed the foundations of buildings, removed the surface soil and even dug canals through the midst of the city in order to turn the site into swampland.[7] It appears to have been one of the more complete and systematic eradications of a major city in the recorded history of ancient warfare.[8] Yet Khor and Egypt were spared this man's capacity for vengeance.)

After the conflict of 701, it is not only Judah that avoided becoming an Assyrian province; none of its Philistine partners in the anti-Nineveh coalition did either. No evidence exists to indicate that Judah or the Philistine city-states continued to contribute to Nineveh's coffers after making the initial payment called for in the settlement; but even if they had, they appear to have enjoyed, in Hayim Tadmor's words, "*de facto* independence" in the years after 701.[9] Egypt had the buffer it wanted,[10] and there is no evidence to suggest that Assyria kept so much as a trade garrison close to Egypt's Sinai border.

Another indication of an understanding between Sennacherib and the allies is that the Assyrians mounted new invasions of Khor and Egypt almost immediately after Sennacherib's death in 681. His successors would have seen the peace-in-Khor policy as something to which an individual ruler had committed himself and to which they themselves were not bound.[11]

In the 33 years up to and including 701, Assyria invaded Khor six times. Now, starting in 679, or within two years of Sennacherib's death, Assyrian armies would return with dogged regularity to Khor. In 679, 674, 671 and 667 Assyria mounted expeditions that reached the Egyptian border or beyond, a policy that climaxed with the capture of Thebes in 663. With this ferocious pattern, it is easier to appreciate how the peace between Assyria and Khor/Egypt that lasted 21 years[12] represented a truly radical shift in Nineveh's foreign policy. No other theory for Sennacherib's withdrawal can account for this extraordinary hiatus. Assyria might have left Judah alone if it were paying bounteous tribute, but that would not explain why during this period the empire did not even try to attack the land that was so patently the apple of its eye—Egypt itself.

Here's another clue to the Kushite Dynasty's role in the region.

Twenty-six years after he led the expedition into Khor and 15 years after becoming pharaoh, Taharqa inscribed a remarkable address to Amon in the walls of a Theban temple.[13] In the message, chiseled in hierogylphics, Taharqa seeks the god's help in a crisis which, while not identified, appears to be Assyrian-tied. The line that concerns us most is that which refers to "your tribute of Khor which has been turned aside from you."[14] The 675 inscription strongly implies that, until Assyria's aggressive return to the region, Khor had been rendering some sort of tribute to the Kushite Dynasty's principal deity.[15]

Tribute in this context does not necessarily imply a *strict* ruler-vassal relationship. What is certain, however, is that receiving tribute means wielding a degree of political influence. It could also mean providing some sort of protection.

This powerful role does not in itself prove that Egypt carried the day against the Assyrians in 701. Had Assyria withdrawn to deal with troubles elsewhere or to flee an epidemic, one could try to argue that Egypt rushed into Khor to fill the vacuum. But tribute is more consistent with the idea that elements in Khor recognized Egypt as instrumental in driving the Assyrians away and as deserving its due. Also, tribute implies that Egypt had a credible ability to continue looking after the region's interests, short of posting a standing army there.

⌐G⌐

THE FATE OF the key city of Gaza is another indication of who came out on top in 701.

In prior decades, Sennacherib's two predecessors, Tiglath-pileser and Sargon, had both captured this southernmost of the five Philistine city-states. Gaza was of special importance to Assyria because of its proximity to Egypt and also because of commercial dealings with Arabia. For caravans from the great desert peninsula, Gaza stood as the gateway to Khor. Tadmor goes so far as to say: "Controlling Gaza, Assyria could extend her control further into Arabia. . . ."[16] For Egypt, Gaza was even more important. It held the key not only to its own caravan traffic (to and from Khor) but to its own defense.

We might reasonably expect the political status of this city, which both Assyria and Egypt so valued, to serve as a test of the new power relationship between these two adversaries in the post-701 period.

In Sennacherib's own record, his annal of 701, he boasts that he installed loyal vassals to replace the rebel rulers of the Philistine cities of Ashkelon and Ekron. One may assume this bombast obscures the fact that, in order to establish a political equilibrium in the region, these vassals were acceptable to Egypt, and that Philistia became, in Tadmor's words, a "semi-neutral buffer area between Assyria and Egypt."[17] But what is striking is this: in his list of cities that swore loyalty to him, Sennacherib omits Gaza.[18]

Some historians have claimed that in the years after the conflict of 701 Sennacherib was still the overlord of Khor generally. For this, they offer no hard evidence; but if for the sake of argument one allows that they are right, these historians cannot possibly extend this hypothesis to the specific city-state of Gaza.[19] Sennacherib himself does not make the claim.

The 25th Dynasty, then, was indisputably able to deny Sennacherib any sway over this strategic city so valued by both sides.

ANOTHER SIGN OF Egypt's influence in Khor is trade.

In 734, having made themselves masters of the eastern Mediterranean coast, the Assyrians had prohibited the Phoenician city of Sidon from selling Lebanese lumber to Egypt or its Philistine intermediaries.[20] Assyria had wanted the wood for itself. The famous cedars were a valued commodity in that country as well as Egypt. Lacking suitable trees themselves, both nations required foreign sources of high-quality lumber for colossal construction projects and ships. No import-export records exist for this period, but when Taharqa rebuilt the temple to Amon in Kawa, he left behind a list of donations of precious objects that he had made to the temple: the list includes prized cedar of Lebanon to build the massive doors, as well as juniper and acacia woods that also appear to have come from Khor. From this record, Anthony Spalinger draws the reasonable conclusion that in his first decade as pharaoh (690-680), Taharqa was able to show "complete disregard" for the import ban as well as to exhibit "close connections" with Phoenicia.[21]

Excavators' discoveries also buttress the idea that Khor and Egypt enjoyed robust commercial ties under the 25th Dynasty.[22] The most compelling is the finding of a distinctive system of weights.

Weights, of course, are an integral part of commerce: buyers and sellers need to measure the quantities of goods. Archaeologists have collected more than 200 such weights, inscribed with hieratic numerals, scattered about in territory that corresponds to southwestern Khor. They found most of these in Jerusalem, but significant numbers have also come to light in the Lachish region and the Negev; while the majority hail from Judahite territory, a few have also turned up in such Philistine centres as Ekron and Gezer. The weights are dome shaped and made of limestone. In a meticulously researched book on these artifacts published in 1998, University of Haifa historian Raz Kletter says that the level at which these objects were buried clearly indicates that their use began in the late eighth century BC, during Hezekiah's reign, and they became commonly used in the seventh century BC.[23]

One important thing, says Kletter, is puzzling: the weights' shape, hieratic numeral inscriptions and units of measure all indicate that the weights were based on a system that Egypt had devised centuries before and was still using at the time.[24] The weights would thus have been useful for trade with Egypt: because the heavier of them bear numerals that match Egypt's own weight units, the historian deduces they may have been used for trade in metals like gold, silver and copper, and also perhaps for incense and spices.[25] For Kletter, the finding that Judah would have begun to borrow the weight system in the late eighth century presents no problem, since the kingdom at that time was trying to break away from its status as vassal to Assyria and was friendly with Egypt. What he finds curious is that the boom in usage of the Egyptian-style weights came later, in the first half of seventh century. Operating on the widespread assumption that Assyria had regained control over Judah at that time, Kletter says, "One would expect a vassal kingdom to show closer relations with the ruling empire, rather than with Egypt."[26] Yet no appreciable traces of Mesopotamian weights have turned up in the region.

Of course, if one assumes that after 701 Assyria did not have a major presence in Khor and that Egypt did, the situation instantly becomes logical.

Adoption of the new system attests to the likelihood that Judah's trade relations with Egypt were strong. It is no simple matter for a country to adopt an unfamiliar system of measure—witness North America's qualms about "going metric." To accept such a change in habits, ordinary people would have had to feel it was in their economic self-interest. For Kletter, the archaeological evidence is consistent with a high degree of popular acceptance. He notes that while some of the weights have been found in government buildings and "public" locations, which indicates that royal officials used them, most were discovered in domestic sites. This would suggest, he says, that it was not just a thin layer of civil servants under the king's command that used them, but the "population as a whole."[27]

These weights, in short, represent first-class evidence that Egypt's post-701 profile in the commercial life of Khor was robust and pervasive.

IN THE AFTERMATH of the conflict of 701, then, Kushite Egypt enjoyed political and economic benefits that are thoroughly consistent with having bested Assyria militarily. In offering an alternative explanation for these benefits, the various alternatives —surrender, troubles elsewhere and disease—all fall flat. Indeed, it strains the imagination to think of any other circumstance, besides a military stalemate or defeat when confronting 25th-Dynasty forces, that could have compelled Sennacherib to make such strategic concessions not only in Judah but in Khor generally.

AN ADDITIONAL REASON for thinking that Kushite Egypt repelled Sennacherib is its subsequent reputation for extraordinary military prowess.

After Sennacherib's withdrawal, there is little question that in the next 20 years or so Egypt did include much of Khor within its sphere of influence. The term "sphere of influence" is used here in a loose sense: It does not mean that Egypt would necessarily have been an occupying power or have exercised outright control over the area, but rather that it had free commercial access to it, not necessarily to the exclusion of Assyrian traders. During Sennacherib's reign, Khor may have been a demilitarized, or lightly militarized, zone for all parties; neither Egypt nor Assyria, nor their respective allies in the region, would have maintained enough troops in the region to represent a potential offensive threat to the other. (That could explain why Hezekiah relinquished his best soldiers to Assyria as part of the peace agreement.) If either Egypt or Assyria maintained military personnel in the region at all, they may well have been there as monitors, making sure the other side did not cheat.

Taharqa's strategy toward Assyria would have been two-pronged. He would have sought at all costs to avoid rousing the imperial beast and giving it a reason to attack. At the same time he would have sought to avoid appearing to be a military weakling, a monarch unwilling to protect his realm's commercial and security-related interests in Khor. Reconciling these stances would have meant walking a fine line. The philosophical basis for this cautious strategy would have been the need to uphold *ma'at*, behaving in an upright manner to achieve harmony. Assyria would have represented the ultimate example of *isfet*, or chaos. *Ma'at* was the best way, perhaps the only way, to hold it back. The outcome of the earlier confrontation with Sennacherib may also reflect this same philosophy. Just as Taharqa's father, Piye, had forgiven his enemies, including the traitorous Namlot, after his conquest through Lower Egypt, so the Kushite leadership may have calculated that allowing Sennacherib's safe return to Nineveh, with a face-saving diplomatic arrangement, was the best way to achieve political harmony. With generosity can go self-interest.

That Kushite Egypt played so important a role in Khor after 701 does not in itself prove it would have acquired that prominence because of its performance in Judah in 701. Theoretically, it is barely possible (though hard to imagine) that Egypt would have been ineffective against Sennacherib and yet, somehow, have become a major factor in Khor only a few years later. It requires far less effort, how-

ever, to regard Egypt's clout as the natural consequence of a strong
military showing in 701. That is the simplest solution.

To understand the true strength of that dynasty's forces, we
need to bypass historians' dismissive assessments, go back to ancient sources and take a closer look at Assyria's relentless series of
aggressions against Egypt in the post-Sennacherib period. Because
we have no Kushite or Egyptian records of those attacks, which
eventually shattered Kushite control of Egypt forever, Mesopotamian texts will have to do.

In 679, according to an Assyrian annal, Sennacherib's son, King
Esarhaddon, campaigned into Khor as far as the Egyptian border.
Near that frontier, he destroyed an obscure town that was loyal to
Egypt. The annal offers no motive for the campaign, but Tadmor
makes the reasonable surmise that this was "essentially a show of
force demonstrating that Assyria alone ruled in Philistia and warning Tirhaka against any attempt to assert himself in that area."[28] In
677-676, he returned to the Mediterranean, warring against
unbowing Phoenicia. He destroyed one great port city, Sidon, and
intimidated the other, Tyre, into paying tribute.[29]

Then in 674 he took the great step of invading Egypt itself.
Taharqa turned him back by defeating him outright.

Assyrian texts shed no light on the political situation that produced the offensive. Nor do they say how far into Egypt the army
advanced. They do not even mention the failed 674 campaign at
all. It is only from a cursory reference in a Babylonian record that
we even know of Assyria's expedition. (Our entire knowledge of the
abortive invasion is limited to these few words by the Babylonian
chronicler: the "army of Assyria was defeated in Egypt."[30])

That various rulers in Khor saw this Egyptian victory as no
lucky fluke is clear from an annal for 671. By way of explanation
for laying siege that year to stubbornly insurbordinate Tyre,
Esarhaddon says that this city-state's king, Ba'lu, had "put his trust
upon his friend Tirhakah" and had "thrown off the yoke of Ashur,
answering my admonitions with insolence."[31] Clearly, Tyre had
confidence in Egypt's ability to stand up militarily to Assyria. It was
not alone. Farther south along the coast, the Philistine city-state
of Ashkelon also aligned itself with Egypt.[32]

So, perhaps, did Judah. The king at that time was Hezekiah's son, Manasseh. The Bible says that the "commanders of the army of the king of Assyria . . . took Manasseh captive in manacles, bound him with fetters, and brought him to Babylon."[33] The text does not suggest when this would have taken place or why,[34] but the arrest may well have stemmed from Judah's pro-Egyptian sympathies in the decades following 701. Cogan says that Manasseh had "presumably sided with the anti-Assyrian coalition" of Tyre, Ashkelon and other cities aligned with Taharqa.[35] This expert on the period adds: "We can only imagine the terms under which Esarhaddon reinstalled Manasseh on the throne; but if similar reports from the annals are any indication, a renewed pledge of loyalty and increased tribute headed the list." This idea that Assyria forced Manasseh to renounce a pro-Egyptian foreign policy is eminently plausible.[36]

Assyria's Esarhaddon himself feared Egypt. On a rock near Beirut, bits of an inscription he ordered written have survived. The inscription, which has been dated to 671,[37] is in the form of a series of questions that King Esarhaddon poses to the oracle god, Shamash, in the hope of learning whether it would be wise for the Assyrian army to proceed to Ashkelon. Referring to himself in the third person, the king asks apprehensively, "Will he return [to Assyria] safe and sound?" Then he asks an additional question. If he "pitches his camp in the region of Ashkelon," will the Kushite-Egyptian forces "plan and strive to wage war in any way . . . ?" Referring again to himself, the king's anxiety peaks: "Will they defeat him?—Thy Great Divinity Knowest!"[38] His trepidation before Egypt's might is plain. (The correct answer to Esarhaddon's urgent question would turn out to be that no, Taharqa apparently did not send forces to confront him at Ashkelon—or, for that matter, elsewhere in Khor.[39])

These events yield three solid pieces of evidence that in early decades of the seventh century BC Egypt possessed military capability of the first magnitude.

First, in 674 Taharqa's army vanquished Assyrian aggressors on Egyptian soil.

Second, Tyre and Ashkelon aligned themselves politically with Egypt as late as 671. Other kingdoms may also have done so, including Judah. That these states preferred Egypt to Assyria may reflect their confidence in Taharqa following his success against Esarhaddon's invasion of 674. Yet it would surely have been difficult for Tyre's king to place his "trust" in the 25th Dynasty *if*, as most historians insist, Egypt had let Khor down in 701. Similarly, if Egypt had turned out to be the weak reed that the Rab-shakeh had predicted in his speech at Jerusalem's wall, it is hard to imagine that Judah might want to lean again on it so soon.

Finally, in the Ashkelon-related inscription of 671, the ordinarily cocky Assyrian king revealed to a deity his severe anxiety about again clashing with Taharqa. Egypt's obvious might that year is fully consistent with the idea that Egypt was strong enough to have turned back Sennacherib. The fact that later in 671 Assyria went on to defeat Taharqa inside Egypt (a severe setback from which the Kushite pharaoh would recover a few years later) takes nothing away from the sense that Egypt under the 25th Dynasty was for Assyria a most worthy battlefield opponent.

Still, a skeptic might note that this prowess in 674 does not prove anything: even if Kushite Egypt had failed against Sennacherib in 701, it still had 27 years in which to recover and improve its army greatly.

In theory, so thunderous a comeback from a dire defeat is perhaps possible. But by looking at Kushite Egypt's enduring reputation for military prowess even after its ultimate defeat by Assyria in the 660s, we can appreciate the slimness of that possibility. Two different ancient texts uphold this reputation.

The first is a statement by the biblical prophet Nahum, who preached in the seventh century BC. One of his themes was Assyria's destruction in 663 of Thebes, the political capital of Upper Egypt and, because it was Amon's city, the cherished spiritual capital of the 25th Dynasty. Nahum says of Thebes before her destruction, "Kush and Egypt were her boundless strength."[40] One translation calls this strength "infinite."[41] By Egypt, of course, Nahum means the Egypt of the 25th Dynasty (which in 663 was still in power in Upper Egypt). Would a Judahite living so recently after the siege of Jerusalem be apt to exalt Kushite Egypt's military power if it had failed against Sennacherib?

The second text is from Strabo. The Greek historian of the first century BC compiled a kind of honor roll of underrated military leaders of earlier centuries. Strabo reflects on how some great figures of the past are no longer household names: certain "expeditions of princes to lands far remote" are, because of their distance in time, "not . . . matters of off-hand knowledge to everybody." Strabo then adds: "I refer to Madys the Scythian, Tearko the Ethiopian, Cobus the Treran, Sesostris and Psammetichus the Egyptians, and to Persians from Cyrus to Xerxes."[42] Tearko is Taharqa.

The company in which Strabo places Taharqa is elite.

Cyrus the Great was founder of the Persian Empire and liberator of the Jews in the sixth century BC. Xerxes was one of his successors who, prior to the Greeks' celebrated victory against him in the naval battle at Salamis, had put down revolts in Egypt and Babylon. An army of Psammetichus II, also known as Psamtik, the 26th Dynasty pharaoh, invaded Kush and inflicted upon it a serious defeat in 591.

While Sesostris is little-known to us today, he was a truly mighty figure of Egyptian legend. His persona was a composite of several historical pharaohs. Alan Lloyd sees him as an amalgam of Sesostris I and Sesostris III, both of whom expanded Egyptian hegemony over Kush and defeated Libyans on Egypt's western frontier. The British Egyptologist describes the two as "monarchs of outstanding capacity and energy whose activities inside and outside Egypt left an indelible mark on Egyptian history."[43] As well, Lloyd detects in this composite hero the presence of perhaps the most famous of all pharaohs, Ramses II, who led a military expedition as far as Syria.[44] Regardless of the precise historical elements the legend may contain, what matters is that at the time of Strabo many Egyptians would have regarded "Sesostris" in terms that Lloyd describes as the "embodiment of the pharaonic ideal."

It is too bad, however, that Strabo does not identify the heroic events that lead him to mention Taharqa in the same breath as these other military figures. If we apply rigorous logic, we cannot jump to the conclusion that the Napatan necessarily joined this illustrious circle of military leaders because—or even partly because—of success against Sennacherib in 701. Conceivably, Taharqa could have earned his laurels for achievements sometime in the next 37 years of his life.[45] We have, however, scant evidence of what those exploits might have been.[46]

In the unlikely event that Strabo does have in mind some foreign expedition in the 690s or 680s BC, such a feat would have been *in addition* to a strong performance in 701. It is hard to imagine a scenario in which Kushite Egypt, having fared poorly against Sennacherib, might somehow vault only a few years later into the ranks of super-achievers on foreign soil.[47]

⌖

FOUR ANCIENT SOURCES, then, each from a different culture, attest to the military muscle of Kushite Egypt in the aftermath of the Deliverance. One source, Babylonian, indicates Taharqa defeated an Assyrian army inside Egypt. A second text, from an Assyrian king, suggests Taharqa was strong enough for the great trading center of Tyre to place its trust in him. Another source, a Judahite prophet, says that Kush's might seemed limitless. And the fourth, a Greek, says Taharqa's foreign exploits rank among the great feats of military history.

While none of these sources specifically states that Kushite Egypt turned back Assyria in 701, its capability to have done so is obvious. We're rather a long way from the view of the influential William Adams, dean of specialists on Kush and champion of the epidemic theory, that Taharqa is "one of the most unsuccessful military commanders in history."[48]

CHAPTER THIRTEEN

Evidence for the Kushites, V

SKEPTICS MIGHT WELL point out that if the Kushites were *really* responsible for saving Judah, it would follow that the Judahites of that time and of the next several generations would have a positive attitude toward them. They might note that several passages in the Bible that deal with Kushites are, in the opinion of the overwhelming majority of biblical experts, decidedly hostile toward that African people. For example, one internationally respected authority on the biblical texts in question, Denmark's Erling Hammershaimb, makes this flat assertion about Kush: "Its dark-skinned inhabitants were held in contempt by the Israelites."[1] Since these biblical texts were written within several centuries of Sennacherib's invasion, wouldn't their anti-Kushite tone severely undermine the idea that Kushites had helped Hebrews?

Yes it would. But there is one problem. The premise for such a conclusion is false. Mainstream scholars' view that the Hebrew Bible/Old Testament expresses contempt for the Kushites is a delusion. In fact, the experts have it backwards. The opposite of contempt is honor, and that's just what the Bible shows.

Generally speaking, the Hebrew Bible treats the people of foreign nations pejoratively. As is the case with the Philistines, Canaanites and Hittites, often this reflects the fact that the Bible says that the Hebrews were at war with them, or, as in the case of

Lower Egyptians in the Moses story, that the Hebrews were suffering under their oppression; but even in situations that are free of conflict, as in Isaiah's allusions to Judah's attempt to obtain military aid from Lower Egypt, the Bible's tone in describing other nations is frequently scornful. In many cases, these foreign nations' isolation from Yahweh would explain the attitude.[2]

No such negativism exists in regard to Kushites. While the final version of the Hebrew Bible does not explicitly give credit to the Kushites for Jerusalem's rescue, it nonetheless depicts them in exceptionally generous terms. While this respectful attitude does not necessarily attest to Hebrew recognition of Kush for services rendered in 701 BC, it is consistent with such recognition.

The Old Testament mentions "Kush" or "Kushite" and the ancient synonyms "Ethiopia" or "Ethiopian" a total of 56 times. These occur in 29 different passages.[3] I cannot find a single passage that clearly reflects negatively on Kushites.

Those who see the Hebrew Bible as scornful of Kushites often cite Amos 9:7 in support of their view. That verse reads:

> "Are not you Israelites the same to me as the Kushites?" declares the Lord. "Did I not bring Israel up from Egypt, the Philistines from Caphtor and the Arameans from Kir?"[4]

Amos preached in Israel in the mid-eighth century BC, but this particular passage appears to have been added sometime within two centuries after 701.[5]

Hammershaimb, author of a book on Amos and professor of Semitic studies at the University of Aarhus, says that Yahweh is refuting those who boast that the Lord's preference for Israel will prevent it from coming to harm. Following the deep-seated view of prominent biblical scholars on both sides of the Atlantic,[6] Hammershaimb says the meaning of the passage is that Yahwists "must not think they have an advantage at all, even over so despised a nation as the Kushites."[7]

James Luther Mays, of the Union Theological Semininary in Richmond, Virginia, is of the same opinion, saying that the comparison to the lowly Kushites is shameful to the Israelites. He writes: "On the evidence, one can say no more than that the Kushites were a distant, different folk whom the Israelites knew mostly as slaves. 'You are to me,' says Yahweh, 'as these Kushites are to you.' What the comparison does is to humiliate Israel completely with respect to Yahweh, to reduce them to the role in Yahweh's order of things which the Kushites played in their own society."[8]

One U.S. theologian noted for his progressive views on racial issues is Abraham J. Heschel (1907-72), who was active in the civil-rights movement and marched in Selma in 1965 next to Martin Luther King, Jr. A professor of Jewish ethics and mysticism at the Jewish Theological Seminary of America, in New York, Heschel has this to say on the Amos passage:

> The nations chosen for this comparison were not distinguished for might and prestige—countries such as Egypt and Assyria—but rather, nations which were despised and disliked. The color of the Ethiopians is black, and in those days many of them were sold on the slave markets.[9]

Indeed, even a scholar with a disposition so manifestly sympathetic to Kushites as Edward Ullendorff, professor of Ethiopian studies at the University of London, perceives hostility in Amos 9:7. "The climactic inference of these words," he says, "can only be fully appreciated if the Ethiopians serve, in the present context, as the epitome of a far-distant, uncivilized, and despised black race."[10] He makes this observation in a book entitled *Ethiopia and the Bible*; his view surely qualifies as "expert opinion."

Perhaps the most weighty of all the opinions is that of David Noel Freedman, professor of Hebrew biblical studies at the University of California, San Diego, and editor-in-chief of the scholarly Anchor Bible. Freedman is one of the most eminent and prolific biblical experts in North America. Yet his 1989 commentary on the Book of Amos, co-authored by Francis I. Andersen, of Fuller Theological Seminary in California, also regards the passage's likening of Hebrews to Kushites as unfavorable to Hebrews. Their commentary says:

> The dialectic of [verse] 7 could be, "Aren't you like the Kushites, *just another enslaved and exploited people* under the Egyptians?" Answer: "No! There is a difference. You (Yahweh) delivered us (Israel) from bondage in Egypt." The response is, "But I also did the same for other peoples—the Philistines and Aramaeans (to name but the two most familiar to Israel)" [emphasis added].[11]

In other words, Freedman & Andersen view Kushites as a people so undistinguished that Hebrews shrink from being compared to them.

Two other recent American commentaries on Amos state similar opinions, one going so far as to say that the passage "serves to desacralize Israel."[12]

This consensus view that the verse casts Kushites as contemptible or lowly is simply missing its point.

In equating Israelites and Kushites, the biblical writer is *not* putting Israelites down. Other interpretations present themselves. One is that the comparison is neutral. Today someone might say to Americans, "Why should God look out for the United States' interests any more than, say, Mexico's? Or Japan's?" That would not necessarily imply contempt toward those countries.

Another possibility—or likelihood—is that the comparison reflects on the Israelites in a manner that is actually quite positive.

Far-fetched? Let's see.

TO BACK UP his contention that the Hebrews felt outright contempt for Kushites, Hammershaimb presents just one other piece of evidence—Jeremiah 13:23. Addressing sinful Judahites, the prophet of the late seventh and early sixth centuries BC says:

> Can the Ethiopian change his skin or the leopard its spots? Neither can you do good who are accustomed to evil.

There is no more hint of scorn for blacks here than there is for leopards. A white person today who used such an example might be deemed insensitive, but only because racism is all around us; the racial climate in the eastern Mediterranean region in ancient times was relatively benign.

It is a mistake to project back to those times, as many biblical experts do, today's widespread racial attitudes. In ancient times, the racial climate was unlike anything we know today.

In his 1990 investigation of racial views in the Middle East, Bernard Lewis, of Princeton University's department of Near Eastern studies, is emphatic: "[R]ace was of minor importance in antiquity." He adds: "Like every other society known in human history, the ancient Middle Eastern peoples harbored all kinds of prejudices and hostilities against those whom they regarded as 'other.'"[13] But, Lewis stresses, the evidence suggests the "other" was primarily defined by cultural differences. The Mediterranean world had some contacts with Ethiopia and China, which were "both respected, and there is no real evidence in Jewish, Greek, or Roman sources of lower esteem for darker skins or higher esteem for lighter complexions."[14] Other researchers have reached similar conclusions.[15] After steeping myself in Hebrew, Assyrian and Greek texts that deal with inter-racial situations, these assessments ring utterly true to me.

In the 24 other passages referring to Kush and its people, not once does the Hebrew Bible cast aspersions on the Kushites' national character, way of life or religion.

Most of the Kushite references are brief—a verse here, a line there. The longest is the Book of Numbers 12. All 16 verses of that chapter describe the aftermath of Moses' marriage, during the Exodus, to a Kushite woman. In this story, Moses' sister and brother, Miriam and Aaron, oppose the marriage for unspecified reasons (but presumably because the woman is from outside the Hebrew fold). The narrative almost certainly dates from well after 701.[16]

It is important to stress that the Numbers story is remarkably supportive of the marriage: in response to Miriam's criticism of the betrothal, Yahweh afflicts Miriam with leprosy, and her skin turns as "white as snow." Moses, let us remember, was not just another heroic figure, like Joshua or Solomon: he was *the* Hebrew nation's lawgiver, the mortal whom Yahweh chose to show people how to be. It would be hard to overemphasize the moral weight implicit in such a figure's choice of spouse.

One of the 20th century's most acclaimed biblical scholars, Martin Noth of Germany, has written that the term "Kush" in the story refers not to the African nation but to Cushan, an area of Arabia or possibly present-day Jordan. Noth is one of several Moses specialists who scoffs at the likelihood of an interracial marriage.[17] Such views may testify to mainstream scholarship's unfamiliarity with Kush's role in eastern Mediterranean affairs.

Might it make sense to do as Martin Luther did in the 16th century and, taking the story at face value, see Moses' wife as African?[18] Yes.

Consider, first, that the story could have had Yahweh punishing Miriam in thousands of different ways. Yet the story employs the one that renders her skin "white as snow." In terms of irony, is there a more perfect form of retribution?[19] It is also significant that Flavius Josephus himself, the Jewish historian of first century AD, appears to believe the woman to be from Kush, not Cushan.[20]

Another of the Bible's favorable references to Kush comes in the Book of Jeremiah, the same prophet whom Hammershaimb sees, in effect, as racist. Prior to the Babylonian army's destruction of Jerusalem in 586, Jeremiah here predicts the Babylonians' victory and urges the people of the city to flee for their lives.[21] Fearful that such talk would make soldiers lose their courage, royal officials lower the prophet into an empty cistern—a well-like cavity, often the size of a room, used for storing water. Because they give him no food, this is like a death sentence. The king of Judah, Zedekiah, gives his assent to this punishment. The only person to object is a Kushite eunuch, Ebedmelech, who works in the royal palace. He protests to the king. "Your Majesty, what these men have done is wrong." Although Ebedmelech probably occupies a senior position at the court,[22] for him to challenge a royal decision would take considerable audacity. The king duly orders the prophet raised.[23] In the subsequent slaughter and deportations at the hands of Babylonians, Yahweh spares the caring Ebedmelech. Yahweh tells him: "I will keep you safe, and you will not be put to death. You will escape with your life because you have put your trust in me."[24] Like

Moses' wife, Ebedmelech is only a minor biblical character, but his portrayal is highly sympathetic. Nothing in these two characterizations supports the prevailing scholarly view that ancient Hebrews looked askance at Kushites. Quite the contrary.

LET US LOOK at one of the Bible's most misinterpreted passages. It is in the Book of Genesis.

In past centuries, people of European background used the text to justify slavery. In the mid-20th century, some white Americans invoked it to justify racial segregation. Fortunately, many modern scholars and clergy have correctly interpreted the text and have labored to puncture the myth it has created.

The passsage (Genesis 9:18-27) tells the story of Noah after the flood waters have receded:

> The sons of Noah who went out of the ark were Shem, Ham and Japheth. Ham was the father of Canaan. These three were the sons of Noah; and from these the whole earth was peopled.
>
> Noah, a man of the soil, was the first to plant a vineyard. He drank some of the wine and became drunk, and lay uncovered in his tent. And Ham, the father of Canaan, saw the nakedness of his father, and told his two brothers outside. Then Shem and Japheth took a garment, laid it on both their shoulders and walked backward and covered the nakedness of their father; their faces were turned away, and they did not see their father's nakedness.
>
> When Noah awoke from his wine and knew what his youngest son had done to him, he said, "Cursed be Canaan; lowest of the slaves shall he be to his brothers." He also said, "Blessed by the Lord my God be Shem; and let Canaan be his slave. May God make space for Japheth, and let him live in the tents of Shem; and let Canaan be his slave."[25]

By designating him as the flood's survivor, Yahweh had given Noah—and humanity—a second chance. But now he becomes a drunk. His nakedness underscores his shame. We recall how, earlier in Genesis, Adam and Eve's sudden awareness of their nakedness is presented as a symptom of their loss of innocence. After he learns that his son Ham has seen him naked and, in addition, has cruelly told his brothers of the spectacle, Noah feels doubly humiliated. So strong is his bitterness that the patriarch sets this terrible curse on Canaan and all of his descendants.

For many centuries, this has been known as the "curse of Ham." Ham was commonly deemed to be the progenitor of the black race. Ham is the father not only of Canaan but also of Kush, Egypt and Put[26] (commonly identified as either Somalia or Libya). Because Noah declared that Canaan should toil as the "lowest of slaves" for Shem and Japheth, who were seen as progenitors of other races, some whites—in the southern United States and elsewhere—have seen this as legitimization of black slavery and, more recently, of separation of the races.[27]

Many enemies of racism have pointed out the blatant fallacy of seeing in the Ham story a justification for subjugation.[28] Noah never curses Ham. Instead, he curses one of Ham's four sons, Canaan, who became the ancestor of the Hebrews' Canaanite neighbors[29]—who happen to be as Semitic as the Hebrews themslves. A.F. Walls, director of the Centre of Christianity in the Non-Western World, in Great Britain, sums up this distortion pithily: "Despite a long tradition of perverted exegesis in some quarters, there is nothing to connect the curse of Ham with a permanently divinely instituted malediction on the negroid people; it is explicitly applied to Canaanites."[30]

Looking today at the notorious curse of Ham, one can see its very existence to be grotesque nonsense, a transparent instance of text-twisting. It is a wonder that it could have become so widespread.[31]

Yet some other Kushite-discrediting interpretations of the Bible are also preposterous. And, unlike the curse of Ham, they have maintained their credibility and are still prevalent.

IT IS IN the Book of Isaiah that one finds the *closest* to truly unfavorable references to Kushites. The references concern events leading up to the crisis of 701. Most scholars deem them all to be authentic to the historical Isaiah. These passages show the prophet's skepticism (not the same thing as negativism) toward the capacity of Kushites to cope with the mighty Assyrians.

One passage (Isaiah 18:1-6), which may date from some months or possibly even years prior to Assyria's invasion, describes an event that takes place as ambassadors from Kush[32] visit Khor.[33] If, as many bibical scholars assume, the prophet had once been a diplomat or member of Judah's royal court, he might have been in a position to be aware of the nature of the envoys' purpose. In this passage, Isaiah bids the ambassadors return home: he says they should report back (presumably to the pharaoh) that if the Kushites engage the enemy, their corpses will be left to the "birds of prey and to the wild animals." The implicit reason, which he spells out elsewhere, is that the Lord is using the Assyrians as an instrument to crush the Hebrews: resistance to Yahweh's will is futile.[34]

For all this, however, the prophet is respectful of Kush itself.[35] He speaks to the ambassadors of "your strong and powerful nation, . . . your tall and smooth-skinned people, who are feared all over the world." Another translator says people "of glossy skin."[36] Still another speaks of "polished-gleaming" skin.[37] Nothing here is pejorative.

In another statement (Isaiah 31), the prophet refers to Kushite Egypt in a similar vein; here the date may be early in 701 BC, probably after Hezekiah has become aware that Sennacherib will soon invade.[38] Judah's desperate appeal to Kushite Egypt[39] for military help, Isaiah says, is doomed. Arms and troops are not what will stop Yahweh who (acting through his Assyrian agents) will "rise against the house of the evildoers, and against the helpers of those who work iniquity."[40] Some scholars seem to assume that the prophet includes Egypt in his condemnation of those who "work iniquity." He is not. What he is denouncing is the Judahite establishment for its evil and iniquitous deeds. "Egypt's" forces will suffer not because they have done wrong but because, as the Hebrew kingdom's "helpers," they're in the way. They're innocent victims.

A third passage (Isaiah 20) shares this theme. Explicitly composed at least three years after the Assyrians' victorious campaign in 713-712 against the rebellious Philistine city of Ashdod, and at a time when Egypt is under Kushite rule, the prophet warns against relying on Kush and Egypt in any future conflict with Assyria. As in the previous passage (Isaiah 31), he anticipates that mounting tensions in Judah-Assyria relations (perhaps because of Hezekiah's attempts to enlarge his kingdom) will lead to war. Isaiah also foresees Judah calling to Kushite Egypt for help. The prophet says that Yahweh warns that in such a conflict the Assyrians will lead away Judah's Egyptian and Kushite allies "with buttocks uncovered, to the shame of Egypt."[41] This vivid image of POWs is one of humiliation, yet there is no hint of negative sentiments toward these people themselves. On the contrary, Isaiah presents these prospective allies from the Nile simply as potential victims of Judah's folly. He predicts that the rebellious people of the Philistine coast may look at the Kushite and Egyptian prisoners of war being marched off and say, "See, this is what has happened to those in whom we hoped and to whom we fled for help and deliverance from the king of Assyria! And we, how shall we escape?"[42] This is strong compassion for these Kushites and Egyptians, whom the prophet fears Judah's hawks may soon lead to disaster.[43]

It is precisely because Judahites have a high regard for Egypt under the 25th Dynasty that Isaiah is theologically troubled. Thus in still another passage set in the the 701 crisis (Isaiah 30), Yahweh denounces as "rebellious" the Judahites "who set out to go down to Egypt without asking my counsel, to take refuge in the protection of Pharaoh, and to seek shelter in the shadow of Egypt."[44] Francolino Gonçalves makes this acute observation on the prophet's thought: "In seeking their security in Egyptian power, Judahites are exchanging Yahweh, their only true refuge, for Egypt, and that makes them guilty of real idolatry." For Isaiah, says this commentator, this idolatry is "more subtle than that which involves the worship of idols made of metal and wood but it is no less grave and dangerous."[45] Again, the prophet is in no way upset with Kushite Egypt for what it is, only with what it isn't—that it is not Yahweh.[46]

These passages on Egypt of the 25th Dynasty date from before Sennacherib's retreat. It is clear that they show that Judahites in general during this pre-Deliverance period looked up to Kushite

Egypt and that the prophet himself had a fairly open attitude toward it. But does First Isaiah (that is, the first 39 chapters of the Book of Isaiah) contain any hints of how it views Kushites in the *post*-invasion time period? If the Kushites played the role in repelling the Assyrians that I think they did, one would have to assume they would receive attention that was still more positive. When the words of Isaiah were edited some time later, a process about which little is known, the opportunity existed for adding positive comments on the Kushites.

I know of only one clear-cut instance where, after the historical Isaiah's lifetime, a positive comment appears to have been added to statements that were authentic to the prophet. But that single case is significant. This late addition (Isaiah 18:7)[47] says:

> A time is coming when the Lord Almighty will receive offerings from this land divided by rivers, this strong and powerful nation, this tall and smooth-skinned people, who are feared all over the world. They will come to Mount Zion, where the Lord Almighty is worshipped.[48]

In other words, the Kushites are more than military allies: they are also potential theological allies. They go to Zion itself, Jerusalem, to pay respect to Yahweh. The verse describes a noble solidarity between Hebrews and Kushites and, interestingly, it does so in the context of Assyrian confrontation (to which the preceding verses allude).

Another post-701 allusion to Kush is found in Psalm 68:

> Let envoys come from Egypt; let Kush eagerly stretch forth her hands to God.[49]

This psalm's presentation of Kushites as worshipful of Yahweh is highly favorable to them. It reinforces the sense (seen in Isaiah 18:7) that Kush possesses a most unusual, and commendable, respect for Zion.

One of the most puzzling of all biblical allusions to Kush relates to the Garden of Eden.

The Book of Genesis describes the four rivers that water the corners of the earth but whose headwaters are in Eden:

> A river flows out of Eden to water the garden, and from there it divides and becomes four branches. The name of the first is Pishon; it is the one that flows around the whole land of Havilah, where there is gold; and the gold of that land is good; bdellium [a resin used for incense] and onyx stone are there. *The name of the second river is Gihon; it is the one that flows around the whole land of Kush.* The name of the third river is Tigris, which flows east of Assyria. And the fourth river is the Euphrates[50] [emphasis added].

By linking the four rivers to paradise, this passage in Genesis 2 gives extraordinarily lofty status to each. The Tigris and Euphrates, of course, are two celebrated rivers of the ancient world whose ties to the Hebrews, according to a later chapter of Genesis, go back to Abraham, who journeyed to the Promised Land from the Mesopotamian city of Ur. The identity of the Pishon River and land of Havilah, however, is uncertain: one hypothesis is that they refer to Arabia.[51] Iran was advanced several decades ago as the location for both the Pishon and the Gihon.[52] In a 1998 book, a best-selling British writer, David Rohl, has attempted unconvincingly to locate the Gihon, the Pishon and Eden itself in another part of Iran, the Adji Chay valley in the northwestern corner of the country, just west of the Caspian Sea.[53]

One can understand modern researchers' reluctance to identify the Gihon River of Genesis with the Gihon Spring of Jerusalem. The Gihon Spring's gushing flow is equivalent to that of a modest brook—negligible compared with that of the great Tigris and Euphrates.

Yet for Jerusalem the Gihon, which in Hebrew means "a bursting forth," was of seminal importance. Without this unique source of water, the city—located as it is amid arid hills—would never have been founded *c.* 3000 BC.[54] It was vital in theological terms as well. Many peoples of that part of the world revered what one specialist in the subject, Richard J. Clifford, has called a "cosmic mountain," a sacred elevation "involved in the government and stability of the cosmos."[55] These mountains were, among other things, the "source of water and fertility." For many Jerusalemites, of course, the sacred mountain was Mount Zion, and it was the Gihon that gushed from it. A psalm about Zion gives the Gihon a joyously sacred function: "There is a river whose streams make glad the city of God, the holy habitation of the Most High."[56] Indeed, the Gihon Spring was of such sacramental importance that, according to First Kings 1, the elderly David, failing in health, saw to it that his son Solomon was made king at a ceremony at the Gihon, anointed there with holy oil. Clifford supports the identification of the river in Genesis with Jerusalem's stream.[57]

Jon Levenson, author of a book on Zion as the cosmic mountain, also suggests Genesis means just what it says when it names the Gihon as one of the four rivers of paradise. The professor of Jewish studies at Harvard points out that "it is naive to read a description of the primordial paradise in terms of scientific cartography."[58] He adds that "the mythic mind makes associations according to a logic of its own, which is impressionistic and not scientific. To say that the mind of ancient Israel did not make the equation between the Gihon of Genesis 2:13 and the Gihon of First Kings 1 is indeed to strain the imagination. . . ."[59]

Now to the reference in Genesis 2, to the place to which the Gihon flows—"Kush." Where would "Kush" have been located?

The question is important. The Genesis text appears to say, in effect, that "Kush" is the destination of the waters of Zion. Such a context would suggest that the writers of Genesis saw "Kush," whatever its real geographical identity might have been, in an extremely favorable light.

Taken at face value, "Kush" would correspond to the land south of Egypt. Yet literalists would see a problem with this: no brook, they say, could roll from Jerusalem across the Sinai and into the heartland of Africa. Also, those who see ancient Hebrews as disdainful of Kushites would see this sacred linkage between the two nations as theologically absurd. This may help explain why some scholars have struggled to find other interpretations of "Kush."[60]

Yet two prominent biblical scholars say "Kush" is probably the familiar Kush of Africa. They are Claus Westermann, of the University of Heidelberg, and Brevard Childs, of the Yale Divinity School.[61] However, neither Westermann nor Childs (despite having written a thoughtful book on the 701 crisis) discerns significance in this symbolic association between Zion and Kush. Neither explores its possible ramifications.

The origin of the rivers-of-Eden passage is probably post-701.[62] It would be reasonable, then, to suggest that the allusion to Kush as the Gihon's destination reflects the special relationship that flourished between Jerusalem and its southern ally during Hezekiah's reign. One scholar who thinks so is Manfred Görg, of the University of Munich. He says not only that "Kush" should be taken as that African kingdom but that it is "possibly an allusion to the *special contact of Jerusalem under Hezekiah [with] the Egyptian neighbor dominated by the 25th Dynasty*"[63] [emphasis added]. Görg continues:

> This view may be strengthened by considering the prophetic vision of a spring gushing forth from under the Temple (cf. Ezekiel 47) as a utopic description of a river growing up to a stream of universal relevance.

In the light of this book's presentation of the events of 701, Görg's conjecture gains credibility. I am not aware, however, of any significant discussion by scholars of this important symbolic linkage.

The simple solution to the puzzle over Eden-related topography is to accept "Gihon" and "Kush" at face value. In numerous other passages, when the Hebrew Bible says "Gihon" it means the brook that nurtures Jerusalem and when it says "Kush" it means the African nation. The success of the Jerusalem-Napata alliance provides the necessary logic for this metaphorical relationship. What we may have here, in other words, is the Bible paying an exceedingly high compliment to the Kushites.

Indeed, the Gihon does not only go to Kush, it "flows *around* the whole land of Kush," as if embracing it.

GENESIS ALSO CONTAINS another generally underappreciated tribute to Kush.

A few verses after discussing Noah's three sons in relation to the drinking incident, Genesis 10:6-7 describes those sons' own descendants. This represents the beginning of the Bible's famous "Table of Nations"—that is, the Book of Genesis's explanation for the origins of the various peoples of the world.

A common assumption among scholars is that, aside from the B[1] writer's passing reference to Taharqa, the Hebrew Bible mentions by name no Kushite monarch.[64] The assumption reflects the widespread confidence that in the Hebrew view of the outside world the 25th Dynasty had only a minuscule presence .

Interestingly, however, after recounting the curse of Ham—or, more accurately, the curse of Canaan—Genesis goes on to present the Table of Nations and to name the descendants of Noah's three sons. Sandwiched between the account of Japheth's progeny and Shem's is a listing of Ham's line. It begins this way:

> The descendants of Ham: Kush, Egypt, Put and Canaan. The descendants of Kush: Seba, Havilah, Sabtah, Raamah and Sabteca.[65]

Each of the two sentences is of unusual interest. In listing the sons of Ham in the first sentence, the author of the passage places Kush at the beginning—giving it precedence over the great civilization of Egypt.[66] To be sure, the order of the countries could be chance, so let's not make too much of it. But look at the second sentence. As we saw in Chapter 8, Michael Astour proposes that the name *Sabteca* "certainly" refers to Shebitku. But here's something else: Astour's linguistic analysis also leads him to conclude that *Sabtah* would "probably" allude to Shabako.[67]

If Astour is right, the passage would mean that these two 25th Dynasty pharaohs carried significant weight in Hebrew tradition. For a monarch to merit a place in the genealogical tree of humanity is already quite extraordinary, and here we have two contemporaries from the same nation. As we saw in Chapter 6, it is likely that these pharaohs ruled jointly, as co-regents, during a period that included the crisis of 701. Shebitku, the younger and more vigorous of the pharaohs, would have planned the audacious expeditions to Khor, while Shabako, as the senior sovereign, would have had to apply his seal of approval to the treaty with Sennacherib (Chapter 12).

THE BIBLE'S VIEW of Kushites, then, is anything but derogatory. The Bible neither glorifies nor scorns the Kushites, but treats them sympathetically.[68]

This positive depiction already existed in passages describing events immediately prior to 701. And, as prophecies of Kushite deference to Yahweh suggest in Isaiah 18 and Psalm 68, in subsequent generations the Bible's respectful view of Kush only gathered strength.[69]

Against the background that this book is presenting of a Kushite rescue of Jerusalem, the idea in Genesis 2 of connecting Zion's sacred waters to Kush—breathtaking as that symbolism is—makes sense.

Let us go back to the verse from Amos with which this chapter began:

"Are not you Israelites the same to me as the Kushites?" declares the Lord. "Did I not bring Israel up from Egypt . . . ?"

Does a positive interpretation of Kush in this passage still seem so far-fetched? Far from such a comparison being humiliating to Judah, it is, to say the least, glowingly favorable.

Both peoples have a relationship to Yahweh that is special.

CHAPTER FOURTEEN

Evidence for the Kushites, VI

O NE WAY TO test a theory is to examine why people have rejected it in the past. Who knows, perhaps the reason does contain truths that would deal the theory a fatal blow.

The Kushite-rescue theory needs such a test now.

To see why modern scholarship, in the main, has been so skeptical of the Kushites' military performance, let's go back to the "father of American Egyptology,"[1] James Henry Breasted (1865-1935). Although not the originator of the notion that the Napatans were duds in Judah, he embraces that view and, long after his death, he remains one of its most influential advocates. Several aspects of the Illinois native's career command admiration: the depth of his erudition, as seen in his translations of innumerable hieroglyphic texts; his derring-do fieldwork in Egypt and Sudan; his organizing (with financial aid from John D. Rockefeller) of the University of Chicago's Oriental Institute in 1919 as a hotbed of archaeological research, and his ability—as a popularizing scholar of the highest order—to communicate his admiration of ancient Egypt to a wide audience. All these things make Breasted one of the 20th century's leading historians, in any field.

The main vehicle for Breasted's enduring influence today is his book *A History of Egypt*. Ever since its publication in 1905, this thick volume has served as the standard primer for new generations of Egyptologists; it has been hailed as a "masterpiece and probably the best general history of Pharaonic Egypt ever published."² Although after a century some of the contents have inevitably become dated, today's scholars frequently still cite many of the book's core conclusions with confidence.

The Yale-trained scholar devotes an entire chapter of *A History of Egypt* to the Kushite Dynasty. Quick excerpts will show his attitude. When looking for a "strong ruler" to defend against Assyria, ordinary Egyptians "looked in vain during the supremacy of the inglorious Ethiopians."³ In 701 BC, Sennacherib's army "disposed of Taharqa's without difficulty." The reason Sennacherib withdrew, explains the book with impressive-sounding detail, was that "plague-infested winds from the malarial shores of the eastern Delta had scattered death among his troops." In describing how the 25th Dynasty subsequently persisted in trying to foment trouble, the book asserts: "The Syro-Palestinian princes, . . . were so thoroughly cowed [by Assyria] that the inglorious Ethiopians were thenceforth unable to seduce them to rebellion." When, decades later, the Assyrian invaders closed in on Thebes, Taharqa "ingloriously withdrew southward," seeking "ignoble security on the upper Nile." During the Kushite period, Egypt was nothing less than a "decrepit nation." Indeed, by its failure to repel the Assyrians, the 25th Dynasty demonstrated that "there was never a line of kings so ill-suited to their high destiny." Under Taharqa's successor, Tanwetamani, the dynasty never had a chance: "His whole career was characteristic of the feeble and inglorious line from which he sprang." During this eight-page stretch, Breasted employs the word "inglorious" to describe the dynasty a total of four times.

On what evidence does this renowned scholar base his view that disease blown from the eastern Delta caused Sennacherib's departure? He cites none.

On what evidence does he conclude so insistently that the 25th Dynasty was such a pitiful failure? In support of his hostile view of Kushite pharaohs, Breasted cites *one* source. That source is the verse in Second Kings (18:21) where the Assyrian king's envoy, the Rab-shakeh, tells the Jerusalem's beleaguered populace: "Now behold, thou trustest upon the staff of this bruised reed, even upon

Egypt; whereon if a man lean it will go into his hand and pierce it; so is Pharaoh king of Egypt unto all that trust him." (Breasted uses this King James translation.) The Rab-shakeh, Breasted proclaims, spoke "the truth."[4]

A second expert who has helped shape today's common view of the 25th Dynasty is William Adams. Published in 1977, his landmark work, *Nubia: Corridor to Africa*, remains the most comprehensive book to date on the history of the upper Nile. Where does the University of Kentucky scholar, who endorses the epidemic theory, get his view of Kush's military failure in 701? Significantly, it is precisely the same place as Breasted (to whom he shows indebtedness in endnotes). After opening his chapter on the 25th Dynasty by also solemnly quoting the Rab-shakeh's weak-reed statement, Adams comments:

> These words . . . aptly suggest the estate to which Egypt's imperial fortunes had fallen in the eighth century BC. The passage, despite its mocking tone, is dear to the hearts of historians of Nubia, for it recalls the one brief appearance of Kush upon the stage of world history.[5]

The stamp of approval that Breasted and Adams award the Rab-shakeh's speech is typical of modern scholarship. Thus, for example, Nicolas Grimal, in his recent book, *A History of Ancient Egypt*, is as categorical as Breasted and Adams in accepting the Assyrian's scornful characterization of Kushite Egypt as a "bruised reed" or, according to some translations, "broken reed." The Egyptology professor at the Sorbonne says the Rab-shakeh "painted a portrait of the strength of [Hezekiah's] Egyptian ally which, though unflattering, was undeniably close to the truth."[6] In the 1991 edition of *The Cambridge Ancient History*, T.G.H. James also invokes the reed passage in order to reach his conclusion about the dynasty's "abortive campaign of 701."[7] The well-known British Museum Egyptologist makes this severe assessment of Kushite pharaohs:

> Their adventures in foreign affairs, almost invariably disastrous, were, it seems, not prompted by any consistent policy, but by mis-

guided interest in the machinations of Palestinian and Syrian states, compounded with a misjudgment of the competence of their armies in opposition to the well-organized might of Assyria.[8]

In a 1995 article, Kenneth Kitchen—one of the most impressively painstaking researchers I've come across—likewise cites the Rab-shakeh's speech in asserting that the Kushites' performance in Khor was "incompetent."[9]

Of the many other scholars who scoff at that dynasty's ability, not all explicitly invoke the broken-reed statement, but they do not have to: the reputation of the dynasty as politically and militarily hapless is so firmly entrenched that it no longer requires substantiation.[10]

My reading of many scholarly texts dealing, to a greater or lesser extent, with the events of 701, leads to this conclusion: that the Rab-shakeh's statement is the keystone upon which the case for Kushite futility depends.[11] Without this single jeering statement, in other words, the argument for the unreliability of Taharqa's army loses its best evidence. The argument simply falls apart.

How are these scholars interpreting the broken-reed passage?

To see, we must look not only at the verse containing that statement but also—which the scholars do not do—*the verses that come after it.* The biblical writers have almost certainly theologically reshaped the Rab-shakeh's original message. Because it is easy to follow, let us use the translation of the New International Version.

Speaking to Hezekiah's officials within earshot of the Jerusalemites crowding the city's walls, the Rab-shakeh declares:

"Tell Hezekiah:

"This is what the great king, the king of Assyria, says: On what are you basing this confidence of yours? You say you have strategy and military strength—but you speak only empty words. On whom are you depending, that you rebel against me?

"Look now, *you are depending on Egypt,* that splintered reed of a staff, which pierces a man's hand and wounds him if he leans on it! Such is Pharaoh king of Egypt to all who depend on him.

"And if you say to me, *'We are depending on the Lord our God'*—
isn't he the one whose high places and altars Hezekiah has removed,
saying to Judah and Jerusalem, 'You must worship before this altar
in Jerusalem'?. . . .
     "The Lord himself told me to march against this country and
destroy it."

Notice the parallel construction, which I have italicized (and which
is also apparent in other translations). The text's point is that
Hezekiah is depending on Egypt *just as he is depending on Yahweh.*[12]
Yes, the Assyrian is ridiculing the Judahite king's trust in Egypt, but
he is *also* questioning his trust in Yahweh.

It would be hard to shrug off this literary construction as unin-
tentional. The Second Kings narrative employs parallel construction elsewhere: as we saw in Chapter 4, it uses an extensive
variation of the literary device in order to contrast the religious
practices of the kings of Israel and those of Hezekiah.[13] There
should be no question that the biblical writers were sophisticated
enough to use such a construction for a specific purpose, and not
by mere happenstance.

Here, the biblical writers use the story of Jerusalem's salvation
to demonstrate that the mighty Assyrian king was wrong to question the soundness of Hezekiah's faith in Yahweh. Simultaneously,
they use the city's rescue to show that the Assyrian king was equally
wrong to question Hezekiah's dependence on Egypt. Far from
impugning Egypt's reliability, the story fully vindicates Judah's
dependence upon that country.

The pithy part of the Rab-shakeh's speech that has just been cited
also contains another striking element: ecclesiastical politics. The
passage presents Hezekiah as the king who removed Yahwist temples from elsewhere in Judah and who commanded his subjects to
worship Yahweh exclusively at Jerusalem. Whenever the centralization of the religion actually took place (whether it was during
Hezekiah's reign or, as some scholars suggest, several generations
later), it is certain to have been controversial. Priests from outside
the capital would have lost their franchises and perhaps told the population that an angry deity would bring down misfortune.

The passage aims to legitimize this centralization. It introduces the issue by having the the Rab-shakeh express skepticism about making Jerusalem the exclusive place of worship. As one prominent British translator of biblical texts, Israel W. Slotki, has noted of the envoy's remark, "The argument runs thus: How can you expect help from your God in the face of Hezekiah's abolition of all His local places of worship in favor of a single altar in Jerusalem?"[14] The city's eventual rescue thus serves to refute that skepticism and to confirm the theological correctness of the ecclesiastical reorganization. All scholars agree on that, yet the analogous logic of extending the argument to Egypt's reliability eludes them.

The outcome of the overall narrative demonstrates that:

- Yahweh's people can depend upon him.
- Yahweh supports the Davidic Dynasty unconditionally.
- Hezekiah was right to centralize worship at Jerusalem, for it is Yahweh's favored city.
- Judah was right to rely on Egypt for help.

The first three conclusions are self-evident. Today, the final one is not because Breasted and the others take out of context the verse that speaks of Hezekiah's misguided reliance on Egypt. Given the symmetry with which the very next verse speaks of Hezekiah's misguided reliance on Yahweh, the passage implicitly anticipates the pharaonic army's *success*.

Indeed, this parallelism has an echo effect. Just after the passage cited above, the Rab-shakeh urges Hezekiah to make a wager with Sennacherib: if Hezekiah can find riders, Sennacherib will give him 2,000 horses for a battle. Cockily, the envoy boasts that Assyria's charioteers and cavalrymen are invulnerable. He says:

> "How can you repulse one officer of the least of my master's officials, even though you are depending on Egypt for chariots and horsemen? Furthermore, have I come to attack and destroy this place without word from the Lord?"

Here, the parallel is different. No longer does the Assyrian equate the folly of Hezekiah's trust in Kushite Egypt with that of his trust in Yahweh. The envoy claims that Assyria, not Hezekiah and his

people, possesses Yahweh's favor. The Rab-shakeh says that because Assyria serves as the instrument of Yahweh's will, the empire's adversary will fail to drive away even a single member of
Assyria's forces. The final outcome, of course, will show the reverse
to be true: Yahweh will be loyal to Jerusalem and it is Assyria's
forces that will be set back. And *who* will set them back? The passage's logic would suggest that the "chariots and horsemen" of
Egypt would be responsible. It is the 25th Dynasty, not Assyria,
that will serve as the instrument of divine will.

The irony is rich. The very evidence that the scholarly establishment gives for doubting the Kushites' abilities turns out, when
examined more thoroughly, to be ammunition that clinches the
case for the Kushites.

The key passage presents the Rab-shakeh as hostile to three
things: Hezekiah's dependence on the pharaoh, Hezekiah's
dependence on Yahweh and Hezekiah's exaltation of Jerusalem.
Critics cannot choose which of these hostilities are justified and
which are not. According to the passage's internal logic, the three
are joined and indivisible.

If critics still insist on dismissing the importance of the 25th
Dynasty in saving Jerusalem, fine. But then they might usefully
submit their own theory to this test: show that the point of the Second Kings' Deliverance story is that Yahweh is undependable—the
same Yahweh whom the entire Hebrew Bible presents as invincible and omnipotent. And then they would have to show that the
Bible never intended to depict Jerusalem as the holy city.

Unless the critics can demonstrate this, it seems clear that in
relying so heavily upon the "broken-reed" passage as the source of
their premise, they have themselves leaned on specious evidence.
The reed has indeed snapped, and in so doing punctured their
premise.

HERE, TO RECAPITULATE, are the chief reasons for crediting
the Kushite-Egyptian army as the key agent in the rescue of
Jerusalem. First, the consensus view that the biblical account of the

Deliverance was put together in distinct layers indicates, when those layers are separated, that this advancing army prompted the invaders' retreat. Second, in the centuries following the rescue, both Herodotus and biblical oracles present the Assyrians as fleeing under conditions of duress, pursued by an armed foe. The only adversary in that theater of war capable of causing such distress was the Kushite-Egyptian expedition. Third, in the years immediately following Assyria's withdrawal, Egypt under the Kushite pharaohs enjoyed extraordinary political and commercial influence in Judah and elsewhere in Khor, influence that is consistent with having emerged from this conflict with the upper hand. Fourth, a variety of ancient texts—Assyrian, Judahite and Greek—show that in this period Kushite Egypt also possessed a reputation for exceptional military prowess, which is consistent with having forced Assyria's departure. And finally, in addition to the implicit message of Second Kings' broken-reed passage, the Hebrew Bible in several places accords Kush great honor. No other nation receives such special treatment, and no explanation presents itself other than the Kushite Dynasty's help to Judah against Assyria.

CHAPTER FIFTEEN

How the Kushites Could Have Pulled It Off

So far, we have explored *what* forced Sennacherib's withdrawal. Now, a subsidiary aspect: *how* might the 25th Dynasty's forces have managed to force that withdrawal?

I believe my thesis—that Kushite Egypt turned back Sennacherib—is unshakable. My musings on how this might have happened are, however, in another class entirely. Caution says to keep quiet about them—so that, if they are wrong, these musings do not contaminate the thesis's credibility. But the temptation is irresistible, and perhaps useful, too, in that it may help get the ball rolling and provide other people with something to argue against. Perhaps eventually a reasonable explanation satisfactory to most may emerge.

The ideas described so far do not depend on those that follow in this chapter: if the following scenario should be devastatingly critiqued, the premise upon which it is built—that the Kushites played the pivotal role in causing Assyria's withdrawal—should not necessarily suffer. The premise is as independent of the scenario as a tree is of a treehouse.

MY ASSUMPTION HAS been that Kushite Egypt's forces in the showdown of 701 were weaker than Sennacherib's. Any scenario, therefore, has the burden of demonstrating how this weaker party might have been able to outmatch the stronger.

In earlier chapters, I have been careful so far to avoid suggesting that the Kushite-Egyptian success took the form of an outright (as distinct from *de facto*) "victory" or "triumph": such terms would assume that after the clash at Eltekeh a major battle (or battles) took place that produced a decisive military outcome for the pharaonic army. I subscribe to the near-unanimous view[1] that, sometime well after Eltekeh, the Assyrians brought their campaign to a halt before any such *major* confrontation involving Sennacherib's main body of troops necessarily took place. There is simply no evidence of such a battle.[2]

I believe a combination of factors caused the Assyrians to disengage.

The first was the advance of a second Kushite-led force, made up of mostly fresh troops and perhaps with some veterans of the battle of Eltekeh. The second was a desperate and successful effort by the people of Judah themselves, particularly their engineers and manual workers, to improve their fortifications and to deprive the besiegers of water supplies (while ensuring their own). Many scholars have noted with justified awe the magnitude of this industriousness—the water tunnel in particular. The projects may well have caused significant disruption to the besiegers' plans, although not to the extent of abandoning the siege.

The final factor—and a critical one—was the disarray of Assyrian forces. Sennacherib's army was dispersed, making itself vulnerable to Taharqa's post-Eltekeh army.

Here is my "core scenario" for what is likely to have happened.

After the Rab-shakeh's departure to confer with Sennacherib at Libnah, the besiegers kept only a modest contingent at the capital. That is partly because of the Assyrian strategy of deploying forces in several areas simultaneously and partly because of the Jerusalemites' success in limiting their besiegers' access to water. Taking advantage of the fact that Assyrian forces were thin at Jerusalem, Taharqa's army moved on to that city and sent the besiegers fleeing. (This would explain the frantic-flight motif in Herodotus and in the Book of Isaiah's oracles.)

Sennacherib was still in control of much of the rest of northern Judah. He himself remained in the Lachish-Libnah area. Taharqa advanced on him. Sennacherib's troops were not at full strength, their ranks having been depleted both by the action at Jerusalem and by combat at Eltekeh, Gath, Lachish, Libnah and other locales in Judah, Philistia and Phoenicia.

Rather than fight, the Assyrians and their opponents agreed to an arrangement whereby Judah remained viable, although this kingdom shrank in size and paid a heavy penalty to Assyria. The details of this arrangement were probably reached not on the spot but, rather, after Sennacherib's impromptu departure, when diplomats and other representatives of the various parties could meet.

WITH ALL PRUDENCE thrown aside, here is a somewhat playful elaboration of that "core scenario."

This embellished version will stick closely to the B[1] text, mining it for possible clues. The Hebrew Bible's stories often contain details for a purpose: their pertinence may emerge only considerably later in a story.[3] I am assuming that in the drastic editing of the Deliverance narrative, the revisionists not only added a large section of new material (the B[2] wedge) but, in order to give the story a semblance of coherence, also deleted some of the original (B[1]) story. In constructing this scenario, I will therefore assume that reasons exist for certain of the story's seemingly trivial and pointless details—for example, the curiously exact description of the three Assyrian envoys standing near, of all places, a ditch. As the original version of the story unfolded, the relevance of such particularities might have become apparent.

Let's start at the moment when Hezekiah gets word that Sennacherib aims to quell the rebellion.

His first move would have been to appeal for help from Egypt, sending with his envoys that caravan of precious gifts to which Isaiah refers. One can readily imagine the sort of debate that this plea would have set off among Shebitku, Shabako and their advisers. One side would have argued for sticking with the existing strategy of waiting for Assyrian forces to reach Egypt. This approach allowed the Kushites to pick the area of battle, build defensive positions if necessary and confront the invading army when it was weary after its march across the Sinai Desert. Proponents would have pointed out that intervening abroad with maximum force was an extreme gamble that would require draining both Egypt and Kush of almost all troops, so that in the event of their defeat on foreign soil the Nile Valley would have been all but defenseless. The other side would have made the case that Assyria would simply not expect any kind of pre-emptive strike outside Egypt, no Egyptian army having marched much beyond the country's frontier in at least two centuries.

The pharaohs' decision to intervene would have called for a three-part strategy. First, Hezekiah is to play for time. Too weak to confront the invaders on the field of battle, Hezekiah is to fortify the walls of his towns, stock them with garrison troops and food and, with the approach of the enemy, bring into these centers the peasantry, whose survival is vital to the kingdom's agricultural economy. Second, the pharaohs are to send a small advance force composed largely of elite chariotry and cavalry. Its mission: slow down the Assyrian advance. Third, in the interim Shabako and Shebitku are to organize a much larger second force composed of every soldier and militiaman they can find in Lower Egypt, Upper Egypt and Kush and its environs. Hezekiah's objective is to have his kingdom's various forts and walled towns hold out long enough to detain the invaders' progress and allow for the arrival of this second, Taharqa-led contingent.

After smashing through Phoenicia and Philistia, the Assyrian army enters Judah loaded with tribute and plunder. Major tasks remain. The army must still besiege two large cities belonging to King Hezekiah—Lachish and Gath—and many smaller ones including Libnah, about six miles north of Lachish, and Azekah, several miles farther north than that. Finally, and most importantly, Assyrians must conquer the capital, Jerusalem, 30 miles northeast of Lachish. That is where Hezekiah is holding out, where the Assyrian-loyalist king of Ekron, Padi, is imprisoned and, not least, where most of the kingdom's treasure lies. Sennacherib, with his zest for battle, places himself at the heart of the action. He is in charge of attacking Lachish and nearby towns, including Libnah and perhaps Azekah.[4] He delegates to others the preliminary phase of the Jerusalem siege, much of it involving routine engineering to encircle the city. It makes sense for Sennacherib to remain in the general area of Lachish: it is roughly midway between Jerusalem and the Mediterranean and, as the kingdom's second largest city, six roads go out from it in different directions.[5] The location is ideal for keeping alert for a possible advance up the coastal plain by a second Egyptian force, and at the same time it is well-suited for sending out warring parties to many of those 46 walled towns and forts, as well as the many villages, that the king would later boast in his annals of having taken.

While at Lachish, Sennacherib sends the three high-ranking aides—the Tartan, the Rab-saris and the Rab-shakeh—to Jerusalem with "a large force."[6] Possibly, the army that the three men are leading meets up at Jerusalem with another Assyrian force, perhaps smaller, that has approached from Samarina to the north.[7] The Assyrians set up camp on a ridge of Jerusalem's Northwest Hill.[8] They build their earthwork around much or all of the city.

Sennacherib's three envoys seek a parley with Hezekiah. The Judahite king responds by sending three officials of his own to speak to them just outside the outer wall. The lengthy description of the meeting in Second Kings 18:18-37 shows how the Assyrians use various ploys to manipulate the crowd of Jerusalemites that is listening to the discussion from the ramparts. Much of the Rab-shakeh's speech is a reading of a letter by Sennacherib.[9] The speech is complex and layered; while it contains theological coloring, its core appears to be authentic.[10]

Several seemingly innocuous parts of the B[1] account of his performance are telling.

The Rab-shakeh mocks the Jersualemites for holding out against the besiegers in the hope that Egypt would rescue them. He has an interest, of course, in poormouthing Egyptian power. He wants to lower the Jerusalemites' morale and resistance. One reason the Assyrian wants a rapid settlement is water. There is very little of it near Jerusalem. Second Kings may subtly signal that fact when it emphasizes a curious, seemingly insignificant detail in the three envoys' actions. The B¹ narrative says of the trio: "They went up and came to Jerusalem. *When they arrived, they came and stood by the conduit of the upper pool,* which is on the highway to the Fuller's Field"[11] (emphasis added). Why would they do that? The site is not near their presumed camp, nor is it where they will later parley with the Jerusalemites.

Why does the B¹ account stress that these all-important visitors stop at this ditch? Because, I suggest, the ditch may be dry. This is the result of Hezekiah's elaborate plan, as Second Chronicles describes it, to close or divert springs and streams in the vicinity of Jerusalem.[12] The effort has included a truly spectacular effort, the digging of the long tunnel through the limestone hill upon which the city stands. The tunnel diverts water from a source, the Gihon Spring, to a new reservoir built for this purpose inside a new wall. Other pools may accommodate the Gihon's flow as well.[13] Although Hezekiah has constructed the thick new wall to protect these precious resources, this fortification is vulnerable to the sort of assault the Assyrians mounted at Lachish.

The Gihon Spring, says T.C. Mitchell, is the "upper pool" to which 2 Kings 19:17 alludes. Mitchell, an expert on biblical archaeology at the British Museum, says that the precise place where the Rab-shakeh, Tartan and Rab-saris stood

> cannot be certainly identified, but the implied combination of a water conduit and a fuller's field, that is to say, a field in which cloth was cleaned by treading or beating, almost certainly with the aid of water, suggests the area at the foot of the eastern wall of the ancient city which, until the cutting of Hezekiah's tunnel, could have been watered from the aqueduct running southwards from the Gihon spring.[14]

Subsequently, another historian, Dan Bahat, has speculated that the site of the envoys' inspection might have been several hundred yards north of the spring; he says Hezekiah might have previously built a conduit there which brought water into the city from a small dam the king had erected across the Beth Zetha Valley to block floodwaters.[15] This alternative, though it has nothing to do with the Gihon Spring, is perfectly acceptable. Presumably the envoys would have noted that the conduit was dry, either because it was the dry season or because Hezekiah had sabotaged it, or both.

The lack of water, then, has a profound impact on the besiegers. Little wonder that, upon their arrival at Jerusalem, the envoys give attention to the conduit. They see firsthand that their men will have had little drinking water. Also—and this is significant— their horses, which require vast amounts of it, will not have had enough. If this phase of the campaign is taking place in the height of summer, as seems very likely,[16] this shortage would be acutely felt. That is the period when, of course, animals are most thirsty; in temperatures in the mid-80s degrees F, a 1,000-pound horse may consume upwards of 25 gallons of water per day.[17] It is also the time of year in which the alternate source of water, precipitation, is the most scarce. Between May and September, Jerusalem ordinarily receives no rain.

A final observation on this hydro-engineering ploy. My guess is that Hezekiah would divert the water into the city at the last moment. For two reasons. First, of course, in war the element of surprise is always an advantage, forcing the enemy to depart from earlier plans. Secondly, the reservoir, located inside the walls at the southern and downhill end of the city, will eventually fill up and overflow. When that happens, the surplus water will spill beyond the city's southern walls. Mitchell says confidently that this water would not pose a problem: "[I]t would not have been difficult to disperse [the water] on down the valley, where tangled vegetation would have obscured it."[18] Complete concealment seems almost too good to be true, but what is probable is that the Jerusalemites would seek to delay the overflow as long as possible.[19]

The Assyrians, then, have an added disincentive for a protracted siege: drought. Even if they could catch a bit of the reservoir's run-off, the prospect of a siege like the one more than 20 years before in Israel, when Assyrians camped outside the capital Samaria for two or three years before finally conquering it, would represent a severe strain on their most basic need. The extraordinary effort that Sennacherib musters to overcome Lachish quickly (including the building of a massive ramp of earth and rock at the very base of that city's wall) shows how determined he is to keep his campaign from dragging on.

HAVING INSPECTED THE dry ditch, the Assyrian envoys open their talks with Hezekiah's three officials within earshot of the Jersualemites crowding the city's rampart. Midway through his remarks, the Rab-shakeh says that he is not only addressing Hezekiah's three representatives: "I am also talking to the people who are sitting on the wall, who will have to eat their excrement and drink their urine, just as you will."[20] He is postulating that the city faces an acute shortage of food and water. He is evidently impressed by the disappearance of the reputed water supply outside the city's walls. He seems unaware that the Jerusalemites have so much water they could go swimming.

After describing the meeting, the B¹ account says, "The people [on the wall] kept quiet, just as King Hezekiah had told them to."[21] That is an odd command. One can see why the Assyrians want to speak within hearing of the citizenry, for propaganda purposes, but why is the king anxious that the people restrain themselves from talking back? Several possibilities come to mind.

One is that the king does not want his people to hurl insults that might provoke the attackers to deal extra-harshly with the city.

Another possibility concerns Taharqa's advance. The success of the Kushite strategy depends on keeping Hezekiah from surrendering before the rescue unit arrives. Presumably, to keep the king's hopes up, the Kushites would have tried to communicate secretly with Hezekiah to tell him about their firm intention to arrive within a given time period.[22] Presumably, too, Hezekiah—anxious to boost the morale of his own people and thus reduce intense pressure on himself to surrender—would have passed the news on to the population. The besieged may have known a lot more about the advancing force's strength, timetable and itinerary than the besiegers, and Hezekiah would not have wanted any of his subjects to blurt out such information.

Another possible reason the king insists on silence on the walls is that he may want to keep people from shouting defiantly that they have plenty of water. If the Assyrians discover early on that Jerusalem faces no drought, that intelligence could be dangerous to the city. The besiegers would realize that if they aimed to inflict privation on the city they could be there a long time. They might decide to attack instead. And Hezekiah is playing for time until the Kushite-Egyptian force arrives.

In the event that the Assyrians are aware of the water situation, how soon would it take them to launch a full-scale attack on Jersualem? Not immediately. The Jerusalemites have built a stout new wall beyond the perimeter of the existing one.[23] Despite the desertion of some top soldiers, the city can put up more than a token defense. It has no lack of people to dump rocks, boiling liquids and whatnot on attackers. So it is likely that the Assyrians will want to amass a larger force for this attack. They will wait until those forces in and around Lachish, Libnah and elsewhere are free and can gather at Jerusalem. Given the invasion's advanced state, however, this might not be far in the future.

The point underlying all this verbal fencing between the shrewdly inquisitive Rab-Shakeh and the coy Jerusalem officials is that the city has adequate water supplies and its besiegers have little, probably far less than they had originally anticipated.

IN THAT SAME address to Hezekiah's delegates and to the people on the wall, the Rab-shakeh makes an offer: "I will make a bargain with you in the name of the emperor. I will give you 2,000 horses if you can find that many men to ride them!"[24] Many scholars rightly see this as a sneering put-down, a jeer that implies that Jerusalem lacks an adequate cavalry or chariot corps. But the taunt may suggest something else as well: the Rab-shakeh has, truly, more horses than he knows what to do with.

The Assyrian army placed enormous emphasis on horses. Chariotry was its main strength on the battlefield, and its cavalry was also formidable. But in attacks on fortified cities, both the chariotry and the cavalry were useless.

The Rab-shakeh, in short, finds himself with an embarrassment of horses—not only elite battle horses but also work horses. In the opening phases of the siege, a large number of work horses have been useful for transporting men and supplies to Jerusalem and for hauling rocks and soil to make the earthwork. After that, however, relatively few are needed for carrying supplies and doing errands and, once the city has fallen, for pulling equipment and booty back to Assyria.

The Assyrians' construction of an earthwork effectively prevents Hezekiah's troops from confronting the besiegers on an open field of battle. (If Hezekiah should propose such a battle, the Assyrians can allow his men to pass over the earthwork unmolested. But it is highly unlikely Hezekiah will seek this. He has already rejected the offer—assuming the Rab-shakeh had not made it in jest—of free horses and chariots and, if he does not confront the enemy with them, it is hard to imagine he will want to confront the Assyrians without them.) Of what utility, then, are many of the horses? The end of the campaign seems in sight. That the Assyrian forces are so scattered indicates they expect no serious threat from outside.

One of the puzzling aspects of the conflict of 701 is the question of why there was no battle, or at least no record of a battle, between the rescuers and the besiegers. And yet both Herodotus and the several of the Book of Isaiah's oracles appear to describe the foe being put to flight. How does one reconcile these two things? One explanation is that there was in fact a pitched battle that our sources somehow failed to mention. That is possible but improbable: such a battle would have been a great event, so it seems unlikely Herodotus' Egyptian sources would have passed over it. Consider another explanation.

So far, everything in this scenario derives from a close reading of Second Kings and, to a lesser extent, of Sennacherib's writings. Now I venture further into conjecture and suggest something that appears in neither of those sources. In a decision that might prove to have serious consequences for their campaign, the Assyrians may have sent away many of their battle horses from Jerusalem,[25] probably back to Mesopotamia.[26]

There are excellent reasons why it would have made sense from the Assyrians' viewpoint to dismiss a large quantity of their horses. As already mentioned, at this point in the campaign horses are of little military value. Why keep cavalry and chariotry horses *en masse* at a besieged city if no major open-field battles are foreseeable? Meanwhile, the siege at Lachish has effectively bottled up another major part of equestrian corps belonging to Judah's defenders, for the city is probably a center for chariotry.[27] The siege and destruction of Lachish have thus removed another justification for keeping Assyria's war horses in Judah.

A second reason for wanting fewer horses is that the camp at Jerusalem has an acute water-supply problem. Not only are the Assyrians deprived of the waters of the Gihon Spring but, as noted earlier, Second Chronicles tells us that Hezekiah stopped up "all" the springs. It is hard to tell just how many miles this sabotage of water sources extended, but presumably it is over a substantial distance.[28] (Although the underground water would eventually have leaked out elsewhere in the limestone terrain, the location of these openings would probably have been unpredictable and perhaps hard to find, and inconvenient for water-wagons and the like to reach.)

Also, by August, grazing has largely dried up. If the Judahites have gone to the trouble of blocking wells, it is safe to assume they also destroyed supplies of hay and grain in a broad area around Jerusalem.[29] No fodder.

A more positive reason for wanting to send the horses away is that on the trip home, they can be useful hauling vast amounts of plunder to Nineveh as well as their own wounded. Indeed, the members of the chariotry and cavalry might well have more useful things to do elsewhere, such as escorting those captives on their forced marches or simply getting home to see families and enjoy their booty. In pursuing its expansionist goals, Assyria is generally in a state of almost constant war and depends on its standing army's good morale.

HAVING UNSUCCESSFULLY TRIED to threaten and manipulate the Jersualemites into surrendering, a frustrated Rab-shakeh reports back to Sennacherib. Second Kings says:

> The Rab-shakeh returned, and found the king of Assyria fighting against Libnah; for he had heard that the king had left Lachish. . . . [T]he king heard concerning King Tirhakah of Kush, "See, he has set out to fight against you". . . . [Account B[2] interrupts here for 25 and a half verses.] Then King Sennacherib of Assyria left, went home, and lived at Nineveh.[30]

As we saw in Chapter 9, Frank Yurco and Kenneth Kitchen, in their separate articles, plausibly propose that the arrival of Taharqa's army coincides with the dispersal of Sennacherib's army: one Assyrian force is at Libnah, another at Jersualem, and others elsewhere. Kitchen goes so far as to say that Taharqa is deliberately rushing north to try to exploit the "sudden golden opportunity" that Assyria's scattered forces presents.[31] Up to this point, I believe that Kitchen is right.[32]

The Rab-shakeh leaves the besieging army at Jerusalem and goes to Libnah to consult Sennacherib. They will have had much to consult about: the determined resistance of the Jerusalemites, the availability of water and food for the horses, the question of how much water the Jerusalemites themselves possess, the state of the city's fortifications and the measures that would be needed to storm the walls.

At this point in the narrative Taharqa's force materializes on the horizon.[33] Where does this army come from?

Yurco quite reasonably speculates on the two Kushite-Egyptian forces in these terms: "The Kushite troops in the unit that fought at Eltekeh may represent personnel stationed in Memphis and throughout the Delta who logically would be the first to be called up for operations in Philistia. By contrast, Taharqa's group was mobilized from Kush. . . ."[34] Although this second contingent would have been composed largely of Kushites,[35] it is quite possible that also taking part were other sub-Saharan peoples, including tribal groups, who were allies or vassals of the kingdom of Kush. As well, native Egyptian security forces stationed at Thebes and elsewhere in the Two Lands could have been enlisted en route. Just as the Assyrian army was an amalgam of people of different national backgrounds, so probably was the force the pharaohs had cobbled together to fight it. In the latter part of the march, within Khor, veterans of the force that had already fought at Eltekeh could have also joined.[36]

The Bible makes the report of Taharqa's advance sound sudden and unexpected by the invaders. One has to assume that the Assyrians, highly competent as they were in military affairs, have their share of spies, but their intelligence network might not understand the true destination of the forces coming down the Nile from Kush. The Assyrians may simply assume that these forces are intending to gather in the eastern Delta or the general region of the Sinai and remain there, establishing an essentially defensive position to discourage an anticipated Assyrian invasion of Egypt. It is easy to imagine that Sennacherib may receive only modest advance notice that the Kushite-Egyptian army is actually pushing on to Khor.[37]

As he approached Khor, where would Taharqa direct his forces? He has two principal choices: the Libnah-Lachish area or Jerusalem. Sennacherib is at Libnah, yet that town itself is only of modest importance; Lachish, which is just six miles or so farther and important, has just fallen and is thus a lost cause. From Taharqa's perspective, the reasons for making Jerusalem the priority are compelling. The two things necessary for the potential buffer state's viability are holed up there: the monarch (as well as his heirs, presumably) and the vast majority of the kingdom's leadership class and tradespeople that Assyria has not already killed or claimed as booty. If Jerusalem falls, so will Judah. As suggested here, the Assyrian forces besieging the capital may also be weak and vulnerable. A significant number of equestrian units may have set off for home; work horses may also have departed, hauling field-battle ordnance, treasure, wounded.

Taharqa hastens toward the capital. The Assyrian army, perhaps caught by surprise or unable to get reinforcements in time from Sennacherib, flees, probably without making a stand. If Herodotus, and also the Book of Isaiah, are accurate, the Kushite-Egyptian forces give them pursuit and inflict significant losses.[38]

THE CITY'S PEOPLE go "to the housetops"—the better to view the Assyrian forces' flight, and to celebrate. Jerusalem, reports Isaiah, becomes "full of shoutings, [a] tumultuous city, exultant town."[39]

But the war is not over. Sennacherib is still in the area of Libnah and Lachish. It is likely the main body of his forces are available to him there. If Sennacherib's troops are indeed dispersed at Lachish, Libnah and perhaps elsewhere, he can regroup them at this time. Yet no evidence exists of a battle. Why would there not have been one? Why would Taharqa prefer to let Sennacherib leave peaceably and to negotiate a treaty with him?

Perhaps one reason is that no one is ever certain of winning a fight, especially against troops more experienced than one's own. Taharqa's army represents Egypt's and Kush's last hope for security: if Taharqa's army lost this battle, Assyria could amble up the Nile Valley almost at will.

Secondly, the first Kushite-Egyptian fighting force has seen some of its ranking members taken prisoner at Eltekeh. In his annal, Sennacherib speaks of having captured "Egyptian charioteers with their princes and also the charioteers of the king of Ethiopia."[40] One can readily imagine that the 25th Dynasty will want these prisoners returned. The charioteers are the army's elite, and the Egyptian princes, whose very presence in Khor demonstrates their loyalty to the dynasty, are likely valuable to the Kushites for Egypt's continued unity. Between the pharaonic family and the captured Kushite princes, close political and personal ties probably existed

Further, a defeat of Sennacherib might not mean a permanent defeat of Assyria. Its war machine might have been capable of renewal. Even *if* Taharqa could strike a mortal blow to the empire, he has to bear in mind that Assyria is not the only militaristic threat to the region. Babylonia is emerging as another threat, witness Merodach-baladan's strength. Babylon might simply replace Assyria as the next imperial predator, which is exactly what happens after Nineveh's overextended empire crumbles in the late seventh century BC. In 701, therefore, the 25th Dynasty might prefer to make peace with the enemy it knew, than to destroy it and open the way for more trouble.

Nor is it the ethos of the Kushite Dynasty to go for the jugular. Witness how Piye in 728 dealt with his foes—Tefnahkt and others. Instead of annihilating them and their forces, he achieved a *modus vivendi* with them. In return for forgiving them and letting them keep some of their privileges, he was spared casualties, received bountiful tribute and gained a political situation that, if uncomfortable (notably because of Tefnakht's comeback in Lower Egypt), he could at least live with. When he went to war against Tefnakht, Piye states that his objective was not to destroy the rebel but to "make him turn back from fighting, forever."[41] In making peace with Sennacherib, the co-regents Shabako and Shebitku may have a similar goal. This merciful quality also may have had an ethical dimension consistent with the Kushites' "kinder, gentler" variation of *ma'at*. What is certain is that for the rest of his life Sennacherib abstained from fighting in Khor. Never again did he pose a threat to Egypt.

$$\boxed{G}$$

THE MOST RELIABLE part of the Bible's entire description of the events of 701, the archivally-based Account A in Second Kings, explains what happened next:

Hezekiah sent a message to Sennacherib, who was in Lachish: "I have done wrong; please stop your attack, and I will pay whatever you demand." The emperor's answer was that Hezekiah should send him ten tons of silver and one ton of gold. Hezekiah sent him all the silver in the Temple and in the palace treasury; he also stripped the gold from the temple doors and the gold with which he himself had covered the doorposts, and he sent it to Sennacherib.[42]

One can imagine the preliminary negotiations. Account A may imply that Sennacherib located these talks at Lachish.[43] If that is the case, it suggests a shrewd effort at seizing a psychological advantage. The city, once the "most formidable citadel in Judah,"[44] is now a charred ruin. The emperor's conquest of it is a "great military achievement, since no other victory was ever recorded by Sennacherib in such lavish display," points out archaeologist David Ussishkin, alluding to the famous bas-relief.[45] The proximity of that city's tragic remains serves as a poignant reminder to Assyria's negotiating adversaries of the fate that might await Jerusalem if it provokes the empire's displeasure in the future.

Thus did Sennacherib save face and Taharqa save, among other things, Judah.

LET'S CONSIDER ONE last element of the campaign.

Taharqa's strategy depended on surprise: catching Sennacherib with his forces divided, Taharqa's army probably headed first for Jerusalem, neutralized whatever Assyrian forces were there, and then turned west to confront Sennacherib, who had been in the general area of Lachish and Libnah. To do this, the army would have had to find a road enabling it to approach Jerusalem from the "back door"—that is, not from the normal direction, from the coast, where lay the main highway, the so-called Way of the Sea. Did such a back road exist?

Only after roughing out the core scenario did I realized that my ignorance of such a route's existence represented a gaping hole in the hypothesis. My assumption that a serviceable back road "had" to exist was gratuitous, based on nothing more than conjecture.

The problem that Taharqa would have faced as he emerged from the Sinai was this. The plain and the hills that lay between the Way of the Sea and Jerusalem were crawling with Assyrians and their local allies. How could Taharqa elude them without causing delays and other problems?

Certainly small roads crisscrossed Judah, and some of them would have permitted access to Jerusalem without passing by the coast. But rugged hills, some of them 3,000 feet high, separated Jerusalem from the Sinai and Negev desert to the south, as well as from the west. To achieve speed and assure surprise, however, Taharqa's army needed a road through this hill country that was not meandering. All country roads were unpaved, so the army would also require one that was in good enough condition for vehicles ranging from chariots to supply wagons. The road also had to be broad enough to accommodate these vehicles. Finally, for reasons of speed, the route ideally should not be steep. Did such a route exist?

Yes, according to *The Roads and Highways of Ancient Israel*, a book that uses painstaking detective work to reveal just where Judah's and Israel's roads were located during this era.[46] Author David Dorsey, who spent three years of hiking to discover this transportation network, does not mention the events of 701. But he shows that one road in particular would have been ideal for Taharqa's army.

This is the so-called "national highway" that links Beer-sheba, a city at Judah's southern frontier, with Jerusalem.[47] Starting from Beer-sheba, the highway went north to Debir, Hebron and Bethlehem before passing less than a mile west of Jerusalem. The road from Beer-sheba to Jerusalem was about 44 miles long. (After the capital, the road continued on into Israel, going to Bethel, Shechem and Jezreel.)

To reach this highway, and thereby bypass Gaza and the region around Lachish, Taharqa could have used the road called the "Way of Shur" through the north-central Sinai, resupplied his forces at Beer-sheba and then barreled up the national highway to Jerusalem.

To judge from Dorsey's map, this bow-shaped route would appear to add no more than 10 to 20 miles to any of the more direct Sinai-Jerusalem routes that used the coastal road. Dorsey estimates that ancient armies typically marched 14-15 miles per day.[48] So this route's additional 10 to 15 miles might have added only about a day to Taharqa's army's travel time. The disadvantage would have been a minor one.

This itinerary would have bypassed those areas along the coast and the general area of Lachish where the presence of Assyria and its Philistine allies was strongest.[49] The Beer-sheba-to-Jerusalem leg cleaved to ridges or high plateaus—the watershed for most of Judah. This meant that the road's physical condition was far better than for routes located on hillsides or valleys. By occupying the watershed, the road was immune to fallen rocks, and erosion from rains earlier in the year would have been minimal.

True, about 12 miles south of Hebron (or about one-third of the way to Jerusalem), the national highway briefly left the watershed and descended into a series of valleys. Dorsey, however, says that a secondary branch remained along the watershed.[50] So the army would have had that roadway as an option. This sustained ability to remain on a watershed is rare, if not unique, for long-distance itineraries on Judah's roads.

The route's easy grades presented little challenge for weary horses and foot soldiers[51] even as it offered a welcome measure of security. By constantly occupying the highest point of land, the route would have given Taharqa's army the best possible tactical position in the event that word of its advance brought out a force to intercept it. In short, by detouring through Beer-sheba, the Kushites would have been able to strike at Jerusalem swiftly and with minimal interference.[52]

How fast could Taharqa get to Jerusalem? Although the typical daily progress of armies in ancient times was, as mentioned, about 15 miles, when pressed they could go much faster. Alexander the Great's army was capable of marching 45 miles in a single day.[53] And in one instance, the Roman army is believed to have been able to sustain a daily average of 46 miles over a period of a week.[54] By leaving his supply train behind, then, Taharqa could have dashed to Jerusalem in just one day, or more likely two (given the army's condition after the desert march and possible combat in the Beer-sheba region). He could well have caught Sennacherib flat-footed and unable to bring fresh troops into position at the capital.

Plausible though this scenario is, it is but pure speculation and not really essential to the book's thesis.

PART III

Why History Has Distorted the Kushites' Achievement

[I]f anything historically true is in the Bible, it is there not because it is historically true but for different reasons. The reasons have presumably something to do with spiritual profundity or significance. And historical truth has no correlation with spiritual profundity, unless the relation is inverse.

Northrop Frye

The Great Code: The Bible and Literature

CHAPTER SIXTEEN

The Ancient Revisionists' Motive

THE B² ACCOUNT, that huge mass of text that intrudes awkwardly into the Second Kings' invasion narrative, reflects theological ideas of monumental importance, but for purposes of understanding what happened in 701 BC it is completely useless. For all its great size—it fills almost half the narrative—it contains no historical facts. Its presence obscures the role of Taharqa's army and raises questions that we cannot ignore. Why did these later writers cloud the historical truth? What did they perceive as truth? Did they downgrade the role of the Kushites in the rescue of Jerusalem because of ill will toward them?

That last question is particularly pertinent here, because if the B² writers did have such a negative view of Kush it would contradict the earlier argument that the Hebrew Bible is favorably disposed to it.

For them, as with people of antiquity generally, truth had little to do with factual history. The B² writers had a higher agenda. Like all writers of what eventually would become the Bible, they wanted prophetic and historical texts to serve the religious needs of their community. As societal conditions changed, so these needs would change and thinkers would gain new interpretations of Yahweh's will. To reflect these freshly revealed divine truths, it was necessary to adjust those texts.[1] The ancients saw the revision of texts (or the writing of entirely new ones) as essential precisely in order to be truthful. For them, there was nothing sacrilegious about this. The B[2] writers did not see themselves as tampering with Holy Scripture. If anything, by adjusting the story of Sennacherib's campaign they were perfecting it.

A more involved question: Why would the B[2] writers rework the B[1] text and in a way that renders the decisive role of Kush (or Kushite Egypt) less apparent?

In modern society, with racism all around us, it may seem only natural to suspect that disdain for black Africa tainted the B[2] writers' perspective. But, again, let's be wary of falling into the trap of ascribing today's all-too-common mentality to ancient people.

Most specialists agree that the bulk of the B[2] account probably originated sometime during the 100-year period that started shortly after 622 BC, the date that conventional historians give for the emergence of the Book of Deuteronomy.[2]

The difference between the later Judahite perspective on Egypt and that which existed in 701 was like night and day. The period in question includes some of the most bleak and turbulent years in all of Hebrew history. And, unlike the time of the Kushite Dynasty, Egypt now was part of the problem.

At the time of the writing of the B[1] account, Egypt had been Assyria's enemy and Judah's ally. By the time of B[2], the reverse was true: the 25th Dynasty of the Kushites was long gone, and Egypt had become Assyria's ally and Judah's enemy.

This Assyrian-Egyptian partnership began during the reign of Sennacherib's grandson, Assurbanipal. After defeating the Kushites in Egypt and permanently pushing them back to Kush itself in *c.* 656, Assurbanipal set up a Sais-based family as Egypt's docile 26th Dynasty.[3] Whether this family had actual blood ties to the 24th Dynasty of Tefnakht and Bakenranef, who were also Saite, is not known, but both dynasties shared an emphatic hostility toward Kush. This new regime's indebtedness to its creator is especially evident in its stalwart efforts to help the Assyrians keep their empire from crumbling. In 616, Egypt sent an army to the

Euphrates to bolster Assyria against the Babylonians. Although three years later the Babylonians conquered Nineveh, the Assyrians fought on and in 609 the Pharaoh Necho II dispatched a new army to aid the beleaguered emperor. Judah's nationalistic monarch, Josiah, opposed this attempt to prop up his kingdom's age-old oppressor, and he tried to intercept the Egyptians as their army marched through Judah. In the battle, the victorious Egyptians killed the popular Josiah.

Most Judahites of the *late* seventh century—the start of the probable time period in which B² was composed—would have regarded Egypt as a source of tribulation. Not only did they see an Egyptian military expedition slay, not save, their monarch, but they then went through a period in which Egypt dominated Judah politically.[4] Because King Josiah's son and successor displeased him, Pharaoh Necho deported him to Egypt after the young man had ruled just three months and replaced him with his more pliable half brother. The prophet Jeremiah denounced this king, Jehoiakim, as a petty despot: "You can only see your selfish interests; you kill the innocent and violently oppress your people."[5]

In the early years of the sixth century, after Assyria's collapse, Egypt's 26th Dynasty and Judah's compliant government were allies. In this second phase of the relations between Saite Egypt and Judah, the two nations together resisted the westward advances of a common foe, Babylonia. In a prelude to the Exile, in 597 Babylon captured Jerusalem, deporting perhaps 10,000 people,[6] but it chose not to destroy the city or to threaten the continuity of the state. Necho's son and successor, Psamtik II, encouraged Judah to pursue an anti-Babylon policy; the new pharaoh failed in 586, however, to deliver adequate military support when it mattered, leaving Jerusalem in the lurch and making it easy for Babylon to carry out its final, fatal conquest of the city. We can appreciate how in the early sixth century Judahites' attitude toward Egypt might have changed from the late seventh century, veering from outright enmity to bitterness at its unreliability.

During the ensuing Exile, many deported Judahites would have associated Egypt with bitter and profound setbacks. If Francolino

Gonçalves, Ronald Clements, Paul Dion and many others are right in dating B² to the Exile, then those responsible for that text would likely have personally lived through this cataclysmic period of successive invasions and deportation. That the B¹ account would have presented Egypt as a hero of 701 would have posed a problem.

One might argue that the B² writers could have made a distinction between Kush and Egypt. But let us recall B¹'s vocabulary: it quotes the Rab-shakeh as referring three times to *Egypt* as Judah's looked-for savior. Many if not most members of the rescuing Egyptian army would have been Kushites, including Taharqa and other leaders, but the army did nonetheless represent Egypt. While the 25th Dynasty might itself hail from Kush, it had become Egypt's own royalty. From the Judahite perspective in the aftermath of Josiah's death, the fact that different dynasties ruled Egypt in 701 and 609 must have seemed a secondary matter. Whether people of Kushite, Libyan or old-stock Egyptian origin ruled, Egypt was always Egypt.

It is interesting that many historians now think that the Exodus story would have been written at about this same period of time. In that story, the chief villains are of course the Egyptian pharaoh and his cohorts, who are presented as being as cruel and repugnant as any people in the Bible. That is the contemporary image of Egypt. It is with a wholly free conscience that later biblical writers could have obscured Egypt's role as Jerusalem's savior.

More questions. Why would the B² writers have awarded a starring role in the story of Jerusalem's salvation to a divine agent who was supernatural? Why didn't they depict Yahweh as intervening by, say, using a phenomenon of nature such as a storm, drought or an epidemic? Or, given the writers' strong nationalism, why didn't they give the credit to, say, a divinely assisted Hebrew army?

To understand why it was essential to make the agent's identity supernatural, it is necessary to know the biblical writers' reason for changing the story of the rescue in the first place. They would have had something else in mind other than obfuscating the role of a political enemy. These writers were nothing if not idealistic.

In the period that began with Josiah's death and that includes the Exile, the very survival of Hebrew society hung in the balance. The purpose of the Deliverance narrative, as the B² writers revised it, was to introduce some rays of hope. The story's power to strengthen the spirit lives on: in their darkest hour during World War II, Jewish prisoners in concentration camps turned to the story of Jerusalem's rescue to pray for deliverance of any kind.[7]

After many years of mulling over the reasoning for the B² text, Clements has become confident that it was composed during the Exile when many deportees saw Jerusalem, reduced to rubble, as "discredited and no longer suitable as a focus of hope and protection." The idea behind the B² account was to show that "when the right precondition of faith and obedience on the part of the king was present, God may give a miraculous victory."[8] Hence the idealization of Hezekiah and the miraculous reward—survival—that he and his subjects receive. The B² revisionists are also quite political. In depicting Yahweh as saving Jerusalem partly "for the sake of my servant David," they present a divine endorsement of the Davidic royal family's right to the throne.[9] (At least one male family member was among the exiles in Babylon.[10]) In this bleak time, the B² writers felt a desperate need for monarchs who were strong, righteous and piously Yahwist. Only such leaders, they believed, could rally public support, keep Hebrew society intact and obtain Yahweh's powerful favor.

That same desire permeates Second Kings and those other biblical books that form what scholars call the Deuteronomistic History. As we've seen, that history gets its name because its strong philosophical viewpoint reflects that of the Book of Deuteronomy. This history is an amalgam of old and new texts. The books' authors and editors, the Deuteronomists, inserted chunks of the old material, such as the A and B¹ accounts, into the main body of their own freshly minted work. In its description of Hezekiah's 29-year reign, this new material includes not only the B² account but also three shorter passages. One of them portrays the young Hezekiah in his confident pre-invasion years (18:1-12). Another depicts him on his sickbed (20:1-11) and the third presents him showing off his treasures to Babylonian envoys (20:12-19). (Whether all Deuteronomistic texts were composed at precisely the same time by the same people is a matter of great scholarly conjecture and need not detain us.)

The Book of Deuteronomy purports to have been authored centuries before by Moses himself shortly before his death. It represents his farewell instructions to his people. The Deuteronomists used the ostensibly venerable text to promote obedience to Yahweh, to Moses' Ten Commandments and to his many other laws. In order to show Judahites how it was in their self-interest to heed the early prophet's teachings, the Deuteronomistic History reviews the reigns of each of Israel and Judah's monarchs in a manner that reflects Deuteronomy's philosophy that good things happen to Hebrew society when it is under the rule of kings who respect Yahweh, and that misfortune erupts when kings ignore him.

Those who wrote the Deuteronomistic History would have found that the already existing texts on Sennacherib's invasion (that is, the tersely archival A account and the action-oriented B[1]) failed to measure up to this didactic standard. They therefore adjusted the invasion story so as to make the respective fates of Hezekiah, Sennacherib and Jerusalem illustrate this philosophy.

Because of its relevance to the B[2] revision, one passage in the Book of Deuteronomy—in particular, Chapter 7—deserves special attention. This is no ordinary passage: few texts anywhere in the Bible have been more influential in shaping the core identity of the Hebrew people. Let us see how the Deuteronomistic historians revamped the story of Sennacherib's invasion to reflect ideas and motifs that appear in that passage.

In Chapter 3, we saw how the Deliverance story contains the seed of the concept of divine election. It is in Deuteronomy 7 that the Bible formally reveals Yahweh's uniquely high regard for the Hebrews: Moses makes the climactic announcement to his Exodus followers that Yahweh "has chosen you out of all the peoples on earth to be his people, his treasured possession."[11] In addition to making Moses' followers the Chosen People, this identity seals their right to rule the Holy Land[12]—so long as they abide by certain conditions.

At first sight Deuteronomy 7 has nothing to do with the Assyrian aggression. About half a millennium separates the ostensible time of Moses' speech from Sennacherib's campaign. And although in this passage the prophet predicts many future occurrences, never does he refer to any actions that sound like the events of 701. Yet that passage and the B² account have an almost hand-and-glove relationship.

Deuteronomy 7 presents Moses as addressing his followers as they are about to begin the Conquest, at that moment when their 40-year Exodus wandering is over and the Hebrews are about to enter the Promised Land and battle the existing inhabitants for its possession. The Conquest is most popularly known as the occasion when, under the leadership of Joshua, they cross the Jordan River and use rams' horns as trumpets to make the walls of the enemy city of Jericho come tumbling down. Using more conventional weaponry, the Hebrew forces then overcome numerous other enemy strongholds and make all of the Promised Land their own, a campaign that the Book of Joshua describes in often realistic-sounding detail. In recent years, suspicions have been growing among historians that the Conquest as a whole, like the account of the Exodus journey, is largely fictional.[13]

Yet the Conquest and Deliverance stories have this in common: both are about territorial strife between the Chosen People and foreigners, and in both the Chosen People owe their success to their leaders' respect for Moses's instructions. In Deuteronomy, Moses tells his people, who are soon to invade the Promised Land under Joshua, that they "must follow *exactly* the path that the Lord your God has commanded you, so that you may live, and that it may go well with you, and that you may long live in the land that you are to possess" (emphasis added).[14] In Second Kings, the Deuteronomistic historians transform the story of Sennacherib's threat to the Promised Land into an exemplification of the same vital principles that Moses had given his followers.

In Deuteronomy 7, Moses tells his followers that because they are a Chosen People they have certain obligations and, if they are obedient, will win rewards. He therefore tells the Hebrews that when they enter the Promised Land they must destroy pagan temples (7:5). In the Second Kings' story, in remarkably similar descriptive language, Hezekiah does precisely that after he becomes king (18:4). In Deuteronomy, Moses stresses that Yahweh is loyal to those who "keep his commandments" (7:9); in Second Kings, Hezekiah "kept the commandments that the Lord had commanded Moses" (18:6). In Deuteronomy, Moses says that Yahweh will remove all sickness from those who are loyal to him (7:15); in Second Kings, Yahweh cures Hezekiah precisely because the desperately ill king has been so faithful (20:1-7). As well, Deuteronomy warns that Yahweh does not delay in paying back those who reject him (7:10). Sure enough, Second Kings conforms to this idea of speedy justice, making Sennacherib's death appear as though it occurred right after his retreat from Jerusalem (19:36-37). As we've seen earlier, however, he in fact died about 20 years later.

These parallels are all close. But here's the most striking correspondence of all. In mid-siege, Hezekiah enters the Temple where Yahweh dwells, takes Sennacherib's blasphemous letter and "spread it out before YHWH" and then proceeds to address the deity in most peculiar terms. He says: "Turn your *ear*, O YHWH, and *listen*; open your *eyes*, O YHWH, and *look*. *Listen* to the messsage that Sennacherib has sent to taunt the living God" (emphases added).[15] This sustained physiognomical imagery seems strained. For storytelling purposes, it's wholly unnecessary. The entire scene has long baffled experts.[16] But if you look at Deuteronomy 7 its logic leaps out. There, in another odd turn of phrase, Moses says Yahweh insists on paying back with death "those who hate him to his face" (7:10).[17] The two facial allusions seem made for each other.

We see, then, just how closely the Deliverance story demonstrates the practical value of abiding by Moses' instructions—not just approximately but "exactly."

But why did the B² writers insist on an intervention that is supernatural?

One of the biblical books that the Book of Deuteronomy relates to most closely is the Book of Exodus. In Deuteronomy, Moses looks back on the harrowing, just-concluded Exodus experience and draws great lessons from it. Thus, still in Deuteronomy 7,

Moses gives Exodus-based advice that will prove to be as pertinent to the circumstances of the Conquest as to those of the Deliverance. He tells his followers that when they are in conflict with stronger nations,

> do not be afraid of them. Just remember what the Lord your God did to Pharaoh and to all Egypt, the great trials that your eyes saw, the *signs and wonders*, the mighty hand and the outstretched arm by which the Lord your God brought you out. The Lord your God *will do the same* to all peoples of whom you are afraid[18] [7:18-19, emphases added].

What does "will do the same" mean? The Exodus story teems with "signs and wonders." The most famous are the "ten plagues" that Yahweh inflicted on the Egyptians to pressure Pharaoh into freeing the Hebrews from bondage and letting Moses take them away. In chronological order, these plagues are: the transformation of all the Nile's water into blood; a blanket of frogs over Egypt; a monstrous swarm of gnats over the land; a similar presence of flies; an affliction that kills the Egyptian livestock; an outbreak of soot-caused boils on humans and animals; heavy hail that kills all humans, animals and plants that are in open spaces; a devastating cloud of locusts; dense darkness for three days and, finally, the terrible blow that forces Pharaoh to relent—the deaths of all first-born children in Egyptians' families. The term "plague," then, is clearly metaphorical; a better term for it would be "disasters." (Only the livestock deaths, the boils and the infants' deaths are possibly illness-related. As well, only one of these three involves death to humans, the last one, and the cause of death is not clearly disease: Yahweh vaguely "strikes down" the children.) What do all 10 of these diverse calamities have in common? None of them is a realistic "natural disaster" as we know the term.[19] None of them involves humans working on Yahweh's behalf. All are thoroughly supernatural.

The same applies to the Exodus story's other "signs and wonders." For our purposes, the most pertinent of these is the Exodus's angel of Yahweh. It is no common angel. The angel of Yahweh is like another form of Yahweh himself.[20] The same angel also appears in other momentous biblical events. It is this angel who, for example, orders Abraham to refrain from slaughtering his only son, Isaac,[21] ancestor of the Hebrew people. It is the angel of Yahweh who appears before young Moses in the form of a burning bush and mandates him to liberate "my people."[22] More pertinently, the angel of Yahweh also reappears to play a major role in the Hebrews' liberation: as the Egyptian army pursues them, the angel works in tandem with the divine "pillar of cloud" to prevent Pharaoh's men from overtaking the fugitives.[23] In the Conquest, too, this angel will play a major role. Yahweh will direct the angel to lead the Hebrews into Canaan and into victorious battle against its occupants.[24]

The Deuteronomistic History must be true to the reassuring prophecy that in the future Yahweh always will use "signs and wonders" that are "the same" as those of the Exodus to save his people. In its account of the Deliverance, the history therefore uses the identical supernatural agent as in the Exodus. No natural phenomenon or human agent could ever be so sure. Placing a human army—even one that was Hebrew or exclusively Kushite (without Egyptian contamination)—in the heroic role of repelling Sennacherib would not have held the same theological message of infallibility. Indeed, for a contemporary audience a Hebrew or Kushite army would not have been even remotely credible. In the decades preceding the Exile the Judahite forces were weak, having been beaten by Egypt in 609 and later by Babylon. During the Exile itself they were nonexistent. As for the Kushite army, since well before the Deuteronomistic period it had had no presence of any kind in the Mediterranean world.

Despite the fact that, historically speaking, it is total fabrication, B[2] does not spring from a calculated effort to "cover up" as such the Kushite accomplishments. Its Deuteronomistic authors do not attempt to suppress the facts out of any evident antipathy for Kushites. For didactic purposes, the use of the angel of Yahweh as intervenor is very effective. The angel gives majesty to the Deliverance story and helps elevate it to a high level of significance.[25] Yahweh's use of the same agent against Assyria that he employed to save the fugitives from the wicked Egyptian army and to vanquish the Canaanite pagans transforms the story of Jerusalem's survival into a hard proof of Deuteronomy 7's promise that Yahweh "maintains covenant loyalty with those who love him and keep his commandments . . ." (7:9). It is hard proof because Sennacherib's retreat was, unlike the stories of the Exodus or the Conquest, a very real occurrence that was only several generations removed and that all Judahites would have heard of from their elders.

In short, the function of the B² revision of the rescue story is to turn it into a vivid illustration of the truth of Moses' instructions. The revision was tailor-made for comparisons with the Exodus story, and indeed clergy over the millennia have been alert to parallels between the two.

A brilliant example of such a cleric is Alfred Edersheim, (1825-1889), a Presbyterian minister in England and a prominent biblical academic at the University of Oxford. Toward the end of his seven-volume biblical history, he makes this lucid commentary on the parallels:

> There is one event in the history of Israel which the Divine judgment on Sennacherib and the deliverance of Judah must recall to every mind. It is Israel's miraculous deliverance at the time of the Exodus and of the destruction of the army of Pharaoh in the waves of the Red Sea. Then, as now, was the danger extreme, and it seemed as if Israel were defenseless and powerless before the mighty host of the enemy. Then, as now, was the word of the Lord clear and emphatic; then, as now, it was the night season when the deliverance was wrought; and then, as now, was it Israel's birthtime as a nation. For now, after the final transportation [*i.e.*, deportation of *c.* 720 BC] of Israel, did Judah stand forth as the people of the Lord, the inheritors of the promise, the representatives of the kingdom of God. As then, so now was Judah saved without drawing sword or bow, only by the interposition of the Lord. And so it has to all times remained by the side of the miracles of the Exodus as the outstanding event in the typical [*i.e.*, paradigmatic] history of the people of God. . . . [26]

We've seen that Cecil Roth, an eminent biblical historian of the mid-20th century, likened the Deliverance to the Exodus, saying the rescue of Jerusalem was second only to the flight from Egypt as an instance of Yahweh's intervention to help his people. So if, as much belief-neutral research now holds, the Exodus is largely myth (and at best an inflation of a minor migration from Egypt), and if the date of the Exodus narrative's composition was long after 701 BC (as is now widely acknowledged), then it would follow that the rescue of Jerusalem was far more important *as an historical event* than a journey from Egypt in shaping the Hebrew identity as a Chosen People.

As a factual event that shaped the Hebrew identity as the Chosen People, the city's rescue would be in a class by itself.

IN TRYING TO understand the B[2] writers' motivation, I am reminded of a chapter in U.S. popular culture. When I grew up in New Jersey in the 1940s and 1950s, the media and classroom alike glorified World War II. At the movies, in war-hero comic books and in school textbooks, all I would see was how the Americans won the war—with a slight bit of help from the Canadians, the British and the Free French. I never heard anything about the Soviet Union's enormous contribution in defeating Nazi Germany. In the Cold War of my youth, our new enemy's past heroics did not merit our thanks, acknowledgment or even awareness. But, though the Hollywood establishment blacklisted some moviemakers suspected of communist sympathies, I don't think most Hollywood producers—or writers of history textbooks or popular comic books—consciously decided to write the Soviet Union out of the glory of World War II. Personally, many of them felt disdain for and fear of the Soviets: why, they might have asked, should they go out of their way to acclaim the Soviets for their achievements in an earlier, pre-Cold War time? They devoted their energies to showing what they felt to be true—that Americans had starred in the war. The war's outcome demonstrated the superiority of the "American way of life." Little wonder that even the Canadians, the

British and other "good" allies received only minor supporting roles. Of the many books and movies on the war, some were clearly designed for building national pride—but the writers and producers were hardly people who did not believe in what they were doing. Their works resonate with conviction.

So too, perhaps, did the B² writers simply follow their own understandable biases. They saw no point in glorifying Egypt, which in intervening years had become first a bitter enemy, then an untrustworthy ally. In glorifying Yahweh instead, they were simply showing the obvious—that Yahweh was all-powerful, that he could intervene in human affairs and that he would help his Chosen People by means of an angel. After all, that was the assurance of Moses, he whom the Deuteronomists deemed the greatest prophet of all.²⁹

A STRANGE LINE occurs in this same rich passage that we have been examining, Deuteronomy 7.

Immediately after saying that Yahweh will use Exodus-based "signs and wonders" to overcome the Chosen People's enemies, Moses declares:

> Moreover the Lord your God will send hornets among them [*i.e.*, enemy peoples], until those who are left and who hide themselves from you are destroyed.

Hornets that defeat the Hebrews' foe? What can this possibly mean?

In Hebrew, the word in question is *tsir'ah*, or *sir'â*. The above translation of 7:20 is that of the Revised Standard Version of 1952.

But the presence of hornets in this context so perplexed the translators of the *New* Revised Standard Version, published in 1989, that they changed the word to "pestilence." In this, they are in the spirit of the American Translation, which renders it "leprosy." Yet this is a minority view. The majority—represented by the Anchor Bible, King James Bible, New International Version and Schocken Bible—agrees with the Revised Standard Version and translates it as "hornets" or, preferably, "hornet."

Some commentaries see the passage as referring to the use of insects as warfare agents;[28] others see the hornet as a metaphor for terror or panic.[29]

But another metaphorical meaning is attractive. And if there is anything to that surprising possibility it would represent supporting evidence for the thesis that it was Egypt's 25th Dynasty that drove out the Assyrians.

Three archaeologists have separately endorsed the idea that the hornet is a symbol of Egypt.

The first to do so was John Garstang in 1931; the University of Liverpool scholar excavated extensively in both the Nile Valley and Jerusalem. Although conventional wisdom has long held that the ancient symbol for Lower Egyptian kingship was the bee, just as for Upper Egyptian kingship it was the reed, the Briton argued that what archaeologists have commonly taken to be a bee in Egyptian depictions is in fact a hornet.[30] A half century later Yigael Yadin, head of the Hebrew University's Institute of Archaeology, rallied to that view. So, more recently, has Oded Borowski, director of the Program in Mediterranean Archaeology at Emory University's Department of Middle Eastern Studies.[31] The view has endured, then, for three generations, and its advocates all have solid reputations. (Indeed, such is Yadin's respectability that in the 1970s he served as deputy prime minister of Israel.)

The word *tsir'ah* occurs in only two other places in the Hebrew Bible,[32] and in both these passages, the context is similar to Deuteronomy 7:20: as the Hebrews enter the Promised Land and commence the Conquest, *tsir'ah* will drive all their enemies out of their way. All three passages would have been written no earlier than the seventh century BC. These archaeologists propose that the writers of three biblical passages used the hornet as a code word for the invasion of Canaan by New Kingdom pharaohs. After Egypt had overcome the Canaanite peoples, these scholars suggest, its eventual departure enabled the Hebrews to settle there. Borowski places this inadvertently helpful Egyptian activity in the 13th century BC.

Why would the writers of these biblical passages employ a code word instead of stating openly that Egypt prepared the way for Hebrews? Garstang explains:

> The religion of the Israelites, and in particular the ideals of those who set down and arranged these records, could not tolerate the notion that any power other than that of the God of Israel might influence their destinies. No direct allusion is made throughout these books [of the Bible] to the supreme temporal power in the land, that of the Pharaoh, which had held Canaan in vassalage almost continuously for 400 years. That side of the picture is veiled from view, and only at rare intervals does a chance reflection betray what is there concealed.[33]

Borowski expands on why the biblical writers employed a code word:

> [It] should be remembered that Egypt was always considered Israel's enemy. The fact that Egyptian activities in Canaan had paved the way for the Israelite conquest had to be concealed but could not be denied; therefore Egypt appears under a code-name as an agent of Yahweh.[34]

These ideas chime with my own on why the Kushites vanished from the Deliverance account.

If these three members of successive generations of mainstream archaeologists are right about the event disguised by the code-name "hornet" being an Egyptian offensive, an obvious question arises. *Which* offensive did the writers of Deuteronomy have in mind?

Were they, as these conventional historians propose, thinking exclusively of an event that took place an enormously long time (six or seven centuries) before the composition of this passage in Deuteronomy? Or might these biblical writers be referring to a far more recent event unknown to these archaeologists, the 25th Dynasty's successful campaign?[35]

To raise the question is to answer it.

Skeptics might ask, however, whether a symbol of *Lower* Egypt could aptly denote the 25th Dynasty's army. That force's manpower, after all, would have consisted less of Lower Egyptians than of Kushites and Upper Egyptians. The response has to be an emphatic yes. The 25th Dynasty's pharaohs were true rulers of the Two Lands—both Upper and Lower Egypt. Shebitku and Taharqa both made their political capital in Lower Egypt. In fact, following the tradition of many dynasties, the Kushite pharaohs used the hornet as part of their official identification, giving it precisely the same prominence as the reed.[36] The symbol shown on page 221 is from Taharqa's pharaonic insignia.

It would be too much to claim that an incontrovertible connection exists between the hornet of Deuteronomy 7 and the Kushite Dynasty's action of 701 BC. Nonetheless, such symbolism would have considerable logic: as we have seen, although this biblical chapter deals explicitly with the Conquest, it pertains indirectly to the Deliverance. To be conservative, it is enough to say that the hornet's link to the events of 701 is intriguingly plausible.

CHAPTER SEVENTEEN

Scapegoating the Kushites

The history of Africa needs rewriting, for up until now it has often been masked, faked, distorted, mutilated, by "force of circumstance"—*i.e.*, through ignorance or self-interest. Crushed by centuries of oppression, Africa has seen generations of travellers, slave traders, explorers, missionaries, governors and scholars of all kinds give out its image as one of nothing but poverty, barbarism, irresponsibility and chaos.

J. Ki-Zerbo,
UNESCO's General History of Africa,
vol. 1 (1981)

WE'VE SEEN HOW modern scholarship either discounts or plays down the Kushite Dynasty's success in Judah in 701 BC. But that is only part of what history has to say about the Kushites' dealings with Assyria during that general time period.

Most scholars also make this bold assertion: that the 25th Dynasty, far from being a reluctant participant in the invasion crisis, actually provoked Sennacherib's attack on Khor in the first place. They say it did so by instigating the ill-fated anti-Assyrian rebellion of Judah and its neighbors. When it sent troops to Khor in 701, then, the Kushite Dynasty in effect would have been attempting to put out a fire that it had itself ignited.

Making this stinging judgment are many top-tier historians. The prevailing scholarly view of Kushite leaders in the period leading up to the Ashdodite rebellion of 713-712 and continuing past 701 is that they were vainglorious bumpkins in over their heads in the Mediterranean world or, worse, slick diplomatic conmen. Almost no scholars have suggested that, in sending troops to Khor, the 25th Dynasty may simply have been acting in self-defense or responding to calls for help from within that region.[1]

Because it is so common, let us explore the view that this African people essentially flubbed their only known important sortie from their continent, inadvertently bringing misery to the nations they encountered. If good evidence exists for it, this conclusion would raise real questions about this people's ability to participate in the ancient world's geopolitics. If this negative verdict lacks supporting evidence, however, it would add weight to questions already raised in this book about Western scholarship's ability so far to assess the Kushites' role in history.

ONE OF THE first authorities to blame Kushite Egypt for provoking Sennacherib's invasion was James Breasted. In his *A History of Egypt* (1905), he asserts that the Kushite Dynasty "attempted an imperial role" and sought to "seduce" Judah and neighboring states to rebellion.[2] The view still dominates scholarly thought. Here, in chronological order, is a sampling of reputable scholars' views:

■ Abram Leon Sachar, founding president of Brandeis University, in *A History of the Jews* (1965): In *c.* 714, just prior to the Ashdodite conflict, the envoys "who came from Egypt [to Jerusalem] were the most importunate. They urged the creation of a strong alliance to break the humiliating hold of Assyria on the world. . . . The arguments were plausible and were presented with the glibness and smoothness of practised diplomats." After Sennacherib succeeded Sargon in 705, "Egypt was again on the alert, planning, plotting, exhorting."[3]

■ William Adams, in the standard work *Nubia* (1977): "[Shabako's] imperial ambitions led him to intrigue with the petty rulers of Palestine and Syria against the empire of Assyria. These imprudent efforts only provoked the scornful Assyrian response. . . ." Referring to the pharaoh's "machinations," the University of Kentucky scholar says, "Their immediate upshot was the devastation of Judah. . . ."[4]

■ J. Maxwell Miller and John H. Hayes, in *A History of Ancient Israel and Judah* (1986): "Egypt was a strong supporter, if not an instigator of the revolt."[5]

■ Francolino Gonçalves, the Isaianic specialist (1986): Egypt sought "to foment or organize an anti-Assyrian uprising."[6]

■ J. Alec Motyer, principal of Trinity College in Bristol, England, in *The Prophecy of Isaiah* (1993): Egypt was "vociferous in promising backing to a rebellion."[7] In leading Khor astray, Egypt behaved as "nothing less than an evil genius."

■ Amélie Kuhrt, in her acclaimed two-volume *Ancient Near East* (1995): Egypt "fomented revolts."[8]

■ Kenneth Kitchen, one of the most cited of modern Egyptologists (1995): the Kushite pharaohs' "meddling" in 701 and "incompetent interference in Palestinian affairs was disastrous for Egypt and Palestine alike."[9]

Of all these scholars, it is interesting that only two actually cite a primary source for reaching their judgments. These are Gonçalves and Motyer.[10] So entrenched in academic circles is the shabby image of the Kushite Dynasty that it no longer requires supporting evidence.

The source that both Gonçalves and Motyer give is Isaiah 18.[11] (The other critics of the Kushites can only be using that text, too.

It is the principal primary source that makes explicit references to Kushite Egypt actively seeking to communicate with Judah.) Here is the key portion:

> Ah, land of whirring wings
> which is beyond the rivers of Ethiopia;
> which sends ambassadors by the Nile,
> in vessels of papyrus upon the waters!
> Go, you swift messengers,
> to a nation, tall and smooth,
> to a people feared near and far,
> a nation mighty and conquering,
> whose land the rivers divide.[12]

The passage deals with African ambassadors' journey to Khor aboard a reed boat at a time of crisis. Some biblicists see such a vessel as crude and flimsy, suggestive that the Kushites were relatively primitive. Yet this was a common Egyptian sea-going craft. (In fact, when in 1970 Norwegian ethnologist Thor Heyerdahl built a close replica of such an ancient Egyptian vessel, based on depictions found in tombs, it proved to be sturdy enough to carry him and seven men across the Atlantic from Morocco to Barbados.) Much of the rest of the biblical passage, however, is genuinely puzzling.[13] One uncertainty is the date. While it seems probable that the diplomats' visit came just before the invasion of 701, it is possible that it took place at the time of some earlier crisis with Assyria such as the Ashdodite rebellion.[14] Another enigma: the passage does not state the mission's purpose. This, however, has not prevented scholars from making elaborate and confident inferences. As with Gonçalves and Motyer, Ronald Clements sees the envoys as trying to instigate trouble: "[They] had been sent to Jerusalem to enlist [Hezekiah's] support in the planned revolt of Egypt-Ethiopia against Assyria."[15] He does not say how he deduces that.

There is nothing to support this view. If this mission does in fact pertain to Ashdod's defiant movement against Sargon, as Clements believes, the envoys might well be advising Judah *not* to take part in it. After all, we know that Judah early on had been tempted to join that coastal city-state's rebellion, but in the end decided against it. Also, we know that the Kushite co-regency was no active supporter of Ashdod's revolt. (The evidence: Sargon's annal says that after Ashdod's uprising failed, its leader, Iamani, fled to Kushite-controlled territory for safety, yet—as we saw in Chapter 6—Shebitku extradited that rebel at Sargon's request to Assyria, a sign that Kush sought no problems with the empire.) Since Kush was against provoking Assyria, it would seem logical that its reason for sending ambassadors to Hezekiah would have been to talk him *out* of rebelling. The alternative scenario, which the usually cautious Gonçalves endorses, calls for Isaiah 18 to describe a Kushite attempt to incite Judah to rebellion in the 705-701 period. That view is equally weak. At that time the reverse was happening: it was Judah that was seeking to drag Kushite Egypt's army into Khor. If, as is very plausible, the passage does pertain to the time when Sennacherib was about to thunder down on Khor, the envoys' mission may have been to decide with Hezekiah on a common defense strategy: "Yes," the ambassadors may have said, "Egypt will respond to your call for help, but in the meantime prepare for siege, refuse to surrender and stall for time."[16]

For a glimpse of how scholars have misconstrued the innocent language of Isaiah, consider Sachar's pointed reference to the Kushite diplomats' "glibness and smoothness." While he gives no source, it would appear to be the Revised Standard Version's translation of Isaiah 18, quoted above, which describes Kushites as a nation or people "tall and smooth."[17] The context, however, suggests that the word "smooth," as we saw in Chapter 13, is not meant to convey unctuous, insincere talk but rather a physical characteristic; the American Translation accordingly uses "sleek." The source for Sachar's allegation that envoys were "planning, plotting, exhorting," however, is inexplicable. So is the basis for Adams' pejorative assertion of Kushite "machinations." Motyer's finding of an "evil genius" is simply gratuitous.

So much for the case that Kush was stirring up trouble. Now let's look at what the evidence really says about Khor's behavior during this conflict-filled period of 713 to 701.

Some of the best testimony is to be found in other parts of the Book of Isaiah. In a passage explicitly dealing with the lead-up to the Ashdodite rebellion, the prophet speaks of people along Khor's coast who turned to Kush and Egypt for assistance. He depicts these people as saying, in their own words, that these are allies *"to whom we fled for help and deliverance* from the king of Assyria!"[18] (Emphasis added.) It could not be clearer: people in Khor went to them, not vice versa.

In another passage, whose action Clements, Gonçalves and Brevard Childs reasonably place in the period just prior to the 701 invasion, we see the same sort of thing, only this time those seeking military assistance are clearly Judahites. The prophet deplores Judahites "who go down to Egypt for help."[19] Against this evidence, the claim that the Kushites had seduced Judah into breaking away from Nineveh is baffling.

To appreciate how baseless this enticement scenario is, consider a final passage from the same period. In a straightforward manner, it speaks of Judah's envoys who travel across the desert to Egypt in order "to make an alliance."[20] They bring with them precious gifts in the hope of obtaining the "protection of Pharaoh." Elaborating, the prophet describes how these envoys "carry their riches on the backs of donkeys, and their treasures on the humps of camels, to a people who cannot profit them" (that is, to a people who cannot be of real help). That Judah was using all its powers of persuasion to pull Kushite Egypt into the fray could hardly be clearer.

And yet the specialists don't see it. Gonçalves's confusion typifies that of the scholars in general. In his generally estimable *L'expédition de Sennachérib*, he allows that this passage deals implicitly with Judah-Egypt diplomacy in the period of 705-701,[21] yet elsewhere in that same book he states that the 25th Dynasty "probably encouraged" the revolt by Judah and her Philistine and Phoenician neighbors.[22] Most bizarre.[23]

For the *coup de grâce* on assumptions of Kushite meddling in the 713-701 period, look at what Assyrian kings themselves have to say.

First, in his annal dealing with the Ashdodite rebellion, Sargon attests that the king of Judah and the rulers of several neighboring kingdoms "sent evil words and unseemly speeches with their presents to Pharaoh king of Egypt, a prince who could not save them, to set him at enmity with me, and asked him for military aid."[24] Again, the entreaties flow from Khor to Egypt, not from Egypt to Khor.

As for the Assyrian campaign of 701, Sennacherib's annal is just as clear. It states that the Khor rebels "had become afraid and had called for help upon the kings of Egypt and the bowmen, the chariot-corps and the cavalry of the king of Kush." A more recent translation uses a more dramatic verb for the rebels' communication to Egypt: it says they "implored" Egypt for help.[25]

What modern scholars appear to have done to the relationship between Khor and Egypt, then, is to turn it upside down. They claim that Egypt talked Khor into taking a path of conflict with Assyria when all the evidence points to Khor beseeching Egypt to do so.

As for the accusation that the Kushites coveted Khor for imperialistic motives, no evidence exists of such a mentality among the Kushite kings of this period. Piye set the tone of Kushite governance outside of Kush. Having subdued Lower Egypt in c. 728, Piye made no attempt to impose himself as master of the entire Nile Valley (Chapter 6). He instead returned almost immediately to Napata, treated Egypt as a remarkably loose trusteeship and permitted the muted return to power in Lower Egypt of his former adversary. So long as the country enjoyed political stability and Assyria could be kept at bay, the Kushites were loath to intervene. Piye's successor, Shabako, likewise showed no imperialistic mindset. According to Herodotus, after his conquest of Lower Egypt in 712, that pharaoh even yielded his rule over Egypt and returned to Kush because he found the exercise of power to compromise his religious principles.[26] As for Shebitku and Taharqa, no evidence exists that their policies as pharaohs sought to absorb Khor into any kind of empire.

Hezekiah appears to have sowed the seeds of his own near-destruction. His pre-701 territorial expansion into parts of Philistia is a matter of record.[27] His annexation of Gaza and Gath, cities loyal to Assyria, would have been provocative indeed. And no contemporary source, either biblical or Assyrian, suggests Egypt's involvement, even behind the scenes.

If any outside agent appears to have wanted to foment rebellion in Khor it was the Babylonian leader, Merodach-baladan. There is no reason to question the Bible's assertion that this dynamic king, forever in conflict with Assyria, sent envoys to Jerusalem.[28] The scholarly consensus seems credible in maintaining that this diplomatic visit probably took place sometime prior to the rebellion against Sennacherib, reflecting a strategy of encouraging simultaneous revolt in different parts of the empire.

To be sure, ties between the new Kushite masters of Egypt and the anti-Assyrian element in Khor would have been friendly. They had common trade interests and a common enemy. Anti-Assyrian rulers in Khor may also have felt emboldened by Shabako's conquest of Egypt: he had the military capability (as distinct from the desire) to fight Assyria. This, however, is not the same thing as Egypt actively provoking the region to insurrection. Tough conditions under Assyrian domination would have been reason enough for many people in Khor to rebel. Modern scholarship's widespread assumption that Judah and its allies needed to be manipulated by Kush into rebelling would imply that Judah and its neighbors were putty, possessing too little initiative to consider such action on their own.[29]

The Kushites' initial reluctance to get involved militarily in Khor in 701 also conforms to a pattern. As far back as 726-725, when King Hoshea of Israel had appealed for help, the Kushite monarchy had refused to intervene militarily in the region.[30] Twenty years later, it was so anxious to avoid angering Assyria that it handed over Ashdod's fugitive leader to Sargon.[31] In 701, the need for Judah to ply it with largesse shows that its first reaction was to stay put. Then, perhaps because of an additional factor, the possibility or probability that Assyria intended an invasion of Egypt, the Kushite monarchy decided to head the enemy off at the pass in Khor rather than wait on its side of the border for the invasion to take place.

G

IN MY READING of modern historians and biblical commentators, I have encountered very little criticism of King Hezekiah for approving the rebellion and thus provoking Assyria's retaliation. I have come across no criticism of Babylon's King Merodach-baladan for encouraging that revolt. I have seen no criticism at all of Egypt's later Saite Dynasty for genuinely provoking Judah to rebellion against Babylon, then abandoning it in 586 and leaving the way clear for Babylon's King Nebuchadrezzar to destroy Jerusalem and the rest of the kingdom. Indeed, I have seldom come upon disapproval of the Assyrians and Babylonians themselves for their own unabashedly voracious imperialism; most historians treat their destructiveness with a kind of empires-will-be-empires shrug.

I am not suggesting that scholars should start hurling feverish invective at these various parties. I would simply note a double standard that is glaring. The scholarly consensus is as indulgent vis à vis the Assyrians' foreign policy, despite copious evidence of its inhumanity, as it is reproachful of the Africans' foreign policy, even though not a scrap of evidence exists for the latter's alleged faults and follies.

In the quotation at the start of this chapter, J. Ki-Zerbo, a professor of history at the Centre d'Enseignement Supérieur in Ouagadougou, Burkina Faso, makes the point that generations of Western scholars have helped to mask Africans' accomplishments in history and to assign Africans a false image of inherent irresponsibility.[32] Although I know too little about Africa's overall past to evaluate this generalization, his view is eminently applicable to that sliver of history with which I am familiar. That he made his observation a generation ago and that the same attitudes still prevail, make the situation all the more discouraging.

In past chapters, we have seen how, without evidence, many modern experts ascribe military failure to the Kushites and insist that the Hebrews despised them, not just as soldiers but as people. In this chapter, we see how they have even concocted out of thin air the notion that incendiary Kushite actions are to blame for the devastation of Judah and much of Khor.

The injustice here is not simply that a bogus reputation for ineptitude hangs over a people who did remarkable deeds long ago.

That might just be a matter of "ancient history." The problem is that the injustice is ongoing. The longer sub-Saharan Africa retains its image as History's nonentity the more likely the rest of the world, often unconsciously, will maintain its dismissive or patronizing attitudes and policies toward it.

CHAPTER EIGHTEEN

The Real "Epidemic":
An Outbreak of Modern Amnesia

ANYONE AT ALL familiar with Egyptian-Hebrew relations in antiquity knows—*knows*—that pre-20th-century scholars have utterly nothing of significance to say about that period. In the course of my first seven years of research, I had looked at several hundred books and articles by 20th-century scholars, and virtually none had alluded to the work of their predecessors of the 19th century, much less of the centuries before that. I say "virtually" because of very few exceptions: the main one is Bernhard Stade's frequently cited article, distinguishing B^2 from B^1, that was published toward the 19th century's close.

Until I had nearly finished the research for this book, I shared the general assumption that today's scholarship, for all its weaknesses, has nothing to learn from the pre-modern era—a time when archaeological discoveries were few and when, as I believed, methodological primitivism, racial intolerance and religious dogmatism were widespread. Then one evening, paying what I thought would be a final visit to McGill University's main library, I chanced upon a leatherbound book so old as to make me wonder what it was doing there. Fingering its dried-out pages, I found it had been published at Oxford in 1838 and written by one A.H.L. Heeren. The volume, which was translated from the German, bore a tedious title: *Historical Researches into the Politics, Intercourse, and Trade of the Carthaginians, Ethiopians and Egyptians.*

Idly leafing through it, I was immediately struck by its extraordinary tone when describing Kush/Meroë/Ethiopia. It was one of respect. In the course of his surprisingly detailed, 150-page treatment of that ancient culture, Heeren speaks of the "lustre of the Ethiopians" in Greek literature. He observes how, in his own day, they continue to command "admiration." Indeed, the German says, "the pen of cautious, clear-sighted historians often places them in the highest rank of knowledge and civilization." Heeren praises the "piety and justice of the Ethiopians" and goes on to deduce that "they are the first virtues which would be cultivated in a nation whose government was established by religion and commerce, and not by violence and oppression."[1] Amazing.

I kept reading, compelled to see what conclusions this open-minded approach might produce when tackling the crisis of 701 BC. It turned out that Heeren devotes just one sentence to the conflict. But that sentence is even more stunning:

Tarhaco was the contemporary of . . . Sennacherib, and deterred him . . . from the invasion of Egypt, merely by the rumor of his advance against him.[2]

In one pithy sentence, Heeren says it all: that the 25th Dynasty's expedition was exclusively responsible for turning back Sennacherib. He also implies that in challenging Assyria the dynasty was not engaging in imperialistic meddling but rather in self-defense against the "invasion of Egypt."

That lone sentence also contains something that is just as surprising but more subtle: an off-hand manner. It seems to hint that no further elaboration is necessary. Could it be, I wondered, that the expedition's successful outcome was, in Heeren's pre-industrial Europe, common knowledge?

If so, I knew my research would be far from over. It would take on a new puzzle, as unsettling to me as it was intriguing. No longer would there be just the one question to answer: "What saved

Jerusalem?" There would also be a compelling follow-up question: "Having once known the answer, why has the West lost it?"

HEEREN, IT TURNS out, was no eccentric writer whose views stood outside mainstream contemporary thinking. Born in Bremen in 1760, he was an establishment academic of the first order. For his illustrious career as historian and professor of philosophy at the University of Göttingen, King William IV of England knighted him and King Louis-Philippe of France made him a member of France's Legion of Honor.

How common was Heeren's opinion that the 25th Dynasty had played a big role in 701?

To the sentence about Taharqa, Heeren's translator attaches a footnote. It refers the reader to "Mant's Bible."

An 1817 edition of that Bible, prepared by the Rev. Richard Mant and the Rev. George D'Oyly, both chaplains to the Archbishop of Canterbury, contains commentaries by earlier experts.[3] In a note to Second Kings 19:7, these editors cite one "Bishop Patrick" as subscribing to the idea that pestilence had weakened Sennacherib's army. But they go on to quote Patrick as saying this about Isaiah's prophecy of a report:

> Perhaps, after that [pestilential] stroke, the report was renewed, that Tirhakah was coming against him [i.e, Sennacherib]; which made him hasten away with the remains of his army to his own country.

This espousal of a joint epidemic/Kushite-rescue solution—with the Kushites getting credit for the *coup de grâce*—is not whispered in the fine print of an obscure publication where only a few other specialized scholars will see it. On the contrary, the information could hardly be more prominent: it is published in a widely circulated edition of the Old Testament that, says the title page, is "for the Use of Families." And for other clergy and lay people alike the source could not be more impeccable. The editors were members of the official entourage of the Church of England's highest cleric.

As for the bishop himself, Simon Patrick, he was a staunch mainstream figure in Anglican circles. Born in 1626, he was bishop of Ely, near Cambridge. Earlier in his career he was, in the words of a church history, "among the great London preachers of his time."[4]

In his original commentary, published in 1705,[5] Patrick says two countries are called Kush, one known as Ethiopia and the other located in Arabia. For logistical rather than racial reasons, the prelate opts for the Arabian Kush: it "was near," says Patrick, observing that the "far off" Ethiopian monarch would have had to take his army "through Egypt before he could fight with Sennacherib."[6]

In a posthumous edition of Patrick's commentary, however, this view changes. Published in 1730 and edited by another Anglican cleric, William Lowth (1160-1732), chaplain to the bishop of Winchester, this edition comes out squarely in favor of an African location for Kush.[7] Lowth sees merit in the idea that Taharqa's army created a "diversion" for "Sennacherib's forces just when they were ready to fall upon the Jews."[8] It is plain, in other words, that in early 18th-century England it was quite respectable to believe that Africa had played a significant role in saving Jerusalem.

The legitimacy of this view goes back further still.

One of the most influential figures in the Protestant Reformation was, of course, French theologian John Calvin (1509-1564). The austere preacher is best remembered for having organized in the city-state of Geneva a theocratic government that enforced the biblical ideals of morality. In reading bits of his extensive analyses of the Bible, it is hard not to be impressed by the breadth of his learning, even by today's standards.

The founder of the University of Geneva saw such theological significance in the events of 701 that he devoted fully 70 pages to them in his commentary on the Book of Isaiah.[9] That text makes for astonishing reading. The author shows an understanding of the politics behind the conflict of 701 that is, in my opinion, far more penetrating than that of any modern scholar. It says much about the aptitude of our age that Calvin was able to put together that analysis on the basis of data that was much more meager than what is available today. He relied on the Hebrew Bible and Herodotus only. The discovery of the Assyrian annals and the emergence of Egyptology (which, with Piye's stela and other findings, showed the Kushites' military heft) were still centuries away.

According to Calvin's analysis, Egypt and Kush became politically linked for the specific purpose of opposing Sennacherib. They "saw that his power was becoming excessive, and that his invasion of other countries had no limit."[10] In his broadminded view, Kush and Egypt acted "wisely in joining their forces and meeting him early; for separately they would easily have been subdued and destroyed." The Kushite monarchy's involvement in Egypt and its later intervention in Judah were, for him, part of a defensive strategy against Assyria. By consolidating their military forces, Egypt and Kush could "repel the power and violence of that tyrant." The 25th Dynasty's involvement in Khor, then, was a sensible pre-emptive strike against "that tyrant" Sennacherib, not a foolish attempt at self-aggrandizement. The analysis is brilliant.

Calvin's analysis of the actual conflict of 701 is less so. Theology gets in his way. Assyria's reversal, he suggests, came in two stages. First, he says, the report of Taharqa's approach "compelled Sennacherib to withdraw" from Jerusalem. Taking Herodotus at face value, Calvin goes on to say that Sennacherib might have marched to Pelusium in Egypt, where he became "entangled in a hazardous war against Egypt."[11] The second stage occurred when, after retreating from Pelusium, Sennacherib went back to Judah. Feeling "ashamed" of having failed in his first siege of Jerusalem,[12] the Assyrian king sought to attack the city a second time. Before he could do so, the angel struck, causing Sennacherib to return home.[13] The angel, Calvin insists, was real and not a mere metaphor for disease. The idea that a plague was responsible is, for him, nothing less than an "invention by which Satan, through profane historians, has attempted to obscure this extraordinary judgment of God." He refrains from speculating on how, if not via disease, the deity achieved victory.

While Egypt's army did "give some relief to the Jews," for Calvin it would have been unfitting for the "hand of man" or "natural causes" (such as disease) to deliver the decisive blow against the invaders.[14] For this subscriber to Deuteronomic thought, the angelic role means that "all the praise is due to God alone, of whom the angels are only instruments."[15] Still, in his treatment of the pharaoh's forces, Calvin is generous, crediting them with driving off Sennacherib *twice*—once by the report of their advance, and the second time by force of arms at Pelusium.

At least as far back as the 16th century, then, some Christians espoused the idea that Kushite-Egypt had played a critical (though supporting) role in an event whose importance was, for them, theologically momentous.

By the 19th century, one finds a willingness to credit Kushite-Egypt with having played the *leading* role. The Kushite-rescue theory attracts many supporters besides Heeren. For example, in *The Imperial Bible-Dictionary*, a massive reference volume published in London in 1867, the Rev. Henry Constable, of Cork, says that Taharqa achieved a "midnight overthrow" of Sennacherib.[16] And in the 1878 edition of his three-volume study of ancient Egypt, the vice-president of the British Archaeological Association, Sir J. Gardner Wilkinson, refers unequivocally to Taharqa's "successful opposition to the power of Assyria" in Judah. Wilkinson, who first visited Egypt in 1821 and was one of the founders of British Egyptology, credits Taharqa with the "defeat of the numerous army of Sennacherib."[17] Adding authority to this view is the fact that, according to the title page, this edition of Wilkinson's famous work[18] was "revised and corrected" by Samuel Birch, a luminary in the field who carried the important titles of "Keeper of the Egyptian and Oriental Antiquities in the British Museum, President of the Society of Biblical Archaeology."

One illustrious Western thinker of that time was Heinrich von Ewald (1803-1875), whom *Britannica* describes as "one of the foremost" Christian theologians of 19th-century Germany. He does not give exclusive credit to Taharqa, preferring to ascribe Sennacherib's "wild flight" to a combination of "terror at the approach of the Ethiopian army" and a "desolating plague."[19] Nonetheless Ewald, who taught at the University of Göttingen a generation after Heeren, casts a positive light on the 25th

Dynasty's diplomatic dealings with Judah prior to the invasion. The "powerful Ethiopian king," he says approvingly, sent a "solemn embassy to Jerusalem in this period of [Judahite] depression to proffer friendship and assistance."[20] There is nothing about a wheedling 25th Dynasty provoking rebellion.

In Jewish circles, we encounter the same sort of thinking. Important rabbinic commentators of past centuries credit Taharqa with a vital role in causing Sennacherib's departure. In giving these two commentators' views, I am quoting from a 1980 annotation of Second Kings by Rabbi A.J. Rosenberg:[21]

■ Radak[22] (approximately 1160-1235), a rabbi from France: "[T]he words 'and he will return to his land' [Second Kings 19:7] refer to Sennacherib's return to Assyria to defend it against Tirhakah, king of Kush." Radak's scenario may be highly imaginative, calling for Taharqa to have launched a strike against Mesopotamia, yet the medieval rabbi still credits the Kushite with liberating Jerusalem.

■ Malbim[23] (1809-1879), an eastern European rabbi: "Sennacherib's withdrawal from Jerusalem was in itself a series of miracles. First, Sennacherib heard but a rumor, not an official report, that Tirhakah had marched on Assyria. Yet he believed it. . . . Second, he returned to his land, taking the entire army with him. He did not leave any portion of his vast army to lay siege to Jerusalem."

In the United States, one of the pioneers of reform Judaism was Rabbi Isaac Mayer Wise (1819-1900). He was the founding president of Hebrew Union College, the oldest rabbinical seminary in the United States, and he has been called one of the country's two most important Jewish religious leaders of his time.[24] Wise, who was also a vigorous critic of the curse-of-Ham theory as a justification for American slavery,[25] says Taharqa forced the Assyrian army's departure after disease had enfeebled it.[26]

The point, then, should be made emphatically. Prior to the 20th century, those who stated that the Kushite Dynasty had played some sort of major role (whether supporting or leading) in turning back Sennacherib included some of the West's leading figures in Christian and Jewish thought.

This respectful view of Kush is on glowing display in the arts. Giuseppe Verdi's 1871 opera *Aida* is the best-known example. Egypt's Ottoman viceroy commissioned the Italian composer to write the opera for the opening of the new Cairo opera house, and the eminent French Egyptologist Auguste Mariette helped write the scenario. The title character of this interracial love story, which immediately enjoyed huge popularity in Europe, is of course a Kushite slave in the Egyptian pharaoh's court; she and the Egyptian captain of the pharaoh's guard are in love. While the plot features an invasion of Egypt by the Kushite king, Verdi presents Kush as militarily competent and culturally respectable, and indeed the sympathetic Aida herself turns out to be the daughter of the Kushite king. It is significant that Mariette's regard for Kushites was shared by his earlier countryman, Jean-François Champollion, decipherer of Egyptian hieroglyphics and the perhaps most celebrated Egyptologist of all time. This historian and linguist, who visited Nubia, concluded in 1829—more than a century prior to the emergence of Afro-centrism—that Nubians had been the founders of pharaonic Egypt.[27] (Later invaders, he said, were responsible for changing much of the population's physical appearance.) Although he did not address the campaign of 701, Champollion had nothing but good things to say about the 25th Dynasty: its rule was "gentle and humane."[28]

In sculpture and painting, too, European open-mindedness toward Africa flourished in the heart of the 19th century. In Paris's Musée d'Orsay, for example, stands a towering bronze statue made in 1872 of "The Four Parts of the World Holding up the Globe." The allegory by Jean-Baptiste Carpeaux, one the leading sculptors of France's Second Empire, shows the planet lifted by four women—Caucasian, Amerindian, Oriental and African. Each is noble and majestic. A few feet away is a bronze bust of "A Sudanese Negro" with a turban and piercing eyes. In this sculpture made in 1857 by Charles Cordier, the man looks at least as distinguished as any of the same artist's aristocratic European subjects. Meanwhile in England, much the same was occurring. The pre-Raphaelite artists are famous for their uplifting idealizations of figures from Greek myths and the Arthurian legends, but they did not limit their search for heroic subjects to Europeans. In an imposing 12-foot-high oil, begun in 1881, the pre-Raphaelite painter Edward Burne-Jones portrays a black African king, clad in armor, wooing a white maiden. A poem by Tennyson, based on an Elizabethan legend, inspired the scene. Burne-Jones presents the young man, King Cophetua, in as upright and lordly a manner as in other paintings he depicts Perseus or Galahad.

And then, suddenly, within a decade or two of *Aida's* triumphant debut this sense of equity wilts. Respect for Africa makes way for disdain. This is not to suggest that before this time all European intellectuals regarded black Africans with a sense of fair play,[29] nor that afterwards they all ceased to do so, but generally speaking a societal sea change took place in both in the arts and in scholarship. Among the generation of Egyptologists that succeeded Mariette (1821-1881), it is hard to imagine anyone capable of devising an *Aida*-like plot. As support for the Kushite-rescue theory wanes, scholars' acceptance of rival theories surges.

To be sure, these alternative theories do not arrive out of thin air. The epidemic theory, for example, had received approval from Josephus as early as the first century AD and, according to Calvin, it enjoyed some support in the 16th century. Lord Byron also seems to hint at the idea in his 1815 poem "The Destruction of Sennacherib," and in 1853 a book by Nineveh's celebrated discoverer, Austen Layard, backed the notion.[30] But now, in the late 19th century, alternatives to the Kushite-rescue theory gain an unprecedented degree of acceptance.[31]

James Breasted's 1905 bestseller, with its ostensibly erudite reference to "plague-infested winds" and its insistence on the Napatan pharaohs' "inglorious" rule, popularized this dismissive view of Kush. But scoffing at the Kushites had become common well before then.

In 1897, for example, one of the most popular of the English-speaking world's religious writers, Cunningham Geikie of England, suggested that the conflict had disgraced the Kushites. After the Eltekeh clash, the Presbyterian minister said, "Tirhakah had been been hurled back ignominiously toward Egypt," thus "leaving Hezekiah, so far as he was concerned, to fall into the hands of his terrible foe."[32] Message: Taharqa was not only a military weakling but, to save his skin, he had unmanfully abandoned his helpless ally. And Stade himself in his 1886 article declared that the rumor of Taharqa's advance that had caused Sennacherib to depart was in fact a false rumor, an explanation that had the effect of nullifying Africa's true performance.

One of the most famous of all the historians of the day was Leopold von Ranke, a religiously motivated German who is sometimes called the father of modern history writing; in the 1885 English edition of one of his books, this devout Lutheran, who sought to juggle objectivity with a desire to show the "truth" of God's hand in history, endorsed the theory that troubles elsewhere in the empire had drawn Sennacherib away.[33] About this same time, many other internationally influential historians, often clerics or strongly religious laypeople, threw their weight behind the epidemic theory. Among these leading lights were: Franz Delitzsch, a Christian intellectual at the University of Leipzig;[34] Alfred Edersheim, the Oxford scholar and Presbyterian minister,[35] and George Adam Smith, Scottish preacher and principal of the University of Aberdeen, who received a knighthood for his prolific biblical scholarship.[36] Other examples abound.[37]

By 1908, it had become so *de rigeur* to diminish the Kushite role at Jerusalem that in a biblical commentary, one William Emery Barnes went so far as to vilify Taharqa as Assyria's "contemptible foe."[38] The book could hardly have had more respectable credentials: the Cambridge University Press published it, and Barnes was a professor of divinity and associate of the Bishop of London. In 1910, a famous excavator of Kushite and Egyptian remains, George Reisner, of Harvard and the Boston Museum of Fine Arts, concluded of Kush: "Its very race appears to be a product of its poverty and its isolation—a negroid Egyptian mixture fused together on a desert river bank too far away and too poor to attract a stronger and better race."[39]

This has been a light sampling of scholarship from medieval times onward, not a systematic review of it, but what it suggests is that in the course of the 1880s two things happen: the tradition of writings that are supportive of the Kushites tends to taper noticeably,

soon to peter out, and writings that marginalize the Kushites' role
at Jerusalem enter a boom period.

Puzzled by this blizzard of Kushite-demoting opinions starting
in the decade of the 1880s, I opened some history books to see
what might explain such a sea change.

THE ANCIENT WORLD was free, or relatively free, of what we
today call racism. A major cause of racism's emergence was the rise
as early as the 16th and 17th centuries of European colonialism.[40]
Yet slavery took place out of sight of Europe itself. There, the practice was largely frowned upon and the racist premise of European
superiority more muted. Despite the energetic presence of many
Englishmen in the African slave trade, for example, the law banned
slavery in England itself. Many Western intellectuals and clerics,
as noted, were not particularly hostile to the Kushites and were
often quite positive.

Indeed, early in the 19th century, Europe's sympathy for
Africans was on the upswing. In Britain, Parliament in 1833 abolished slavery in all British colonies. In 1848, France followed suit
in its colonies. Why, then, this sudden arrival in the 1880s of
antipathy toward Kush?

Much of the answer has to do with the advent at this precise
time of colonialism in Africa. That tumultous process began late—
centuries after the conquest of the Americas and East Indies, and
about a century after that of India. For an ideologically dispassionate view, here is *Britannica:*

> By the turn of the 20th century, the map of Africa looked like a huge
> jigsaw puzzle, with most of the boundary lines having been drawn
> in a sort of game of give-and-take played in the foreign offices of
> leading European powers. The division of Africa, the last continent
> to be so carved up, was essentially a product of the new imperial-
> ism, vividly highlighting its essential features. In this respect, the
> timing and pace of the scramble for Africa are especially note-
> worthy. *Before 1880 colonial possessions in Africa were relatively few and*

limited to coastal areas, with large sections of the coastline and almost all the
interior still independent. By 1900 Africa was almost entirely divided into
separate territories controlled by European nations[41] [emphasis added].

The turn-around in the European assessment of the ancient
Kushites, then, coincides almost perfectly with Europe's subjugation of all of Africa in the century's last two decades. As early as the
mid-1880s the British press first dubbed the spirited process the
"Scramble," and the name has stuck.

To be sure, colonialism was not the only cause of the intensification of Western racism in the late 19th century. Ivan Hannaford's
groundbreaking 1996 book, *Race: The History of an Idea in the West,*
shows other influences. The British researcher says the publication
in 1859 of Charles Darwin's *On the Origin of Species,* which introduced evidence for evolution, laid some of the intellectual groundwork for racism. Says Hannaford:

> If evolution and natural selection were the principles of natural
> existence and therefore applicable to social life, it must be true [in
> the view of some of Darwin's followers] that the poor and the
> Negro were in their natural condition because of some deficiency
> in their physical and intellectual capacity. . . . Notable was the per-
> sistence of the argument that the peoples living in simple ways
> were in such a state because of the original corruption of Ham or
> some "scientific" variant of it.[42]

In addition, says Hannaford, among the English in the second
half of the 19th century there "arose a romantic consciousness of
the spiritual force of race and a scientific hereditarism that both
explained and justified the advance of Anglo-Saxon civilization in
all corners of the world."[43] By the century's end the British Empire
covered almost one-quarter of the world's land surface and was the
home of more than a quarter of the world's population. In other
countries, Hannaford points out, other factors came into play.
After France's defeat in 1879 in the Franco-Prussian War, for
example, some of that country's influential writers—such as
Edouard Drumont in an 1886 book, *La France Juive*—blamed

Jewish financiers for victimizing the "Aryan" people of France.[44] Hannaford deals with various precursor ideas to modern racism in the medieval and Renaissance periods, including the Inquisition and other violent expressions of anti-Jewish feeling. Making a subtle distinction between anti-Jewish feelings and anti-Semitism, he finds that religion—as distinct from ethnic/racial considerations—largely determined the former. He says of the Inquisition and other early persecutions of Jews: "Because their idolatrous ways were seen as a threat to the true faith, their extirpation from the face of the earth could be justified."[45] Drawing considerably on Hannah Arendt's analysis, Hannaford concludes "that there was no fundamental historical movement of racial and anti-Semitic ideas until after 1880."[46] The observations certainly raise further questions about the historical evolution of these ideas, and the nuances between the attitudes of various periods. But what's interesting is that Hannaford sees a watershed intensification of European hostility toward the Other at precisely the same time that the Kushite-rescue theory falls from grace.[47]

We begin to see, then, the kind of intellectual soil in which grew the trend toward minimizing and often disparaging the Kushites' place in history. It is easier for a society to subjugate another if it can convince itself that the subjugated people are not just economically but also morally inferior.

A final thing is striking about the viewpoint that Heeren represents: it predates Stade's discovery of B^1-B^2 textual cleavage. That means pre-1880s thinkers often were able to discern Taharqa's decisive role without their having the benefit of Stade's useful insight.

When, taking my very first step in trying to discover what had happened to the pharaoh's army in the territory that is now Israel, I repeatedly read the Second Kings account, I had the suspicion that Taharqa's army was a significant cause of Sennacherib's withdrawal. Yet I did not trust my interpretation. Who was I, I asked myself, a rank novice reader of the Bible, to go against the prevailing opinion among experts? Only upon later learning of Stade's division of the main part of the narrative did I come to feel confident about the decisive role of Taharqa's army.

The experts of the pre-modern era had firmly grasped the meaning that I had been fumbling toward, and they did so without the help of Stade's breakthrough in textual analysis. That many people—such as Calvin, Heeren, Wise and Wilkinson—had been able to penetrate the murky narrative prior to that sophisticated insight means two things.

It demonstrates that the B^2 writers did *not* erase the credit that the B^1 writers would have given to Kushite Egypt's forces. Their theologically motivated insertion of the angel may have impeded a reader's view of the role of those forces, but it did not entirely block it. They may have rendered the Deliverance story's historical denouement inconspicuous, but they had the integrity to leave it in.

Second, the ability of early experts to reach such a conclusion *without* distinguishing between B^1 and B^2 fortifies the view that the Bible itself indicates Taharqa's army played a vital role in saving Jerusalem.

It is an ironic coincidence that Stade's important paper should have been published in the same decade as the mass abandonment of the Kushite-rescue theory. Logically, Stade's finding should have helped cement the case for Kushites' determining role. Its failure to do so, thanks to such feeble rationalizations as that the report of Taharqa's advance was false, shows the grip of Europe's colonial adventure on the thinking of serious historians—intellectuals whom one might like to think of as too bright, too reflective and (especially among the large number of those religiously inclined) too humanitarian as to vault so readily aboard a popular, narrow-minded bandwagon.

CHAPTER NINETEEN

How Colonialism Twisted History's Judgment

I F THE WORLD ignores the Kushite record, the responsibility lies with many of the experts on the period. Why are today's Egyptologists, biblical historians, biblical commentators and Assyriologists so blind to Kush's vital participation in saving Judah? With their relatively sophisticated resources, why can't they perceive an historic role that many of their counterparts in pre-colonial times discerned simply by reading two elementary research tools, the Bible and Herodotus?

The modern experts, as their citations and footnotes show, derive their view of Kush's insignificance in 701 BC from their late 19th- and early 20th-century predecessors. They seem to accept their assumption that Kush—and ancient sub-Saharan Africa as a whole—is irrelevant to the study of serious history. While they readily acknowledge that sub-Saharan Africa is where the human species began, they act as though nothing of much consequence happened there between the time early people migrated out of the continent and the arrival of European and Arab explorers and slavers in the last millennium.

To be sure, the racism that is so overt in these colonial-era writings has not been visible in later scholarship for the last two or three generations. Modern experts are retaining their predecessors' core dismissiveness toward the 25th Dynasty while rinsing out the explicitly racist tint. So deeply entrenched is this view of Kushite incompetence that most experts today do not question it. In the extraordinary conditions of the colonial era, political pressures and social conditions gave rise to a form of intellectual corruption that has outlasted the era itelf.

IN THE PREVIOUS chapter, we saw how the hurricane of colonialism blew Western thinking about Kushite history off course. The 1880s' rush to dominate the African continent, the so-called Scramble, created a climate in the West that made disdain for colonized peoples almost psychologically necessary in order justify their subjugation.

Yet this explanation is not totally satisfying. Nagging questions remain. How could so many scholars get so caught up in that mentality? How could they in good conscience produce "expert findings" that actively contributed to the perceived legitimacy of the colonizing mindset?

The scholars of that day, after all, were no dullards. Far, far from it. As we've seen, many of those who rejected Kush's role against Assyria were true intellectual luminaries, hardly the kind of people politicians might readily manipulate. Most of these archaeologists, historians and biblical experts were products of classical educations, with backgrounds in history, language and literature that were designed to engender balanced judgment. In their books, these experts often evince a breadth of learning and command of language that is really quite awesome.

They also tended to be members of academic communities that valued internationalism and humanitarian ideals. Most of these scholars, for example, would have supported the antislavery movement which continued in Europe decades after the emancipation of slaves in the United States and which focused on slavery of Africans by Africans. Most were also strongly committed to the Judeo-Christian faith. Indeed, many were actual clerics of religious denominations that had sent missionaries to Africa to save souls.

Archibald Henry Sayce (1845-1933) is an apt example of a scholar in the eye of colonalism's storm.

He was from Britain, the first country off the mark in the Scramble, and during the period was actively working in the Nile Valley. He was a man of Oxbridge, spawning ground of many of the day's intellectuals, and was himself one of his generation's most admired experts on the ancient world's history, archaeology and, especially, philology. A cleric, he served as president for many years of the Society of Biblical Archaeology and was a prolific contributor to its prestigious research journal. Among scholars visiting Egypt and the Sudan in the late 19th century, his erudition, social skills and the length of his stay combined to make him a near-legendary figure, an insider *par excellence*.[1]

Indeed, as much as any of his contemporaries, Sayce might be said to incarnate the ideal of scholarly respectability of the Victorian and Edwardian times. His obituary in *The Times* speaks effusively of his benign, gracious character:

> His was one of the lovable personalities of the world; his presence, ever genial and stamped with old-fashioned courtliness, which endeared him to all, will for long be an Oxford tradition.[2]

Among his many friends were some of Britain's intellectual and artistic giants—poet Robert Browning, novelist George Eliot, philosopher Herbert Spencer, poet and scholar Matthew Arnold, explorer-scholar Sir Richard Burton and writers Walter Pater and John Ruskin.[3] It is interesting that in all the books and articles I have seen that deal with Sayce, never is anything the least bit negative said about his character. The closest thing to an adverse remark is an American archaeologist's comment that he was "prissy," but this colleague adds in the next breath that he was "kindly."[4] As concerns his work, *Britannica* is typically appreciative. Its 1998 edition hails the Bristol native's "many valuable contributions to ancient Near Eastern linguistic and archaeological research."[5]

As for Sayce's status as ordained deacon in the Church of England, nothing was unusual about that. At Oxford, where he was a student and fellow (at Queen's College) and spent his teaching career, such a background was natural for faculty: until the mid-19th century, that university allowed only Anglican clergymen to teach undergraduates, all of whom—as at the University of Cambridge—had to be Anglican as well.[6]

Throughout Sayce's lifetime, the Anglican Church saw itself as a compassionate and caring presence in many non-Christian countries. While he himself appears not to have proselytized,[7] Sayce was always proud of his clerical identity: some of his books on ancient history identify him as "The Rev. A.H. Sayce." And although early in his career he declined appointment as a suffragan bishop (the assistant to the bishop of a diocese) in favor of pursuing his research on the ancient world, he insisted on wearing his clerical garb even when traveling to the hottest, dustiest of digs abroad. In his churchman's long-tailed black coat, high collar and black felt hat, the slightly built Welshman cut a striking figure at archaeological sites across the Fertile Crescent and Nile Valley.[8]

A colleague has described Sayce as a "genius." He could, for example, write decent prose in 20 or more ancient and modern languages.[9] Holder of the chair of Assyriology at Oxford, he published the first grammar in English of Assyrian and translated numerous Mesopotamian records, including Sennacherib's annals. A major achievement was the decipherment of ancient Armenian cuneiform ("Vannic"). Another coup was his revelation of the existence in Anatolia of the great Hittite Empire; some critics believed Sayce's arguments to be preposterous, yet later discoveries proved him right.[10] Sayce was also active in Jerusalem. Shortly after someone else had discovered the workmen's inscription in Hezekiah's Tunnel (see Chapters 4, 5 and 15), he waded through the channel and, after clearing away the lime deposit that obscured them, copied the words by candlelight. He later published the first copy and translation of the famous text. The subjects of his writings show the scope of his learning: he wrote separate books on the ancient cultures of Assyria, Persia, Babylonia, Israel, Greece and Syria.

One can only marvel, then, that in addition to all that work, Sayce devoted some of his most productive years to delving into two other ancient civilizations—Egypt and Kush. Partly because his weak lungs benefited from warm dry air, starting in 1879 and extending over a period of four decades Sayce spent 17 winters in the Nile Valley.[11] Here, too, he did remarkable work, scouring the countryside for hieroglyphs and translating them. To reach archaeological sites on the lower Nile, the professor acquired his own private houseboat. Crewed by 19 sailors, not including his two servants,[12] this spacious sailing vessel became the bachelor scholar's home for many years; he used it to visit sites up and down the Nile. He stocked it with 2,000 books and wrote many of his works there. It also helps explain his influence in shaping intellectual opinion: for many fieldwork-weary archaeologists, including Breasted, the vessel was an oasis of comfort and scholarly discussion.

Late in his career, Sayce journeyed to Sudan, where he became the first person to make a positive identification of the ruins of Meroë, a city whose importance as a Kushite center grew after the 26th Dynasty's destruction of Napata. He returned to oversee the city's excavation.

But it is this learned man's views on race that require a close look here. His autobiography, published after World War I, offers a virulently anti-Semitic interpretation of contemporary history. The Russian revolution, he writes, was a time when "the wild dreams of the Slav and the long-treasured revenge of the Jew upon the Gentile would combine in an orgy of destruction."[13]

It is in earlier writings, however, that he fashioned his most analytical opinions on race.

In a book published in 1891, entitled *The Races of the Old Testament*, this icon of scholarly rectitude has this to say:

■ "The brains of the higher races are distinguished by more complex convolutions than those of the inferior races."[14] "The black coloring matter of the Negro extends to . . . even his brain, the convolutions of which are comparatively simple."[15]

■ "The greater the projection of the jaws beyond the line of the face, the more animal-like is the latter." Measurement of this forehead-to-jaw angle leads to this conclusion about one of the "lower races": "The Negro, in fact, stands about as much below the European as he stands above the orang-outang. . . ."[16]

■ "The [ancient] Egyptian is a member of the white race."[17]

■ Inhabiting the southern valley of the Nile are "two black races, the Negroes . . . and the Nubians. The Nubians, in spite of their black skins, are usually classed among the handsomest of mankind, just as the Negroes are among the ugliest."[18]

■ Shabako, Taharqa and other Kushite "kings, like the court which surrounded them, belonged to the white race. They were of Egyptian descent. . . ."[19]

In a book published in 1895, *The Egypt of the Hebrews and Herodotus*, Sayce revises the Kushites' racial identity. A captive Kushite king or prince depicted on an Assyrian stela has recently come to his attention, he says, and this royal personage possesses "all the physical characteristics of the Negro." Sayce concludes that "we now know [the Kushites] were Negroes in reality."[20] This tallies with Breasted's own view of the Kushite dynasty, which he gives in his book a decade later. In another book published in 1899, Sayce makes a similar affirmation.[21] (In neither work, incidentally, does Sayce try to reconcile how Nubians can be among the "handsomest" of people while at the same time belong to a race that is "among the ugliest.")

In both books, Sayce also states flatly that this Negro dynasty had played a hapless role in the events of 701 BC. "Again and again the Egyptian armies were defeated at the borders of Canaan," he writes, freely pluralizing the Eltekeh experience, "and Taharqa was saved from invasion [of Egypt by Assyria] only by the disaster which befell Sennacherib during his siege of Jerusalem."[22]

How can we explain such an eruption of racist scorn?

It did not occur in a vacuum. Starting in 1882, the don found himself in the very cauldron of the first great conflict of Europe's imperialist assault of Africa. When Sayce first arrived there at the age of 34, European powers were still in the background. Egypt and Sudan were part of Turkey's Ottoman Empire. In 1882, however, Britain's Prime Minister William Gladstone ordered naval ships to bombard the Delta city of Alexandria with cannon fire. As it turned out, this was the act that launched the Scramble.[23]

London's motivation had little to do with coveting new territory or markets.[24] Notes one historian: "Imperialism was immoral [for

Gladstone], a form of wrongdoing. Unless there was a strategic necessity, why extend the formal British Empire when most of the world was open to British trade?"[25] Gladstone's government would have been content to let the Ottoman Empire, which with only brief interruption had ruled Egypt since the 16th century, continue to run the country as a vast province. But that empire was in decay, and a rising Egyptian-nationalist movement seemed poised to overthrow it. That would have jeopardized important British financial investments in the Egyptian economy. It also threatened the Suez Canal, upon which the British had grown dependent since its construction by the French a decade earlier. If nationalists were to seize the waterway, London feared that access to India, the British Empire's most prized possession, would greatly suffer.

Despite deep misgivings, then, Britain stumbled into an imperial role in Africa. One historian deftly describes its policy as "imperialism without impetus."[26] The cannonading of Alexandria backfired: instead of cowing the nationalists, it galvanized them, provoking them to riot against Europeans and prompting Britain's occupation of the country while leaving the Ottoman viceroy in nominal control. Gladstone wanted Britain to extricate itself as soon as conditions permitted, but straightening out Egypt's finances was harder than anticipated. Soon, the white-man's-burden rationale seeped into Gladstone's thinking: two years after the occupation had begun, he told the House of Commons that Britain's task in Egypt was "one which we are executing not alone, on our behalf, but on behalf, if I may say, of civilized mankind."[27]

Technically, Britain never practiced outright colonialism in the Nile valley: Turkey was always in charge—officially. Still, for 24 years starting in 1883, Egypt's *de facto* ruler was Britain's man in Cairo, Lord Cromer. In time, he would become known for his scornful views of what he called "the subject races." Britain's domination would persist throughout the period best recalled for the exploits of Lawrence of Arabia and end only after World War I, in 1922.

While the conflict in Egypt between nationalists and the Anglo-Turkish-Egyptian forces often involved great bloodshed, its casualties did not approach those in Sudan. In this seldom remembered theater of war, the number of Sudanese combatants and civilians who died either in fighting or from war-related causes such as starvation reached staggering proportions. According to a well-placed British official at that time, the Sudanese death toll approached six million.[28] And that is out of a total Sudanese population that this official estimated at eight million.

This catastrophe took place over the last two decades of the 19th century. First the Ottomans, with the active help of the British and Egyptians, sought to subdue the Sudanese in order to modernize the territory and at the same time suppress (at British instigation) the slave trade on which much of the indigenous economy relied. This intervention by outsiders—particularly the Christian British—provoked widespread religious and nationalistic outrage in the Muslim population. In 1883, the Sudanese annihilated a 10,000-man Egyptian army under the command of a British colonel. Two years later an event took place that rocked the British Empire. Under the leadership of the religious leader Muhammad Ahmad al-Mahdi, Sudanese forces conquered their country's capital, Khartoum, that had been held by British troops under the command of one of the empire's most illustrious figures, Gen. Charles Gordon. Killed by a Sudanese spear, Gordon immediately achieved warrior-saint status in Britain.

More than any other event, the fall of Khartoum—a national humiliation—caused Gladstone to commit Britain to deep immersion in Africa.[29] Queen Victoria's anger spoke for that of many of her subjects: in a letter to the minister of war, she said she was appalled to see her troops "retreating before savages" and making Britain "the laughing-stock of the whole world."[30] Such was Britons' humiliation after the Gordon debacle that, according to one historian, "Even 13 years later it was felt necessary to appease popular emotions over Gordon's death by reconquering the Sudan and *collectively punishing the Sudanese* in this most uncivilized 'civilizing mission'" [emphasis added].[31]

Finally, in 1898, British forces under the command of another national hero, Gen. Horatio Herbert Kitchener, were able to avenge Gordon by defeating the Sudanese rebels. In the joint rule that Britain and Ottoman Egypt now exercised over Sudan, Britain was the dominant partner. Sir Reginald Wingate, a general who had fought alongside Kitchener, became governor general (1899-1916). "The Sudan," wrote Sayce, "was now restored to the civilized world."[32]

As we've seen, the Kushite-rescue theory's decline coincided with Europe's *overall* conquest of Africa in the 1880s. But the correlation between the two was even closer than that. The early stage of this continent-wide subjugation contained a particularly violent conflict that happened to take place in the *precise region* that had been part of the Kushite homeland. Indeed, the British waged this war against forces whose members would have included direct descendants of the various peoples who lived under the Kushite monarchy.[33]

To understand the intensity of many Britons' contempt for their enemy, one has to understand the role of religion. Gladstone called the Sudanese conflict a "Christian war."[34] Robert Salisbury, the Conservative whose terms as prime minister alternated with those of the Liberal Gladstone, called Islam a "false religion" and said it was "capable of the most atrocious perversion and corruption of any religion on the face of the earth."[35] For him, a policy objective in the Sudan was "to extirpate from the earth one of the vilest despotisms . . . ever seen."

The British military historian Brian Robson adds this disturbing note: "Killing the wounded, while it happens on occasion in any army, has never been a British tradition; indeed, the reverse is true. Yet, in [the campaigns of eastern Sudan], it became the norm for probably the first and, hopefully, the last time in our history."[36] Desperation may help explain this. Although the Sudanese were poorly armed, Robson calls their army "the most formidable that the British army had ever encountered, and overwhelming disaster hovered on at least two occasions."[37]

Sayce's own religious and academic institutions were hardly intellectual adversaries to this official climate of religious intolerance against the Sudanese. Both institutions—the Anglican Church and Oxford—were effectively satellites of the state. In her capacity as monarch, Queen Victoria was of course also the head of the Church of England, and she took this dual role with uncommon seriousness.

She insisted on exercising her right to select all Anglican bishops who were consecrated in her reign.[38] Far from acting as a rubber stamp, she sometimes defied her prime ministers' advice on whom to appoint, and she was anxious to stamp out any theological trends within the Church that she saw as unhealthy. The Church was identified largely, though not completely, with the State: it inculcated reverence for the State and saw to the State's Christian character.[39]

As we saw earlier, Oxford was still a clerical milieu; it, too, like the Church, was remarkably close to government. Prime Minister Gladstone himself—reflecting Her Majesty's wishes—would even personally intervene in appointments of professorships, including those in religion-related fields. He called this "ecclesiastical patronage."[40] Says his biographer: "Gladstone habitually took such immense pains over ecclesiastical appointments that even a minor one was liable to disrupt the routine of his office for days on end."[41] Oxford's intellectual environment, then, was hardly conducive to thinking independently about any subject dear to the government[42]—and it would be hard to think of any subject more dear to the British Empire than imperialism.

One of the most striking things to emerge from Sayce's autobiography is the proximity that existed on a social level between his world of scholarship and that of government.

Already as a young Oxford scholar—in pre-Scramble days— Sayce had established a friendly relationship with the learned Gladstone himself, who was the member of Parliament for Oxford. Gladstone, 36 years older and author of a three-volume work on the Homeric age, shared with Sayce an avid interest in classical literature, and when prime minister he would sometimes invite the Oxford prodigy for breakfast at his London home.[43] Years later, when Sayce had become a respected authority on biblical matters, the two collaborated on a deluxe edition of the Bible; the professor and the retired politician wrote the introductions to the Old Testament and New Testament respectively.

But it was in Egypt and Sudan that Sayce's contacts with the imperial establishment reached full flower. Government and ancient history needed each other. From the government's viewpoint, biblical and classical history were not dusty subjects far from the attention of the public. This history helped nourish society's religious, artistic and intellectual interests. This was also true of nations other than Britain. Important discoveries by a Western country's archaeologists often became fuel for that country's nationalism, the sort of role that space exploits would assume during the Cold War. Earlier in the 19th century, France's Champollion (decipherer of the Rosetta Stone), England's Layard (discoverer of Nineveh) and Germany's Heinrich Schliemann (excavator of Troy and Mycenae) became heroes of their respective countries. Many ancient artifacts—the Egyptian obelisks, Sennacherib's Lachish relief, the Elgin marbles—were hauled back to Western capitals like trophies.[44]

To be successful, people involved in archaeological research needed more than just scholarly skills. To receive permission to excavate or remove artifacts, to obtain funding, to get the protection of soldiers when travelling to isolated sites at times of civil unrest, to receive permission to export their treasures, they needed the favor of authorities. On friendships and networking much depended.

At such socializing, Sayce excelled. Earlier, my sketch of Britain's presence in Egypt and Sudan mentioned four individuals who stood out as pillars of the Empire's presence in those countries during Sayce's 30 years there. With each, the professor enjoyed cordial, rewarding relations.

The first was Egypt's master, the autocratic Lord Cromer.[45] The earl relied on Sayce as a kind of political fixer in international archaeological circles.[46] Sayce also profitably traded on his influence with Cromer: in return for interceding with him on behalf of a wealthy Egyptian, who needed the great man's approval on a private matter, Sayce purchased from the Egyptian the sumptuous houseboat—spanking new—at less than half its construction cost.[47]

As for Charles Gordon, Sayce may have been the last British civilian to see the celebrated martyr-general alive.[48] Such was Sayce's standing with Gordon's family that years later the general's widow helped finance Sayce's excavations at Meroë.[49]

Sayce describes as a "good friend" that other great British military hero, Gen. Kitchener. After being named commander-in-chief of the Anglo-Egyptian army in 1892, Kitchener was a frequent luncheon guest on Sayce's vessel. When Sayce wanted to reach archaeological sites in enemy territory, the general arranged for many British troops to accompany him on camelback. Such was the relationship that he confided to the professor astonishing war secrets.[50]

Another central figure Sayce befriended was Gen. Wingate, successor to Gordon and Kitchener as Sudan's governor general. While lunching with Wingate at the war hero's home in Scotland, Sayce planned with the general his trip to Sudan.[51] After his arrival in that country, he spent a week at Sir Reginald's palace at Khartoum and made use of his personal steamer for a 350-mile trip up the Blue Nile. Wingate's station was hardly humble. As Breasted's son would later write of him, "from his white-washed mud-brick palace at Khartoum, [he] ruled like a king over a territory about one-fourth the size of Europe."[52]

Sayce, in other words, lost all critical distance between himself—as a scholar and cleric who was originally probably quite devoted to ideals like truth and justice—and empire. He became the cosseted adjunct of a colonial regime.

The following story says much about the situation's effect on his personal behavior.

While on an archaeological trip through central Egypt in the winter of 1884-85, the clergyman was asked by the provincial governor for advice on what to do with 130 brigands who had been arrested on suspicion of robbing and killing peasants. In a telegram, British authorities in Cairo had insisted upon trials, but the governor feared that the difficulty in finding witnesses could result in many acquittals. Sayce counseled the governor to execute the prisoners at once and to tell Cairo that the telegram had arrived only later.

What is even more shocking is that, as he recounts the advice to the governor 35 years later in his autobiography, Sayce shows not even a twinge of remorse. From his tone, he seems almost pleased to have helped rid the world of so many felony suspects.[53]

Sayce's scholarship is another reflection of this conflict's dehumanizing effect. In wars, each side tends to deny the moral worth of the other. It makes killing easier. If a hostile people is inherently without value, then so must be its history. Britain at that time was a profoundly churchgoing society and its people knew biblical history thoroughly. An appreciation that the Sudanese were heroes, having saved Jerusalem and thus enabling the Judeo-Christian tradition to emerge, would hardly have abetted the war effort. As the empire's resident intellectual on the scene, Sayce lent himself to the erasure of that history. This required no effort. He identified completely with the imperial rulers, received their moral approval and owed his princely lifestyle to his symbiotic relationship to them.

It is interesting to recall that it was just when the war was at a fever pitch, in the early 1890s, that his views on the Kushites harshened. While before he had regarded them as the "handsomest" of people, at that time he demoted them from their prior status as whites and classified them as Negroes, who to him were subhuman. At that time he also said the Kushites when confronting Sennacherib had been big losers.

Once the smoke of war vanished from Sudan, something strange happened to Sayce's view of the Kushites. After the pacification of Sudan, Sayce in 1908-1909 traveled through that vast land. It was in the course of a trek by dromedary that he located Meroë,[54] and less than a year later, Sayce returned to the site to organize the first dig.[55] The excavation had great influence on his opinion of Kushite/Meroitic civilization. Upon his return home, he wrote the preface to a friend's book, published in 1911, on contemporary Anglo-Egyptian Sudan. In his brief comments, Sayce expresses enthusiasm for ancient Meroë's cultural sophistication. Archaeology, he writes, "has brought to light a new and unexpected civilization of high order."[56] Sounding like Heeren, he says that "the Greek writers were correct in the accounts they gave" of, among other things, the Meroë region's "high culture."

Sayce then goes on to make this startling assessment of a civilization with whose descendants the empire was now at peace:

In later days Ethiopia still exercised an influence upon the history of the world. *It was the Ethiopian king, with his black levies from the land of the sadd* [or "sudd," southern Sudan], *who prevented Sennacherib from destroying Jerusalem, and therewith the religion of Judah, before the reforms of Josiah and the preaching of the great prophets and enabled it to withstand the disintegrating forces of exile and dispersion.* Though Tirhakah was compelled to retreat to Egypt after the battle of Eltekeh, the Assyrian army was too shattered to follow him or to return to the siege of Jerusalem with any prospect of success. The season had grown late, and disease broke out in the ranks of the invaders. Sennacherib found himself obliged to lead the survivors of his army back to Nineveh, with his rebellious vassal unsubdued. *The Negroes of Africa had saved the city and temple of Jerusalem.*[57] [Emphases added.]

This is the most forthright statement I have encountered by any scholar in the 20th century that recognizes both a) the decisive role of Taharqa's forces in turning back Assyria *and* b) the impact of that event on history.[58]

But wait. If one reads the above passage carefully, one notices that nowhere does Sayce say that Taharqa himself is "Negro"— only his conscripts or militia were. Is this missing racial identification of Taharqa a mere oversight? No, in another book published the same year, 1911, we see that the scholar no longer considers Taharqa to be Negro.[59]

A revealing correlation, then, emerges from Sayce's zigzags. When he declares Taharqa to be Negro he sees the Kushite commander's expedition to Khor as a fiasco. It has no bearing on the Assyrians' withdrawal. But when Sayce deems Taharqa to be *not* Negro (and presumably white), then his expedition has the effect of leaving Assyria's forces "too shattered" to capture Jerusalem: Taharqa is responsible for the survival of both the city and Judah's religion.

Sayce's generosity toward Taharqa and his conscripts, "the Negroes of Africa," however, appears to have been remarkably discreet. As mentioned, his statement occurs in the preface to a friend's book. The friend was His Excellency Yacoub Artin Pasha, a high Ottoman official in Egypt's education ministry in Cairo. The book, entitled *England in the Sudan*, consists of a collection of letters that the pasha, a Christian of aristocratic Armenian descent, had written to his wife while accompanying Sayce on that 1908-1909 journey through Sudan. The result is a volume—essentially, a vanity book—whose limited circulation would have been mostly outside Europe and would have included the retired official's many Turkish, Egyptian and Sudanese associates. It is unlikely such a book would attract many, if any, scholars' attention, and indeed I have not seen any scholar cite it. In short, Sayce's pro-Taharqa statement was in the form of an off-stage aside.

Sayce's public stance on Taharqa's success in 701 did not last. He reverted (at least on the record) to his original view. In 1925, a revised edition appeared of his 1891 book, *Races of the Old Testament*. In it, Sayce conserves his crudely racist statements about the inferiority and ugliness of "Negroes." He also lets stand his insistence that Kushite kings were white.

Did he give approval to republication without reflection? No. In a preface to the new edition, he writes that he has re-read the book and "I find little to alter in it."[60] Was he, at the age of 80, no longer alert? No again. For another six years he was still producing articles and book reviews for scholarly journals.

In a revised edition in 1926 of still another book, this one on ancient Assyria that had been first published 40 years before, Sayce seems to confirm that he is back where he started. In referring to Sennacherib's withdrawal, he offers no clue as to its cause. He passes up a golden opportunity to speak of Taharqa's influence, which he had acclaimed in 1911.[61] A reader of these 1925 and 1926 editions of his books, or indeed of his 1923 autobiography,[62] would see the Kushites as wholly irrelevant to the conflict of 701.

Sayce's silence late in life is puzzling. Had he promoted the Kushite-rescue theory with any vigor, he might have helped the theory to regain in the 20th century the credibility that it had so recently lost. Few people, after all, had better credentials than the expert who had helped to unearth Meroë. Also, it would be difficult to find anyone more strategically placed to publicize such a view. At the time of his pro-Taharqa insight, he was still the head of the Society of Biblical Archaeology. Then again, Sayce's reticence is no more puzzling than the general failure of subsequent scholarship to come to grips with the obvious solution to the so-called mystery of the Deliverance.

There is something sadly ironic about the Scramble's generation of scholars. That generation made exciting discoveries of Kushite ruins. Thanks to these archaeologists, the world was in a position to know more about this ancient civilization than ever. Yet also because of this same generation, recognition of Kush's contributions to history sank from public view. Archibald Sayce personifies the paradox. As important as he was as an excavator of the Kushite past, in effect he was equally one of its buriers.

IT WOULD BE wrong to leave the impression that all modern scholarship has been unfair.

Several scholars have been exceptionally balanced in their presentation of Kushite culture. Jean Leclant and Fritz Hintze are among the first in the 20th century to demonstrate such fairness. In a book by Leclant published in 1958, for example, this French expert on ancient art says the Kushite Dynasty had, among other things, "brought to light the old traditions and given them new life" and provided the "last vision of great power in Egypt."[63] Another unusually unbiased assessment of the 25th Dynasty by a modern writer is that of Rex Keating.[64] Bruce Trigger, of McGill, is also notably even-handed, as is László Török, of the Hungarian Academy of Sciences, author of prolific research in the 1990s. The refreshing absence of negative bias toward Kush that characterizes their writings is also becoming apparent in the recent work of other specialists in the region such as Derek Welsby and Robert Morkot. One hopes this signals a trend. Various museums have presented Kushite civilization to the public in an unbiased light; Boston's Museum of Fine Arts, for which archaeologist Timothy Kendall has done exciting research at Napata, and Toronto's Royal Ontario Museum have been models.

CHAPTER 16 EXPLORED the ancient B² revision of the Kushite record of 701. Now we have seen the modern-day revision. We can detect honor in the motivation behind the earlier revision. In the second, that quality is conspicuously missing.

Insofar as it connotes deliberate or conspiratorial cunning, the term "cover up" does not really fit. There was no need for a conscious effort by Western historians, archaeologists and biblical commentators a century ago to deny this chapter of Africa's past. Rather, the denial sprang from a common mindset. Sharing their society's support for overseas expansion, the scholars set aside ideas that clashed with the imperial premise of Africans' inherent unworthiness. If, like Archibald Sayce, one believed "the Negroes of Africa" to be midway between Europeans and apes, it was hard to swallow the idea that members of such a sorry genetic background could have accomplished so heroic a feat as to save Jerusalem.

That a scholar—and man of the cloth—like Sayce could recommend the mass killing of prisoners was of course extreme and atypical, but that he could speak openly of such cold-blooded behavior with neither shame nor fear of condemnation from peers says much about the effect of that terrible conflict on the most basic morality. With their great academic and religious institutions functioning as handmaidens of goverment, it took no great effort for Sayce and other scholars to help kill the enemy's history.

Today, more than a century later, those intellectuals' successors possess no such excuse.

Conclusion

The idea of Zion is rooted in deeper regions of the

earth and rises into loftier regions of the air, and

neither its deep roots nor its lofty heights, neither

its memory of the past nor its ideal for the future,

both of the selfsame texture, must be repudiated.

Martin Buber

On Zion (1952)

CHAPTER TWENTY

The Roots of the Zion Concept

IN 1933, ALDOUS Huxley described Jerusalem as the "great slaughterhouse of religions." With tensions ever mounting since then, the summit of the original Zion hill itself has become the most potentially explosive piece of real estate on earth. A major threat to Jerusalem's security comes from Iraq, the same territory where Assyria once lay.

Few ideas are more influential in geopolitics today than the concept of Zion, and certainly none is so ancient. The Zion concept predates even the emergence of the monotheisms with which it has been closely entwined—Islam, Christianity and, the oldest of the three, Judaism.

As is widely known, originally the Zion idea was the belief that Yahweh's caring presence pervades the hill, called Mount Zion. The Hebrew Bible/Old Testament says that it was atop this elevation, on which the oldest part of Jerusalem grew, that King Solomon built the original Temple of Yahweh. As one of the psalms affirms, "For the Lord has chosen Zion and desired it for his home: 'This is my resting-place for ever; here I will make my home, for such is my desire.'"[1] It is a place name that possesses great flexibility. Sometimes the Bible also uses "Zion" to include the entire city of Jerusalem, which came to cover more than a single hill. Sometimes, starting with the Babylonian Exile in 586 BC, it employs the word poetically to refer to the entire Hebrew home-land, the former kingdoms of Judah and Israel alike.

It is Yahweh's devotion to Mount Zion as his "dwelling"[2] and to the larger territory that explains the terms Holy City and Holy Land. In the Hebrew Bible, this devotion is no abstract emotion. It has a vividly practical application. Because Yahweh is so strong, says the Bible, he is able to demonstrate his love for the city by protecting it against all enemies. Another psalm, for example, calls the city Yahweh's "high stronghold" and declares, "God is in that city; she will not be overthrown" by earthly forces.[3] In the centuries following the composition of those lines, numerous invaders have conquered Jerusalem and thus discredited the belief in a divine defense; nonetheless, the sense of holiness that is an integral part of that belief remains strong. For millions of people today, Jerusalem is as much a spiritual capital as it was for the psalmist who wrote: "God reigns over the nations, God is seated on his holy throne"[4]—that is, on Zion.

And yet, despite the visceral feelings millions have for Zion, and the violence that erupts over the question of to which people it properly belongs, no one really understands this idea. The histor-ical impetus that lies behind this concept of a Holy City has remained unresolved. Just how the writers of the Bible would have arrived at this perception that an omnipotent deity had chosen Zion as his abode and would guard it against even the most pow-erful of attacking foes has been a puzzle.

In recent generations the Zion concept has sometimes been reduced to a functional role—as a divine land title. Tracing its early development and its original *raison d'être* will remind us that it is much more than that.

Typical of the vagueness enveloping the idea, even the hill's geographical location is commonly misunderstood. The "Mount Zion" that appears on many Jerusalem maps and in the city's guidebooks is not the original Mount Zion. Because the Bible speaks effusively of Zion's great height,[5] the widespread assump-tion arose many centuries ago that Zion must be the sprawling city's westernmost hill. In fact, of course, the original Zion is the eastern hill;[6] it is here, where the glittering Dome of the Rock now rises, that the Bible says Solomon built the first temple to Yahweh.

Centuries after the Bible was written, early rabbis amplified the Zion concept: Talmudic literature makes the hill the navel of the world, the place where earth and heaven meet and where mortals, wherever they happen to be geographically, can route their messages to the divine. It becomes the most important place in the entire cosmos.[7] In the New Testament, too, Jerusalem acquires additional holiness: because the Gospels describe Jesus of Nazareth, himself a Jew, as worshipping his divine father at Jerusalem and as dying and then rising from the dead in Jerusalem, the city has become a focus for the Christian faith. The city's importance in the story of Jesus explains why on maps many medieval Christian cartographers placed Jersusalem at the world's geographical center, making it the very pivot of the world, and why the Crusaders struggled to wrest control of it. Some early Christian and Jewish texts also depict Jerusalem as the terrestrial prototype for a heavenly Jerusalem, making the city the axis of a future apocalypse. Like Christians, Muslims accept the Hebrew Bible's depiction of Zion and see later events as adding to its holiness. Although Mecca and Medina have superior status for Muslims, in their tradition it is from Zion's summit that the Prophet Muhammad ascended to heaven and returned. The 1,300-year-old Dome of the Rock commemorates the spot.

More recently, the Zion concept has acquired still another dimension. Inspired by the idea of Zion as homeland, and pushed by the rise of virulent anti-Semitism, the Jewish nationalist movement known as Zionism in late-19th-century Europe sought to create a Jewish state in Palestine. With the founding of the modern state of Israel in 1948, it succeeded.

Despite the term's close association with Jewish patriotism, "Zionism" can sometimes have a much broader, more universal meaning. The German-Jewish religious philosopher Martin Buber (1878-1965) said that planners of the new state of Israel should remember the roots of the Zion idea. He meant that they should know that Zion involved "an eternal purpose" that transcends nationalism.[8] Buber, who became editor of the Zionist weekly *Die*

Welt in 1901, saw Zionism as having a "supranational mission" in which the power of the spirit would replace power politics. It would, he said, spark a new sense of community among nations. In Israel, a "deep and lasting solidarity" would emerge between Jews and Arabs. A Zion that is based on mutual respect and good will among states, he said, will become "the new sanctuary of the nations," and the people who helped achieve that "will become the priest" in that sanctuary.[9] Buber resided for 17 years in the new state of Israel and served as the first president of Israel's Academy of Arts and Sciences.

He died a disappointed man, but it is noteworthy that at his state funeral in Jerusalem a delegation of the Arab Students' Organization placed a wreath on his grave.

THE FIRST SETTLEMENT of Jerusalem may have been about 3000 BC when practical motives—rather than religious ones—dictated the choice of the site. The Gihon Spring was the main source of water for many miles, and the hill above that stream offered a defensible slope on three of four sides. The belief in a divine presence looking out for the welfare of his people came later. The Canaanite people who would have lived in Jerusalem prior to the Bible-described conquest of the city by David (*c.* 1000 BC) had used the word "Zion" for the hill on which they built their town; the word probably meant fortress or rock. The hill was the home of their deity, Shalem, a West Semitic god.[10]

According to the Bible, after the Hebrews took over the hill they continued to call it Zion (in Hebrew, *Tsiyyon*), but they considered that it was the residence of their own deity, Yahweh.[11] The newcomers also retained the town's venerable name, Yerushalim (pronounced "Yerushalayim"), meaning the "foundation of Shalem."

Prior to the late eighth century BC, was Mount Zion special? Not particularly. The ancient world was full of sacred hills and mountains. Khor, Mesopotamia, the Sinai Peninsula (as with Mount Sinai) and even Kush (witness Amon's sacred mountain,

Gebel Barkal, at Napata) contained various heights that were regarded as cosmic places where the earth touched the divine sphere.[12] In the northern kingdom, such elevations included Mount Carmel, Mount Tabor and Mount Gerizim; they could be sacred in either Yahweh's name or in the names of Canaanite gods.[13] Many other peoples had their counterparts to Mount Zion, and Judahites saw Jerusalem's religious status as conforming to a larger international pattern.[14] The people of Judah at that time believed in the existence of many gods, and they would have harbored no illusions about their national deity being the mightiest and his abode therefore the safest.

The most in-depth investigation of the origins of Jerusalem's sacred status is by Ronald Clements. His astute 1980 book, *Isaiah and the Deliverance of Jerusalem*, concludes that Jerusalemites of the late 8th century BC would have seen Mount Zion as somewhat special, but not *uniquely* so—a vital nuance. Describing the people of this period, he says that they

> held special beliefs about the presence of Yahweh in the sanctuary [Temple] there. [. . .] The inhabitants of Jerusalem were certainly encouraged to believe that their God would protect them in time of war and bless them with peace and prosperity. Yet these ideas were fundamental elements in almost all the cult-traditions of the ancient Orient. There is little to indicate that Jerusalem was especially unique in this regard. If we had fuller information about the ancient cults of Bethel, Shechem and elsewhere [Bethel and Shechem being centers for worship of Yahweh in the northern kingdom] we should no doubt find that there were many features in which they were closely similar to that of Jerusalem.

The professor at King's College, University of London, who based his research mostly on biblical texts, adds:

> There is no reason why we should be especially surprised therefore that the old Jerusalem cultus [*i.e.*, organized religious practice] was linked with a mythology about a sacred mountain. . . . Nor is it at all surprising that the citizens of Jerusalem believed that their God

would guard and protect them in time of war, since this must have been one of the most deeply embedded of all early man's religious convictions.[15]

In the generations prior to 701, then, there is little to suggest that Hebrews would have seen Jerusalem as any more deserving of divine protection than other Hebrew cities.

Starting in 738 BC, a generation of people in the Hebrew, Philistine and Phoenician kingdoms of the eastern Mediterranean region lived in profound fear. Eight times over a period of 37 years, Assyria, history's first military state, had dispatched armies to the region to conquer its people and, when they dared rebel, punish them by ravaging the land. Five of these onslaughts struck at Hebrew territory; one of them, in 720, annihilated the restive vassal state of Israel.

In the thinking of people of that time, military conflicts always had a strongly religious dimension: if Assyria had so easily bested other kingdoms by force of arms, it meant that its main deity, Ashur, was vastly stronger than the national gods of the defeated peoples, including Yahweh, Israel's national god.

In 701, that dynamic changed. The army of Ashur was on the verge of obliterating the only remaining Hebrew kingdom, tiny Judah, when a Kushite-led army from Egypt drove the invader from the gates of Jerusalem and saved the nation. The 11th-hour rescue enabled Judah to survive another 115 years, a vital period in which it was able to nurse itself back to economic and demographic health.

It is also during this grace period that Yahwism, the local variant of the polytheism that thrived in the region, would greatly develop and begin a process of theological reflection that would continue to ripen during and after the Exile. The stimulus of much of this reflection had been the rescue of 701. That event cried out for a religious explanation: How had Yahweh overpowered the supposedly invincible Ashur? And why? For several generations, Judahites pondered these questions. The answers they found have gone far toward defining the dominant religious tradition of the West.

Yahweh was a great beneficiary of the rescue. Judahites interpreted the outcome of the Assyrian invasion as demonstrating that their national deity was mightier than Ashur. That Yahweh had saved Jerusalem and not any other city—including Samaria, the relatively grand Israelite capital which the Assyrians had besieged before destroying—meant that he had a special love for Jerusalem and its people.[16] It would take one or two centuries for this perception to mature, but eventually Yahweh would be seen as a deity who was indeed so powerful that his realm could not be confined to one nation but could only be universal.

Indeed, later generations would see Jerusalem's miraculous survival as the Deliverance through which Yahweh had demonstrated his commitment to them. From this grew a confidence among Hebrews that they were the deity's Chosen People—an identity to which, eventually, many Christians and Muslims would see themselves as heirs.

The Deliverance also laid the groundwork for what has become one of the modern world's most politically charged ideas—the concept of Zion, closely related to the idea of election.

It is in biblical texts that originate after 701 that we find a new appreciation of Zion, a conviction that Yahweh had revealed his love for the city by saving it from an Assyrian army under the personal command of the mighty emperor Sennacherib. Jerusalem came to be seen as forever impregnable. Yahweh was now in a position to offer such a guarantee: having triumphed over Ashur, the powerhouse in Assyria's pantheon, Yahweh was no longer a minor deity but an indomitable one.[17] Yahweh's proven prowess over Assyria becomes, as Clements puts it, "the basis for a larger and more universal hope" that the deity will always protect Zion from *all* nations.[18] In other passages of the Book of Isaiah that deal with a hypothetical future, Yahweh chases away threatening nations as easily as the wind blows dust.[19] As the character of the Hebrew godhead changed in response to the Assyrians' retreat, so did that of his "dwelling place," Jerusalem. It was in this post-701 period that the worship of Yahweh may have become centralized in Jerusalem,[20] institutionally anchoring the city's religious importance.

This belief in the city's providential safety became almost dogma; scholars call it the "doctrine of Jerusalem's inviolability." This belief, reflected in many biblical passages, is the key step in Jerusalem's ascension to the holy status that it possesses to this day.

Like most other experts on the period, Hayim Tadmor argues that "the concept of the inviolability of Jerusalem . . . stemmed from the outcome of the siege of 701." He explains:

> [T]he fact that Sennacherib and his huge army could devastate most of Judah but not take its capital was considered by the following generations as indeed a miracle. Until then, the Assyrian military machine had seemed invincible, crushing every western rebel, annexing its territory and exiling its people.[21]

The example a few years earlier of the annihilation of Israel, militarily stronger than Judah and also a worshipper of Yahweh, added to the city's extraordinary aura. As Tadmor's colleague at the Hebrew University, Sara Japhet, puts it, Sennacherib's retreat showed that "Jerusalem had a unique position in the earthly world. It was indestructible, for the Lord's presence and special grace protected it from all evil."[22]

The argument that Jerusalem's survival in 701 gave enormous impetus to the Zion concept is eminently logical and very widely accepted. Where I differ, however, is on the *cause* of that survival. Clements, for one, argues that Hezekiah would have surrendered the city and mollified Sennacherib with a large indemnity. That makes no sense: a banal payoff to the Assyrians would not have inspired a psalm to say that in Mount Zion's citadel "God has shown himself a sure defense" who makes attacking kings flee "in panic."[23] As well, in theological terms such a capitulation would imply that Ashur had cowed Jerusalemites—and hence that the city's survival in effect sprang from infidelity to Yahweh.

The doctrine of inviolability did not crystallize overnight. It probably took the better part of the ensuing century. The Deliverance was also seen as demonstrating another of Yahweh's great loyalties, this one political. Not only would Yahweh always protect his city, but he would also protect David's dynasty—and never bless any other aspirants to the throne. In the B[2] account, which may have been written a generation or more after Josiah's time, Yahweh announces he will defend Jerusalem "for the sake of my servant David."[24] The deity's rescue of David's descendant, Hezekiah, from Sennacherib, then, was presented as proof of the solemnity of Yahweh's promise to David in the Deuteronomistic History that his descendants would rule forever,[25] a promise known as the "Davidic covenant" (as distinct from *the* Covenant). The blessing that Yahweh gives to the City of David meshes closely with the blessing that he grants to the family of David. One of the lessons in the Bible's story of the Deliverance, Clements notes, is that "the salvation of Israel is assured through the Davidic dynasty."[26]

But why should anyone *today* care about either the doctrine of Jerusalem's inviolability or the Davidic covenant? Didn't both concepts soon prove to be groundless?

Yes and no. Within a few decades of the doctrine's formulation, Babylon's conquest of Jerusalem made it obvious that Yahweh's protection was not absolute. As well, Yahweh's promise to David that his descendants would rule in perpetuity proved to be inaccurate. After Babylon destroyed Jerusalem, no member of David's line ever again became monarch.

Yet, remarkably, Judah's downfall discredited neither idea. In trying to reconcile the collapse of both Jerusalem and the House of David with their own theology, Hebrew thinkers during the Exile decided that Yahweh's love for both the city and David's line had to be conditional. That is, Yahweh's loyalty depended upon the Chosen People's loyalty to him. If God's people accepted the rule of their divine overlord they would prosper, if their fealty to him weakened they would be punished. This Deuteronomic theology explains why the Deuteronomistic History blames Judah's destruction on ungodly and cruel policies of King Manasseh,[27] Hezekiah's son, even though this scapegoat's reign had ended more than half a century before.[28]

The importance of this Deuteronomic idea in Western thought is hard to overstate. For two-and-a-half millennia it has provided believers with an incentive system for respecting religion and for practicing good behavior. Indeed, through the Ten Commandments and other rules, it has greatly helped to define "good." To appreciate this approach's revolutionary impact, recall that the Deuteronomic school replaced an old system of currying favor by means of making sacrifices to the gods or behaving in other ways that were quite distinct from ethics. In an indirect but nonetheless significant manner, the new way evolved from the Deliverance. As Clements puts it, the stimulus for the rise of the Deuteronomic school was the "tension" between the high optimism of the Zion-Davidic theology as it evolved from the Deliverance and the military setbacks that Judah suffered starting about a century later, culminating with Babylon's destruction of Jerusalem in 586.[29]

Several centuries after the Exile and the period of Deuteronomy, the doctrine of inviolability would take on an eschatological dimension. A late addition to the Book of Zechariah says that on the day that "all the nations of the earth" attack Jerusalem, Yahweh will destroy them all, shielding the city's inhabitants while at the same time cleansing them of "sin and impurity."[30] Later still, in the first century AD, the New Testament's Book of Revelation further elevated Jerusalem's mystical standing. At the end of the world, this apocalyptic text foresees "the holy city, the new Jerusalem, coming down out of heaven from God. . . ." Jerusalem, says Revelation, will be a shining city made of "pure gold, clear as glass" with the "glory of God [as] its light" so that the "nations will walk by its light, and the kings of the earth will bring their glory into it" and "nothing unclean will enter it."[31]

Because of our incomplete knowledge of Jerusalem's religious reputation prior to Sennacherib's invasion, caution is in order. Rather than suggest that the survival of 701 was necessarily the genesis of the idea of the city's absolute divine protection, I am saying that this survival represented the *major impetus* to the flowering of that idea. (Clements himself allows that prior to Sennacherib's withdrawal there may have been a sense that a relatively weak Yahweh would do what he could in the face of Assyria's high-powered deity.) The Deliverance does not necessarily deserve all the credit for giving Jerusalem an aura of holiness, but it does merit the lion's share.[32]

Sennacherib's retreat was one of the great turning points in recorded history because if his army had destroyed Jerusalem there would have been no Judaism, Christianity or Islam. But the Deliverance did more than enable those religions to exist. It also affected their content, particularly in the case of Judaism and Christianity. The attribution of supreme holiness to Zion, the concept of the power and character of the godhead and the identity of the Chosen People are all, to a significant degree, traceable to early efforts to explain the "why" of Sennacherib's withdrawal. And later attempts to reconcile the theological first impressions of that marvelous event to the calamitous reality that ensued in 586 BC helped to establish a sense of morality that has influenced the daily conduct of billions of people.

WHAT INTERESTED MARTIN Buber was not the Zion concept's proprietary aspect so much as its ecumenical dimension. A biblical basis exists for that view. In one of its most uplifting passages on Zion, the Bible promises that at some future time "all nations shall stream to it." The text goes on to say that, "Many peoples shall come and say, 'Come, let us go up to the mountain of the Lord. . . , that he may teach us his ways . . .' For out of Zion shall go forth instruction, and the word of the Lord from Jerusalem." While those lines receive little attention, it is immediately after them that we encounter the celebrated verse that the nations "shall beat their swords into plowshares" and "nation shall not lift sword against nation." One of the biblical passages that peace movements in various countries use most frequently, in other words, originates in the specific context of the Zion concept. The passage is from the Book of Isaiah;[33] it would have been composed sometime after that prophet's lifetime when Judahites were assessing implications of the crisis of 701.

This book's examination of the crisis from an historical perspective reveals that it was not, as most scholars suppose, mere microbes that, by infecting Sennacherib's army with disease, "miraculously" saved Jerusalem—and, in effect, permitted the survival of the Hebrew people and led to the flowering of the Zion concept. Nor was it, as others speculate, because some other crisis distracted the attackers' attention or because the Jerusalemites meekly surrendered. None of those three theoretical explanations for the Deliverance has any logical connection to the Zion concept's intrinsic majesty. Rather, the factual explanation advanced here is fully consistent with the Book of Isaiah's depiction of Zion's ultimate character as international, as bringing nations together.[34] If the Zion concept is ultimately ecumenical, so is the historical event that contributed so much to that concept: Jerusalem owed its survival to an alliance of people of different cultures—Judahites, Egyptians, Kushites and, quite possibly, other sub-Saharan peoples with ties to the Kushite kingdom, either as subjects or allies.

THE RAMIFICATIONS OF the conflict of 701 were not so positive for the Kushites.

To be sure, their own performance that summer must be one of the great stories of military heroism. That we lack adequate records of their feat is no reason not to attempt to reconstruct its outlines.

The overriding preoccupation of the two Kushite pharaohs, Shabako and his son Shebitku, who probably ruled in a co-regency arrangement during these crisis years, was to save the Nile Valley from Assyrian invasion. Yet, after hearing desperate pleas from Hezekiah's emissaries to save Judah, the Kushites departed from the prudent strategy that they had used at least twice before[35] of waiting for the Assyrians to reach the Egyptian border before confronting them. Deploying large forces in Judah against Sennacherib represented a huge gamble. If those forces lost and suffered important casualties, Assyria could conquer the Nile Valley with little resistance; if they won, Egypt and Kush might keep Judah and adjacent kingdoms free of Assyrian domination indefinitely and win back trade access to markets in the eastern Mediterranean.

The interventionist strategy appears to have had two prongs. The first took advantage of Kush's celebrated equine prowess:

Shabako and Shebitku sent a small, fast-travelling unit composed mostly of chariotry and cavalry to confront Sennacherib. The Kushite-Egyptian contingent achieved success by slowing Sennacherib's advance and thus delaying his assault on Jerusalem and the completion of his conquest of Judah. This gave time for the pharaohs to prepare the other prong: a larger, slow-moving force composed mostly of foot soldiers and militia and perhaps mobilized from as far away as Kush and led by Shebitku's young cousin, Prince Taharqa. One can imagine the sense of desperation and physical strain as this army traveled more than 1,000 miles through Kush, Upper and Lower Egypt[36] and then another 300 miles east of the Nile across the grueling Sinai Desert under the sun to meet a foe that was more experienced and better equipped than itself—an army that was as strong, demonstrably cruel and insatiably power-hungry as antiquity had produced to that time. Catching Sennacherib flat-footed and out of position, Taharqa's army was able to liberate Jerusalem from siege and free the region from Assyrian imperialism for a generation.

But only a generation.

Kush and its allies within Egypt would pay dearly for their success. In 679, Sennacherib's son and successor, Esarhaddon, stormed back into Judah and its neighbors. And a few years later, when Taharqa was the pharaoh, his fate and that of his people became one of the great tragedies of history. Esarhaddon describes his invasion of Egypt in 671 in these chillingly vindictive terms:

> I fought daily, without interruption, very bloody battles against Tarqû [Taharqa], king of Egypt and Kush, the one accursed by the great gods. Five times I hit him with the point of my arrows, inflicting wounds from which he should not recover. . . .[37]

The victorious king goes on to explain what happened after he captured Taharqa's palace at Memphis:

> I destroyed it, tore down its walls and burnt it down. His "queen," the women of his palace, Ushanahuru his heir apparent, his other children, his possessions, horses, large and small cattle beyond

counting, I carried as booty to Assyria. All Kushites I deported
from Egypt—leaving not even one to do homage to me.

Yet the severely injured Taharqa did not die. He somehow recovered and defended Egypt against further Assyrian onslaughts for
another seven years before dying at age 56.

Impatient to end Kush's dogged hold on Egyptian territory and
on many native Egyptians' political loyalties, in 663 a new Assyrian king, Assurbanipal, marched against the new Kushite pharaoh,
Tanwetamani, Shebitku's younger brother. The pharaoh retreated
south to the great fortified city of Thebes, the religious and political capital of Upper Egypt. Because Thebes was the home of their
great deity Amon, much as Jerusalem was that of Yahweh, successive Kushite pharaohs had restored many of the city's neglected
great monuments and temples and built new ones. Once again,
Thebes had become storied throughout the Western world for its
grandeur, beauty and wealth.

Upon the approach of Assurbanipal's army, Tanwetamani left
Thebes, perhaps to spare the city from destructive all-out battle, and
retreated south again. Assurbanipal describes what happened next:

> . . . I, myself, conquered this town completely. From Thebes I car-
> ried away booty, heavy and beyond counting: silver, gold, precious
> stones, his entire personal possessions, linen garments with multi-
> colored trimmings, fine horses, certain inhabitants, male and
> female. I pulled two high obelisks, made of shining bronze, the
> weight of which was 2,500 talents, standing at the door of the tem-
> ple, . . . and took them to Assyria. Thus I carried off from Thebes
> heavy booty, beyond counting.
>
> I made Egypt and Kush feel my weapons bitterly and celebrated
> my triumph.[38]

The gusto with which Assyria carried out these invasions, and the
manner in which Esarhaddon glories in the severe injuries that
Taharqa himself suffers, testify to an unusual grudge toward the
Kushites. This frame of mind has puzzled historians. T.G.H.
James, for one, points out that the "enmity displayed by the Assyr-

ian kings, directed particularly at Taharqa personally, suggests that something more than simple imperial purposes prompted the successive Assyrian invasions of Egypt."[39] James does not offer a rationale for the punishing fury with which Assyria pursued Taharqa and his people. But with our new grasp of the Kushite role in the events of 701, we can understand the depth of the humiliation that Assyria sought to avenge.

For enabling Hebrew society to survive, Taharqa, his cousin Shebitku and his uncle Shabako are every bit as worthy of recognition as the celebrated Persian emperor, Cyrus the Great, who liberated the Hebrews from their Babylonian captivity in 538 BC and resettled them in the new Persian province of Judea.

THE POSSIBILITY CONCERNS me that some browsers looking at this book's concluding chapter may innocently draw the inference that unsympathetic writers of the Hebrew Bible have concealed the fact that Africans saved Jerusalem. That would simply create resentment—and conceivably add to strains in North America between blacks and Jews—where there is no cause. The point is worth restating: *the Bible has not deleted the Kushite role.*

The original biblical narrative (B¹), perhaps written within about half a century of the Deliverance, gave the credit for Sennacherib's withdrawal to the Kushites. The subsequent account (B²), written considerably later, greatly downplayed the Kushite role without erasing it: careful readers can still see that role. The reasons for this change in the story had nothing to do with the Kushites. One reason was contemporary Egypt: it had come under the control of a new government that was the enemy of Kushites and most Hebrews. The principle reason for obscuring Kush's part, however, was religious: a desire to give greater glory to Yahweh and to show that loyalty to him could bring deliverance. Outside the particular context of 701, the Hebrew Bible in fact praises the Kushites, treating them as pious exceptions in a pagan world, a people who are drawn to the worship of the Hebrews' own deity, Yahweh.

One of the most recent scholars to have perceived this is the French philospher and historian Ernest Renan. "It is remarkable," he writes in his *History of the People of Israel*, "that the Ethiopians [*i.e.*, Kushites] are always represented by the prophets as having a propensity for the worship of Yahweh, and that they for this reason were treated more favorably than the other *goyim* [nations]."[40] The timing of this properly generous insight is significant: Renan (1823-1892) was a member of the last European generation to have reached maturity prior to the colonization of Africa.[41]

If the Kushites' achievement in 701 is unknown to us today, it does not reflect on the integrity of biblical writers. Rather, it reflects on that of Western scholarship beginning in the late 19th century when the Western imperialist adventure in Africa got under way. As that invasion went into high gear, it relied heavily on the idea that if one's own civilization dominates other peoples, they must be inherently inferior. Their history, accordingly, must be worthless. The disdainful outlook has stuck. Ignoring all evidence to the contrary, most leading biblical scholars and Egyptologists claim to this day that the Hebrew Bible is contemptuous of Kushites and that their foreign policy and military performance were pitiable.

IN ITS TELLING of the invasion of 701, the Hebrew Bible makes it very clear that Jerusalem was unexpectedly saved and that the survivors and their descendants were filled with gratitude. The Hebrews had an acute understanding that salvation is too important to take for granted, and they reshaped their theology to account for it. In the invasion story's final version, the introduction of an angel as the agent of salvation symbolizes a caring deity who looked out for his people.

Nothing in this reconstruction of the events of 701 BC should serve to diminish either the deity's stature or Jerusalem's holiness. On the contrary, the reconstruction serves to flesh out the origins of the city's holy status and to show that, if Yahweh intervened to save the city, the deity did so not by acting vertically, through an angel, but horizontally, through people. It is a story that impels us to stand back and reflect that the original cause of Jerusalem's specialness has less to do with religious particularity than with universalism. It is a story that chimes neatly with Martin Buber's understanding of what the Zion concept stands for, a kind of supranational sense of fellowship, of good struggling valiantly for survival.

From the perspective of realism, is it not more credible that the rescue came from humans rather than an angel? From the perspective of religion, is the arrival of a friendly foreign army not a more uplifting explanation than those secular theories that hold that the reason for the city's Deliverance was an abject capitulation by the city's defenders? Or mere germs?

After all, a central tenet of all three religions—Judaism, Christianity and Islam alike—is that people should help each other.

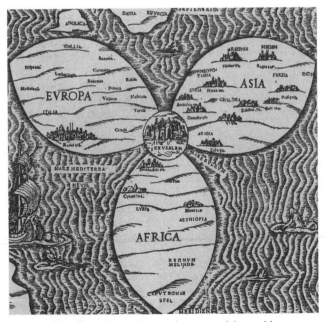

Woodcut of Jerusalem at the center of the world,
by Heinrich Brüntig, 1594

INTRODUCTION

[1] For the view that Egypt's pharaohs were black in many other dynasties besides the 25th, see Cheikh Anta Diop, "Origin of the Ancient Egyptians," in *General History of Africa II: Ancient Civilizations of Africa* (Paris: UNESCO, London: Heinemann Educational Books, Berkeley: University of California Press, 1981), pp. 27-51, and Martin Bernal, *Black Athena: The Afroasiatic Roots of Classical Civilization,* vol. 1: *The Fabrication of Ancient Greece* (London: Free Association Books, 1987), p. 242.

For rebuttals of that view, see: Frank M. Snowden, Jr., "Bernal's 'Blacks,' Herodotus, and Other Classical Evidence," in *Arethusa Special Issue* (1989), pp. 83-93; Kathryn Bard, "Ancient Egyptians and the Issue of Race," in *Bostonia* magazine (published by Boston University: Summer 1992), pp. 41ff.; Mary Lefkowitz, *Not out of Africa: How Afrocentrism Became an Excuse to Teach Myth as History* (New York: BasicBooks, 1996), and *Black Athena Revisited,* ed. by Mary R. Lefkowitz and Guy MacLean Rogers (Chapel Hill, NC, and London: University of North Carolina Press, 1996).

[2] There is unanimity among scholars that the Kushites were dark-skinned and in North American parlance, black.

Contemporary art is often cited in support of this. For example, numerous sculptural depictions exist of Taharqa, the longest-reigning of the four members of this dynasty. James Henry Breasted, *A History of Egypt: From the Earliest Times to the Persian Conquest* (London: Hodder & Stoughton, 1906), has noted that in these sculptures Taharqa's features "show unmistakable negroid characteristics" (p. 554). As well, an Assyrian stela at Zinjirli shows King Esarhaddon of Assyria facing a figure whom scholars commonly identify as either Taharqa or his son; the sculpted figure has distinctively black African features.

Nubia, as the land of the ancient Kushites is often called, corresponds to today's southern Egypt and northern Sudan. British archaeologist P. L. Shinnie, who has excavated Kushite sites, writes in *Meroe: A Civilization of the Sudan* (London: Thames and Hudson, 1967): "Nubia, together with most of the northern Sudan, is today inhabited by a predominantly brown-skinned people of aquiline features having in varying degrees an admixture of Negro, and there is no reason to suppose that the ancient populations were very different" (p. 155).

Historical anthropologist William Y. Adams, *Nubia: Corridor to Africa* (London: Allen Lane, 1977), says he is uncomfortable with any racial pigeonholing of today's Nubians. Adams says that "race is largely in the eye of the beholder; it is more a matter of social ascription than of biology, and its defining characteristics have changed from age to age and from place to place" (p. 8). He says of the Nubians: "They exhibit an old, stable blend of African Negro and Mediterranean Caucasian elements, in which the two strains are about equally represented" (p. 46).

Is there any reason to supppose that modern Nubians are of different background than ancient Kushites/Nubians? Adams, who also studied the evolution of Nubia's 3,000-year-old culture, has an answer. Like Shinnie, he sees population stability (rather than migratory change) as characterizing the region. He concludes: "There is no longer, today, any satisfactory reason for believing that the modern Nubians are a different people from the Nubians of antiquity or of any intervening period. On the contrary, I think everything points to their being the same people. That their numbers have been swelled by immigration, warlike as well as peaceful, from the north and from the south, goes without saying; that the intruders have occasionally and sometimes drastically upset the orderly processes of social and cultural development is likewise apparent. Yet the threads of cultural continuity from age to age are there for all to see. They provide the underlying warp for a tapestry of Nubian history extending from prehistoric times to the present" (p. 667).

In a more detailed discussion, Bruce Trigger, "Nubian, Negro, Black, Nilotic?" in *Africa in Antiquity*, vol. 1: *The Arts of Ancient Nubia and the Sudan* (New York: Brooklyn Museum, 1978), agrees with Shinnie and Adams that population stability has characterized the region but questions the scientific basis for assuming the Nubians are a blend of two racial strains. The anthropologist rejects the traditional classification of three races — white or Caucasoid, black or Negroid and yellow or Mongolian. He sees no reason to think that a "pure" version of each of these races exists and that a people like the Nubians who do not neatly fit into one of these three is necessarily a mixture of two or more of them (pp. 27-35). "Physical traits tend to vary in frequency from one region to another," he says, explaining: "This happens because natural selection operates upon specific genes, and individual characteristics are selected for or against at different rates and for different reasons in accordance with a wide range of environmental variations" (p. 27).

Trigger observes that skin color of the peoples of the Nile Valley, which runs from the Mediterranean to southern Sudan, is like a continuum. It ranges "from light brown to what appears to the eye as bluish black." He adds: "All these people are Africans. To proceed further and divide them into Caucasoid and Negroid stocks is to perform an act that is arbitrary and wholly devoid of historical or biological significance." Trigger goes on: "In the Nile Valley continuum, the modern Nubians occupy an intermediate position. Their skin color is medium brown, with considerable individual variation. Hair is frizzy or kinky, everted lips are common but not universal, and some people have sharp aquiline features" (p. 27).

In saying that all scholars agree that the Kushites were black as that term is commonly used in North America, then, I am not employing a racial categorization based on biology; rather, I am making, as Adams would put it, a "social ascription." My litmus test is simple: If Taharqa could have visited Alabama prior to the civil-rights movement, would he have been able to sit in the front of a bus? All scholars, I think, would agree the answer is no.

[3] Amélie Kuhrt, *The Ancient Near East, c. 3000-330 BC*, vol. 2 (London and New York: Routledge, 1995), p. 419.

[4] 2 Chronicles 28:8 (NRSV and TEV respectively).

[5] 2 Kings 14:13ff.

[6] Five of the families would have established dynasties. Two other kings, Pekah and Hoshea, would not have had the opportunity to pass on the crown to their progeny.

[7] In the last 10 or 15 years, some conventional historians, influenced by archaeological discoveries, have become increasingly critical of the Bible's depiction of the Hebrews as having lived in Egypt prior to the supposed Exodus. They say that a people that had spent centuries in Egypt should, in the generations immediately following their migration to a new land, still show signs of Egyptian acculturation (in architecture, for example, or pottery); yet these scholars note that abundant excavations have yet to turn up any such vestiges. As well, in sifting through the rubble of Canaanite cities that the Bible says the Israelite newcomers toppled, archaeologists have failed to find traces of such destruction in the appropriate time period.

For a critique of the traditional "Exodus-wilderness wanderings-conquest" version, see William G. Dever, "Israel, History of, Archaeology and the Conquest" in the *Anchor Bible Dictionary*, ed. by David Noel Freedman (New York: Doubleday, 1992), vol. 3, pp. 546-557. See also Dever, "Cultural Continuity, Ethnicity in the Archaeological Record and the Question of Israelite Origins," in *Eretz-Israel*, vol. 24 (1993), pp. 22-33. For an overview of more recent theories, see Dever's Anchor text and James D. Martin, "Israel as a Tribal Society," in *The World of Ancient Israel: Sociological, Anthropological and Political Perspectives*, ed. by R.E. Clements (Cambridge: Cambridge University Press, 1989), pp. 95-117).

Why should the biblical version be unreliable? Dever points out that many centuries separate the biblical writers from the 13th century. He goes on to say: "Ancient Israel's problem in comprehending her own history was the same as ours: how to account for the unique reality of the people of Israel. The biblical writers fell back on the only analogy they had, historical experience, which for them was their first-hand knowledge of the power of Yahweh over their pagan neighbors, and his ability to save and shape them as his people. . . ." (p. 557).

Donald B. Redford, "An Egyptological Perspective on the Exodus Narrative," in *Egypt, Israel, Sinai: Archaeological and Historical Relationships in the Biblical Period*, ed. by Anson F. Rainey (Tel Aviv University, 1987), also casts doubt on the historicity of the Exodus. He says a time frame in the 13th century BC is unlikely: the Exodus story's historical material and its place names (for example, "Land of Goshen"), he says, exclude that earlier period as a time of composition. Rather, he says, they point to the sixth century BC or later, at the time of the 26th or 27th dynasties, when the biblical writers would have drawn on contemporary names. He goes on to speculate that the Hebrews' liberation in the Exodus story may not be a "wholly late fabrication" but rather an embellishment of an earlier departure of some Semitic-speaking inhabitants of Egypt — who may not even have been Hebrews but, rather, the Hyskos (p. 150). See also the same writer's *Egypt, Canaan, and Israel in Ancient Times* (Princeton, NJ: Princeton University Press, 1992, pp. 408-422)

[8] Mark S. Smith, *The Early History of God: Yahweh and the Other Deities in Ancient Israel* (HarperSanFrancisco, 1990), p. *xxii*.

See also, Israel Finkelstein and Neil Asher Silberman, *The Bible Unearthed: Archaeology's New Vision of Ancient Israel and the Origin of Its Sacred Texts* (New York: Free Press, 2001): "The early Israelites were — irony of ironies — themselves originally Canaanites" (p. 118).

[9] David Jamieson-Drake, *Scribes and Schools in Monarchic Judah: A Socio-Archaeological Approach* (N.p.: Almond Press, 1991), pp. 139-143.

[10] Thomas L. Thompson, *Early History of the Israelite People: From the Written and Archaeological Sources* (Leiden: E.J. Brill, 1994), pp. 312-313, 412.

[11] Jamieson-Drake, *Scribes and Schools in Monarchic Judah*, p. 139. Also estimating that Judah in the eighth century BC had a population on the order of 100,000 are Finkelstein & Silberman, *Bible Unearthed*, p. 208.

[12] In 1993, the fragment of an inscription was found at Tel Dan, about 100 miles north of Jerusalem. The discoverer, Avraham Biran, dated the inscription to the early ninth century BC. The inscription made headlines around the world because it contains the word *bytdwd*, which some scholars translate as "House of David," or David's dynasty. This was hailed as archaeological proof that David had actually existed.

However, Niels Peter Lemche and Thomas L. Thompson, "Did Biran Kill David? The Bible in the Light of Archaeology," in *Journal for the Study of the Old Testament* 64 (1994), pp. 3-22, contest this interpretation. Calling the original research "pseudo-scholarship," Lemche & Thompson suggest *bytdwd* means "temple of the beloved." They say the text may date almost 150 years later than claimed and propose that the text may refer to Yahweh's temple.

[13] *Ibid.*, p. 19.

[14] *Ibid.*, p. 18.

[15] Herbert Niehr, "The Rise of YHWH in Judahite and Israelite Religion: Methodological and Religio-Historical Aspects," in *The Triumph of Elohim: From Yahwisms to Judaisms*, ed. by Diana Vikander Edelman (Grand Rapids, MI: William B. Eerdmans Publishing, 1996), p. 49.

[16] This affinity is described in vague and cautious terms by Philip R. Davies, *In Search of 'Ancient Israel'* (Sheffield, UK: JSOT Press, 1992): ". . . although we have no extra-biblical evidence that Judah was ever thought of as Israel, it is possible to conceive that the two kingdoms were, in the eyes of Israel and perhaps even in Judah, part of 'greater Israel'. This state of affairs would offer one historical basis for the subsequent adoption of the identity of 'Israel' by inhabitants of the Jerusalem state, if that is what happened" (pp. 69-70).

Thompson, *Early History of the Israelite People*, disagrees. He says that "just as the origin of the ninth- and seventh-century states of Israel and Judah were wholly separate, they were also unlikely to have had any more common an ethnic base than any other two neighboring states of the Southern Levant" (p. 412).

[17] An additional reason that the biblical version of history becomes relatively reliable starting with events in the eighth century BC is that Hebrew culture appears at that time to have first used alphabetic writing. The earliest inscriptions from Judah and Israel that archaeologists have found date from that period, according to Nadav Na'aman, "The 'Conquest of Canaan' in the Book of Joshua and in History," in *From Nomadism to Monarchy: Archaeological and Historical Aspects of Early Israel*, ed. by Israel Finkelstein and Nadav Na'aman (Jerusalem: Yad Izhak Ben-Zvi and Israel Exploration Society; Washington, DC: Biblical Archaeology Society, 1994), pp. 219-222. Na'aman speculates that prior to that time the royal courts of Samaria and Jerusalem might have used writing, but presumably largely for record-keeping by a "few professional scribes." Because the "development of historiography is necessarily connected with the emergence of a wide circle of readers who can appreciate the literary quality of the compo-

sition and understand its meaning and objectives," the "earliest possible date for the onset of historical writing" in Hebrew society, he concludes, would have been the eighth century BC.

CHAPTER ONE

[1] Another view, based on taking 2 Kings 18:22 at face value, is that sometime prior to the Assyrian invasion Jerusalem's king would have abolished all outlying places of worship of Yahweh and ordered that the city's temple become the exclusive location for such worship. If this view is correct, however, the centralization of the Yahweh cult at Jerusalem would have been relatively recent, it would have been controversial (especially among disenfranchised priests at these outlying sites) and much of the kingdom's outlying population would not have respected it (as archaeological evidence, to be discussed in Chapter 4, appears to suggest). Whatever singularly holy status Jerusalem might have had among the general population prior to the invasion, then, would have been tentative.

[2] Passages from the Book of Isaiah referred to or quoted from earlier in this chapter are (in order): 10:27-31; 22:3 (NEB); 1:21-23 (NRSV) and 10:1-6; 1:4 (NEB); 10:32; 22:7 (TEV); 22:5 (NRSV); 30:14 (NRSV); 22:2, 13 (NRSV); 10:6 (NRSV); 1:4,9-10; 3:9.

In the Book of Isaiah, some passages' context is unclear; it can be hard to tell to which of several armed conflicts the prophet may be referring. For an analysis that concludes that Isaiah 1:4-9 pertains implicitly to the crisis of 701 BC, see John A. Emerton, "The Historical Background of Isaiah 1:4-9," in *Eretz-Israel: Archaeological, Historical and Geographic Studies*, 24 (Jerusalem: Israel Exploration Society, 1993), pp. 39-40. For the view that 22:7 evokes the Assyrian invasion, see Francolino J. Gonçalves, *L'expédition de Sennachérib en Palestine dans la littérature hébraïque ancienne* (Paris: Librairie Lecoffre, J. Gabalda, 1986), p. 241; also p. 105.

This chapter's reconstruction of events also uses parts of the invasion narrative presented in 2 Kings 18-19/Isaiah 36-37.

Some of the passages in the Book of Isaiah and Second Kings that relate to the invasion, including statements attributed to Isaiah to the effect that Judah's deity would save (not destroy) the kingdom, have not been included in this reconstruction for reasons that later chapters will explain.

Some other parts of this reconstruction of the invasion, including the "bird in a cage" passage, are from the Assyrian record in *Ancient Near Eastern Texts Relating to the Old Testament*, 3rd ed. with supplement, ed. by James B. Pritchard (Princeton: Princeton University Press, 1969), p. 287-288. The fate of Lachish, including that of Assyria's prisoners, is based on Sennacherib's bas-relief on the siege of that city.

[3] 2 Kings 18:5-6, 2 Chronicles 29-32.

[4] Daniel David Luckenbill, *Ancient Records of Assyria and Babylon*, vol. 2: *Historical Records of Assyria from Sargon to the End* (Chicago: University of Chicago Press, 1927), pp. 140, 173, 178-179, 183, 188, 191-194, 196-198. He called himself this on well over a dozen different surviving records, including wall inscriptions.

[5] In his 500-page analysis of the Bible's so-called B² account of the invasion, which was probably written a century or more after the event and which will be described in Chapter 10, Gonçalves, *L'expédition de Sennachérib*, concludes that the story's objective

is to "show that, in keeping his promise to protect Jerusalem and to save it, Yahweh revealed himself as the true God. In preventing Assyria from taking Jerusalem, Yahweh succeeded in doing what no other god had been able to do in support of his own people. The Angel of Yahweh even decimated the Assyrian army, which had previously destroyed the gods of other nations" (p. 479). Gonçalves' reference to the destruction of gods, or idols, is from 2 Kings 19:18, in which the Assyrians pitch idols of conquered peoples into the fire.

[6] R.E. Clements, *Isaiah and the Deliverance of Jerusalem: A Study of the Interpretation of Prophecy in the Old Testament* (Sheffield, UK: JSOT Press, 1980), pp. 72-83.

[7] Bernard J. Bamberger, *The Story of Judaism* (New York: Union of American Hebrew Congregations, 1957), p. 22.

[8] In addition, the Assyrian invasion of 701 BC is summarized in Ecclesiasticus (or the Wisdom of Sirach), one of the books of the "deutero-canonical" category (the so-called Apocrypha), which Roman Catholics deem to be sacred canon but Jewish and Protestant authorities do not. The summary in Ecclesiasticus (48:17-25) dates from the second century BC.

Brief echoes of the invasion also find their way into deutero-canonical works elsewhere: 1 Maccabees 8:41-42 and 2 Maccabees 8:19 and 15:22-24. These date from the second or first centuries BC.

Sennacherib's attack on Judah, in other words, reverberated for centuries.

[9] Exodus 20: 1-17 and Deuteronomy 5:6-21.

The Hebrew Bible makes references to certain events (such as the Exodus journey) many times. So far as extended narratives are concerned, however, only the Deliverance of Jerusalem receives such multiple treatment.

[10] Cecil Roth, *A History of the Jews* (New York: Schocken, 1961), p. 42.

[11] Karen Armstrong, *Jerusalem: One City, Three Faiths* (New York: Alfred A. Knopf, 1996), p. 70.

[12] One scholar whose interest in these ramifications also deserves mention is Sara Japhet, of the Hebrew University: later on, I will be quoting repeatedly from her perceptive 1997 article.

[13] 2 Kings 19:35 (NIV).

[14] Exodus 14.

[15] Robert R. Wilson, "2 Kings," in *The HarperCollins Study Bible*, ed. by Wayne A. Meeks (New York: HarperCollins, 1993), p. 594.

[16] *ANET*, p. 287.

[17] 2 Kings 19:9.

[18] Frank J. Yurco, "Sennacherib's Third Campaign and the Coregency of Shabaka and Shebitku," in *Serapis: The American Journal of Egyptology* 6 (1980), pp. 225-228. Yurco estimates at least a month's interval between the departures of the two armies, the second being from Kush.

For a variation of this, see K.A. Kitchen, *The Third Intermediate Period in Egypt*, 2nd ed. with supplement (Warminster, UK: Aris & Phillips, 1986). He argues that the 25th

Dynasty's forces would have arrived in Philistia in one large group, and then split into two divisions — one confronting the Assyrians at Eltekeh and the second flirting with the idea of a further attack before returning to Egypt. Kitchen sees Kush as the source of this main body of soldiers; Taharqa would have led them on the long journey (pp. 157-158, 557).

[19] That Taharqa at that time was a prince and not the king of Kush, as 2 Kings 19:9 so identifies him, will be discussed in Chapter 8.

[20] K.A. Kitchen, "Late-Egyptian Chronology and the Hebrew Monarchy," *The Journal of the Ancient Near Eastern Society of Columbia University* 5 (1973), pp. 229-233. Kitchen demonstrates that in 701 BC Taharqa was not the youngster of about nine that some earlier scholars had assumed. See also Kitchen, *Third Intermediate Period*, pp. 157-160.

[21] Breasted, *History of Egypt*, p. 552.

[22] Adams, *Nubia*, p. 264.

[23] Kenneth A. Kitchen, "Egypt," in *Baker Encyclopedia of Bible Places*, ed. by John J. Bimson (Grand Rapids, MI: Baker Books, 1995), p. 117.

In his *Third Intermediate Period*, Kitchen says that in the face of Assyria's might Taharqa and his forces "swiftly retired homewards to Egypt." They can, Kitchen says, "hardly be said to have covered themselves with glory by feat of arms" (pp. 385-386).

Another recent and severe judgment is by T.G.H. James, "Egypt: The Twenty-fifth and Twenty-sixth Dynasties," in *The Cambridge Ancient History*, 2nd ed., vol. 3, pt. 2 (Cambridge: Cambridge University Press, 1991). He says that in 701 "Taharqa may have been taught a severe lesson," and that he "presumably led his own force back to Egypt, possibly never having been engaged, and scarcely in triumph" (p. 696). See also Nicolas Grimal, *A History of Ancient Egypt*, trans. from the French by Ian Shaw (Oxford: Blackwell, 1992). He says, "The Assyrians attacked the Egyptian troops and Taharqa chose to withdraw to Egypt" (p. 347).

[24] Chapter 18 will explore their wobbly reliance on 2 Kings 18:21.

[25] Strabo, *Geography*, I.3.21. The version this book is using is *The Geography of Strabo*, trans. from the Greek by Horace Leonard Jones (London: Willam Heinemann; Cambridge, MA: Harvard University Press, 1966), vol. 1, pp. 227, 229. Strabo uses the name "Tearko the Ethiopian" for Taharqa. Strabo also refers to the far-ranging military campaigns of Taharqa, this time spelled "Tearco," in XV.1.16 (vol. 7, pp. 7-9).

CHAPTER TWO

[1] Hayim Tadmor, "Philistia Under Assyrian Rule," in *The Biblical Archaeologist* 34 (1966), p. 88.

[2] A. Malamat, "Introduction," *A History of the Jewish People*, ed. by H.H. Ben-Sasson (Cambridge, MA: Harvard University Press, 1976), notes that the region was "important as a bridgehead, and its conquest was a prerequisite for any attack by one power upon another. It is not surprising, therefore, that Palestine and Syria served as international battlegrounds more often than any other area in the ancient world" (p.6).

[3] The term is used in an inscription of Taharqa's found at Thebes. See Pascal Vernus, "Inscriptions de la troisième période intermédiaire," in *Bulletin de l'Institut français*

d'architecture orientale 75 (1975), p. 31 and a note on pp. 45-46. Also using the form "Khor" is Anthony Spalinger, "The Foreign Policy of Egypt Preceding the Assyrian Conquest" in *Chronique d'Égypte* (Brussels: Fondation Egyptologique Reine Elisabeth, January 1978), pp. 32, 43. Another form of the same term is "Khurru," as translated by Kitchen, Third Intermediate Period, p. 558.

The precise extent of the territory covered by the term "Khor," as it was used by the ancient Egyptians, is unclear. The definition this book gives to the term should not be seen as the original definition.

[4] Kathleen M. Kenyon, *Archaeology in the Holy Land*, 3rd ed. (London: Ernest Benn, 1970 {1960}), points out geography's role in explaining why Israel's proximity to such sophisticated cultures as Phoenicia and Syria helps account for its cultural advance on Judah. "Judah," she notes, "was shut in between Israel, with whom she was usually at war, the backward and warlike kingdoms of Transjordan to the east, and the desert to the south" (p. 260).

[5] T.C. Mitchell, "Israel and Judah from the Coming of Assyrian Domination until the Fall of Samaria, and the Struggle for Independence in Judah," in *Cambridge Ancient History*, vol. 3, pt. 2, p. 326, and E.W. Heaton, *The Hebrew Kingdoms* (London: Oxford University Press, 1968), p. 21, both estimate Israel's population at 800,000 and Judah's at 200,000 in the eighth century BC. John Bright, *A History of Israel*, 2nd ed. (Philadelphia: Westminster Press, 1972), says Judah's population "probably exceeded 250,000" (p. 344).

Traditionalists believe those figures too conservative, while minimalists see them as inflated. At the time of Israel's collapse, the minimalist Jamieson-Drake says Judah may have had just 100,000 people; see *Scribes and Schools in Monarchic Judah*, p. 139.

[6] Israel Finkelstein, "The Archaeology of the Days of Manasseh," in *Scripture and Other Artifacts: Essays on the Bible and Archaeology in Honor of Philip J. King*, ed. by M.D. Coogan, J.C. Exum and L.E. Stager (Louisville: Westminster John Knox Press, 1994), p. 176.

[7] In looking through the conventional lens (and, for that matter, the traditional lens), we would reach the following conclusion about overall Hebrew society at the time of Sennacherib's invasion: never, in the three centuries since the establishment of the united monarchy, would the Hebrew people have been so few in number, controlling so little territory, possessing so little wealth and capable of mobilizing so few soldiers in their own defense.

It is the view of some minimalists that Judah in the years leading up to Sennacherib's attack would have been on an unprecedented upswing. The influx of refugees from Samaria might have given it demographic and economic strength. (Indeed, Judah's rebellious provocation of the Assyrian invasion would itself have been a symptom of new confidence.) Yet Judah was coming from so far back, from the humble status of chiefdom, that despite this progress it was still only a petty kingdom. For Thompson, *Early History of the Israelite People*, Jerusalem itself was more like a "small town" than the capital of a bonafide "nation-state," as in the case of Samaria (pp. 410-412). In terms of soldiery, then, the minimalists' Judah would have been even weaker than almost all historians until recently have supposed: the manpower pool from which it could conscript peasants and others to help defend itself would have been smaller than in the other model.

The two scenarios depict Judah in differing trajectories: both the traditional and conventional perspectives present Judahite society's strength as falling, while the minimalist sees it as ascending, but both curves plot Judah at a point on the scale of political and socio-economic robustness in 701 that is very low. This is especially true of the minimalist vision.

In an enlightening article published in 1996, a conventional historian notably free of rigidity, Nadav Na'aman, reviews minimalist claims for Judah on the basis of his examination of archaeological evidence and his extrapolations of Egyptian documents (the Amarna letters) that pertain to Jerusalem in the 14th century BC. Na'aman, of Tel Aviv University's department of Jewish history, concludes: "Judah in the late tenth-ninth centuries B.C.E. was a peripheral small and powerless kingdom governed by its local dynasty from the highland stronghold of Jerusalem" ("The Contribution of the Amarna Letters to the Debate on Jerusalem's Political Position in the Tenth Century B.C.E.," in *Bulletin of the American Schools of Oriental Research* 304, p. 24.)

Na'aman, one of today's leading specialists on the monarchical period, arrives at a kind of compromise position between the two schools. He says that Judahites would have deemed their rulers to be kings, not chiefs; he therefore makes "kingdom" the preferred term. Nonetheless, he agrees that by the modern sociological definition Judah at that time would have been a "chiefdom." He also agrees that it "was transformed to a state only in the eighth century B.C.E." (p. 25).

[8] 2 Kings 16:7-9.

[9] Yohanan Aharoni, *Land of the Bible: A Historical Geography*, trans. from the Hebrew by A. F. Rainey (Philadelphia: Westminster Press (1962?), pp. 327-328; J. Maxwell Miller and John H. Hayes, *A History of Ancient Israel and Judah* (Philadelphia: Westminster, 1986), p. 343; and Stuart A. Irvine, *Isaiah, Ahaz, and the Syro-Ephraimite Crisis* (Atlanta: Scholars Press, 1990), pp. 298-299. These authors argue that Israel's prime motive for trying to conquer Judah was to mobilize it against Assyria. Mitchell, "Israel and Judah," speculates that Israel and Syria sought to take control from Judah of a valuable south-north trade route from Arabia that ran outside Judah through the Transjordan (p. 329). A desperate desire to marshal a maximum amount of military resistance against Assyrian aggression may better explain the invasion of Judah at this time, though this does not exclude an additional economic motive of such a sort.

[10] As estimated from Aharoni's map, *Land of the Bible*, p. 332.

[11] This is how Miller & Hayes, *Israel and Judah*, interpret Isaiah 8:5-7 and 8:11-15 (pp. 343-344). See, too, Irvine, *Isaiah, Ahaz*. He suggests the polarization would have pitched Ahaz, the royal court, Jerusalem's population and perhaps the military against "most Judeans," who might have seen Ahaz's refusal to join the coalition as "treason against his Israelite superior" (pp. 298-299).

[12] Hayim Tadmor, "Period of the First Temple," in *History of the Jewish People*, ed. by H.H. Ben-Sasson, op. cit., pp. 135-136.

[13] 2 Kings 17:4.

[14] The 723 date, which concurs with an earlier independent calculation by Hayim Tadmor, is from Bob Becking, *The Fall of Samaria: An Historical and Archaeological Study* (Leiden: E.J. Brill, 1992), pp. 38, 56.

[15] Mitchell, "Israel and Judah," p. 340.

[16] This policy is well described by Siegfried Herrmann, *A History of Israel in Old Testament Times*, rev. and enlarged ed. (Philadelphia: Fortress Press, 1975), p. 245, and also by Herbert Donner, "The Separate States of Israel and Judah," in *Israelite and Judean History*, ed. by John H. Hayes and J. Maxwell Miller (London: SCM Press Ltd., 1977), p. 419.

[17] *ANET*, p. 285.

[18] Favoring the later date is I.M. Diakonoff, "The Cities of the Medes," *Ah, Assyria . . .: Studies in Assyrian History and Ancient Near Eastern Historigraphy: Presented to Hayim Tadmor*, ed. by Mordechai Cogan and Israel Eph'al, Scripta Hierosolymitana, vol. 33 (Jerusalem: Magnes Press, Hebrew University, 1991), p. 13. Becking, Fall of Samaria, says the deportation was in 720 but that "it took a few years for the deportees to reach their final destination" (p. 72).

[19] There is no reason to believe the exiles were persecuted in their new homelands; certainly, the thousands of elite deportees from elsewhere in the empire prospered after they replaced the Hebrews in what had been Israel.

As Diakonoff, *ibid.*, points out, when in the sixth century BC the later Judahite exiles were allowed to return to Judah from Mesopotamia, these exiles appear to have made no "attempt to find the 'ten lost tribes' and to repatriate them" (p. 20). He says "most of these must have irrevocably merged with the local population." Herrmann, *History of Israel*, also notes that "we cannot even recognize the deportees as a coherent group at a later date" (p. 243).

[20] 1 Kings 14:25-26.

For Shishak's invasion of Israel, which Kings does not mention, see Nadav Na'aman, "The Contribution of Royal Inscriptions for a Re-evaluation of the Book of Kings as a Historical Source," *Journal for the Study of the Old Testament* 82 (1999). p. 12.

[21] *ANET*, p. 287.

[22] The Assyrians had left in place part of Israel's original population, mostly the peasantry. Doing so ensured uninterrupted agricultural production. After the arrival of masses of newcomers, this remaining population was too dispersed and leaderless to give coherence or continuity to Hebrew society.

[23] 2 Kings 18:31-32.

[24] *Encyclopaedia Judaica* describes Graetz's book as the "first comprehensive attempt to write the history of the Jews as the history of a living people and from a Jewish point of view" (Samuel Ettinger, "Graetz, Heinrich," in *Encyclopaedia Judaica*, vol. 7 {Jerusalem: Encyclopaedia Judaica; New York: Macmillan, 1971}, p. 848.) In this book, Graetz has this to say about Sennacherib's design to conquer Jerusalem: "If this plan had succeeded, Jerusalem would have suffered a fate similar to that of Samaria, and the few remaining tribes would have been carried off into captivity and scattered abroad, to be irretrievably lost amongst the various nationalities" (Graetz, *History of the Jews*, vol. 1, p. 273).

[25] Mordechai Cogan, "Into Exile: From the Assyrian Conquest of Israel to the Fall of Babylon," in *The Oxford History of the Biblical World*, ed. by Michael D. Coogan (New York, Oxford: Oxford University Press, 1998), p. 335.

Just as emphatic is Cogan's Hebrew University colleague, biblical specialist Sara Japhet, "From the King's Sanctuary to the Chosen City," in *Judaism: A Quarterly Journal of Jewish Life and Thought* 182 (Spring 1997): "The historical and political meaning of these events [of 701] cannot be overstated: . . . the conquest of Jerusalem would have meant the end of Judah, and with it the end of the national entity called Israel" (p. 135).

[26] William H. McNeill, "Infectious Alternatives," in *The Quarterly Journal of Military History* 10, 1998, p. 80.

CHAPTER THREE

[1] Japhet, "From the King's Sanctuary to the Chosen City," p. 135.

[2] Isaiah 49:6 (TEV).

[3] H.H. Rowley, *The Biblical Doctrine of Election* (London: Lutterworth Press, 1950), p. 121.

[4] Donald Harman Akenson, *Surpassing Wonder: The Invention of the Bible and the Talmuds* (Montreal and Kingston: McGill-Queen's University Press, 1998), p. 12.

[5] Rowley, *Biblical Doctrine of Election*, p. 147. Rowley adds: "It was in this belief that the Church continued to use the Jewish Scriptures. They were part of its heritage. . . ." (p. 147).

[6] Exodus 19:5 (NRSV).

[7] Exodus 20, Deuteronomy 5.

[8] 2 Kings 18:6 (NRSV).

[9] See, for example, Yehezkel Kaufmann, *The Religion of Israel: From Its Beginnings to the Babylonian State*, trans. and abridged by Moshe Greenberg (London: George Allen & Unwin, 1961), speaks of Moses' "monotheistic revolution." He says: "By making Israel enter a covenant with the only God, he made it a monotheistic people that alone among men was punishable for the sin of idolatry" (p. 230). Irving M. Zeitlin, *Ancient Judaism: Biblical Criticism from Max Weber to the Present* (Cambridge, UK: Polity Press, 1984), also argues that Israel's faith was monotheistic from the time that Yahweh revealed his will to Moses on Mount Sinai (p. 260).

[10] Exodus 20:3, Deuteronomy 5:7 (NRSV).

Moses, and those who followed his precept, would thus not have been monotheistic but monolatrous — that is, worshipping one god to the exclusion of others.

See Theophile James Meek, *Hebrew Origins*, rev. ed. (Toronto: University of Toronto Press, 1950), p. 204 ff., and Roland de Vaux, *The Early History of Israel*, trans. from the French by David Smith (Philadelphia: Westminster Press, 1978), pp. 462-4).

[11] For example, dating the psalm to the 6th century BC is David Noel Freedman, "The Twenty-third Psalm," in *Michigan Oriental Studies in Honor of George G. Cameron*, ed. by Louis L. Orlis (Ann Arbor, MI: University of Michigan, 1976), p. 165. See also Michael L. Barré and John S. Kselman, "New Exodus, Covenant, and Restoration in

Psalm 23," in *The Word of the Lord Shall Go Forth: Essays in Honor of David Noel Freedman in Celebration of His Sixtieth Birthday*, edited by Carol L. Meyers and M. O'Connor (Winona Lake, IN: Eisenbrauns, 1983). These authors find in Psalm 23 themes of the seventh and sixth centuries BC (pp. 97-98, 114-115).

[12] My use of the word "several" is deliberately vague. The perspective to be attributed to these time-travellers would fit many Jerusalemites of the late sixth century BC, according to the conventional view of the evolution of religious thought; however, according to some minimalists' chronology, it would more properly correspond to beliefs and practices as late as the second century BC. See below.

[13] In 701 BC, the typical shrine was a place whose rituals were focused on sacrifice; they required the presence of priests. At the synagogue, on the other hand, it was teachers who were necessary: they gave instruction in Moses' law. Synagogues could therefore have evolved only after 701; it may have been only during the Exile, or later, that they began to evolve. See, for example, T.C. Mitchell, "The Babylonian Exile and the Restoration of the Jews in Palestine," *Cambridge Ancient History*, vol. 3, pt. 2, pp. 424-425. Also: H. Jagersma, *A History of Israel from Alexander the Great to Bar Kochba*, trans. from the Dutch by John Bowden (London: SCM Press, 1985), p. 122; Yehezkel Kaufmann, *History of the Religion of Israel*, vol. 4, *From the Babylonian Captivity to the End of Prophecy*, trans. from the Hebrew by C.W. Efroymson (New York: KTAV Publishing House Inc., 1977), p. 32; Hans-Joachim Kraus, *Worship in Israel: A Cultic History of the Old Testament*, trans. from the German by Geoffrey Buswell (Oxford: Basil Blackwell, 1966), pp. 229-230; Morton Smith, *Palestinian Parties and Politics that Shaped the Old Testament* (New York and London: Columbia University Press, 1971), p. 55. For a recent discussion, see Lee I. Levine, "The Nature and Origin of the Palestinian Synagogue Reconsidered," in *Journal of Biblical Literature* 115 (1996), pp. 425-448.

[14] Many Jerusalemites of that time may have used that day to rest from work, but not to worship. See Morton Smith, *Palestinian Parties*, p. 55, and U. Cassuto, *A Commentary on the Book of Genesis*, pt. 1, trans. from the Hebrew by Israel Abrahams (Jerusalem: Magnes Press, 1978 {1944}), p. 68.

[15] See below.

[16] Robert H. Pfeiffer, *Religion in the Old Testament: The History of a Spiritual Triumph*, ed. by Charles Conrad Forman (London: Adam & Charles Black, 1961) is one of many scholars to identify Second Isaiah, the prophet of the sixth century BC, as the first Hebrew to proclaim monotheism (pp. 171-172). Among the more recent writers who support this view is Norman Cohn, *Cosmos, Chaos and the World to Come: The Ancient Roots of Apocalyptic Faith* (New Haven and London: Yale University Press, 1993). He says: "If one excludes the case of Zoroaster, which is debatable and much debated, Second Isaiah is the first monotheist we know of" (p. 152). (He makes no reference to Akhenaten.) Similarly, Mark Smith, *Early History of God*, asserts, "Texts dating to the Exile are the first to attest to unambiguous expression of Israelite monotheism" (p. 152). Another expert on the evolution of the Yahweh concept, Peter Machinist, "The Question of Distinctiveness in Ancient Israel: An Essay," *Ah, Assyria . . . , op. cit.*) is only slightly less specific: monotheism "is attested only late in Israel, *i.e.*, the late pre-Exilic or, better, Exilic period" (p. 201 n. 19).

[17] Thompson, *Early History*, says monotheism would have emerged in "a mid- and a late-Persian period intellectual milieu in Palestine" — that is, the fifth and fourth centuries BC (p. 422). Thompson in his subsequent "The Intellectual Matrix of Early Biblical Narrative: Inclusive Monotheism in Persian Period Palestine," in *Triumph of Elohim, op. cit.*, says the idea of monotheism may have been further shaped during the third and second centuries BC; nationalist Hebrews of that period may have affirmed the exclusive worship of Yahweh as "indigenous tradition" in the face of the dominating Greek culture (pp. 123-124). See also Diana Vikander Edelman, "Introduction," *Triumph of Elohim, op. cit.*, pp. 19, 23-24.

[18] Morton Smith, *Palestinian Parties*, p. 19.

[19] *Ibid.*, pp. 24-25.

[20] A British writer, Michael Grant, expresses this viewpoint succinctly: "Although the Bible declares it to have been a stark choice between Yahwist monotheism and Canaanite polytheism, the situation was in reality much more blurred. Many people, while accepting Yahweh's pre-eminence, continued to worship the deities of Canaan, on whose side wealth and science and culture stood; while others worshipped Yahweh himself as though he was a Canaanite deity." See Grant, *The History of Ancient Israel* (New York: Charles Scribner's Sons, 1984), p. 61.

[21] Though the Bible presents Yahweh as a celibate, non-sexual deity, these historians suggest that in this early period the goddess Asherah would actually have been his consort. This divine couple, they say, would have been at the summit of a pantheon of lesser deities. See Susan Ackerman, *Under Every Green Tree: Popular Religion in Sixth-Century Judah*, Harvard Semitic Monographs 46 (Atlanta: Scholars Press, 1992), pp. 215, 217; Lowell K. Handy, "The Appearance of Pantheon in Judah," *Triumph of Elohim, op. cit.*, p. 39ff.; Niehr, "Rise of YHWH," pp. 60-63, and Thompson, "Intellectual Matrix," p. 119, n. 13.

[22] J. Alberto Soggin, *Introduction to the Old Testament: From Its Origins to the Closing of the Alexandrian Canon*, 3rd ed., trans. from the Italian by John Bowden (London: SCM Press (1989), compares the biblical version of history with scholars' understanding of it. The "argument" of the Hebrew Bible, he observes, is that the "religion of Israel was originally already monotheistic, pure and incorrupt; it would then have been contaminated in contact with that of Canaan, giving rise to unacceptable forms of syncretism." This last word describes the polytheistic tendency of combining the worship of Yahweh with that of other deities. Referring to the idea of Moses-era monotheism, Soggin says: "But this concept is based on the presupposition of a glorious past which gave way to decadence, and thus on a variant of the myth of the golden age, so it cannot be sustained on a historical-critical level. If we can trust the few pieces of information at our disposal, the process must have been precisely the opposite" (pp. 262-263).

[23] Morton Smith, *Palestinian Parties*, p. 18.

[24] Says the minimalist Handy, "Appearance of Pantheon in Judah": "The religious vision of the state of Judah was of a piece with that of her neighbors . . ." (p. 42). Niehr, "Rise of YHWH," also notes that the religions of Judah and Israel "have to be judged as local variants of northwest Semitic religions in Palestine during the first millennium BCE" (p. 50).

²⁵ See Isaiah 1:11-20.

²⁶ Bright, *History of Israel*, p. 276, citing Isaiah 1:10-17.

²⁷ Micah 3:11 (NEB).

²⁸ That is the common interpretation of 2 Kings 18:4: as part of his Yahwist reform upon taking power, Hezekiah "broke in pieces the bronze snake that Moses had made, which was called Nehushtan" (TEV). The bronze snake was evidently based on the tradition, in Numbers 21:4-9, that Moses had made a "metal snake and put it on a pole, so that anyone who was bitten would look at the bronze snake and be healed" (TEV). Meek, incidentally, observes that this worship of the bronze snake up to Hezekiah's time undercuts some scholars' claim that Moses was a monotheist; if Moses was a monotheist, Meek argues, "tradition would assuredly never have connected him with the bronze serpent" (*Hebrew Origins*, p. 211).

²⁹ R.E. Clements, *Deuteronomy* (Sheffield, UK: JSOT Press, 1989), pp. 10, 69ff. Also, Joachim Becker, *Messianic Expectation in the Old Testament*, translated from the German by David E. Green (Philadephia: Fortress Press, 1980 {1977}), notes in passing that "the Sinai tradition . . . is not yet known to Isaiah, who is steeped in the tradition of Jerusalem" (p. 28). Indeed, despite their emphasis on the right conduct for Yahwists, Isaiah's authentic oracles allude neither to Moses nor to the Exodus. (Isaiah 10:24-26 is widely seen as inauthentic.) Chapter 4 will discuss what is meant by the Book of Isaiah's "authentic" passages.

³⁰ Clements, *Deuteronomy*, pp. 41-42; Pfeiffer, *Religion in the Old Testament*, p. 54; Soggin, *Introduction*, p. 148, and John Van Seters, "'Comparing Scripture with Scripture': Some Observations on the Sinai Pericope of Exodus 19-24," in *Canon, Theology and Old Testament Interpretation: Essays in Honor of Brevard S. Childs*, ed. by Gene M. Tucker, David L. Peterson and Robert R. Wilson (Philadelphia: Fortress Press, 1988), pp. 127-128.

³¹ See R.E. Clements, *God's Chosen People: A Theological Interpretation of the Book of Deuteronomy* (London: SCM Press, 1968), pp. 24-25, and Robert H. Pfeiffer, "Canon of the Old Testament," in *The Interpreter's Dictionary of the Bible*, vol. 1, op. cit., 498. Pfeiffer observes: "Every sentence in the Old Testament was profane before it became canonical scripture" (p. 499).

³² Pfeiffer, "Canon." p. 499.

³³ Although she is a minimalist, Edelman, "Introduction," probably does not differ from many conventional scholars in describing the process this way:

"It is important to realize that the text of the Hebrew Bible is the product of a long, editorial process. Its final shapers were monotheistic and they wanted the inherited traditions to reflect their own religious beliefs in a single creator deity, Yahweh, who had at his command various lesser divine beings who also populated heaven, the angels. Had they created the texts themselves, they almost certainly would not have included the scattered references to Asherah, Nehushtan, Plague, Pestilence, Death, Sun, Moon and other lesser deities, which they have gone out of their way to turn into cultic objects used in the worship of Yahweh or turn into mere abstract qualities. Having inherited sources that were used to create the texts, if not some of the texts themselves, they apparently felt constrained to maintain these references, yet obligated at the same time to neutralize them in a way that would make them acceptable within their own, later religious world view. This suggests that some texts already enjoyed the status of 'classics' and so could not be discarded wholesale. Earlier generations may have had more freedom to edit such texts more extensively and delete direct references to deities other than Yahweh that were not easily understood within an emerging monotheistic framework, before certain texts became 'classics.' It is unknown, then, how much information about the cult of Yahweh during the period that the state of Judah existed . . . has been deliberately excised from the books that make up the Hebrew Bible through the centuries. We are extremely fortunate to have the few remnants that remain, even though they have been altered from their original meanings and referents in the vast majority of cases" (pp. 16-17).

[34] See, for example, Kraus, *Worship*, who says circumcision "came to the fore during the exile as a sign of the covenant and of the confession of faith" (p. 230).

[35] H. Reviv, "The History of Judah from Hezekiah to Josiah," in *The World History of the Jewish People*, vol. 4: *The Age of Monarchies: Political History*, ed. by Abraham Malamat (Jerusalem: Massada Press, 1979), pp. 202-203.

[36] Pfeiffer, *Religion in the Old Testament*, p. 55.

Just as categorical is John Van Seters, "'Comparing Scripture.'" He declares unambiguously: "There is no longer any basis for supporting the notion of a pre-exilic Sinai theology of law and covenant. It is possible that the giving of divine law was first associated with Moses and the wilderness period by Deuteronomic reformers in the late monarchy [towards the end of the seventh century BC and the start of the sixth], but there is no evidence that this notion rested on a cultic tradition of a covenant renewal festival or law making. The understanding of Israel as a covenant community is an exilic, and primarily a diaspora, form of corporate identity that became significant in Israel's religious life only after the demise of the monarchy and the state" (pp. 127-128).

Clements, *Deuteronomy*, adds a nuance, acknowledging that there may have been some earlier precedents for the late seventh-century doctrine of the covenant. But then he goes on to say: ". . . in developing the idea of covenant in the way that they did, the Deuteronomists accorded it a much increased theological significance as a definition of the meaning of Israel's claim to a relationship to Yahweh as its God" (p. 58) Similarly, Soggin, *Introduction*, concludes that "it is only with Deuteronomy that [the covenant] came to represent a central concept" (p. 141).

[37] Sheldon H. Blank, *Prophetic Faith in Israel* (New York: Harper & Brothers, 1958), p. 8.

Max L. Margolis and Alexander Marx, *A History of the Jewish People* (New York: Atheneum, 1972), also observe that it was only during the sixth-century BC Exile in Babylon that Hebrews became "conscious of the religious uniqueness which set them apart from all other nations" (p. 115).

Clements, *Chosen People*, would mainly agree. However, he nudges the start of this process a few decades earlier to the late seventh century BC. Prior to this period, he says, Judahites might have felt that Yahweh had chosen David's dynasty as the recipient of divine favor and that Yahweh had also chosen as his dwelling place the site of the Temple of Solomon, but no one felt that the entire nation was the object of Yahweh's special choice (pp. 45-46). He dates this insight to the Deuteronomic period.

Minimalists would advance the date to sometime after the Exile.

[38] See, for example, Pfeiffer, *Religion in the Old Testament*, p. 167, and Morton Smith, *Palestinian Parties*, pp. 55-56.

[39] Edelman, "Introduction," p. 24, and P. Davies, "Scenes from the Early History of Judaism," in the same book, *Triumph of Elohim*. *op. cit.*, pp. 176-180.

[40] The Bible discusses aspects of the invasion in other places — for example, in oracles in the Book of Isaiah, snippets of which were quoted at the start of Chapter 1, as well as in a narrative of the Book of Isaiah that repeats most of the Second Kings' account. But Second Kings constitutes the core text.

[41] Clements, *Isaiah and the Deliverance*, p. 16.

[42] 2 Kings 22.

[43] 2 Kings 23.

[44] Ackerman, *Under Every Green Tree*, pp. 213-214, and Niehr, "Rise of YHWH," p. 59.

[45] P. Davies, *In Search of 'Ancient Israel'*, p. 89. Favoring a sixth-century date is Akenson, *Surpassing Wonder*, pp. 38, 51-52, 62.

[46] While Davies says that the Deuteronomistic History and most other books of the Bible would have been produced no earlier than the fifth century BC (*Ibid.*, p. 92), he agrees with conventional historians that these texts contain numerous "nuggets of historical fact" — "relics" based on written and oral literature that date from well before the fifth century BC (pp. 75, 94-95). In later chapters, I will make a nuance between these different narrative segments; they contain different levels of factual reliability.

CHAPTER FOUR

[1] R.E. Clements, "Isaiah," in *The Books of the Bible*, vol. 1. *The Old Testament/Hebrew Bible*, ed. by Bernhard W. Anderson (New York: Charles Scribner's Sons, 1989), p. 248.

[2] Isaiah 20 (NRSV).

[3] Isaiah 31:3-5, 8 (NRSV).

[4] For the lack of unanimity among scholars on this point, see Chapter 7, note 9.

[5] R.E. Clements, "Beyond Tradition-History: Deutero-Isaianic Development of First Isaiah's Themes," in *Journal for the Study of the Old Testament* 31 (1985), p. 98.

[6] J.L. McKenzie, *Second Isaiah: Introduction, Translation, and Notes* (Anchor Bible 20; Garden City, NY: Doubleday, 1968), pp. *xx*, 12.

[7] Clements, "Beyond Tradition-History," p. 98.

[8] Among others, Bright, *History of Israel*, is also of this opinion (p. 280). Also, it stands to reason that, in order to make his point, Isaiah also may not have had to parade through Jerusalem for three years continuously but, rather, only periodically.

[9] Isaiah 8:16 alludes to the prophet's disciples.

¹⁰ See, for example: Clements, *Isaiah and the Deliverance*, pp. 34-51; Blank, *Prophetic Faith*, pp. 11-14; Moses Buttenwieser, *The Prophets of Israel: From the Eighth Century to the Fifth Century* (New York: Macmillan, 1914), pp. 268-296, Gonçalves, *L'expédition de Sennachérib*, pp. 540-541, and (in remarks limited to Isaiah 29:1-8) Jon D. Levenson, *Sinai and Zion: An Entry into the Jewish Bible* (Minneapolis, Chicago, New York: Winston Press, 1985), p. 164-165.

These scholars suggest that while Isaiah predicted the Assyrian empire's eventual collapse sometime in the future, he never deviated from his repeated predictions that Sennacherib's invasion would crush Judah.

Buttenwieser, a professor of biblical exegesis at Hebrew Union College in Cincinnati, gives an especially powerful argument. He says that if Isaiah had really changed his mind and believed that Sennacherib would fail, as many scholars contended during Buttenwieser's time a century ago (and still contend today), it is inconceivable that the prophet would have denounced Jerusalemites for celebrating Sennacherib's surprise withdrawal, as in Isaiah 22. In verses 1-3 and 12-14, widely regarded as authentic, Isaiah says that instead of being joyous his fellow citizens should grieve about the destruction wreaked on much of the rest of the country; he also predicts that Yahweh will not forgive them — presumably for their disloyalty to him. If Isaiah really had predicted Sennacherib's failure, says Buttenwieser, he would have "exulted in the fact that YHWH had proved Himself more victorious than ever before" (p. 292). So far as I am aware, those who argue that Isaiah changed his mind have not seriously dealt with this argument (which Blank has later also used) but have ignored it.

Buttenwieser also says that if Isaiah had in fact swung to the view that Yahweh would save Jerusalem, "It would be at variance with those basic views from which his whole preaching proceeds . . ." (p. 268). That is, he says, it would contradict the prophet's guiding principle, the need for faith in Yahweh: without faith, one cannot endure (Isaiah 7:9). Ergo, Jerusalem should fall.

Clements' own lengthy anaylsis concludes: ". . . there is no justification at all for arguing that Isaiah had foretold the miraculous defeat of Sennacherib's assault on Jerusalem in 701 BC. Those passages in the book of Isaiah which have been thought to support such a contention are not authentic to Isaiah . . ." (p. 51).

Blank, whose earlier book shares this view, rightly notes that this would indicate the fictive nature of one of the biblical narrative's emphasized aspects of the siege of Jerusalem, Isaiah's prophecy that Sennacherib would withdraw (Isaiah 37:5-7, 29, 33-35/ 2 Kings 19:5-7,28,32-34).

¹¹ Some minimalists express skepticism on whether the prophets ever existed. Referring to the original Isaiah among others, Thompson, *Early History the Israelite People*, has this to say: "[I]n dating the prophets — Amos, Hosea, First Isaiah, Ezekiel — we too quickly identify the characters of stories as historical persons and assume that the prophetic traditions had original nuclei deriving from actual events and persons narrated by the traditions. . . . In fact, however, we know historically little of any such events or persons. External confirmatory evidence we have for these assumptions is both fragmentary and oblique" (p. 399). P. Davies, *In Search of 'Ancient Israel'*, goes further. Speaking of prophetic writing, he says : "I do not at all resist the idea that there is real anger, real morality, real passion in this poetry. But I see no reason to attribute it to 'prophets' nor to anyone before the fifth century BCE." (p. 124).

I cannot respond to these historians' remarks on the other prophets, but I believe their generalizations are untenable as they apply to the original Isaiah, the only prophet on which this book concentrates. As evidence, consider the Book of Isaiah's two radically different predictions regarding Jerusalem's future in the face of the Assyrian invasion. The prediction that Yahweh would successfully seek the city's destruction and the prediction that he would save it from being even touched by the invaders do not reflect a mood swing but rather a profound theological contradiction. It is hard to suppose that centuries later biblical writers would have composed the pessimistic prediction when they knew it to be false. After all, the minimalists say these writers would have been trying to put Isaiah on a religious pedestal. Why, then, would those writers have made him look so confusingly and erroneously contradictory?

[12] Isaiah 8:1-3, 7:3.

[13] R.E. Clements, *Isaiah 1-39; New Century Bible Commentary* (Grand Rapids, MI: Wm. B. Eerdmans Publishing; London: Marshall, Morgan & Scott, 1980), p. 13.

[14] Isaiah 1:16-17 (TEV).

[15] The message was not entirely original among the Hebrews. Isaiah's contemporary in Israel, the prophet Amos, for example, had also stressed the primacy of righteousness: "Seek good, not evil, that you may live. Then the Lord God Almighty will be with you . . ." (Amos 5:14 [NIV]).

[16] Micah 6:7-8 (NRSV).

[17] Ernest Renan, *History of the People of Israel: From the Time of Hezekiah till the Return from Babylon*, vol. 3 (Boston: Roberts Brothers, 1891), pp. 84-85.

[18] Isaiah 2:4 (NRSV).

[19] Clements, *Isaiah 1-39*, says Isaiah 2:4 may come from the fifth century BC (p. 38). Others who see Isaiah 2:4 as a late insertion include Becker, *Messianic Expectation* (p. 72), and Otto Kaiser, *Isaiah 1-12: A Commentary*, 2nd ed., completely rewritten, trans. from the German by John Bowden (London: SCM Press, 1983, {p. 252}). For a discussion of this common view, see Marvin A. Sweeney, "Micah's Debate with Hezekiah," in *Journal for the Study of the Old Testament* 93 (2001), pp. 111 ff.

[20] It is Sennacherib, *ANET*, p. 288, who mentions the existence of Hezekiah's daughters and concubines.

[21] 2 Kings 18:5-6 (NRSV).

[22] 2 Chronicles 29-32.

[23] Many scholars assume that Isaiah 9:2-7, the famous passage that speaks glowingly of a monarch who will uphold his authority "with justice and with righteousness" (NRSV), was written for Hezekiah at his coronation. There is no persuasive evidence for this assumption. Even if this assumption is correct, however, the passage would describe the expectations for Hezekiah's future reign; it would not be an assessment of his past record.

One part of the Book of Isaiah that speaks very well of Hezekiah is chapters 36-39. This segment is, however, not authentic to the prophet; it is borrowed wholesale from Second Kings, as Chap. 8 will discuss.

[24] Isaiah 10:1-2 (NRSV).

[25] Isaiah 1:23 (NIV). NEB also gives "rulers," NRSV "princes."

[26] Micah 3:11.

[27] Micah 3:1, 9-10 (NIV). NEB and NRSV also give "rulers."

[28] Isaiah 22:3.
Some translations of Isaiah 22:3 imply that those who fled were civic leaders (*e.g.*, the RSV's and NRSV's "rulers"). The NEB renders deserters as "commanders" and "stoutest warriors." Clements, *Isaiah 1-39*, approves of the NEB and says "army commanders" and "best warriors" fit best here (p. 184).
Clements' reasoning, however, can be questioned. He says he is influenced by Sennacherib's annal (*ANET*, p. 288). The *ANET* and *ARAB* translations say that Hezekiah's elite soldiers deserted him. However, Mordechai Cogan and Hayim Tadmor, *II Kings: A New Translation with Introduction and Commentary* (Anchor Bible 11; N.p.: Doubleday, 1988), challenge this rendering; they propose that the annal really says that Hezekiah gave to Sennacherib some of these troops as part of his tribute (p. 247, n. 2). The version of the text reproduced in Chapter 7 reflects this latter view.
In rendering senior army leaders, I am following the NEB but I do so without conviction. There is room for disagreement on whether these deserters were military or civilian. What is clear is that they were important people.

[29] Breaking what had been the virtual unanimity among historians and archaeologists on this point are John Rogerson and Philip R. Davies, "Was the Siloam Tunnel Built by Hezekiah?" in *Biblical Archaeologist* 59, September 1996. They point out that "no biblical text can be said to ascribe the tunnel, or any tunnel, to Hezekiah" (p. 145). They suggest that 2 Kings' allusion to Hezekiah's construction of waterworks may refer to the so-called "Warren's Shaft," another project affecting access to the Gihon Spring. They prefer to date the construction of the tunnel to the Hasmonean period several centuries later.
It is hard for me to evaluate the Rogerson & Davies dissent. This book will go along with the tradition that Hezekiah indeed had had the tunnel built. In the event Rogerson & Davies are right, it would not significantly affect this book. It would downgrade the credit I give Hezekiah for building so ambitious and successful a project as the tunnel. It would also require adjusting this book's scenario for the events of 701 as proposed in Chapter 15 — to what extent that scenario would require modification would depend on a new understanding of the function of Warren's Shaft.

[30] William H. Shea, "Commemorating the Final Breakthrough of the Siloam Tunnel," in *FUCUS*, *op. cit.*, pp. 441. He cites Sennacherib as an example of a monarch who saw to it that inscriptions commemorating his waterworks gave him, the king, a starring role.

[31] It is possible to infer from Isaiah 22:10-11, an unclear passage, that the general population had a low regard for the monarch. The passage, after describing the celebrations that accompany Sennacherib's withdrawal, recalls how prior to the invasion Jerusalemites had built the Siloam Pool and torn down houses to use the stone to strengthen the city's fortifications. The prophet adds reprovingly: "But you [Jerusalemites] did not look for him who did it, or have regard for him who planned it long ago" (NRSV). To whom does the pronoun "him" refer? Some translations assume it is Yahweh. But John H. Hayes and Stuart A. Irvine, *Isaiah the Eighth-Century Prophet:*

His Times and Preachings (Nashville, TN: Abingdon Press, 1987) suggest it is Hezekiah. They favor the interpretation that Isaiah "condemned the [civic] leaders for having constructed the tunnel under the city without consulting Hezekiah, who had planned the project earlier" (pp. 282-283). The prophet may be scolding the public for neglecting to give the king credit for plans that kept the enemy at bay. The point seems plausible: it fits the pattern of low public regard for the king, particularly as the invaders approached.

[32] 2 Kings 20:1-7. Coming as it does after Sennacherib's retreat and death, the passage's placement gives the false impression that the illness took place after the Assyrian invasion. In verse 6, however, Yahweh tells the stricken Hezekiah: "I will let you live 15 years longer. I will rescue you and this city Jerusalem from the emperor of Assyria" (TEV). The future tense in the second sentence suggests the city's survival was in question at the time of his sickness.

Whether this illness preceded or followed the dramatic visit of the Assyrian delegation is uncertain. 2 Kings 19:1-4 presents Hezekiah as at least ambulatory. As soon as his aides inform him of the enemy's surrender terms, he goes directly from his palace to the neighboring Solomon's Temple. There is, at this point, no hint that the king is an invalid.

We should bear in mind that 2 Kings 20 is part of the Deuteronomistic History; later chapters will show that, in the context of 701, we should take its 'factual content' with caution. However, it may be that while 2 Kings 20 embellishes the story of the illness, at some point during the invasion the king was genuinely sick.

[33] Those who say Hezekiah came to power in 727 BC include: Hayim Tadmor, "The Chronology of the First Temple Period: A Presentation and Evaluation of the Sources," in *World History of the Jewish People*, vol. 4, *Age of Monarchies, op. cit.*, p. 58; Barnes, *Studies*, pp. 114-116, n. 124, n. 127; p. 134); John H. Hayes and Paul K. Hooker, *A New Chronology for the Kings of Israel and Judah, and Its Implications for Biblical History and Literature* (Atlanta: John Knox Press, 1988), pp. 71-80, and Reviv, "History of Judah," p. 193. Putting the year at 725 is R.E. Clements, "Isaiah."

Favoring an accession date of 715/714 are David Noel Freedman, "The Chronology of Israel and the Ancient Near East: A. Old Testament Chronology," in *The Bible and the Ancient Near East: Essays in Honor of William Foxwell Albright*, ed. by G. Ernest Wright (London: Routledge & Kegan Paul, 1961), p. 211, and Edwin R. Thiele, *A Chronology of Hebrew Kings* (Grand Rapids, MI: Zondervan Publishing House, 1977), p. 67. Those who accept this date include: H. Jagersma, *A History of Israel in the Old Testament Period*, trans. from the Dutch by John Bowden (London: SCM Press., 1982), p. 163; Mitchell, "Israel and Judah," p. 346, and Andrew G. Vaughn, *Theology, History, and Archaeology in the Chronicler's Account of Hezekiah* (Atlanta, GA: Scholars Press, 1999), p. 14.

Gonçalves, *L'expédition de Sennachérib*, sees a period of joint rule between Ahaz and Hezekiah as the "most probable" scenario (p. 59). He suggests they would have reigned as co-regents starting in about 729-727 to 716-714. Hezekiah would have governed as sole king between 716-14 and 700-698 (pp. 58-60). Closely resembling this is a proposal by J.A. Motyer, *The Prophecy of Isaiah* (Leicester, UK: Inter-Varsity Press, 1993). He suggests an Ahaz-Hezekiah co-regency between 729-715 and sees Hezekiah as reigning alone between 715-696. In 696, Hezekiah and Manasseh would have ruled as co-regents until 687 (pp. 276-277, n. 2).

³⁴ M. Broshi. "The Expansion of Jerusalem in the Reigns of Hezekiah and Manasseh," in *Israel Exploration Journal* 24 (1978), pp. 25-26.

³⁵ 2 Kings 17:7-23. The translation is Cogan & Tadmor's.

³⁶ 2 Kings 18:4-7 (Cogan & Tadmor).

³⁷ 2 Chronicles 29:3 says that Hezekiah began his religious reform in the first month of his reign. Cogan & Tadmor, *Ibid.*, comment "that this date is a literary convention, indicating Hezekiah's early piety, and cannot be used for chronological purposes" (pp. 219-220). They date the start of the reform to some years after Hezekiah's enthronement and in the aftermath of Samaria's collapse.

³⁸ 2 Kings 18:22 puts this statement in the Rab-shakeh's mouth, but nowhere does the Bible challenge its accuracy (TEV).

³⁹ See 2 Chronicles 29-31.

⁴⁰ Cogan & Tadmor, *II Kings*, do make a plausible case for religious reform as a logical response by Judah to the northern kingdom's collapse: "The political and religious leadership in Jerusalem saw in the downfall of Israel a foreboding lesson: Was it not Israel's apostasy that brought about its demise? Could not similar deviations from the prescribed cult be pointed to within Judah?. . . . Hezekiah's reform, then, can be viewed as directed against such practices, in the hope that Judah would be spared the divine wrath" (p. 220). Cogan & Tadmor place this reform in the decade or so after Assyria's invasion of Israel in 722-720.

Cogan & Tadmor define this reform, however, as involving concentration of worship "at the single altar in the Temple of Jerusalem" (p. 218). Their lesson-from-Israel argument would certainly favor an intensification of cult worship in Judah; it would not, however, necessarily involve centralization of that worship. That is, if Yahweh was Judah's god as he had been Israel's, why would worshipping him only in Jerusalem be advisable? Cogan & Tadmor do not address this.

⁴¹ Tadmor, "Period of the First Temple," p. 146.

Miller & Hayes, *Israel and Judah*, also observe: "By making the other cities religiously dependent upon the capital city, Hezekiah may have been seeking to tie their political and religious allegiance more firmly to himself . . . and to the state cause which he espoused" (p. 357).

⁴² Carl D. Evans, "Judah's Foreign Policy from Hezekiah to Judah," in *Scripture and Context: Essays on the Comparative Method*, ed. by Carl D. Evans, William W. Hallo and John B. White (Pittsburgh: Pickwick Press, 1980), p. 162. Evans bases this on the Second Chronicles' account of the reform. Yet even if one is skeptical of that account, it is likely that a modest centralization would have produced the kind of effect that Evans describes.

These various scholars' view that religious centralization was designed to have broader implications might not hold up if the centralization had been a last-minute, improvisation. L.K. Handy, "Hezekiah's Unlikely Reform," *Zeitschrift für die alttestamentliche Wissenschaft* 100 (1988), presents a variation on this idea of an historical foundation for Hezekiah's reform. He suggests that it may have been as the Assyrians under Sennacherib were actually approaching Judah that Hezekiah ordered the removal of the statues of gods and silver cultic objects from shrines in outlying areas.

Handy says the king's motive would not have been spiritual but simply pragmatic: Hezekiah would not have wanted the enemy to capture the statues of these gods, since Assyria's possession of these idols might mean they had gone over to its own side (pp. 111-115).

Additionally, says Handy, Hezekiah would have sought to keep the precious metals in Judah's hands.

[43] 2 Kings 23:13. Whether these altars had in fact been built by Solomon, or whether they were simply ancient, or indeed whether the entire allusion is an invention, is something we need not get into. If one were to accept at face value Second King's description of Hezekiah's reforms, it would be fair to apply the same standard to what it says about Josiah's reforms.

[44] In 2 Kings 23:13, the term "Mount of the Destroyer" refers to the Mount of Olives. See Cogan & Tadmor, *II Kings*, p. 289.

[45] Nadav Na'aman, "The Debated Historicity of Hezekiah's Reform in the Light of Historical and Archaeological Research," *Zeitschrift für die alttestamentliche Wissenschaft* 107, 1995, p. 193. Na'aman finds evidence that a cultic shrine persisted well beyond 701 at another site, Tel Arad, in Judah's south (p. 185).

See also Oded Borowski, "Hezekiah's Reforms and the Revolt against Assyria," in *Biblical Archaeologist*, Sept. 1995. Borowski describes evidence that shrines at Tell Halif, in southern Judah, and at Lachish, were still in use in 701 and that they almost certainly owe their demolition that year to Sennacherib (p. 152).

[46] Na'aman, "Debated Historicity," pp. 189, 194.

[47] Referring to 2 Chronicles, Gonçalves, *L'expédition de Sennachérib*, observes that the "absolute revival of Yahwism attributed to Hezekiah is as implausible as the total apostasy imputed to Ahaz. . . ." (p. 95).

[48] Na'aman himself notes that "lack of positive evidence does not indicate that reform did not take place . . ." (*ibid.*, p. 189).

As well, that some shrines persisted at least until 701 in a few outlying areas, well removed from Jerusalem, could mean nothing more than that the head of state was unable to get subordinates to execute his orders comprehensively, a chronic condition of governments everywhere.

Also: the Bible's evident confusion in ascribing similar deeds to Hezekiah and Josiah could simply be a minor slip, not weighty enough to cancel out the general thrust of what else it says about the earlier king's religious policy.

A further consideration: if minimalist skepticism is justified, before the invasion Hezekiah may not have had firm control over these areas well-removed from Jerusalem in the first place.

[49] Isaiah 1:11-16, Micah 6:6-7.

[50] For example, Bright, *History of Israel*, says, "A return to strict Yahwism would of necessity have involved an attempt to remove economic abuses that had existed . . ." (p. 282).

[51] *ARAB*, vol. 2, p. 105. See also, *ANET*, p. 287.

⁵² Bustenay Oded, "Judah and the Exile," in *Israelite and Judean History*, ed. by John H. Hayes and J. Maxwell Miller (London: SCM Press Ltd., 1977), p. 444.

If one accepts the thrust of 2 Chronicles 30, Hezekiah may also have sent messengers far and wide to invite remnants of the northern tribes hard hit by deportation to come to Jerusalem for festivals honoring Yahweh. Such an attempt to rally all Hebrews to centralized worship in Jerusalem would not have pleased the Assyrian empire of which the former state of Israel now comprised several provinces. According to Bright, *History of Israel:* "It was hoped that religious unification, the reactivation of Jerusalem as a national shrine of all Israel, would serve as a prelude to political unification" (p. 281).

⁵³ 2 Kings 18:8 (NRSV).

⁵⁴ Nadav Na'aman, "Sennacherib's 'Letter to God' on His Campaign to Israel," in *Bulletin of the American Schools of Oriental Research*, April 1974, pp. 34-35.

⁵⁵ See, for example, Cogan & Tadmor, *II Kings*, p. 221.

⁵⁶ 2 Kings 20:12. The placement of the passage after the account of Sennacherib's invasion may make it seem that the envoys arrived sometime after 701 BC. But historians are virtually unanimous in saying that diplomatic mission took place sometime before. Where they disagree is on just when.

For example, Hayes & Irvine, *Isaiah the Eighth-Century Prophet*, assign it to a 721-710 time-slot, and probably just before the Ashdodite rebellion of 713 BC (pp. 385-386). Barnes, *Studies*, also favors an early date, c. 714 (pp. 115-118, n. 127, n. 128.) Cogan & Tadmor, *II Kings*, point to 713 (p. 261).

Many scholars, however, prefer a later date. For example, Evans, "Judah's Foreign Policy," favors the period between 704 and 702 (p. 164). Clements, *Isaiah and the Deliverance*, also says it is "most probable" that the visit was a prelude to Hezekiah's revolt of 705-701 (pp. 66-67).

⁵⁷ K.A. Kitchen, "The Philistines," in *Peoples of Old Testament Times, op. cit.,* pp. 67-70.

⁵⁸ D. R. Ap-Thomas, "Phoenicians," *Peoples of Old Testament Times*, ed. by D. J. Wiseman (Oxford: Clarendon Press, 1973) pp. 263-264.

⁵⁹ Sennacherib's annal identifies the rebel Phoenician king, Luli, as king of Sidon. However, Luli was in fact king of Tyre, which had hegemony over Sidon, according to Gonçalves, *L'expédition de Sennachérib*, p. 113.

⁶⁰ Renan, *History*, p. 81-82.

⁶¹ *ANET*, p. 287; *ARAB*, vol. 2, p. 119.

⁶² See, for example: Aharoni, *Land of the Bible*, p. 337; Bright, *History of Israel*, p. 283; Cogan, *Imperialism and Religion*, p. 66; Herrmann, *History of Israel*, p. 257; Nadav Na'aman, "Forced Participation in Alliances in the Course of the Assyrian Campaigns to the West," in *Ah, Assyria, op. cit.,* pp. 94-95; Spalinger, "Foreign Policy of Egypt," p. 35, and Tadmor, "Period of the First Temple," p. 141.

⁶³ With repetition it becomes more exaggerated. A 1990 reference book that is part of the Anchor series goes beyond saying that Hezekiah simply persuaded neighboring kings to rebel. Amihai Mazar, *Archaeology of the Land of the Bible: 10,000 B.C.E.-586*

B.C.E. (New York: Doubleday, 1990), says Hezekiah "forced Ekron . . . to enter into an alliance with him" (p. 405). There is no argumentation.

An exponent of such a view might argue that the fact that Padi was imprisoned in Jerusalem suggests that Hezekiah must have been the master-schemer. But this might simply mean that Padi was safer from rescue there than in his native Ekron, where he would have had sympathizers.

[64] So far as I know, the only scholar who shares my view of Luli's leadership in the coalition is H. Jacob Katzenstein, *The History of Tyre: From the Beginning of the Second Millenium B.C.E. until the Fall of the Neo-Babylonian Empire in 538 B.C.E.* (Jerusalem: Schocken Institute for Jewish Research, 1973), p. 246). In a passing reference, Katzenstein credits Luli and Hezekiah as co-leaders.

[65] H.W.F. Saggs, "The Assyrians," in *Peoples of Old Testament Times, op. cit.*, p. 163.

[66] *ARAB*, vol. 2, p. 116. In a later text, Sennacherib boosted the count to 89 strong cities and 820 small ones (p. 134). *ARAB* says small cities are hamlets (p. 134).

[67] Sennacherib says he carried off a total of "208,000 people, male and female, 7,200 horses and mules, 11,703 asses, 5,230 camels, 80,100 cattle, 800,509 sheep, an enormous spoil" (*ibid.*, p. 134.) The young king's campaign had, however, one major failing: in a clash on the plain of Kish, just south of present-day Baghdad, he was unable to capture the redoubtable Merodach-baladan. In his annal, Sennacherib sneers at his enemy's flight, portraying it as almost cowardly: "In the midst of that battle he forsook his camp and made his escape alone; so he saved his life" (*Ibid.*, p. 116).

[68] *Ibid.*, pp. 117-118.

[69] True, the annals are partly propaganda exercises intended to give members and visitors of the royal court a favorable view of what happened during these remote military campaigns. Yet, even if the annals magnify a monarch's exploits and downplay or omit his failures, they provide us with an idea of what the king thought was important for people to know. That tells us a lot about his priorities, his mentality and the image he desired for himself.

[70] *ARAB*, vol. 2, p. 115.

John Malcolm Russell, *Sennacherib's Palace without Rival at Nineveh* (Chicago and London: University of Chicago Press, 1991), says this of Sennacherib's choice of titles: "Because of its conventional character, it is tempting to view the titulary as little more than a formality, devoid of real meaning. This would be a mistake, however, for Sennacherib evidently took his titulary seriously and chose each of its components and epithets with care" (pp. 241-242).

[71] *Ibid.*, p. 261.

[72] *ARAB*, vol. 2, p. 117.

[73] *Ibid.*, p. 122.

[74] *Ibid.*, p. 127.

[75] *Ibid.*, p. 117.

CHAPTER FIVE

1 Yurco, "Sennacherib's Third Campaign," estimates that Sennacherib's departure from Assyria would have probably have taken place sometime between late March and mid-April, but possibly as late as early May (p. 226, including n. 46). He further calculates that the march from Assyria to the Mediterranean coast, would have taken a minimum of 16 days.

2 *The Harper Encyclopedia of Military History: From 3500 BC to the Present*, 4th ed., ed. by R. Ernest Dupuy and Trevor N. Dupuy (New York: HarperCollins Publishers, 1993), pp. 10-11.

3 Herrmann, *History of Israel*, p. 244.

4 Trevor N. Dupuy, *The Evolution of Weapons and Warfare* (Indianapolis and New York: Bobbs-Merrill, 1980), pp. 6-7.

5 A.K. Grayson, "Assyrian Civilization," in *The Cambridge Ancient History*, vol. 3, part 2, 2nd ed. (Cambridge: Cambridge University Press, 1991), p. 217.

6 These foreign troops probably had few complaints about fighting for their former adversary. The opportunities for pillage would have been frequent. A change in allegiance would also have been theologically defensible: the god of a victorious people was widely seen as more powerful than that of the defeated.

For reasons perhaps of language and morale, the foreigners were often concentrated into organizational units according to nationality rather than scattered and integrated into Assyrian-dominated units. From Isaiah, we know that Sennacherib's army included cavalry from Elam from what is now southwestern Iran and other troops from Kir, in Mesopotamia (Isaiah 22:6). Early in his reign, Sargon speaks of having absorbed 50 chariot crews from Samaria in Israel, 300 chariot crews and 600 cavalry from Hamath in present-day Syria, and 50 chariot crews, 200 cavalry and 3,000 foot soldiers from Carchemish in what is now southern Turkey (*ANET*, p. 285).

7 Stephanie Dalley, "Foreign Chariotry and Cavalry in the Armies of Tiglath-pileser III and Sargon II," in *Iraq* 47, 1985, p. 32.

8 *Ibid.*, pp. 38-39.

9 See 2 Kings 16:5, 2 Chronicles 28:5-8.

10 In the following discussion of the army's make-up, I am largely indebted to Yigael Yadin, *The Art of Warfare in Biblical Lands*, vols. 1 and 2 (New York: McGraw-Hill, 1963), especially vol. 2, pp. 291-328.

11 Edward McEwen, Robert L. Miller and Christopher A. Bergman, "Early Bow Design and Construction," *Scientific American*, June 1991, explain how the composite bow utilized these materials: "The sinew on the back handles tensile stress. The horn, with a maximum strength of roughly 13 kilograms per square millimeter (about twice that of hardwoods), bears compressive loads. Horn also has a high coefficient of restitution, or the ability to return to its original shape after being distorted. The flexibility of these materials gives the bow short, lightweight, reflexed limbs capable of storing a large amount of energy under tension. In addition, the flexible limbs enable the composite bow to be drawn much farther relative to the overall length of the weapon. The combination of extended draw length and short limbs enables the composite bow to

shoot an arrow faster and farther than can a wooden self-bow of equal draw weight" (p. 80).

[12] John Keegan, *A History of Warfare* (New York: Alfred A. Knopf, 1993), p. 162.

[13] Yadin, *Art of Warfare*, vol. 1, p. 8.

[14] The first known usage of stirrups was by Hindu cavalry in the first century BC, according to T.N. Dupuy, *Evolution of Weapons and Warfare*, p. 38.

[15] Yadin, *Art of Warfare*, vol. 2, p. 297.

[16] The many months it would have taken to build both the tunnel and the wall suggest the Jerusalemites anticipated the invasion before Sennacherib's army left Assyria.

[17] Gabriel Barkay, "The Iron Age II-III," in *The Archaeology of Ancient Israel*, ed. by Amnon Ben-Tor, trans. from the Hebrew by R. Greenberg (New Haven and London: Yale University Press; Open University of Israel, 1992), pp. 348-349, and Mazar, *Archaeology of the Land of the Bible*, pp. 457-458.

[18] 2 Chronicles 32:2-5 (TEV). As a rule, one should approach the Book of Second Chronicles with great caution when attempting to use it for its historical content. In a note to Chapter 15, I will give reasons for giving the benefit of the doubt to the historicity of these water-related verses (32:2-5 as well as 32:30).

[19] 2 Chronicles 32:30 (TEV).

[20] See Isaiah 22:10. Brevard S. Childs, *Isaiah and the Assyrian Crisis* (London: SCM Press, 1967), p. 23, note 9, and Clements, *Isaiah 1-39*, pp. 182-183, are among many scholars who say that Isaiah 22:8b-11 is not authentic to the prophet but represents a later addition. Nonetheless, this passage which deals with siege preparations at Jerusalem is still useful to us. Verses 9-11 deal with collecting water inside the city and with fortifying the defensive wall. Clements says that while the authorship of these verses dates from after 586 BC, the writer looks back to the "details of the building up of the siege defences of Jerusalem during the period of Isaiah's ministry . . ." (p. 186).

While the information about the preparations against Sennacherib's invasion is second-hand, I believe that it is so specific (in talking about tearing down houses in order to strengthen the defences, for example) as to justify the assumption that it is based on fact.

For discussion of the wall's construction, see, among others, Yigal Shiloh on excavation results in "Jerusalem," *New Encyclopedia of Archaeological Excavations in the Holy Land*, vol. 2. ed. by Ephraim Stern (Jerusalem: Israel Exploration Society and Carta; New York: Simon & Schuster, 1993), pp. 704-708, and Mazar, *Archaeology of the Land of the Bible*, pp. 420-423.

For recent discoveries relating to the outer wall and Gihon tower, see Hershel Shanks, "Everything You ever Knew about Jerusalem Is Wrong (well, almost)," in *Biblical Archaeology Review*, Nov.-Dec. 1999 (pp. 20-29).

[21] The circumstances by which Hezekiah would have done this are murky. So is the timing. It is probable, but not certain, that the appeal to Egypt would have been made in conjunction with the coalition partners.

[22] Isaiah 19:2 (TEV).

[23] Isaiah 19:15 (TEV).

[24] Isaiah 31:1-3 (TEV). Clements, *Isaiah and the Deliverance,* p. 29, and Gonçalves, *L'exépedition de Sennachérib,* p. 534, date this oracle to the period immediately prior to the invasion of 701 BC (although Gonçalves proposes that the passage also contains a snippet of post-exilic editing, p. 161).

Note that Isaiah never criticizes Hezekiah directly. He adroitly targets only the emissaries.

[25] Isaiah 10:5-6.

[26] Just which members of the coalition sent for help? Sennacherib's annals explicitly credit Ekron with the appeal to Egypt for aid (*ANET,* p. 287, *ARAB,* vol. 2, pp. 119, 142). But Sennacherib does so within a larger context of Ekron and Judah working in concert against him — specifically, in jointly seeing to the incarceration of his vassal Padi. Hezekiah's participation in the appeal, mentioned in the same breath as Padi's imprisonment, can be assumed; Sennacherib's awkward, run-on sentence structure, that is, allows the inference that the Assyrian is lumping Hezekiah in with Ekron in the plea for help.

We know that Judah was not passive: Isaiah 30:2 and 31:1-2 describe Judahite envoys travelling to Egypt in search of assistance.

My assumption, then, is that both Ekron and Jerusalem sent to Egypt. Whether they did so together or separately, or if one of them did so while acting for both, is unclear.

There is no evidence to suggest that Tyre participated in this last-minute appeal to Egypt. Although it was a very major member of the rebel alliance, Tyre's absence from any SOS mission would have been understandable for geographical reasons. Of all the allies, Phoenicia was located the farthest from Egypt and, in terms of travel routes, the closest to Assyria; it was thus the most vulnerable to Assyrian attack. That Tyre's king sailed to Cyprus at Sennacherib's approach suggests that his emergency plan called for flight rather than a long wait while under siege for an Egyptian rescue.

CHAPTER SIX

[1] To look at a map, one might wonder if ancient Kush was actually sub-Saharan. In characterizing it as such, I am relying upon archaeologists specializing in the region. See, for example, Timothy Kendall, "Discoveries at Sudan's Sacred Mountain of Jebel Barkal Reveal Secrets of the Kingdom of Kush," in *National Geographic* 178 (1990), p. 105.

[2] This standard dating has gone virtually unchallenged until the 1990s. It still enjoys very wide currency.

A rival timetable that moves the 18th Dynasty forward by two or three centuries has been proposed by Peter James, *Centuries of Darkness: A Challenge to the Conventional Chronology of Old World Archaeology,* in collaboration with I.J. Thorpe, Nikos Kokkinos, Robert Morkot and John Frankish (New Brunswick, NJ: Rutgers University Press, 1993).

The standard chronology is based on the description of ancient dynasties by Manetho, an Egyptian priest of the third century BC. According to the length of reigns that Manetho assigns to each dynasty, scholars' standard calculation would put the 18th Dynasty at 1567 to 1320 BC, or thereabouts. James, however, would move this reign to about 1290 to 1040 BC (p. 195). This revisionist chronology compresses the duration of several subsequent dynasties with the result of "an overall lowering of the dates for the New Kingdom (18th-20th Dynasties) by some 250 years" (p. 257).

Many scholars have received this thesis cooly. Yet it is interesting that some critics who dispute the book's conclusions nonetheless acknowledge that the existing chronology may be wobbly. In his book review in *American Historical Review* 99 (1994), Bruce Trigger calls *Centuries of Darkness* a "highly polemical study" and questions its methodology, particularly the "extremely arbitrary" treatment of radiocarbon dates (pp. 872-873). The anthropologist goes on to say, however, that "James and his associates have performed a useful service in drawing attention to the problems that beset Late Bronze and Early Iron Age chronology throughout the Mediterranean region. Far too many dates are based on circular reasoning and inadequate data." In his book review in the *Journal of Interdisciplinary History* 26 (1994), Philip L. Kohl also disputes *Centuries of Darkness'* methodology and conclusion. But the Wellesley College scholar says that this is a "valuable study" that "forces scholars to reconsider the ambiguous, archaeologically derived chronological sequences worked out for different regions, many of which need critical reexamination, if not revision" (p. 275).

In short, even if James's alternative chronology is wrong, important defects may exist in conventional chronology. While this book will, in discussing Egyptian history prior to the 25th Dynasty, employ the dating system that is a fixture in mainstream scholarship, readers should bear in mind that these dates are not airtight.

If James' time frame, or something close to it, were someday to win wide acceptance, what effect would that have on this book? Very little.

That is because James alters the standard chronology only up to the 25th Dynasty. In James' view, that dynasty's reign represents the point at which the standard chronology becomes reliable. The main reason is that this is the period in which Assyrian records begin to refer to Egypt in concrete terms. By putting Manetho's data alongside the Assyrian records, it is possible to assign confidently the reign of the 25th dynasty to the late eighth and early seventh centuries BC.

If James' chronology is correct, one minor consequence would be that Kush's exposure to Egyptian colonization would have gone back less far than widely believed; it would also mean that when the 25th Dynasty looked back to the New Kingdom for religious and cultural ideas (a practice that historians have often remarked upon), this inspirational model was far less removed in time than believed.

James and his collaborators' ideas on Egypt and Kush have much in common with the minimalist views of Hebrew history, described earlier. While the two schools' assumptions and research are independent and draw heavily on separate archaeological work, they both question the standard interpretation of events during the centuries leading up to the late eighth century BC. What is most pertinent for our purposes is that both schools agree that much of the historical uncertainty surrounding these ancient times ends abruptly with the tumultuous events that this book deals with: the series of threats that Assyria posed to Hebrew and Egyptian societies. For anyone trying to reconstruct the history of the ancient world, the reigns of Hezekiah and the 25th Dynasty have in common this welcome trait: they both stand on a kind of terra firma, a point in history of which we can speak with more confidence than of the preceding periods in their respective cultures. That Sennacherib (backed up by the Bible, with its passing reference in 2 Kings 19:9 to "Tirhakah") describes the dynasty in the same breath as Hezekiah, allows us to establish that dynasty and that Judahite monarch alike in a timeframe that is unshakable.

[3] David O'Connor, "Early States along the Nubian Nile," in *Egypt and Africa: Nubia from Prehistory to Islam*, ed. by W.V. Davies (London: British Museum Press, 1991), p. 147. O'Connor's estimate of 460,000 is for the Bronze Age, a period that would have elapsed several centuries before the eighth century BC, but there would probably have been no great change in population.

Given the slender nature of the available demographic evidence, it is wise to treat all estimates of Kush's population with great caution.

[4] Favoring a population of 2.5 million for Egypt is Karl W. Butzer, *Early Hydraulic Civilization in Egypt; A Study in Cultural Ecology* (Chicago and London: University of Chicago Press, 1976), graph on p. 85. Butzer derives his estimate from the amount of land under cultivation.

Preferring a higher figure is David O'Connor, "The New Kingdom and Third Intermediate Period, 1552-664 BC" in *Ancient Egypt: A Social History*, ed. by B.G. Trigger, B.J. Kemp, D. O'Connor and A.B. Lloyd (Cambridge: Cambridge University Press, 1983). He estimates that Egypt's population may have been between 2.9 million and 4.5 million in the period of 1500-1000 BC and that by 300 BC it would have risen to 7 million (p. 190). He does not deal with the in-between period. If one assumes a generally upward (if uneven) rate of growth, one might hazard that Egypt in 701 BC would — following O'Connor's model — have had a population in the neighborhood of 5-6 million people.

[5] Bruce Trigger, *Nubia under the Pharaohs* (Boulder, CO: Westview Press, 1976), p. 149, and Stuart Tyson Smith, *Askut in Nubia: The Economics and Ideology of Egyptian Imperialism in the Second Millenium B.C.* (London and New York: Kegan Paul International, 1995), pp. 174-174.

[6] S.T. Smith, *Askut*, goes so far as to suggest that "gold extracted from Nubia during the New Kingdom [16th-11th centuries BC] was critical in the maintenance of Egypt's economic and political relations with the Near East. Indeed, gold replaced silver as a standard of value in Mesopotamia as a result of these shipments" (p. 16).

[7] Bruce G. Trigger, *History and Settlement in Lower Nubia* (New Haven: Department of Anthropology, Yale University, 1965), p. 111.

[8] S.T. Smith, *Askut*, p. 182. Smith also finds that the Egyptians reorganized the culture "into a stratified society along the lines of Egypt" (p. 173). See also László Török, *The Kingdom of Kush: Handbook of the Napatan-Meroitic Civilization* (Leiden: Brill, 1997), pp. 100-101, 110-111.

[9] *Ibid.*, p. 173.

[10] Exotic resources such as ivory and ebony, says Smith, became "a powerful source of legitimization for the [pharaoh], helping him establish patronage relationships with the Egyptian elites" (*Ibid.*, p. 170).

[11] Joyce L. Hanes, *Nubia: Ancient Kingdoms of Africa* (Boston: Museum of Fine Arts, 1992), says: "No doubt some of the Egyptian gods that were adopted into Nubian religion were combined with local Nubian deities. For example, the ram god played an important role in Nubia. One can find statues of a ram-headed sphinx at Kerma [in

northern Kush, just south of the Nile's third cataract], as well as burials containing elaborately decorated rams. This worship of the ram was well-established in Nubia before the cult of Amon arrived from Egypt. Very likely, the Nubians linked Amon to their ancient ram deity and considered him as their own. Many scholars believe that the ram connection to Amon originated in Nubia and was later brought to Egypt" (p. 35). See also Dietrich Wildung, *L'Égypte*, trans. from the German by Jean-Baptiste Sherrer (Paris: Editions Citadelles, 1989), pp. 207-208. Wildung says that in the second millenium BC the Theban god Amon "borrowed" the ram identity from the Kushites. For further discussion, see Miriam Maát-Ka-Re Monges, *Kush, the Jewel of the Nubia* (Trenton, NJ, and Asmara, Eritrea: Africa World Press, 1997), pp. 178-182.

The Amon/ram relationship is evident in statuary and in sacred texts. In Egypt of the 14th-11th centuries BC we find, for example, a hymn that says of Amon, "his divine face is ram-headed." Cited by Jan Assmann, *Egyptian Solar Religion: Re, Amun and the Crisis of Polytheism*, trans. from the German by Anthony Alcock (London and New York: Kegan Paul International, 1995), p. 197.

Amon also took sacral forms other than the ram — including the bull and the Nile goose.

[12] The precise time of the Egyptian withdrawal is disputed among even those historians who use the standard chronological frame of reference; most favor the 12th or 11th century. Recent support for the 1060s comes from László Török, "Kush: An African State in the First Millenium BC," in *Proceedings of the British Academy: 1994 Lectures and Memoirs* (Oxford: Oxford University Press, 1995), p. 2.

In his revisionist chronology, P. James, *Centuries of Darkness*, would place Egypt's departure from Kush in the ninth century BC (p. 213). He bases this revision largely on radiocarbon tests on material at Kurru and other Kushite sites (pp. 212-216). By bringing forward Egypt's departure, James would explain the perplexing gap in the known history of Kush between the time of Egypt's departure and the rise of the independent state of Kush in the early eighth century BC. Under James' proposal, these "centuries of darkness" between the eleventh and early eighth centuries, when little textual or archaeological evidence exists to show what Kush was up to, would disappear.

[13] Adams, *Nubia*, p. 250.

[14] This is not to say that internal politics were always smooth. Referring to these 11 centuries, David N. Edwards, *The Archaeology of the Meroitic State: New Perspectives on Its Social and Political Organization* (Oxford: Tempvs Repartatvm, 1996), notes: "Ultimately, it is only the sequence of royal tombs that provides us with an appearance of continuity over this great span of time. Even here, the possibility remains that this neat sequence may not be as straightforward as we have tended to suppose" (p. 1). He adds that, notwithstanding that possibility, the "existence of a large and culturally sophisticated kingdom dominating the Middle Nile throughout this period cannot be doubted."

[15] Török, "Kush: An African State," explains the fall this way: "The crisis of Roman Egypt in the third and fourth centuries AD deprived Kush of her principal trade partner and delivered her northern provinces to the incursions of barbarians. The end was also prompted by the emergence of Ethiopia in the southeastern neighborhood, bringing about a mass movement of peoples toward the central territories of Kush and, finally, it was actual Ethiopian invasions that destroyed her political unity" (pp. 34-35).

¹⁶ Trigger, *Nubia under the Pharaohs*, p. 150.

¹⁷ I.E.S. Edwards, "Egypt: From the Twenty-second to the Twenty-fourth Dynasty," in *Cambridge Ancient History*, Vol. 3, Part 1, *op. cit.*, p. 570. Edwards says Kashta maintained "his sovereignty over Upper Egypt for perhaps 12 or more years until his death." Kitchen, *Third Intermediate Period*, says Kashta died in 747 (p. 468).

¹⁸ Török, "Kush: An African State," p. 27, citing Jean Leclant. See also Török, "The Emergence of the Kingdom of Kush and her Myth of the State in the First Millenium BC," in *Actes de la VIIIe Conférence Internationale des Études Nubiennes, Lille 11-17 Septembre 1994*, vol. 1 (Université Charles-de-Gaulle, Lille III), *op. cit.*, p. 207.

See also Adams, *Nubia*. Referring to Thebes, Adams says: "To the Egyptian priests, threatened as they were from the north and long accustomed to rely on Nubian troops for their protection, the rise of a new and effective Nubian commander may well have appeared as a deliverance" (p. 261).

¹⁹ Redford, *Egypt, Canaan, and Israel*, p. 288.

²⁰ O'Connor, "New Kingdom and Third Intermediate Period," pp. 242-243.

²¹ Kitchen, *Third Intermediate Period*, p. 372.

²² O'Connor, "New Kingdom and Third Intermediate Period," p. 276.

²³ P. James, *Centuries of Darkness*, dissents from this view. His revised chronology places Sheshonk later than the 10th century BC. James says that the biblical "Shishak" therefore has to be another pharaoh; he proposes none other than Rameses III of the 20th Dynasty. He writes: "The biblical name 'Shishak' could well be a corruption of the Egyptian 'Sessi', the common abbreviation of the name Rameses" (p. 257).

²⁴ 1 Kings 14:25-26 (NRSV). See also 2 Chronicles 12:2-10.

²⁵ Trigger, *Nubia under the Pharaohs, p. 145*; Kitchen, *Third Intermediate Period*, p. 363, and Adams, *Nubia*, p. 262.

²⁶ Referring to Tefnakht's threatening advance, Adams, *Nubia*, speculates: "The military officials at Thebes implored Piankhi [Piye] to protect the domains of Amon against the intruder" (p. 261).

²⁷ The year 728 is from Kitchen, *Third Intermediate Period*, p. 175. This date is several years later than the earlier prevailing view.

A later examination by Alberto R.W. Green, "The Identity of So — an Alternative Interpretation," in *Journal of Near Eastern Studies* 52, April 1993, submits evidence in favor of 727 (pp. 105-107).

²⁸ One English translation is by Miriam Lichtheim, "The Victory Stela of King Piye," in *Ancient Egyptian Literature: A Book of Readings*, vol. 3 (Berkeley: University of California Press, 1980). Another is by James Henry Breasted, "The Piankhi Stela," in *Ancient Records of Egypt*, vol. 4 (Chicago: University of Chicago Press, 1906).

²⁹ Looking for a historical parallel for Piye's liberation of Egypt from turmoil, British writer Rex Keating has suggested the English Civil War — a time "when the Puritans felt it their duty to put an end to the loose and riotous behavior of the Stuart

Court." See Keating, *Nubian Rescue* (London: Robert Hale; New York: Hawthorn Books, 1975), pp. 167-168.

[30] Kitchen, *Third Intermediate Period*, p. 372.

[31] Adams, *Nubia*, p. 262.

[32] See, for example, Alan Gardiner, *Egypt of the Pharaohs: An Introduction* (London: Oxford University Press, 1961): "It is strange that after his defeat of Tefnakht, [Piye] appears to have retired to his home at Napata, leaving hardly a trace of himself in Egypt" (p. 340).

[33] Particularly disdainful is T.G.H. James, "Egypt: the Twenty-fifth and Twenty-sixth Dynasties": "In political matters the Nubians behaved with extraordinary naivety, failing wholly, it would seem, to grasp the reality of the exercise of power within Egypt. The title of King of Upper and Lower Egypt, which represented so potently the over-all dominion of the pharaoh throughout Egypt, was accepted as a supreme dignity, but its political implications were ignored. The unity of the north with the south in the understanding of the Egyptian monarchy since the First Dynasty meant the physical control of the whole of Egypt; it was not simply titular. This fact seems never to have been appreciated by the Nubians, and their acceptance from time to time of the sub-mission and formal loyalty of the Delta rulers reveals how little they were able to jus-tify, in the terms of long-established practice, their assumption of the supreme pharaonic designation. It is perhaps not unlikely that they were never in a sufficiently strong position to impose a true unity on the whole of Egypt. They could not have done so without radically changing the administration of the state of Lower Egypt" (p. 703).

This is a historian who, as we will see in Chapter 14, describes the 25th Dynasty's handling of foreign affairs as "almost invariably disastrous." Here, in his assessment of the dynasty's performance in Egypt, James seems to scoff at the Kushites for not try-ing forcefully to impose a unitary regime over the entire country — even though that is something which, in his last two sentences, he acknowledges would have been beyond their military capabilities.

An attempt to subjugate all of Egypt, as James would have had the Kushites do, would have encountered such resistance — in the Delta in particular, where the marshy terrain would have hindered pursuit — as to plunge the country into a most difficult and draining war. A loose-rein policy that James calls naive was simply realistic.

[34] Kitchen, *Third Intermediate Period*, p. 372.

[35] Edwards, "Egypt," p. 570.

[36] Yurco, "Sennacherib's Third Campaign," p. 221. Yurco also cites Anthony Spalinger and Klaus Baer in support of this date. Kitchen, *Third Intermediate Period*, says 715 is the probable date of Shabako's conquest (p. 155) but allows that it is possible it could have been as late as 712 (pp. 144, 553). In terms of trying to render some coher-ence to Egypt-Khor relations during this period, the Kushites' control of Egypt start-ing in 712 BC — after the Ashdodite rebellion — makes the most sense.

[37] Isaiah 19:2 (NRSV). The description might also fit the period immediately pre-ceding Piye's conquest of *c.* 728 BC (see below), but this is less likely.

[38] 2 Kings 17:4.

[39] The main argument for Osorkon is that "So" might be an abbreviated form of his name, (O)so(rkon), and that, residing as he did in the eastern-Delta city of Tanis, he would have been the first point of all for messengers journeying from the east. (See, for example, Kitchen, *Third Intermediate Period*, pp. 373-375, and Edwards, "Egypt," p. 576.) The problem is that Osorkon was so feeble militarily he would have been no help at all. The case for Tefnakht is that he was more militarily capable than Osorkon and thus was a far more logical ruler to look to for help; also, "So" sounds a bit like Tefnakht's city, Sais. (For example, see Redford, *Egypt, Canaan, and Israel*, p. 346.) The problem with that idea is that Tefnakht was probably not strong enough so soon after his defeat in *c.*728 to be of much assistance; as well, he may have been more of a friend than a foe to Assyria. In the 1990s some scholars have revived an earlier idea that enjoyed currency in the early 20th century: that "So" must correspond to a Kushite king. Hoshea would have had to send his mesengers to Piye, reasons Alberto Green, "Identity of So", because "it was clear where the power lay" (p. 106). A year earlier, in 1992, Becking, *Fall of Samaria*, also favored Piye. Some scholars of earlier generations have suggested that So was Shabako (a choice that reflects the chronology of Kushite kings in use at that time). See, for example, Sir E.A. Wallis Budge, *A History of Ethiopia, Nubia and Abyssinia*, vol. 1 (London: Methuen, 1928), p. 33.

[40] For the unusually close ties between Piye and Osorkon's 23rd Dynasty, see Donald Redford, *Pharaonic King-Lists, Annals and Daybooks: A Contribution to the Study of the Egyptian Sense of History* (SSEA Publication IV; Missisauga, Ont.: Benben Publications, 1986). Redford points out that the daughter of Osorkon III, Shepenwepet, had been the Divine Wife of Amon in Thebes, effectively in control of the Theban priesthood, when she adopted Piye's daughter. This arrangement eventually enabled this Kushite princess, Amenirdis, to assume this important role herself (pp. 312-317). Despite the membership of Osorkon IV in Tefnakht's coalition in *c.* 728 (a membership that may have predated Piye's declaration of war against the coalition), Piye subsequently forgave the deferential monarch and let him retain his pharaonic standing, such as it was. Redford argues that "the family of Shepenwepet I had been grafted on to the family tree of the Sudanese kings" (p. 316).

It would have been logical, then, for Hoshea to route via Osorkon any appeal for help to the geographically remote Piye.

[41] 2 Kings 17:4-5.

[42] Kitchen, *Third Intermediate Period*, p. 373, n. 743. The view is not unanimous. For example, Tadmor, "Philistia," favors the resurgent Tefnakht, p. 91.

[43] *ARAB*, vol. 2, p. 26; see also *ANET*, p. 285.

[44] *ARAB*, vol. 2, p. 3; see also *ANET*, p. 285.

[45] Paul K. Hooker, "The Location of the Brook of Egypt," in *History and Interpretation: Essays in Honour of John H. Hayes*, ed. by M.P. Graham, W.P. Brown and J.K Kuan (Sheffield, UK: JSOT Press, 1993), citing an inscription by Sargon (ND 3411) published in 1954 by C.J. Gadd (p. 207).

[46] Kitchen, *Third Intermediate Period*, basing himself on Sargon, *ANET*, deduces the Assyrians went as far as the "Brook of Egypt" (p. 286).

As to whether or not Raphia was on the Egyptian side of the border, there is room for debate. Hooker, "Location of the Brook of Egypt," argues that the location of the border may have shifted by about 35 kilometers — from one stream to another — in the course of the late eighth and early seventh centuries BC (pp. 203-214). Becking, *Fall of Samaria*, favors 715 rather than the commonly supported 716 for the date of Sargon's campaign (p. 54).

[47] See Kitchen, "Egypt," p. 122.

[48] Barnes, *Studies*, p. 100; Grayson, "Assyrian Civilization," p. 89; Kitchen, *Third Intermediate Period*, pp. 143, 376, and Tadmor, "Philistia," p. 92.

[49] *ANET*, p. 286.

[50] Sargon wrote in 716 that he was receiving gold, jewels, ivory, herbs, horses and camels as tribute from several lands including Egypt and Arabia. He identified the Egyptian donor in question as the "pharaoh," probably Osorkon (*ARAB*, vol. 2, pp. 7-8. For the dating of this text to 716 and the identification of Osorkon, see Mitchell, "Israel and Judah," p. 345).

[51] A. K. Grayson, "Assyria: Tiglath-pileser III to Sargon II," *Cambridge Ancient History*, 2nd ed., vol. 3, pt. 2, *op. cit.*, p. 89.

[52] *ANET*, p. 287. The reference to "Pir'u" means pharaoh.

[53] *ANET*, p. 286, and *ARAB*, vol. 2, pp. 31-32. Robert G. Morkot, *The Black Pharaohs: Egypt's Nubian Rulers* (London: Rubicon Press, 2000), sees in Sargon's annal a suggestion that Iamani was in Kushite-controlled territory (p. 202).

[54] Even Kitchen, generally dogged in establishing a portrait of the period, draws a blank: "Precisely why . . . Shabako marched north to the reconquest of Egypt is unknown" (*Third Intermediate Period*, p. 378).

[55] T.G.H. James, "Egypt: Twenty-fifth and Twenty-sixth Dynasties": "It is possible only to surmise at his reasons for moving north, but among them may well have been the desire to match the brilliant campaign of Py [*i.e.*, Piye] . . . , and the need to demonstrate to the apparently insurgent Bocchoris [*i.e.*, Bakenranef] that his increasingly independent activities in the Delta and in the region of Memphis represented a threat to Nubian dominion which could not be tolerated" (p. 689).

[56] Since writing this, I have seen Török's superbly comprehensive 1997 book, *Kingdom of Kush: Handbook*. It makes the same point obliquely (p. 166).

[57] Tadmor, "Philistia," p. 92.

[58] Other scholars have proposed other sites for Sargon's sealed port. R. Reich, "On the Identification of the 'Sealed Karu of Egypt'," *Eretz-Israel* 15 (1981), *op. cit.*, proposes a location in the eastern Sinai at Tell Abu Salima, near Sheikh Zuweid, where the remains of a fortress have been found. (The English summary of his Hebrew text is on that volume's p. 84.).

More recently, another location in the eastern Sinai has been proposed in two separate reports in *New Encyclopedia of Archaeological Excavations in the Holy Land*, vol. 4., *op. cit.* Eliezer D. Oren, "Ruqeish" (pp. 1293-1294), and Avraham Negev, "Sinai: Northern Sinai" (p. 1392), both suggest Sargon's port would have been at Ruqeish, on the coast near Deir el-Balah, about 11 miles southwest of Gaza. They say the settlement's large size and its fortifications support the idea that this might have been the Assyrian trade center that Sargon says he opened in 716 BC. Oren dates the fortifications to the second half of the eighth century BC.

Neither Oren nor Negev say why the site, located as it is near the traditional Egyptian frontier, would not have been one of those other operations for overland trade that Assyria set up on the border during other campaigns in the last half of the eighth century. Nor do they provide any argument to support the notion that this fairly smooth bit of coastline might long ago have contained a harbor here. And, even if a harbor had existed, they give no indication as to why Assyria would have wanted to create a major port here to deal with Egyptian trade. More than 150 miles of desert separate Ruqeish from populated Egypt, if we define that as beginning about where the Suez Canal now lies.

Kitchen touches briefly on the question in a 1995 article, "Egypt." He says that while Sargon's harbor "could be Pelusium," he prefers the Brook of Egypt as the site (p. 122).

[59] Tadmor, "Philistia," p. 92

[60] Kitchen, *Third Intermediate Period*, p. 145.

[61] Adams, *Nubia*, p. 267.

[62] T.G.H. James, "Egypt, History of," in *The New Encyclopaedia Britannica, Macropaedia*, vol. 6 (Chicago: Encyclopaedia Britannica, Inc., 1975), p. 460.

[63] Adams, *Nubia*, p. 267.

[64] Albeit far smaller that the earlier Egyptian pyramids. The Kushite pyramids' steep sides make their design quite distinct from the familiar Egyptian model.

[65] Jean-Claude Goyon, "An Interpretation of the Edifice," in *The Edifice of Taharqa by the Sacred Lake of Karnak*, by Richard A. Parker, Jean Leclant and Jean-Claude Goyon, trans. from the French by Claude Crozier-Brelot (Providence: Brown University Press; London: Lund Humphries, 1979), p. 85.

[66] See Adams, *Nubia*, p. 267.

[67] Karl-Heinz Priese, "The Napatan Period," in *Africa in Antiquity*, vol. 1, *op. cit.*, p. 88.

[68] Steffen Wenig, *Africa in Antiquity*, vol. 2, *The Arts of Ancient Nubia and the Sudan: The Catalogue* (New York: Brooklyn Museum, 1978), p. 49.

[69] *Ibid.*, p. 48.

[70] John H. Taylor, *Egypt and Nubia* (Cambridge, MA: Harvard University Press, 1991), P. 41.

[71] Dietrich Wildung, *L'Égypte* (Paris: Éditions Citadelles, 1989), p. 208.

[72] W. Stevenson Smith, *The Art and Architecture of Ancient Egypt* (N.p.: Penguin Books, 1958), pp. 244-245.

[73] Jean Leclant, "Introduction," *L'Égypte du crépuscule: De Tanis à Méroé, 1070 av. J.C. — IVe siècle apr. J.-C.*, by Cyril Aldred, François Daumas, Christiane Desroches-Noblecourt, Jean Leclant (France: Gallimard, 1980), p. 5. See also Timothy Kendall, "Kush," in *The Oxford Encyclopedia of Ancient Egypt*, vol. 2, ed. by Donald B. Redford (Oxford

University Press, 2001), who says of the Kushites in Egypt: ". . . their age, therefore, marked the beginning of Egypt's last great cultural renaissance" (p. 252).

74 I should note that another writer touches on the fact that Piye's conquest occurred during the same period that Assyria was threatening Egypt. In passing, Donald B. Redford, "Sais and the Kushite Invasions of the Eighth Century B.C.," *Journal of the American Research Center in Egypt* 22, 1985, speculates that "an engagement with the forces of Asia could be contemplated" by Piye in coming north with his invading force (p. 12). He further suggests that an engagement between Piye's troops and Assyria's "actually took place." I question his reasoning.

Redford does not explain why Piye's stela makes no mention of this clash. This is curious, particularly since Redford believes that Piye's forces would have put Assyria's to flight. If the Kushite king was successful against Assyrians, one would expect that he would have trumpeted the fact or at the very least included it among the list of successes that his army registered in the course of that campaign.

I also disagree with Redford's view of Napata's motivation. He sees Piye's conquest as a precursor to Shabako and Shebitku's "aspirations to extend their hegemony over Asia" (p. 15). This reflects modern scholarship's prevailing view of Kush as a nation with a lust for imperialism. A later chapter will evaluate this.

Incidentally, the same article proposes that Piye's invasion took place as late as 716 BC (pp. 12-13). It also suggests that Hoshea's appeal to Egypt for aid would have been in 724-723 BC (p. 15). I am not the right person to evaluate these claims regarding chronology, but if they are correct they would not change much about this book; they would simply compress time a bit.

75 *ARAB*, vol, 1, p. 293; *ANET*, p. 283.

76 *ARAB*, vol. 1, p. 287. See also, p. 293.

77 *ARAB*, vol 1, p. 294. What's more, Grayson, "Tiglath-pileser III," citing Tadmor, suggests Assyria may have received tribute from the Meunites, a people south of the Brook of Egypt and thus within Egyptian territory (p. 78).

78 Also making this point, but without showing it as reflecting a broader Kushite foreign policy preoccupation leading up to the expedition of 701, is Alviero Niccacci, "Isaiah XVIII-XX from an Egyptological Perspective," in *Vetus Testamentum* 48 (1999), pp. 219, 232-233.

79 This was true not only in strict military terms but in religious terms as well: if *ma'at* — internal peace — could prevail throughout the land, that quality would help repel the forces of chaos. The turmoil that Tefnakht generated was an offence against *ma'at*.

80 The translation is by Lichtheim, *Ancient Egyptian Literature*, vol. 3, p. 71.

81 Adding an interesting nuance is the translation by Breasted, *Ancient Records of Egypt*, vol. 4, p. 427. It says: "When his majesty sailed northward . . . , the terror of his majesty reached to the *end of the Asiatics*, every heart was heavy with the fear of him" (emphasis added). The allusion to people who lived in the far reaches of what the Egyptians knew as Asia indicates that Piye is not referring to the people of Khor or to the populations of other places that were relatively near.

[82] Pauline Albenda, "Observations on Egyptians in Assyrian Art," in *Bulletin of the Egyptological Seminar* 4 (1982), p. 8. Having made this point, however, the article drops it, not pursuing the matter of why the Kushites might have been there.

[83] J.E. Reade, "Sargon's Campaigns of 720, 716, and 715 B.C.: Evidence from the Sculptures," in *Journal of Near Eastern Studies* 35 (1976), p. 100.

[84] Anthony J. Spalinger, "Notes on the Military in Egypt during the XXVth Dynasty," in *The Journal of the Society for the Study of Egyptian Antiquities*, January 1981, p. 47-49.

[85] Possibly, it was even the strongest army in the entire history of Egypt.

[86] See William J. Murnane, *Ancient Egyptian Coregencies* (Chicago: The Oriental Institute, the University of Chicago, 1977), especially pp. 239-265.

[87] The hyothesis of a co-regency has been around for some years, but in the absence of textual evidence it has remained controversial until 1999. That's when the journal *Orientalia* published the translation of an Assyrian inscription that had been discovered in 1968 near the village of Tang-i Var in Iranian Kurdistan.
According to Grant Frame, "The Inscription of Sargon II at Tang-i Var," in *Orientalia* 68 (1999), Sargon was responsible for the inscription, which appears to date from the last year of his rule, 705 B.C.(pp. 34-35). The inscription identifies Shebitku (and not Shabako, as had earlier been assumed) as the head of state who extradited Iamani. This means that Shebitku had become pharaoh by at least 705, which is several years before scholars had earlier supposed. As Donald Redford explains in a companion article, "A Note on the Chronology of Dynasty 25 and the Inscription of Sargon II at Tang-i Var," this means the reigns of Shabako and Shebitku appear to have overlapped; it greatly strengthens the case for a co-regency that started in 705 at the latest (pp. 58-60). Redford proposes that Shabako reigned from 713 to 699.

[88] Herodotus identifies Shebitku as the pharaoh who confronts Sennacherib (see Chapter 7). Also, Sargon names him as the pharaoh who extradites Iamani (see below); the pharaoh who delivered the rebel to Assyria would logically have been the pharaoh closest to the border.

[89] The ancient historian Diodorus (I.65) says that Shabako left Egypt prematurely for religious reasons and returned to Napata to live. That suggests he was still alive when another pharaoh took power.
As for Shabako's responsibility over international affairs, it is noteworthy that it was Shabako's signet impression, and not Shebitku's, that was found on a seal in Nineveh; it may have appeared on a treaty making an end to the hostilities of 701 (see Chapter 12). Both Layard and Breasted say this seal may have been used to make final a diplomatic understanding between the two rulers. The most logical occasion for cutting such a deal would have been the aftermath of Sennacherib's invasion of 701.

[90] *ARAB*, vol. 2, p. 32; see also *ANET*, p. 286. That these texts are implicitly referring to Shebitku, and not Shabako, is plain from Frame, "Inscription of Sargon II," p. 40.

[91] Bright, *History of Israel*, p. 280.

⁹² In his translation of the Tang-i Var text, Frame, "Inscription of Sargon II," presents Shebitku as surrendering Iamani after hearing of Sargon's drive to demonstrate the might of Assyria's gods "over all lands" (p. 40).

⁹³ A.K. Grayson, "Assyria: Sennacherib and Esarhaddon (704-669 B.C.)," *Cambridge Ancient History, op. cit.*, vol. 3, part 2, observes: "In the case of Palestine it is fairly obvious from the circumstances that Sennacherib envisaged the conquest of Egypt, and that all his efforts in the west came to be dictated by this overriding goal, a goal that his son would pursue almost as soon as he took the crown" (p. 122).

⁹⁴ It is pertinent to note that archaeological evidence shows that Assyria constructed precisely such an infrastructure several decades after 701 BC, when it finally did invade Egypt.

Archaeologist Amihai Mazar, *Archaeology of the Land of the Bible*, notes: "The southern part of Palestine was particularly important for the Assyrians during the seventh century B.C.E., since it guarded the road to Egypt, the target of the Assyrian strategy. The archaeological evidence reflects massive Assyrian presence in this region. At Gezer, two administrative documents from the mid-seventh century B.C.E., a group of objects, and some architectural remains indicate that this city was an Assyrian stronghold. Assyrian finds are abundant farther south along the southern coastal plain and in northeastern Sinai, where the land route to Egypt passed. At Tel Sera, part of a large seventh century B.C.E. citadel contained Assyrian metal objects, including a scepter of a type used to decorate Assyrian chariots. Tell Jemmeh, farther to the west along the Gerar Brook, was identified by B. Mazar with Arsah (Yurza), a city conquered by the Assyrians in 679 B.C.E. Mud-brick buildings found here — featuring unique Assyrian-type vaulted ceilings and floors, and containing Assyrian 'Palace Ware' — are the remains of an important Assyrian military and administrative base" (p. 547).

⁹⁵ Barry J. Kemp, "Old Kingdom, Middle Kingdom and Second Intermediate Period c. 2686-1552 BC," in *Ancient Egypt: A Social History, op. cit.*, p. 145.

⁹⁶ Redford, *Egypt, Canaan, and Israel*, p. 337.

⁹⁷ The following list of Kushites' involvement in Khor, gleaned from non-Kushite records, is not meant to be complete.

* In the course of the 23rd century BC, Kushite mercenaries in the army of Pharaoh Pepy I had taken part in Egyptian invasions of that region. (Kemp, "Old Kingdom," pp. 142-143.)

* In the fourteenth century BC, the governor of the Egyptian-controlled city of Byblos twice wrote letters to Egypt pleading for it to send reinforcements, and specifically including a request for 100 Kushite soldiers, for the purpose of lifting a siege of that city. (*The Amarna Letters*, ed. and trans. by William L. Moran (Baltimore and London: Johns Hopkins University Press, 1992), pp. 207, 212.)

* Also in the 14th century BC, the pharaoh posted Kushite troops in Jerusalem, ruled by one of Egypt's Canaanite vassals. He did so for the purpose of helping protect Canaan from an invasion that was then underway. (Kushites were thus defending Jerusalem, even though it did not belong to them, some three centuries before the conventional historians credit the Hebrews, under King David, with having come into possession of the city).

This information comes from a letter that Jerusalem's ruler, Abdi-Heba, wrote to Egypt (*ibid.*, pp. 328-329). The thrust of that letter is to complain about serious misconduct by some of these Kushite troops. The ruler asks Egypt to "please make the Kasites [Kushites] responsible for the evil deed. I was almost killed by the Kasites in my own house." The letter, however, does not say what happened or why.

The invasion of the house could, of course, have been a criminal rampage. Or, possibly, it could have some sort of political tinge to it, perhaps even mutiny: in support of this latter idea, it is worth noting that the letter makes it clear the invaders are a growing force in the region and that Abdi-Heba worries that Egypt will send Jerusalem no reinforcements. The translator comments that Abdi-Heba "fears that the [Egyptian] king is going to abandon Jerusalem to its own resources" (p. 330, n. 14). The letter identifies the attackers as the 'Apiru. There has been a long debate over whether and in what the circumstances the term may denote Hebrews.

* In 925 BC, that pharaoh whom 2 Chronicles 12:3 identifies as "Shishak" overran much of Israel and Judah and looted Jerusalem. (The date is from Kitchen, "Late Egyptian Chronology," p. 231.) The Bible says his vast army included, among others, Libyans, Sukkites and Kushites.

* During the reign of Judah's King Asa (913-873 BC), the Bible says that one "Zerah the Kushite" commanded a "vast army and 300 chariots" that invaded Judah with troops that included both Kushites and Libyans. Judah's forces repelled this army (2 Chronicles 14:9-15; 16:8). It is not clear whether Zerah, possibly in charge of mercenary troops garrisoned in southern Khor, was acting on his own initiative or in concert with Sheshonk's successor, Osorkon I, or, possibly, with the king of Israel (Bright, *History of Israel*, p. 231).

* More recently, however, Kushite soldiers appear to have fought alongside troops of Khor. An Assyrian sculpture, or relief, that glorifies the besiegers' conquest of the Philistine city of Gibbethon *c.* 712 BC during Sargon's campaign against the Ashdodite rebellion, depicts black soldiers as among the defenders of that city. Since the Kushite pharaoh stayed out of that conflict, these may have been Kushite mercenaries. (Mitchell, "Israel and Judah," p. 352.)

The sculpture appears to buttress key information in Isaiah 20, written at the time of the Ashdodite rebellion, telling of how the prophet "walked naked and barefoot": apparently worried that Judah will join the rebellion in the expectation that Kush and Egypt will help them against Sargon, Isaiah says he is protesting against those Judahites who rely on Kush and Egypt. He warns that "the king of Assyria [shall] lead away the Egyptians as captives and the Ethiopians as exiles, . . . with buttocks uncovered" (NRSV). The Gibbethon sculpture suggests black Africans were indeed among the prisoners.

In short, a long and still-vigorous pattern existed for the involvement of Kushite troops in Khor. For Shebitku, sending an army across the Sinai and beyond would not have represented crossing any great psychological threshold.

[90] Lisa A. Heidorn, "The Horses of Kush," in *Journal of Near Eastern Studies* 56 (April 1997), pp. 105, 111-114.

[99] Dalley, "Foreign Chariotry and Cavalry," p. 44.

The number of Kushites associated with the royal stables may have been considerable. Heidorn, "Horses of Kush," calculates that the number of Kushites employed probably ranged from 36 to 60 (p. 108, n. 21).

[100] Dalley, "Foreign Chariotry and Cavalry," p. 43, and also Robert Morkot, "The Foundations of the Kushite State," in *Actes de la VIIIe Conférence Internationale des*

Études Nubiennes, I — *Communications principales, Lille, 11-17 septembre, 1994* (Université Charles-de-Gaulle — Lille III), pp. 237-238.

[101] Dalley, "Foreign Chariotry and Cavalry," p. 46.

[102] *Ibid.*, pp. 43-44.

In this context, it is pertinent to note Isaiah 31:1, in which the prophet refers to Judahites who implore Egypt of the 25th Dynasty for help against Sennacherib; the prophet describes these Judahites specifically as people "who rely on horses, who trust in chariots . . ." (NRSV).

Dalley says that documents from the reign of Sennacherib's son, Esarhaddon, suggest that the Assyrian army relied on two breeds of combat horses in particular: Kushite horses for the chariotry and smaller horses from Iran for the cavalry (p. 43).

It does not necessarily follow from this, however, that Kushites had traded to Assyria large numbers of horses that would be used against them. While Assyria clearly purchased some horses from Kush using normal trade channels, it may have added to these numbers through the conquest of other nations that possessed Kushite horses.

[103] In his examination of Napatan reliefs of Kushite soldiers during Piye's reign, Spalinger, "Notes on the Military in Egypt," pays special attention to the modest protective gear and weaponry of these warriors. He observes: "In all, one receives the impression that, in contrast to the contemporary Assyrian military machine, the Kushites were rather backward militarily" (p. 50). On the basis of what the Napatan artwork and the text of Piye's stela suggest about weaponry and tactics, Spalinger concludes that "the military of the Nile Valley lagged behind the developments in other parts of the ancient Near East" (p. 57). For the period in question, Piye's tenure, the assessment seems fair.

[104] Isaiah 31:1 (NIV). In his highly specialized examination of Isaiah's 701-related oracles, Childs, *Isaiah and the Assyrian Crisis*, also stresses the might of these horsemen. His translation refers to them as "very powerful" (p. 33).

CHAPTER SEVEN

[1] Childs, *Isaiah and the Assyrian Crisis*, p. 120.

[2] The text is available in *ANET*, pp. 287-288, ARAB, vol. 2, pp. 118-121, and Cogan & Tadmor, *II Kings* (Appendix I, pp. 337-339). (The original translation of 1878 was by George Smith.)

Sennacherib also describes aspects of his campaign of 701 in other writings, but these simply retell parts of the main annal. See *ARAB*, vol. 2, pp. 142-143, 147-148, 154.

[3] For a translation of the text and discussion of it, see Na'aman, "Sennacherib's 'Letter to God,'" pp. 25-39.

[4] For the identification of the unnamed city as Gath, see *Ibid.*, p. 35.

[5] The translation is based on that of Austen H. Layard, *Discoveries among the Ruins of Nineveh and Babylon* (New York: Harper & Brothers, 1853), p. 128.

[6] Russell, *Sennacherib's Palace*, p. 262.

⁷ See David Ussishkin, *The Conquest of Lachish by Sennacherib* (Tel Aviv: Tel Aviv University, 1982), pp. 71, 76.

⁸ *ANET,* pp. 287-288.

I have made three modifications.

First, the version printed here incorporates a recommendation of Cogan & Tadmor, *II Kings,* regarding the fate of some of Hezekiah's forces (p. 247, n. 2, and p. 339). They say the annal presents Hezekiah as sending his "elite troops and best soldiers" to Nineveh as tribute; they say that Luckenbill's translation errs in stating that these forces deserted Hezekiah in the course of the invasion. See Chapter 4, note 28.

Second, the Luckenbill translation refers to "Hezekiah, the Jew." The original text employs the term *Ia-ú-d-ai,* which corresponds to "Judahite" and which I am using. Luckenbill's use of the term "Jew" in this period well before Judaism's emergence is anachronistic.

Finally, following other writers, I have changed the Luckenbill translation's two references to "Ethiopia" *(Meluhha* in the original) to Kush.

⁹ Dissents from this consensus that Isaiah 36-39 was drawn from 2 Kings 18-20 have been infrequent. Those few who argue for the primacy of the Isaiah text over the Kings account include K.A.D. Smelik, "Distortion in Old Testament Prophecy: The Purpose of Isaiah XXXVI and XXXVII," in *Crises and Perspectives: Studies in Ancient Near Eastern Polytheism, Biblical Theology, Palestinian Archaeology and Intertestamental Literature* (Leiden: E.J. Brill, 1986), pp. 72-74. For additional discussion of this idea, also see Smelik, *Converting the Past: Studies in Ancient Israelite and Moabite Historiography* (Leiden, New York, Köln: E.J. Brill, 1992), pp. 97-101. Agreeing with Smelik are Christopher R. Seitz, *Zion's Final Destiny: The Development of the Book of Isaiah: A Reassessment of Isaiah 36-39* (Minneapolis: Fortress Press, 1991), p. 97, and Motyer, *Prophecy of Isaiah,* pp. 285-286.

For a recent reassertion of the consensus view, see H.G.M. Williamson, "Hezekiah and the Temple," in *Texts, Temples, and Traditions: A Tribute to Menahem Haran,* ed. by Michael V. Fox, Victor Avigdor Horowitz, Avi Hurvitz, Michael L. Klein, Baruch J. Schwartz and Nili Shupak (Winona Lake, IN: Eisenbrauns, 1996), pp. 47-52.

¹⁰ Two of the most noticeable differences between the two versions are these: 1) the Book of Isaiah drops the opening synopsis of the plot in 2 Kings 18:14-16, and 2) it makes no mention of the Tartan and the Rab-saris as accompanying the Rab-shakeh to Jerusalem, as stated in 2 Kings 18:17.

¹¹ Joel P. Weinberg, "The Book of Chronicles: Its Author and Audience," in *Eretz-Israel* 24, 1993, places First and Second Chronicles in the "mid-second half of the fifth century BCE (though other dates cannot be excluded, this date is preferable) in the Jerusalem Citizen-Temple-Community in the scribal milieu" (p. 218). Tadmor, "Period of the First Temple," p. 159, and Vaughn, *Theology, History, and Archaeology in the Chronicler's Account,* p. 16, suggest they were composed in Jerusalem in the early fourth century BC.

¹² 2 Chronicles 32:6-8 says Hezekiah gave a pep talk to Jerusalemites in the face of the Assyrian offensive, assuring them that Yahweh would protect them. This is not in Second Kings. Most scholars, however, consider this to be a theological addition of doubtful historicity.

2 Chronicles 32:3-5 provides perhaps the only nugget of useful information that is not in the 2 Kings account: it says Hezekiah ordered his men to deprive the Assyrians of water by stopping up streams and a brook in the area of Jerusalem and also to build new fortifications. See Chapter 5, and note 12 in Chapter 15 for why this passage might be worth taking seriously.

[13] Clements, *Isaiah and the Deliverance*, p. 16.

[14] 1 Kings 8:29 (NIV, NRSV).

[15] Clements, *Isaiah and the Deliverance*, p. 16.

[16] *Ibid.*, p. 106.

[17] Steven W. Holloway, "Kings, Book of 1-2," *Anchor Bible Dictionary*, vol. 4, p. 79.

[18] Tadmor, "Period of the First Temple," also notes that the Chronicler's "attempt to glorify the personalities of David, Solomon and other Judean kings, in contrast to the critical attitude prevailing towards them in the books of Samuel and Kings (utilized by him), shows that the period of the Davidic monarchy was looked upon as the Golden Age" (p. 159).

[19] In verse 19:9, I have changed the translation's "king of Ethiopia" to "king of Kush," as it is in the original Hebrew.

[20] Herodotus, *History*, II.141.

[21] See, for example, A.B. Lloyd, *Herodotus, Book II: Commentary 1-98* (Leiden: E.J. Brill, 1976), pp. 7-8.

[22] See, for example, Spalinger, "Foreign Policy of Egypt," p. 40, and Alan B. Lloyd, *Herodotus, Book II: Commentary 99-182* (Leiden: E.J. Brill, 1988), p. 13. (Lloyd uses the name "Shabataka" as a variation of Shebitku.)

[23] Lloyd, *Herodotus, Book II: Commentary 99-182*, says that Herodotus and/or his sources "probably . . . simply *assumed* that the confrontation between the Assyrians and Egyptians, the only two combatants of whom they knew, took place at the gateway to the eastern frontier [of Egypt]" (emphasis in original, p. 103). Herodotus makes no mention of involvement in the conflict by other peoples (*e.g.*, Judahites or Ekronites).

[24] Cogan & Tadmor, *II Kings*, say that Herodotus' "account has nothing to do with Sennacherib's invasion of Judah" (p. 251). Rather, in their hard-to-follow analysis, they propose that Herodotus may really be describing aggression against Egypt by Esarhaddon, Sennacherib's successor. That, they suggest, would explain why in Herodotus' story the Assyrians advance as far as Pelusium. (Although Tadmor had elsewhere, in "Philistia," proposed that Sargon had reached Pelusium, no mention of this is made in this context.)

I have no trouble accepting that Herodotus' account may be an amalgam of Sennacherib and Esarhaddon's campaigns, but I think the hypothesis that the account is exclusively about Esarhaddon's activities contains real problems.

Cogan & Tadmor suggest that Herodotus' version combines two known campaigns against Egypt by Esarhaddon: the first campaign, in 674-673, would have failed, Taharqa having repelled Esarhaddon at an unknown location by unknown means; the second in 671 would, according to Esarhaddon's own annal (*ANET*, p. 292), have included Arabian support. The first campaign would explain the appearance of "Pelusium" in the Herodotus story, they propose, and the second would explain the curious identification of "Sennacherib" as "king of Arabians and Assyrians."

One problem with this is that Esarhaddon penetrated much further than the frontier town of Pelusium. In 671 his army attained the Lower Egyptian hub of Memphis itself, located well inside the country; if Herodotus' Lower Egyptian sources were really talking about Esarhaddon, one would think they would not have forgotten that. The second and larger problem is that in 671 Esarhaddon was not, as in Herodotus' story, defeated: on the contrary, he utterly vanquished the Kushite Egyptian forces at Memphis. Indeed, he introduced the period of decline for the 25th Dynasty that his successor Assurbanipal would complete. (One might argue that Herodotus could have been referring only to Esarhaddon's campaign of 674, when Taharqa did defeat him inside Egypt, but it would be strange for Herodotus' only story about Esarhaddon to be about a temporary setback and to make no mention of his comeback — a comeback that helped alter the course of Egyptian history and that one would assume would have had a large place in folk memory.)

The scholarly consensus is that Herodotus is talking about Sennacherib. See, for example, Lloyd, *Herodotus, Book II: Commentary 99-182*, pp. 99ff.

In the unlikely event that Herodotus is not referring to Sennacherib at all, this would not affect this book's conclusions. These conclusions are reconcilable with the Greek historian's account but they are not dependent upon it.

CHAPTER EIGHT

[1] This description of the Kushite army is based on Spalinger, "Notes on the Military in Egypt," pp. 52-56.

[2] Unlike the other aspects that are described here, our knowledge of three-man chariots comes from a written Assyrian source dating from 671 BC (*Ibid.*, p. 57).

[3] Richard A. Gabriel, *Great Captains of Antiquity* (Westport, CT: Greenwood Press, 2001), expands: "In the Assyrian view, Ashur was the most powerful of all gods and the king was his servant. It was Ashur's will that the lands of all the rebellious gods be restored to him and it was the duty of the Assyrian king to pursue this goal" (p. 60).

[4] Johannes C. de Moor, *The Rise of Yahwism: The Roots of Israelite Monotheism* (Leuven, Belgium: Leuven University Press, 1990), p. 97; see also pp. 45ff.

[5] Lionel Casson, *Ancient Egypt* (New York: Time-Life Books, 1965), pp. 74-75.

[6] O'Connor, "New Kingdom and Third Intermediate Period," p. 242.

[7] I am unaware of any scholars who have sought to link the Kushite challenge to Assyria with *ma'at*. For good discussions of *ma'at* in other contexts of Egyptian foreign policy, however, see Cohn, *Cosmos*, pp. 3-30, and S. T. Smith, *Askut*, pp. 184-188.

[8] Herodotus, II.141.

[9] *ANET*, p. 287.

[10] See, for example, László Török, "Kush and the External World," in *Studia Meroitica 1984, Proceedings of the Fifth International Conference for Meroitic Studies, Rome 1984*, Meroitica 10 (Berlin: Akademie-Verlag, 1988), p. 57.

11 Herodotus II.137. See also Diodorus I.65.

12 *Diodorus on Egypt*, trans. by Edwin Murphy (Jefferson, NC, and London: McFarland, 1985), I.65.

13 Not that such an eradication would have been easy. Veined by rivers and riddled with swamps, the Delta was a good place for fugitives to hide from pursuers. In both 728 and 712, it would probably have been difficult for the Napatans to capture all their defeated foes.

14 For this insight I am grateful to Bruce Trigger, commenting upon my manuscript in 2000.

15 Katzenstein, *The History of Tyre*, pp. 248-249. The passage to which he refers is in *ANET*, p. 287.

16 The following is from *ANET*, p. 287.

17 Spalinger, "Notes on the Military in Egypt," observes: "There is no indication that this coalition was organized for siege warfare or for a major campaign of conquest" (p. 54).
The fast-moving nature of this advance unit represents an additional reason for thinking that foot-soldier conscripts would not have been part of it.

18 *Ibid.*, p. 54.

19 Spalinger, "Foreign Policy of Egypt," p. 36.

20 Tadmor, "Philistia," p. 97.

21 Kitchen, Kenneth A., "Egypt, the Levant and Assyria in 701 B.C.," in *Fontes Atque Pontes: Eine Festgabe für Hellmut Brunner* (Wiesbaden: Otto Harrassowitz, 1983), p. 248; see also p. 250. Sharing this view are Miller & Hayes, *Israel and Judah*, p. 362, and Yurco, "Sennacherib's Third Campaign," p. 224.

22 Seymour Gitin, "Ekron of the Philistines, Part II: Olive-oil Suppliers to the World," *Biblical Archaeology Review* (March-April, 1990), p. 34.

23 *ANET*, p. 288; also, *ARAB*, vol. 2, p. 120.

24 Na'aman, "Sennacherib's "Letter to God," pp. 25-39. The Assyrian king's "letter" describes the capture of two cities under Judahite control. One is explicitly Azekah. While the partly destroyed text does not explicitly identify the second, Na'aman deduces that it is Gath.

25 Sennacherib's annal says the Assyrians "drove out" out of these 46 communities a total of "200,150 people, young and old, male and female" and that he "considered them booty" (*ANET*, 288; see also *ARAB*, vol. 2, p. 120). Many scholars infer from this that there were mass deportations, and there has been scholarly debate as to whether 200,000 deportees is a realistic figure — given that it is seven times the number that Sargon says he exiled from the northern kingdom. For skepticism, see Broshi, "Population of Iron Age Palestine," and Nadav Na'aman, "Sennacherib's Campaign to Judah and the Date of the LMLK Stamps," in *Vetus Testamentum* 29 (1975), p. 85. The consensus is that the figure is exaggerated.

For a view that the 200,150 figure is very plausible, see Baruch Halpern, "Jerusalem and the Lineages in the Seventh Century BCE: Kingship and the Rise of Individual Moral Liability," in *Law and Ideology in Monarchic Israel* (Sheffield, UK: JSOT Press, 1991), pp. 31-33. Halpern argues that the fact that 200,150 is not a round figure makes it seem realistic. Among other things, he also says Sennacherib would have needed large numbers of workers to build his new capital, Nineveh, and that he could have sent others to repopulate parts of Philistia, such as Ekron.

It is interesting that nowhere does Sennacherib's annal say he actually deported any Judahites. Rather, the text says that Sennacherib "drove out" of captured places "200,150 people . . . and considered them booty." Considering people to be spoils of war could be a temporary condition; after all, in the next sentence the Sennacherib says of Hezekiah, "Himself I made a prisoner in Jerusalem, . . . like a bird in a cage," a condition that we *know* was temporary. The second statement is face-saving; so could be the first.

My view is that, even though Sennacherib does not explicitly say there were deportations, some may have taken place. (The Lachish relief does show some people quite clearly departing.) The forced withdrawal of the Assyrians, however, would have cut this process short. Given the preparations (including gathering of supplies) needed for the moving of 200,150 people, many of them over very long distances, and the need to find appropriate destinations for them, a proper operation would have taken many months and perhaps several years. In the summer of 701, Sennacherib and most of his forces were still in a combat mode. Prior to their sudden retreat, the Assyrians would not have had time to execute large-scale deportations.

[26] Layard, *Discoveries among the Ruins,* pp. 126-127.

[27] My account is based on D. Ussishkin, "The Assyrian Attack on Lachish: The Evidence from the Southwest Corner of the Site," English summary of the Hebrew, in *Eretz-Israel* 20, 1989, *op. cit.*, pp. 197-198.

[28] Ussishkin, *Conquest of Lachish,* p. 56.

[29] D.L. Risdon, as cited by Ussishkin, *ibid.*, p. 56.

Ussishkin, describing the findings in the 1930s of Risdon, a British skull expert, makes the following statement:

"Curiously, the crania indicate a close racial resemblance to the population of Egypt at that time. Risdon made comparisons between the Lachish skulls and 21 ancient Egyptian and allied series of skulls. His conclusion was that 'the relationships found suggest that the population of the town in 700 B.C.E. was entirely, or almost entirely, of Egyptian origin, very close connections with some contemporary Egyptian series being found. They show, further, that the population of Lachish was probably derived principally from Upper Egypt. Comparisons of measurements considered singly indicate that the Lachish cranial type has no features which would be unusual for an ancient Egyptian type, other than the prominence of its nasal bones and the curvature of its malar bones.' If so, this is indeed a conclusion of far-reaching implications" (pp. 56-57).

One deduction here is plainly not logical: just because several hundred people whom the Assyrians grouped together were primarily of one stock does not necessarily mean that almost the entire population of the city, which would have numbered several thousand people, were of the same background. The bas-relief shows many civilians leaving the city peaceably. One might argue that the Assyrians executed and/or dumped in one place the bodies of a certain social/ethnic group; the city may have consisted of more than one such group.

Regarding the possible Upper Egyptian background of these victims, there is also another scholar's observation that should be mentioned. When the two observations are taken together, they raise provocative questions.

In her article published in 1982, the same year as Ussishkin's book, Albenda, "Observations on Egyptians in Assyrian Art," indicates no familiarity with Risdon's study or Ussishkin's account. But she makes this comment on the relief:

"In the aftermath of their defeat, processions of Lachishites, together with captured booty, advance toward the enthroned Assyrian king. At the front of this procession are persons quite distinct from the Judeans. They are arranged into three groups: two men are naked and stretched upon the ground to be flayed by Assyrian soldiers; several others advance and raise their hands to the level of their face as a sign of submission; and still other men are shown in a sequence of kneeling actions before the Assyrian king, as they implore mercy. Their physiognomy makes it *almost certain that they are to be identified with the Egyptian/Kushite foes*, since their hair and short beard are composed of rows of tight curls. These persons wear a plain, long garment reaching to the ankle and are barefooted. *Their costume may reveal them to be the charioteers captured by the Assyrian army, and it is quite possible that in this instance the Assyrian artist utilized a single racial type for representing Egyptians and Nubians in the same scene*, similar to the usage on the reliefs of Sargon II" (p. 10, emphasis added).

I have quoted the pertinent passages from both Ussishkin and Albenda in their entirety; neither scholar makes additional argument.

These independent observations perplex me. I am placing this discussion in a note rather than in my main text because I do not know how to assess the importance of these observations — I am not sure they should be called findings.

Before drawing any conclusions, the original 60-year-old analysis of the skulls would benefit from a fresh look by experts. Also, I am not sold on Albenda's interpretation of these figures as being necessarily Egyptian/Kushite. The photos I have seen of the figures do not point conclusively to such a background.

If these scholars' observations are correct, however, the implications are indeed, as Ussishkin says, "far-reaching." It is significant that Risdon identifies the skulls as Upper Egyptian rather than Lower Egyptian; Kush's relations with Upper Egypt were particularly close at this time, given Kush's effective control over Thebes and Upper Egypt generally since the time of King Kashta in the mid-eighth century BC. It is far easier to imagine Upper Egyptians somehow carrying out the 25th Dynasty's foreign policy than Lower Egyptians. One might try to explain the presence of Egyptian/Kushite charioteers at Lachish by supposing that they had repaired to that city after the clash at Eltekeh. But, then, how does one explain the presence there of many women and "immature" people of similar background? One would not expect to find them on a military campaign. Or would they have been there for some other reason?

If the scholars' views are correct, and it is a big *if*, it would seem to strengthen my thesis that strong ties existed between Judah and Egypt at the time of the Kushites.

30 Isaiah 1:7 (NEB).

31 Isaiah 1:8 (TEV).

32 Isaiah 22:3.

[33] 2 Kings 18:18ff, 19:2. The three are the royal steward (Eliakim), the court secretary (Shebna) and the official in charge of records (Joah). As with the Assyrian envoys, their titles probably understate their importance. Cogan & Tadmor, *II Kings*, describe the three Hebrews as "ranking ministers" (p. 230, n. 18).

[34] Aharoni, *Land of the Bible*, pp. 339-340. He bases his case that a second group arrived from the north on Isaiah 10:28-32. Some scholars do not place this passage at 701 BC. However, the passage fits that year better than any other. See also Yohanan Aharoni and Michael Avi-Yonah, *The Macmillan Bible Atlas* (New York: Macmillan Co., 1968), map on p. 99.

[35] Cogan & Tadmor, *II Kings*, p. 229, n. 17.

[36] The translation of these two words, Rab-saris and Rab-shakeh, have been the subject of much debate. Hayim Tadmor, "Rab-saris and Rab-shakeh in 2 Kings 18," in *Word of the Lord Shall Go Forth, op. cit.*, rejects more grandiose earlier translations, such as "field-commander" for Rab-shakeh. Tadmor says research on Assyrian (as distinct from biblical) texts indicates that the titles have these domestic-sounding meanings (pp. 279-281).

[37] Gonçalves, *L'expédition de Sennachérib*, p. 384, n. 59.

[38] Layard, *Discoveries among the Ruins*, p. 127.

[39] 2 Kings 18:26-27.

[40] Cogan & Tadmor, *II Kings*, p. 230, n. 17.

[41] In 2 Kings 18:23-24 and 27, the Rab-shakeh speaks spontaneously and for himself; that he is not reading Sennacherib's letter at that time is obvious from his repeated use of the words, "my master" when referring to the Assyrian king. In the main, however, the Rab-shakeh is speaking for Sennacherib, as when he says, "YHWH said to *me*, 'Attack this country and destroy it!'" (emphasis added, trans. by Cogan & Tadmor.)

[42] The reed also possesses similar symbolic value in Egyptian art. As well, in the official protocol, one of the titles of a pharaoh who claimed power over all of Egypt was "the one who belongs to the Reed and the Bee" — meaning "King of Upper and Lower Egypt." See Georges Posener, *Dictionary of Egyptian Civilization*, trans. from the French by Alix Macfarlane (New York: Tudor Publishing, 1959), pp. 75, 212.

Given the importance of reed symbolism, one can only conclude the Rab-shakeh's choice of metaphor was not accidental.

As for the conventional opinion that the bee was Lower Egypt's symbol, see Chapter 16 for the view that the "bee" may in fact have been a hornet.

[43] Cogan & Tadmor, *II Kings*, say of this passage: "The Hebrew spoken is referred to as Judean, in contrast to the dialect spoken at the same time in the northern kingdom" (p. 232).

[44] See the records of King Tiglath-pileser's reign as discussed by H.W.F. Saggs, *Assyriology and the Study of the Old Testament* (Cardiff: University of Wales, 1969), pp. 16-18.

[45] 2 Kings 19:4 (TEV).

[46] 2 Kings 19:7. The translation is by Cogan & Tadmor, *II Kings*. The NIV also uses the word "report." Many translations use "rumor."

[47] Kitchen, *Third Intermediate Period*, p. 160.

[48] Kitchen, *ibid.*, gives relatively detailed reasons for thinking Taharqa was 20 or 21 at the time of the Judah expedition. He points to inscriptional evidence at a temple at Kawa in which Taharqa, who composed the text after becoming pharaoh, recalls that when he was 20 years old he passed by Kawa on a trip from Napata to Lower Egypt; Taharqa says that Pharaoh Shebitku, who was in Egypt, had summoned him north. Kitchen says military allusions in the text suggest that Shebitku had summoned Taharqa (among others) in order to send him on the expedition against Sennacherib (pp. 157, 164-167). By the time the expedition reached Judah, the prince may or may not have attained the age of 21.

Also using the Kawa text to argue that Taharqa would have been 20 or 21 in 701 is Yurco, "Sennacherib's Third Campaign," pp. 222-223.

For the inscriptional evidence in question, see M.F. Laming Macadam, *The Temples of Kawa*, vol. 1. (London: Oxford University Press, 1949).

[49] Redford, *Egypt, Canaan, and Israel*, p. 353, n. 163. Redford says Taharqa would have been not 20 or 21 but "still a lad" in 701 and absent from the Judah expedition. Redford notes that when Taharqa in his Kawa inscription (see the preceding note) says the Pharaoh Shebitku summoned him north to Lower Egypt he, Taharqa, does not say explicitly that this was in order to prepare for war; Redford says Taharqa probably journeyed to Egypt simply in order to join Shebitku's new pharaonic court. Redford, who maintains Shebitku became pharaoh only in 697 (and here disputes the idea of a co-regency with Shabako starting just prior to the 701 conflict), says Taharqa's trip therefore took place at least four years after Sennacherib's invasion. In 701, according to this argument, the prince would therefore still have been well into his teens. In a later article, "Note on the Chronology," Redford concedes a pre-701 co-regency, however.

[50] Smelik, *Converting the Past*, p. 105, n. 52.

[51] Paul E. Dion, "Sennacherib's Expedition to Palestine," in *Église et Théologie* 20, 1989, p. 24.

[52] Spalinger, "Foreign Policy of Egypt," p. 40.

[53] K.A. Kitchen, *Pharaoh Triumphant: The Life and Times of Ramesses II, King of Egypt* (Warminster, UK: Aris & Phillips, 1982), p. 24. Kitchen, who does not make use of the Ramses parallel in advancing elsewhere his own case for Taharqa's participation in the expedition of 701, assumes that the 14th-century-BC prince was "probably kept clear of the battle lines" during the Delta campaign.

[54] Jean Leclant and Jean Yoyotte, "Notes d'histoire et de civilisation ethiopiennes: a propos d'un ouvrage récent," in *Bulletin de l'Institut français d'architecture orientale* 53, 1953, pp. 18-20.

In the Kawa text, Taharqa, referring to himself in the third person, recalls a time when he "was a young man": Shebitku, who was in Egypt and whom he had evidently not seen for some time, sent for him and other "young men" who were in Kush. When Shebitku was with Taharqa, he — Shebitku — "preferred him" to the other young royals. The context of this meeting between Shebitku and Taharqa is unstated but would fit the circumstances of Shebitku's coronation in Egypt or the preparations for the campaign against Sennacherib. The pharaoh's preference for Taharqa over older kinsmen, including one named Khaliut, would explain his choice of Taharqa as army leader over more senior candidates.

55 *Ibid.*, p. 19. n. 2.

56 Adams, *Nubia*, p. 259. The precise nature of the selection process is not known. Adams speculates: "To some extent the office may have been elective among the eligible brothers and sons, the choice being made either by the claimants themselves or (more probably) by the priesthood of Amon."

57 *Ibid.*, p. 259. Adams believes Taharqa commanded the army in 701 but earned no glory (p. 264). This, however, does not invalidate Adams' deduction that Taharqa must somehow have demonstrated an unusual gift for leadership as a young man. For the view that Taharqa was Shebitku's cousin, and not brother, see Török, *Kingdom of Kush: Handbook.*

58 Michael C. Astour, "Sabtah and Sabteca: Ethiopian Pharaoh Names in Genesis 10," in *Journal of Biblical Literature* 84, 1965, p. 424. Also making the same point, but without discussion, is an earlier book: Emil G. Kraeling, *Rand McNally Bible Atlas* (New York: Rand McNally & Co., 1956), p. 49.

59 Indeed, one might wonder why, if this army had in fact been irrelevant, any mention of the army—let alone its leader—was worth noting in the Bible in the first place, but that's another story.

60 2 Kings 19:35 (Cogan & Tadmor).

CHAPTER NINE

1 A fifth explanation, first proposed more than a century ago, also exists, but it has been widely and persuasively attacked in recent years; it lacks sufficient scholarly support to be included on this list of leading, still-current theories. This fifth theory maintains that Sennacherib staged not one but two invasions of Judah. One invasion would have been in 701, the second *c.* 688 BC. See Bright, *History of Israel*, pp. 296-308. To proponents of this theory, the two conflicts would explain 2 Kings' two parallel accounts.

Scathingly but justifiably, Redford in *Egypt, Canaan, and Israel*, says that this theory "has become such an exercise in ingenuity and a travesty of methodology that it ceases to amuse" (p. 354, n. 165).

The double-invasion theory assumes that Taharqa would have been in his preteens or early teens in 701 BC and thus he too young to take even titular command of any army that year, but old enough to do so a decade or more later, at which time he would have sought to repulse a second Assyrian invasion. As we saw in Chapter 8, however, Kitchen among others has demonstrated that Taharqa was probably 20 or 21 years old in 701, thus giving him the maturity for at least nominal leadership, as the Bible claims. Another weakness with the theory is that there is simply no mention of a second campaign in Assyrian records. One would expect the annals to make some reference to another campaign to Khor, even if it camouflaged a setback. As well, Tadmor says a second campaign sometime after 701 would have been inconsistent with Sennacherib's evident policy toward the west during the remainder of his reign; Tadmor,

"Period of the First Temple," concludes that "the supposition of two campaigns cannot be upheld" (p. 144). See also Cogan & Tadmor, *II Kings*, pp. 249-250.

William H. Shea, "Sennacherib's Second Palestinian Campaign," *Journal of Biblical Literature* 104, 1985, has sought to revive the two-campaign theory (pp. 401-418). In a lengthy examination of Shea's article, Barnes, *Studies*, rightly describes it as "speculative in the extreme" (p. 129).

To Barnes' critique, I would add one point. Shea argues that even if Taharqa was 20 or 21 years old in 701, he would have been more likely to have led an army to Judah during a second campaign *c.* 686 (pp. 403, 416). Shea points out that Egyptian textual evidence clearly shows that it was Pharaoh Shebitku who summoned Taharqa for a campaign. But he argues that Shebitku was not pharaoh in 701, Shabako was. He rejects the view of several writers, including Yurco, "Sennacherib's Third Campaign", that the two would have ruled jointly as co-regents in 701. Shea says that Shabako did not die until *c.* 699 (which itself is plausible), and he proposes that it was only *after* his death that Shebitku succeeded him. Shea's grounds for rejecting the co-regency are simply that "there is no Egyptian inscriptional evidence" for it (p. 416). That argument can also be used to reject Shea's own double-invasion theory.

However, there is Greek textual evidence, which to my knowledge has not been cited in this debate, that would support Yurco. Herodotus (II.139) says that well *before his death* Shabako (whom Herodotus calls Sabacos) voluntarily relinquished power in Egypt and departed, presumably for Kush.

See also Chapter 6, note 87, for recent archaeological evidence that fortifies the co-regency thesis. In the years since Redford's stinging remark in 1992, it has become even harder to argue that Shebitku had not come to power by 701.

For another critique of Shea's two-campaign theory, see Frank J. Yurco, "The Shabaka-Shebitku Coregency and the Supposed Second Campaign of Sennacherib against Judah: A Critical Assessment," in *Journal of Biblical Literature* 110 (1991). Among other things, Yurco points out that at such sites as Lachish and Ekron there is no archaeological evidence of two waves of destruction within the necessary range of dates (p. 36).

[2] Including: Bernhard W. Anderson, *Understanding the Old Testament*, 4th ed. (Englewood Cliffs, NJ: Prentice-Hall, 1986), p. 353; Simon Dubnov, *History of the Jews*, vol. 1, *From the Beginning to Early Christianity*, trans. from the Russian by Moshe Spiegel, 4th definitive and rev. ed. (South Brunswick, NJ: Thomas Yoseloff, 1967), p. 268; Andrew Duncan and Michael Opatowski, *War in the Holy Land: From Megiddo to the West Bank* (Sutton Publishing, 1998), p. 21; Grimal, *History of Ancient Egypt*, p. 347; Hooker, "Location of the Brook of Egypt," p. 212; Morris Jastrow, *The Civilization of Babylon and Assyria* (Philadelphia: J.P. Lippincott, 1915), pp. 177-178; J. Kenneth Kuntz, *The People of Ancient Israel: An Introduction to Old Testament Literature, History and Thought* (New York: Harper & Row, 1974), p. 307; Mazar, *Archaeology of the Land of the Bible*, p. 405; W.O.E. Oesterley, "Egypt and Israel," in *The Legacy of Egypt*, ed. by S.R.K. Glanville (Oxford: Clarendon Press, 1942), p. 229, and Roy A. Rosenberg, *The Concise Guide to Judaism: History, Practice, Faith* (Nal Books, 1990), p. 18.

[3] Luckenbill, *Annals of Sennacherib*, p. 14.

In that year, says Luckenbill, "royal vanity" demanded that a raid against mountain villages northeast of Nineveh be dressed up as a glorious military campaign "recorded in high-sounding phrases" on the walls of his rapidly growing palace at Nineveh.

Grayson, "Sennacherib and Esarhaddon," sets 689 as the time after which Sennacherib was potentially "free to launch a new campaign to the west" (p. 111).

Regardless of the precise date that one picks, the point is that the king had ample opportunity to return to Khor.

⁴ Judah would pay tribute to Nineveh, but it was certainly not a subjugated nation. It retained at least semi-independence. Tadmor, "Period of the First Temple," goes so far as to say that, after his invasion of 701, "Sennacherib consciously acquiesced in the *de facto* independence of Judah and the Philistine cities . . ." (p. 144).

⁵ The Book of Isaiah contains an intriguing passage, 17:12-14, that we will examine more closely in a later chapter. It describes armies of unidentified "powerful nations" advancing confidently, then abruptly retreating like "straw in a whirlwind." There is no scholarly consensus that the passage refers to 701 BC. I would argue that more likely than not it does pertain to that year, since Sennacherib's retreat would be the most vivid example of such a military reversal in Khor by a major power during this general period. What else would the author be thinking of?

If the passage is indeed based on 701, it would strengthen the underlying elements in Herodotus and the Bible's: Sennacherib's withdrawal took place suddenly, under some form of duress and its cause was close by. Responding to a distant uprising would not cause the Assyrians to be "driven away like dust on a mountainside, like straw in a whirlwind" (TEV).

⁶ 2 Kings 19:35, Isaiah 37:36 and 2 Chronicles 32:21.

⁷ For discussion of such efforts, see Cogan & Tadmor, *II Kings*, p. 239, n. 35, and Mitchell, "Israel and Judah," p. 367.

⁸ Supporters of this theory range from those who have given considerable thought to the matter (like Breasted, Kitchen, Lloyd and Rowley) to those who appear to be simply going along with conventional opinion. Several, like Bright, see disease as delivering the *coup de grâce* but in conjunction with another theory, including one that involves two invasions by Sennacherib (see this chapter's note 1).

Supporters include: Adams, *Nubia*, p. 264; A.J. Arkell, *A History of the Sudan: From the Earliest Times to 1821* (London: Athlone Press, 1955), p. 126; Armstrong, *Jerusalem*, p. 70; James Baikie, *The Ancient East and Its Story* (London: T.C. & E.C. Jack, 1929), p. 427; Charles Boutflower, *The Book of Isaiah, Chapters I-XXXIX* (London: Society for Promoting Christian Knowledge, 1930), pp. 284-296; Breasted, *History of Egypt*, p. 552; Bright, *History of Israel,* p. 299; F.F. Bruce, *Israel and the Nations: From the Exodus to the Fall of the Second Temple* (Grand Rapids, MI: William B. Eerdmans, 1963), p. 72; *A Commentary on the Bible by Various Writers*, ed. by the Rev. J.R. Dummelow (New York: Macmillan, 1935), p. 243; François Daumas, *La civilisation de l'Égypte pharaonique*, rev. ed. (Paris: Arthaud, 1987), p. 85; Etienne Drioton and Jacques Vandier, *L'Égypte: Des origines à la conquête d'Alexandre* (Paris: Collection Dito, 1984 {1938}), pp. 549-550; Dupuy & Dupuy, *Harper Encyclopedia of Military History*, p. 11; Peter F. Ellis, "1-2 Kings," in *The Jerome Biblical Commentaries*, vol. 1 (Englewood Cliffs, NJ: Prentice-Hall, 1968), p. 206; Walter A. Fairservis, Jr., *The Ancient Kingdoms of the Nile and the Doomed Monuments of Nubia* (New York: Thomas Y. Crowell, 1962), p. 192; Jack Finegan, *Light from the Ancient Past: The Archeological Background of the Hebrew-Christian Religion* (Princeton: Princeton University Press, 1946), p. 179; Cyrus H. Gordon and Gary Rendsburg, *The Bible and the Ancient Near East*, 4th ed. (London, New York: W.W. Norton, 1997 {1953}), p. 262, and Grant, *History of Ancient Israel*, p. 139.

Also: Abraham J. Heschel, *The Prophets* (N.p.: Jewish Publication Society of America, 1962), p. 77; Philip K. Hitti, *History of Syria, Including Lebanon and Palestine* (New York: Macmillan Co., 1951), p. 199; Sara Japhet, *I & II Chronicles: A Commentary* (London: SCM Press, 1993), pp. 990-991; Paul Johnson, *A History of the Jews* (London: Weidenfeld and Nicholson, 1987), p. 73; Robert W. July, *A History of the African People*, 2nd ed. (New York: Charles Scribner's Sons. 1974), p. 39; Yehezkel Kaufmann, "The Biblical Age," in *Great Ages and Ideas of the Jewish People*, ed. by Leo W. Schwarz (New York: Modern Library, Random House, 1956), pp. 65-66; Werner Keller, *The Bible as History*, rev. 2nd ed., trans. from the German by William Neil (New York: Bantam Books, 1980), p. 281; Charles Foster Kent, *The Kings and Prophets of Israel and Judah* (New York: Charles Scribner's Sons, 1909), p. 179; Kathleen M. Kenyon, *Digging up Jerusalem* (London: London & Tonbridge; Ernest Benn, 1974), pp. 150, 160; Gerhard Konzelmann, *Jérusalem: 40 siècles d'histoire*, trans. from the German by André Muller (Paris: Robert Laffont, 1985), p. 126; Kitchen, "Egypt, the Levant and Assyria," pp. 245, 251; Kuhrt, *Ancient Near East*, vol. 2, pp. 477-478; Antti Laato, "Assyrian Propaganda and the Falsification of History in the Royal Inscriptions of Sennacherib," in *Vetus Testamentum* 45 (1995), pp. 225-226; William Sanford Lasor, David Allan Hubbard and Frederic William Bush, *Old Testament Survey* (Grand Rapids, MI: William B. Eerdmans, 1982), p. 281; Rufus Learsi, *Israel: A History of the Jewish People* (Cleveland and New York: World Publishing, 1949), p. 88; Lloyd, *Herodotus, Book II: Commentary 99-182*, p. 104; Edward Longstreth, *Decisive Battles of the Bible* (Philadelphia and New York: J.B. Lippincott, 1962), p. 111; Mandour El Mahdi, *A Short History of the Sudan* (London: Oxford University Press, 1965), pp. 12-13, and McNeill, "Infectious Alternatives," p. 80.

Also: George E. Mendenhall, "Jerusalem from 1000 - 63 BC," in *Jerusalem in History: 3,000 B.C. to the Present Day*, rev. ed., ed. by Kamil J. Asali (London and New York: Kegan Paul International, 1997), p. 59; *The New Westminster Dictionary of the Bible*, ed. by Henry Snyder Gehman (Philadelphia: Westminster Press, 1970), pp. 386, 847; A.T. Olmstead, *History of Assyria* (New York, London: Charles Scribner's Sons, 1923), p. 309; Harry M. Orlinsky, *Understanding the Bible through History and Archaeology* (New York: KTAV Publishing House, 1972), p. 190; T. Eric Peet, *Egypt and the Old Testament* (Liverpool: University Press of Liverpool; London: Hodder and Stoughton, 1922), p. 177; Giuseppe Ricciotti, *The History of Israel*, vol. 1, *From the Beginning to the Exile*, trans. from the Italian by C. Della Penta and R.T.A. Murphy (Milwaukee: Bruce Publishing, 1955),p. 386; Theodore H. Robinson, *A History of Israel*, vol. 1, *From the Exodus to the Fall of Jerusalem, 586 B.C.* (Oxford: Clarendon Press, 1932); H.H. Rowley, *Men of God: Studies in Old Testament History and Prophecy* (London: Thomas Nelson & Sons, 1963), pp. 125-126; Abram Leon Sachar, *A History of the Jews*, 5th ed. and enlarged (New York: Alfred A. Knopf, 1965 {1930}), p. 58; Moses A. Shulvass, *The History of the Jewish People*, vol. 1: *The Antiquity* (Chicago: Regnery Gateway, 1982), p. 46; Wolfram T. von Soden, "Mesopotamia and Iraq, History of: II. Mesopotamia from 1600 BC to 630 AD," in *Encyclopaedia Britannica: Macropaedia*, vol. 11, 15th ed. (1975), p. 985; *The Standard Jewish Encyclopedia*, ed. by Cecil Roth (Jerusalem and Tel Aviv: Massadah

Publishing, 1958/9), p. 899; and G.W. Wade, *The Book of the Prophet Isaiah, with Introduction and Notes* (London: Methuen, 1911), p. 237, and Derek A. Welsby, *The Kingdom of Kush: The Napatan and Meroitic Empires* (Princeton, NJ: Marcus Wiener, 1998, p. 64).

[9] Exodus 9, 11.

[10] 2 Kings 18:17, 19:8.

[11] Kitchen, "Egypt, the Levant and Assyria," speculates that this additional contingent would have been raiding Mareshah and Adullam, just east of Lachish (p. 250; also, p. 248). See Micah 1:15.

[12] Bear in mind that the Bible clearly indicates the angel targeted just one Assyrian location: the angel "struck the Assyrian camp" (2 Kings 19:35, Cogan & Tadmor).

[13] Yurco, "Sennacherib's Third Campaign," p. 234.

[14] Lloyd, Herodotus, *Book II: Commentary 99-182*, pp. 104.
For a discussion of other descriptions in Greek writings of mice defeating human warriors by nibbling their leather equipment, see W. Kendrick Pritchett, *The Liar School of Herodotus* (Amsterdam: J.C. Gieben, 1993) p. 113-116. The descriptions are in Strabo (13.1.48.) and a commentary on the Iliad by Eustathius, archbishop of Thessalonika, a scholar of the 12th century AD.
Pritchett concludes that, despite the depiction of the mouse by other cultures, the mouse motif told by Herodotus is probably indigenously Egyptian — and *not* a motif borrowed from Greece or, as some have suggested, from Asia.

[15] Lloyd, *Ibid.*, p. 104.

[16] *Ibid.*, pp. 103-104. For Lloyd's reasoning, see below.

[17] Yurco, "Sennacherib's Third Campaign," p. 240, n. 145; see also p. 235. Yurco reasons that rodents symbolized disease for the Philistines; since some Philistines lived in northern Egypt it must have been from them, he says, that Herodotus obtained the story of the mice (p. 234). This is extremely speculative.

[18] Lloyd, *Herodotus, Book II: Commentary 99-182*, p. 104.

[19] Yurco, "Sennacherib's Third Campaign," p. 235. He does not, however, suggest that the Jersualemites would have contaminated the water deliberately.

[20] (NEB)

[21] 2 Kings 18:14 (Cogan & Tadmor).

[22] Clements, *Isaiah and the Deliverance*, pp. 19 ff, 91; Cogan, "Into Exile," pp. 334-335, and in *The HarperCollins Bible Dictionary*, ed. by Paul J. Achtenmeier (HarperSanFrancisco, 1996), pp. 995-996; Gonçalves, *L'expédition de Sennachérib*, pp. 543-544; Miller & Hayes, *Israel and Judah*, p. 362, and Martin Noth, *The History of Israel*, 2nd ed., rev., trans. from the German by P.R. Ackroyd (London: Adam and Charles Black, 1965), p. 268.
Other adherents include: Rainer Albertz, *A History of the Israelite Religion in the Old Testament Period*, vol. 1: *From the Beginnings to the End of the Monarchy*, trans. from the German by John Bowden (Louisville, KY: Westminster/John Knox Press, 1994), p. 163;

John Bowker, *The Complete Bible Handbook* (Willowdale, Ont.: Firefly Books, 1998), p. 143; Peter A. Clayton, *Chronicle of the Pharaohs: The Reign-by-reign Record of the Rulers and Dynasties of Ancient Egypt* (London: Thames and Hudson, 1994), pp. 192-193; Robin Lane Fox, *The Unauthorized Version: Truth and Fiction in the Bible* (New York: Alfred A. Knopf, 1992), p. 325); H.R. Hall, *The Ancient History of the Near East* (London: Methuen, 1913), p. 484, Henry W.F. Saggs, "Sennacherib," in *Encyclopaedia Britannica, Macropaedia*, vol. 16, 15th ed. (1975), p. 542; Smelik, "Distortion of Old Testament Prophecy," p. 85, and Marvin A. Sweeney, *Isaiah 1-39: With an Introduction to Prophetic Literature* (Grand Rapids, MI: William B. Eerdmans, 1996), p. 479.

[23] Clements, *Isaiah and the Deliverance*, describes the theory this way:

"After almost his entire kingdom had been reduced to ruins, Hezekiah surrendered when it was clear that further resistance was useless. By doing so he spared Jerusalem, the preparations for the siege of which had just begun, from experiencing the horrors and destruction which had been meted out to most of the rest of Judah and to Israel and other kingdoms in the course of earlier Assyrian campaigns" (p. 91).

Gonçalves, *L'expédition de Sennachérib*, says that, contrary to the claims of Second Kings, the outcome of the invasion "is due not to any sort of setback to the Assyrians, but to the fact that Hezekiah submitted, and paid the huge sums that Sennacherib imposed upon him. With this, Sennacherib achieved his objective concerning Judah" (pp. 543-544).

[24] Adherents of the troubles-elsewhere theory and epidemic theory would also agree on that.

[25] In Sargon's writings, one does find a single case of forgiveness, but that incident's circumstances are too fundamentally different from the Jerusalem situation to qualify as a precedent.

That event took place in a war against the Manneans, a mountain people of what is now northwest Iran. When Mannean tribal chiefs killed their own Assyria-appointed king, they replaced him with Ullusunu, son of an earlier Assyrian vassal. After Sargon sacked and burned some of the country, he flayed Ullusunu's brother and showed the body to the people. The king of Mannea then journeyed to Sargon from afar, had his people feed the invading Assyrian troops, kissed Sargon's feet, offered tribute and even vowed to fight against one of the chief Mannean rebels responsible for his own accession to the throne. Sargon also notes with relish that Ullusunu and his nobles begged forgiveness while "crawling on all fours like dogs." Sargon pardoned the humiliated wretch and allowed him to keep his throne. (*ARAB*, vol. 2, pp. 5, 6, 27-29, 75-79.)

The difference between this case and the events of 701 is substantial. Ullusunu himself appears not to have been an early fomenter of rebellion, unlike Hezekiah. Ullusunu betrayed the rebels and surrendered while under no immediate personal threat. Hezekiah, while very much under duress, rejected an initial demand for surrender (2 Kings 19:5-7). The Judahite could not give military help to hasten the end of Sennacherib's campaign because with his surrender the campaign would have been virtually over, and besides many of his commanders had already deserted him (Isaiah 22:3).

[26] Clements, *Isaiah and the Deliverance*, proposes only that Assyria would have wanted a deeply-rooted indigenous royal family to provide a "firm and stable government" in the territory of Judah; earlier, the empire did not keep Israel's royal house in place

because, he suggests, unlike Judah with its 300-year-old Davidic Dynasty, the northern kingdom, with its revolving-door royal families, lacked a "stabilizing dynastic tradition" (p. 20.) To be persuasive, such an argument would need to show other cases of comparable leniency by Assyria toward monarchs who had actively rebelled (as distinct from having flirted with the idea of rebellion, as had Hezekiah at the time of Ashdod's revolt).

I would suggest that, in the event he had surrendered, Hezekiah might well have brought little such political stability to Judah. What is more likely is that his position would have been politically untenable. Many of his subjects would have bitterly resented a monarch who had brought down so massive a tragedy upon his kingdom. To ward off revolt, Hezekiah might well have had to resort to repression. That would have been quite contrary to his character, as the Bible presents it.

[27] An observation by Gabriel, *Great Captains of Antiquity*, refers to Sargon in his dealings with vassal states, but it is equally applicable to Sennacherib: ". . . the use of terror by Assyrian kings seems to have been as pragmatic as it was terrible. The horrible fates described in Sargon's annals were by no means universally practiced. A distinction seems to have been made between those peoples who were being newly incorporated into the Assyrian empire and those who had been already incorporated but had broken into open rebellion. The worst of Sargon's terror was visited against the latter, and for good reason. Governing such a large and disparate empire as Assyria with such a small manpower base depended upon the maintenance of order. Rebellion could not be countenanced lest it spread. . . . Terror was a useful weapon in sending the signal to others that there was no real alternative to Assyrian rule" (p. 60).

[28] 2 Kings 18:7 (Cogan & Tadmor).

[29] Granted, despots like Saddam Hussein of Iraq or Kim Il Sung of North Korea might be able to obtain such obsequious praise from intimidated biographers. But the biblical writers in question expressed their praise long after Hezekiah's death, when they had nothing to fear. Indeed, these same writers can be scathing in their criticism of other members of the House of David, notably Hezekiah's own father and son.

Granted, too, it seems a bit much for biblical writers to ascribe an unblemished record of success to a king who recklessly provoked so damaging an invasion. Yet such writers would, in theory, be able to defend that evaluation on grounds that the invader did not actually defeat the king — and that the king, indeed, was able to emerge from the conflict with the appearance of divine benediction. Capitulation, by contrast, would almost inevitably mean humiliation.

[30] 2 Kings 18:5 (Cogan & Tadmor).

[31] Kitchen, "Egypt, the Levant and Assyria," p. 251.

[32] *Ibid.*, p. 252.

[33] Nine pages in length, Kitchen's analysis is many times longer than any other.

[34] Kitchen is not the originator of the idea of two different Kushite-led armies, but he advances it vigorously.

Kitchen prefers to call each of these two contingents a "division" (*ibid.*, p. 250). He speculates that the two would have arrived in Gaza together and used that city as their headquarters.

[35] Kitchen, "Egypt, the Levant and Assyria," p. 250.

[36] Yurco, "Sennacherib's Third Campaign," p. 233.

[37] *Ibid.*, p. 235. On the same page. Yurco also says: "Certainly the presence of mice in Herodotus might suggest that the Biblical divine intervention was a plague outbreak" (p. 235).

[38] *Ibid.*, p. 236.

[39] Lloyd, *Herodotus, Book II: Commentary, 99-182,* p. 103. Because of the weight he gives to disease, I have included Lloyd in the list of supporters of the epidemic theory.

[40] D.J. Wiseman, "The Assyrians," in *Warfare in the Ancient World,* ed. by Gen. Sir John Hackett (London: Sidgwick & Jackson, 1989), p. 52.

[41] Barnes, *Studies,* pp. 123-4. He cites Yurco.

[42] After two cautious sentences suggesting that Taharqa may have been a factor (on pp. 231 and 233), Yurco states in a two-sentence passage that Egypt's presence "very probably was an important factor in Sennacherib's decision to end" the campaign (p. 236). A fifth sentence is more declarative, but it is tucked away in a footnote: "It was the arrival of the army under Taharqa that proved a turning point, with the probable outbreak of pestilence among the troops blockading Jerusalem another adverse turn" (p. 240, n. 145).

[43] Luckenbill, *Annals of Sennacherib,* p. 13.

[44] Redford, *Egypt, Canaan, and Israel,* p. 353.

[45] Here is the passage from Redford, *Egypt, Canaan, and Israel*: "The ease and swiftness with which Shabako led a substantial expeditionary force to the plains of Eltekeh to engage the Assyrians in 701 militates in favor of a large standing army poised in the Delta for precisely this purpose, and certain bases of operation in the northern Sinai and the Philistine plain. Even though our sources for Eltekeh are confined to the Assyria records — Egyptian relief and textual material employ stereotyped images of uncertain application — there can be no doubt that it was an unexpected and serious reverse for Assyria arms, and contributed significantly to Sennacherib's permanent withdrawal from the Levant" (p. 353).

Redford perceptively places the conflict of 701 within a larger context of "an increase in relations, commercial and political, between Judah and Egypt" (p. 356). But the closest he comes to offering evidence to support the idea of a successful Kushite intervention against Sennacherib is in a footnote on the same page. He refers to a Napatan relief, described in my Chapter 6, that shows Kushite soldiers defeating Assyrian troops. Redford says: "It is tempting to see in this scene a 25th Dynasty record of either Eltekeh or one of Taharqa's early campaigns," *i.e.,* after becoming pharaoh (p. 357, note 185). But Redford's reasoning is too thin to be called argument. He disagrees with Spalinger, "Notes on the Military in Egypt," who says says the style of the Assyrian helmets shows that this Napatan art dates from before Sennacherib's reign. Redford says the style of helmet represented in Spalinger's fig. 4 "continued through the reign of Sennacherib and into the seventh century."

The Assyrian art that I have seen would not appear to support that claim. The helmet that the Napatan relief depicts is conical with a knob-like top. One finds these in Sargon's army, as attested by the sculptures in Yadin, *Art of Warfare*, vol. 2, pp. 416-419. But one does not find such helmets in Assyrian art's principal depiction of Sennacherib's invasion of 701, the relief of the attack on Lachish. In that, Assyrian soldiers wear helmets that are conical without the well-formed knob.

It would suit the purposes of my own thesis to agree with Redford that the Napatan depiction of Kushites triumphing over Assyrians may refer to the campaign of 701, but the evidence does not support that. Spalinger's interpretation stands.

[46] Someone defending such a line of thought might argue that Sennacherib would have wanted to backtrack to Eltekeh because that could have been where the Kushite-Egyptian army happened to be. That is unlikely. Why would the pharaoh's army go to an area where Assyria had already consolidated its control? Normally, a defending army tries to prevent an aggressor's further advance.

Of course, someone could then argue that the Kushite-Egyptian army did not know where Sennacherib was located and so it went charging in the wrong direction. But that assumes an egregious blunder in intelligence, not what one might expect from the tradition of Kushite military professionalism. It would have had spies. And, if not, the territory was full of Judahites and Philistines — friends. Any refugees might have reported in which direction the Assyrian army had gone.

On the likelihood of the use of spies in the conflict of 701, see Kitchen, "Egypt, the Levant and Assyria." Recalling the role of spies by Rameses II in his campaign into Khor in the 13th century BC, Kitchen remarks that "it is inconceivable that — half a millenium later — the rival armies did not employ scouts and spies to check on each other's moves, especially as the distances involved were not great" (p. 250, n. 33).

[47] Speaking of Assyrian annals in general, Kuhrt, *Ancient Near East*, vol. 2, notes: "Total falsehoods in the annals are rare — omission of failures and emphasis on successes are used to tilt the picture in a positive direction" (p. 476).

[48] Chaim Herzog and Mordechai Gichon, *Battles of the Bible* (New York: Random House, 1978), pp. 142-143. The "fully revised" 1997 edition of *Battles of the Bible* makes no changes in so far as the events of 701 are concerned. It is published in Toronto by Stoddart Publishing Co. See pp. 211, 213.

[49] It suggests that Hezekiah surrendered and paid heavy tribute to Assyria; yet the authors seem to imply that in submitting to Assyria he somehow did not yield Jerusalem itself. It was in order to crush the hold-out parts of Judah, say the authors, that Sennacherib was still on the scene when Taharqa swept in. Chapter 15 will present another scenario for the sequence of events.

[50] 2 Chronicles 11:5-11.

Second Chronicles is often a dubious historical source, and its account of Rehoboam's widespread strengthening of fortifications is no exception. In an article dealing with this biblical passage, T. R. Hobbs, "The Fortresses of Rehoboam: Another Look," in *Uncovering Ancient Stones: Essays in Memory of H. Neil Richardson*, ed. by Lewis M. Hopfe (Winona Lake, IN: Eisenbrauns, 1994), concludes: "The archaeological data . . . are quite disappointing to those who regard the city-list [of 2 Chronicles 11:5-11] as part of a large defensive system for Judah" (p. 44).

[51] Herzog & Gichon, *Battles of the Bible*, p. 145.

CHAPTER TEN

[1] Here is a summary of current views, from Burke O. Long, "I and II Kings," in *Books of the Bible*, vol. 1, *op. cit.*:

"Scholars of the history of the Bible generally agree that the present form of 1-2 Kings is the result of a long process of collection, editing, writing and revising of diverse materials, some of which could at one time have been transmitted orally. One widely held hypothesis suggests that the preserved text is a pre-exilic history of the monarchy that was revised after 587 B.C.E. in light of the Judean exile, when the hopes vested in King Josiah (640-609 B.C.E.) had come to nothing. Another opinion holds that the Books of Kings belong to a series of writings by a single author (possibly having undergone successive revisions), which include Deuteronomy, Joshua, Judges, Samuel, Kings and a vignette of Judah's last king in Babylonian exile (2 Kings 25:27-30). Adherents of both views assume that an author (or authors) unified this work with theological ideas reflected in, and derived from, the Book of Deuteronomy" (p. 142).

[2] Bernhard Stade, "Anmerkungen zu 2 Kö. 15-21," in *Zeitschrift für die alttestamentliche Wissenschaft* 6 (1886), pp. 122-192.

[3] If one accepts 19:37 as a still later addition, as will be briefly discussed in note 6, it would come to four texts spliced together.

[4] See the discussion in Childs, *Isaiah and the Assyrian Crisis*, p. 73 ff. Writing in 1967, he says: "The last serious attempt to contest the division and to defend the unity of B by Sanda remains extremely unconvincing" (p. 73). The reference is to A. Sanda, *Die Bücher der Könige, II* (Münster, 1912), pp. 289 ff.

However, in writings published in 1986 and 1992 respectively, Smelik, "Distortion in Old Testament Prophecy," pp. 74-85, and Seitz, *Zion's First Destiny*, pp. 70-71, 90, 117, have raised rare objections to Stade's concept of a tiered plot. Nonetheless, these challenges do not qualify as serious. Note 27 at the close of this chapter will examine this claim.

[5] *Ibid.*, p. 73.

[6] Many scholars, including Childs, add verse 37, making it the concluding element in B[1]. More recently, however, Cogan & Tadmor, *II Kings*, have made a strong case for amputating that verse from B[1] (p. 244). The editorial process excerpted verse 37 from a Babylonian chronicle, they say, for the purpose of showing that "the Assyrian was personally punished for his blasphemies" (p. 244, n. 13). They suggest that the responsibility lies with the same editor who reworked the Merodach-baladan tale (especially 2 Kings 20:16-19). Without passing judgment on who was responsible, one may note that the tone of verse 37 does appear to clash with the rest of B[1].

[7] Cogan & Tadmor, *II Kings*, p. 243.

[8] The 50-year estimate comes not from *II Kings* but from Tadmor, "Period of the First Temple," p. 144.

[9] See, for example, Gonçalves, *L'expédition de Sennachérib*, pp. 441, 538, and Clements, *Isaiah and the Deliverance*, p. 68. Clements places the composition of B[1] in

King Josiah's reign which, starting as it did in 640 BC, brings it within the lifetime of people who, while they might or might not have gone through the siege as children, would certainly have heard eyewitness accounts of the great event.

See also Paul Dion, "Sennacherib's Expedition": "The story obviously goes back to an admirer of Isaiah, imbued with the prophet's doctrine of absolute reliance on Yahweh and the condemnation of human pride" (p. 19).

Yet Dion, of the University of Toronto's department of Near Eastern studies, doubts that the writer was an eyewitness to the events of 701. He gives two reasons. One is the anachronistic allusion to Sennacherib's murder in 681 BC; yet that passage is not an integral part of the B¹ account and was likely added subsequently. The other reason is that the B¹ account attributes an "irreproachable faith . . . to Hezekiah and his people [that stands] in contrast to the disapproval voiced in many authentic oracles of Isaiah . . ." (p. 19). This second reason seems more firm. It should be noted, however, that the authentic Isaiah's criticism of Hezekiah is indirect. One has to read between the lines. It is possible that an admirer of Isaiah, reflecting new preoccupations, could have composed an ennobling depiction of Hezekiah without feeling that this betrayed Isaiah's thought.

¹⁰ For example, Gonçalves, *L'expédition de Sennachérib*, citing B. Duhm and several others, deems 2 Kings 18:32b-35 probably to have been added to the B¹ account long after it was first written (p. 387). Dion, "Sennacherib's Expedition," is in agreement (p. 18, n. 70).

¹¹ Gonçalves, *L'expédition de Sennachérib*, pp. 480, 541, and Dion, "Sennacherib's Expedition," p. 22, and R.E. Clements, "Isaiah 14,22-27: A Central Passage Reconsidered," in *The Book of Isaiah/Le Livre d'Isaïe: Les Oracles et leurs relectures: Unité et complexité de l'ouvrage*, ed. by Jacques Vermeylen (Leuven, Belgium: University Press, 1989). Says Clements: "There is much to be said in support of the claim of Gonçalves that the B² account of how Jerusalem was divinely protected in 701 BC has been composed in its extant form after the catastrophe [of 586 BC]. The narrative is designed to show that, under the obedient response of a faithful king, God does act to protect and uphold his people" (p. 261).

These estimates, and others that I have seen, are all by conventional scholars. I am unaware of any minimalist analyses of the invasion text itself.

¹² Dion, "Sennacherib's Expedition," identifies 2 Kings 19:29-31 as an addition made after the Exile (p. 20).

¹³ Childs, *Isaiah and the Assyrian Crisis*, p. 103.

¹⁴ *Ibid.*, p. 106.

¹⁵ See 2 Kings 19:10-13.

¹⁶ Gonçalves, *L'expédition de Sennachérib*, p. 483.

¹⁷ Both terms appear to be acceptable translations, according to Gonçalves. *Ibid.*, p. 427.

¹⁸ Stade, "Amerkungen," p. 174.

¹⁹ *Ibid.*, p. 180. (Stade's word is *getäuscht*.)

Stade's article does not attempt to examine the historical ramifications of the B section's structure. Curiously, it refers to Taharqa only in passing.

[20] Childs, *Isaiah and the Assyrian Crisis*, p. 75.

[21] Clements, *Isaiah and the Deliverance*, p. 55.

[22] *Ibid.*, p. 59.

[23] Cogan & Tadmor, *II Kings*, p. 243.

[24] At least part of the liberating action must have taken place in front of Judahite eyes on Jerusalem's walls. If other causes for the withdrawal occurred elsewhere in the kingdom and thus outside Jerusalemites' direct vision, there must have been friendly witnesses who could have told the Jerusalemites. Even if the decisive moment of the invasion took place in a physically isolated context, the party responsible would have been certain to get the word out. People who drive out the world's most powerful army do not keep it to themselves.

[25] Gonçalves, *L'expédition de Sennachérib*, p. 427.

[26] *Ibid.*, p. 443. In Gonçalves' own words: "Quoi qu'il en soit, le rapport entre l'expédition égyptienne et le départ de Sennachérib obéit vraisemblablement à un souci théologique: en faisant détaler Sennachérib devant l'Egypte si décriée par le Rab-Shaqé, l'auteur du récit souligne l'abaissement de l'orgueuil assyrien. Par conséquent, on peut difficilement s'appuyer sur II Rois, XIX, 9a pour dire que Sennachérib a dû interrompre expédition en raison d'une menace égyptienne."

[27] The most far-fetched is by Smelik, "Distortion of Old Testament Prophecy." It examines Stade's proposal that the all-important report/rumor dealt with the Kushite force's approach (especially pp. 74-85). Smelik's starting premise is that Stade is wrong to divide the B account into separate parts. For Smelik, the B section is a single unit. A second writer, Christopher Seitz, in his 1991 book *Zion's Final Destiny*, endorses many of Smelik's views and develops them.

Their separate treatments of the Kushite-rescue theory are, so far as I am aware, the only critiques of that theory that are more than a paragraph or two in length. Lest I be criticized for avoiding their view, let's look at it.

First, the premise. Smelik sees B as a unified narrative because the repetition of various elements (the Assyrians' two threatening appeals to Jerusalem, Hezekiah's two visits to the Temple, Isaiah's three issuances of prophecies, or oracles) is a deliberate "literary device." The purpose of repetition, he says, is to "enhance the suspense" (p. 81). The stringing out of Isaiah's various oracles (2 Kings 19:9, 28 and 33), he amplifies, "has the function of intensifying the suspense" so that "readers become eager to know what will happen to the arrogant blasphemer whom they will identify with the foreign oppressor of their own time" (p. 84). I find this thesis quite baffling. For me, the dual structure drags things out, produces bewilderment and undermines the story's initial suspense as contained in B[1].

Smelik adheres to the surrender theory. He rejects Stade's idea that the report of the Kushite-Egyptian army's advance repelled Sennacherib. He offers these reasons.

* First, Smelik says that Isaiah's prophecy of a report/rumor that will drive away Sennacherib is "rather obscure." He says: "The reader will at first connect it with the message of Tirhakah's arrival, but Sennacherib's reaction precludes this interpretation. The Assyrian king does not show any fear. Why should he? Egypt is but a broken reed" (p. 83.) (The broken reed refers to the Rab-shakeh's derisive description of the Kushites in 2 Kings 18:21.) Smelik's argument is circular: Taharqa's army will turn out to be weak

because the Assyrians have said it is weak; therefore it cannot possibly have contributed to Sennacherib's withdrawal.

* The closest Smelik comes to explaining just why the incoming army would have been impotent is when he disputes the generally-accepted view, advanced by Kitchen and others, that Taharqa would have been 20 or 21 years old. "Would the Assyrian king who had defeated the Egyptians at Eltekeh," he asks, "have been seized with panic by the appearance of an 18-year-old boy?" (p. 76). Smelik gives *no* argument for thus reducing Taharqa's age.

Chapter 8 discussed allegations of Taharqa's immaturity in 701, but let us suppose for argument's sake that Smelik is correct in suggesting Taharqa may only have been a teenager. Would that fact have made a decisive difference in the quality of the army? Neither the age nor the fighting skills of a figurehead leader necessarily determine an army's capability. If it were, the forces of the teenaged Joan of Arc would hardly have achieved their early battlefield successes.

* Isaiah's prophecy of the report/rumor has a specific literary purpose, Smelik argues. The biblical author intended the prophecy to provide a "deliberate ambiguity." Smelik, and Seitz as well, say that the writer sets up the Taharqa report (in 2 Kings 19:9) as a narrative device *to make readers wrongly suppose* that Judah's alliance with Egypt will prove to be the source of the Deliverance. Smelik says: "By supposing that in the first account [B¹] the news of Tirhakah's arrival ended Sennacherib's attack, Stade actually walked into the trap the author has set for the reader" (p. 77). Smelik and Seitz contend that the story later presents the *real* report. That report is that thousands of Assyrians have been killed at their camp. "The news of this disaster forces Sennacherib to leave," says Smelik, "and not the arrival of Tirhakah" (p. 84). Or, as Seitz puts it, when Sennacherib hears the "notice of the widespread devastation of the Assyrian army," he has the "motivation" to return home (p. 71).

The biblical text, however, makes no reference, even indirectly, to Sennacherib having received any slaughter-related report or rumor — or other form of notice. (Indeed, it is easy to read the terse account of the massacre of the Assyrians and assume that Sennacherib was actually present when it took place. He would then not have needed a report: he would have seen men dying at his feet.) If the biblical writer was the astute literary craftsman that Smelik claims, one would expect that writer to utilize explicitly this report motif in the story's climax.

Seitz praises Smelik for putting all this so "cleverly" (p. 70, n. 73).

CHAPTER ELEVEN

¹ Of course, as Bernhard Stade suggested more than a century ago, the Assyrian army could have been misled by a report that said that the Kushite army was approaching when it really was not (or that grossly exaggerated that army's size and might). But such an explanation assumes a truly egregious blunder on the Assyrians' part — an incompetence uncharacteristic of the Assyrian military tradition. Furthermore, that explanation assumes that the Assyrians were so obtuse that, after withdrawing, they never discovered their error. That's because if they had realized their mistake, they would clearly have felt so humiliated that the "king of the universe," as Sennacherib called himself, would have returned to Judah as soon as possible to redeem himself.

² For example, see: Kitchen, "Egypt, the Levant and Assyria," pp. 247-248; Luckenbill, *Annals of Sennacherib*, p. 13; Miller & Hayes, *Israel and Judah*, p. 362; N. Na'aman, "Sennacherib's Campaign to Judah and the Date of the *LMLK* Stamps," *Vetus*

Testamentum 29 (1979), p. 66; Spalinger, "Foreign Policy of Egypt," p. 36; Tadmor, "Period of the First Temple," p. 142, and Yurco, "Sennacherib's Third Campaign," p.224.

It's also worth noting Sennacherib's annal only claims to have bested the Kushite-Egyptian forces at Eltekeh: it does not claim to have bested them in terms of the campaign as a whole, which one might expect him to say if he had done so.

[3] In addition to Kitchen (see Chapter 9), the Egyptologists include T.G.H. James, "Egypt: The Twenty-fifth and Twenty-sixth Dynasties," p. 693, n. 86; Spalinger, "Foreign Policy of Egypt," p. 36, and Yurco, "Sennacherib's Third Campaign," p. 224. Judah specialists include Na'aman, "Sennacherib's Campaign," pp. 65-66, and Herzog & Gichon, *Battles of the Bible*, pp. 142-143.

[4] For a particularly clear explanation of this reasoning, see Na'aman, "Sennacherib's Campaign," p. 65.

[5] Notice the context in which the annal speaks of the "kings of Egypt": it says the Khor rebels "had become afraid [of Sennacherib] and called for help upon the kings of Egypt."

Were these kings only from the Delta? It is likely the rebels' appeal for help would ultimately have gone to the most powerful of all the various kings of Egypt, the pharaoh or (in the event of a co-regency, pharaohs) of the 25th Dynasty. Therefore, the expression "kings of Egypt" may include both the Delta kinglets *and* the pharaoh(s) of the 25th Dynasty. In referring immediately afterward to the "king of Kush" as the supplier of the army's elite forces, Sennacherib could simply be singling out one of these "kings of Egypt." I don't prefer this interpretation to the other, favored by Na'aman *et al.* Like that other explanation, this one is very inferential—and thus questionable.

[6] 2 Kings 18:20-25.

[7] In recent decades, there appears to be consensus among scholars on this route of advance.

See, for example: Na'aman, "Sennacherib's Campaign," pp. 66-69; Aharoni & Avi-Yonah, *Macmillan Bible Atlas*, map on p. 99, and Kitchen, "Egypt, the Levant and Assyria," p. 250 and map on p. 253.

[8] 2 Kings 18:17.

[9] See Chapter 9. Kitchen, "Egypt, the Levant and Assyria," p. 251.

[10] Clements, "Central Passage Reconsidered," dates Isaiah 31:8 and 14:24-25 after the fall of Jerusalem in 586 BC (pp. 261-262). (This dating supercedes Clements' late seventh-century dating of these same passages in his own earlier book, *Isaiah 1-39*.)

[11] Translation by Childs, *Isaiah and the Assyrian Crisis*, p. 58.

[12] In Chapter 16, we will look closer at this insistence by biblical writers of this later period that only Yahweh — or his alter-ego, the "angel of Yahweh" — can deliver the Chosen People.

[13] Translation by Childs, *ibid.*, p. 38.

[14] The AT also uses this same translation as Childs. The translation is almost the same, "tread under foot," in I. W. Slotki, *Kings: Hebrew Text and English Translation* (London: Soncino Press, 1950).

[15] NEB, NIV, NRSV, TEV, Clements.

[16] As translated both by Slotki, *Kings*, and Joseph Klausner, *The Messianic Idea in Israel*, trans. from the 3rd Hebrew ed. by W.F. Stinespring (New York: Macmillan, 1955), pp. 68-69.

[17] In 18.2, as in 18:7, it is more commonly translated as "conquering."

In the Book of Isaiah, the root *bs* occurs seven times in the form of verb, adjective or participle, according to a Hebrew concordance (Yehuda T. Radday, *An Analytical Linguistic Concordance to the Book of Isaiah* {Missoula, MT: Scholars Press, 1975}). In addition to referring twice to the Kushites in chapter 18, the root is used three times to describe Yahweh's omnipotence (14:25, 22:5 and 63:6), once to describe unnamed "adversaries" (presumably Babylonians) who had "trampled down" Solomon's Temple (63:18, NRSV) and once as independent imagery (14:19). In these last five cases, then, the root conveys a sense of the overwhelming physical force of specific acts.

[18] Also having much in common with Herodotus are two additional passages in the Book of Isaiah. I have omitted them from my main text only for brevity's sake.

These are 17:12-14 and 29:5-7. According to Clements and Gonçalves, both refer implicitly to the events of 701. These passages and the Herodotus story have these similar elements: the Assyrian invaders encounter a sudden and unexpected misadventure, the drama evokes (to varying degree) a night-time context and the invaders suffer humiliating losses while being chased.

The Book of Isaiah thus contains a four-passage pattern of resemblances to the Herodotus account.

[19] See Isaiah 22:2-3, which refers to Jerusalem.

[20] Indeed, Isaiah 1:7 alludes to passivity of Judahites generally: "While you look on, foreigners take over the land . . ." (TEV).

[21] Also, in discussing the rescue-of-Jerusalem theme in Isaiah 17:12-14, Childs, *Isaiah and the Assyrian Crisis*, astutely observes that "Jerusalem plays completely a passive role in the deliverance" (pp. 161-162).

[22] The Bible makes no mention of Moab, Ammon and Edom in its accounts of the conflict. Sennacherib does mention them, but in the context of loyalty: the kings of those three minor countries are included in a list of faithful vassals (including a recently-appointed puppet in Sidon) who brought Sennacherib "sumptuous gifts" and who "kissed my feet" (*ANET*, p. 287).

Some writers, including Yurco, "Sennacherib's Third Campaign," suggest that Moab, Ammon and Edom were early members of the rebel alliance (p. 224). This may be true, but we lack evidence for this view. To reach this conclusion one would have to assume that all kings bringing tribute to Sennacherib were chastened ex-rebels. To demonstrate loyalty, a vassal who had been well-behaved could just as easily pay tribute.

[23] *ANET*, p. 293.

[24] The dates are from Kitchen, *Third Intermediate Dynasty*, p. 406.

[25] László Török, "Kush and the External World,' in *Studia Meroitica 1984*, Meroitica 10, *Proceedings of the Fifth International Conference for Meroitic Studies* (Berlin: Akademie-Verlag, 1988), p. 57.

[26] This stark description of 25th-Dynasty vestiges at Thebes comes from one of the archaeologists who knows them best. J. Leclant, *Recherches sur les monuments thébains de la XXVe dynastie dite Éthiopienne*, text (Cairo: L'Institut français d'archéologie orientale (1965), writes: "The Ethiopian monuments in the Theban region have very often been reduced to a state of simple ruin, delapidation and subjection to the affronts of time: human destruction, wind erosion and the attack of nitre [a salt in some Egyptian soils]. One understands all too well that [modern scholars] who have described Thebes' vestiges have generally scorned these monuments."

Archaeologists, he says, have discovered many of the best surviving fragments only by luck: these fragments had been recycled by later dynasties into new monuments (p. *xv*). Typically, a stone block from a 25th-Dynasty temple might have been used in construction of a later edifice, with the side containing the original inscription turned upside down or otherwise left unexposed.

[27] See Adams, *Nubia*, p. 268, and T.G.H. James, "Egypt: The 25th and 26th Dynasties," pp. 727-729.

[28] Adams, *Nubia*, pp. 271-272.

[29] Torgny Säve-Söderbergh, "The Nubian Campaign: An Appeal after 30 years," in *Actes de la VIIIe Conférence Internationale des Études Nubiennes, op. cit.*, p. 22.

[30] Säve-Söderbergh, *Ibid.*, recounts a still more startling aspect of this already dismaying story:

"Now, after 30 years, we are facing other losses unless something drastic is done.

"In the contracts of the [territorial] concessions [to each of the teams] there was a condition that the results of the investigations should be published in a scientific forum without delay." In other words, when each nation's archaeological team undertook to examine a given piece of land, it pledged to disclose its findings to the researchers around the world — the only responsible thing to do.

Yet after all these years many countries' teams have still not done so. The international conference identified these teams as having failed to publish all their findings: the American, Czecholoslovakian, French-Argentinian, French, German, Italian and Polish. (Paul Van Moorsel, "Once More: ‹Quid novi ex Africa?›," in *Actes de la VIIIe Conférence des Études Nubiennes, op. cit.*, pp. 62-64.) On a more positive note, two teams that received praise at the conference were those of Spain and Scandinavia. As the years pass, of course, the original archaeologists are retiring or dying, creating new — and profound — problems.

Säve-Söderbergh says this of the contracts that the western institutes or states signed: "These obligations are . . . juridically binding. They are moreover moral. Excavations without publication amount to plundering and robbery."

All this is not to suggest that lying under the water of Lake Nasser, or in a forgotten crate in some warehouse, is an inscription that provides smoking-gun evidence of the Kushites' deeds in 701 BC. This is something that we may never know.

[31] This said, material has survived from the time of the 25th Dynasty that is worth noting.

Of particular interest is an inscription found at Kawa, a Kushite site on the Nile about 100 miles downstream from Napata. It was at Kawa that Taharqa, after becoming pharaoh, restored and greatly enlarged a temple of Amon that had been suffering from neglect. Among the numerous inscriptions left by Taharqa is one on the side of a doorway leading to large hall. This inscription's triumphalist tone reflects a literary convention for pharaonic inscriptions, a convention that goes back many centuries. Some of the Kawa text has been has been lost, but the surviving remnant states:

"He has slaughtered the Tjemehu, *he has restrained the Asiatics,* he has (crushed . . . ?) the foreign countries that revolted. He causes them to do the walk of dogs. The dwellers on the sand come, one knows not their place, fearing the king's ferocity" [emphasis added]. (M.F. Laming Macadam, *The Temples of Kawa:* vol. 2, *History and Archaeology of the Site, Text* (London: Oxford University Press, 1955), p. 62.)

Quickly, a few explanations. The Tjemehu are a Libyan people. The parenthetical insertion of "crushed" is by the modern translator. The allusion to "foreign countries" is not clear. (It could, and this is a guess, refer to Kush's vassals in the African heartland that may have rebelled — perhaps when the Kushite military was preoccupied with matters in Lower Egypt and Khor). As for the "walk of dogs," the inscription's translator says that it means "either to walk obediently at their master's heels or to slink away in fear."

The key question, of course, is what the term "Asiatics" refers to. Could that term mean, in this context, the Assyrians? Quite possibly. If it does, it could refer to one of two events during Taharqa's reign:

A. The defeat of Esarhaddon's army in 674 when it invaded Egypt for the first time. Little is known about the circumstances of Taharqa's victory; we know of it only because of a mention in a Babylonian text. (The Assyrian annals, not surprisingly, make no mention of it.) The calm that this victory brought Egypt proved brief: three years later, Esarhaddon returned and captured Memphis and several members of Taharqa's family.

B. The conflict with Sennacherib in 701.

Of the two confrontations, that of 701 appears to fit the best. The verb "restrained" would fit that encounter perfectly: the Kushite-Egyptian army deterred Assyria from approaching Egypt. Words like "expel" and "drive out" would be more appropriate for the events of 674.

As well, work on the Kawa temple appears to have been completed well before 674. Macadam says work at Kawa was completed in the tenth year of Taharqa's reign (*ibid.*, p. 16). Recent dating would put that at about 680 BC. (Taharqa, of course, could have had installed an updated inscription at the temple to hail a late-breaking feat. But the text places the conflict with the Asiatics in no great position of immediacy: the conflict is listed after the defeat of the Libyans and before the clashes with the rebel countries and sand dwellers. The inscription's tone, in short, suggests the confrontation with the Asiatics belongs to the not-too-recent past.)

Finally, we know that probably as early as 675 Taharqa was no longer feeling militarily confident; that may have been the year in which, according to Spalinger, "Foreign Policy of Egypt," Taharqa wrote his gloomy inscription at Karnak in which he expressed concern to Amon over events in Khor (p. 43), presumably as a result of Esarhaddon's reconquest of that region in 679.

While it is tempting to hail the Kawa inscription as a *probable* sign of Kushite Egypt's success in 701, the word *possible* is safer.

Other vestiges have survived that *could* be interpreted as indicating Kushite success against Assyria in 701. But they could as easily be dismissed on grounds of ambiguity. The damaged facade of the Temple of Osiris at Thebes, for example, shows the god Osiris solemnly giving a sword to Shebitku, presumably for some significant military campaign; but the precise context is unstated.

What makes the Kawa inscription less easy to put aside is that it uses the word "restrained" to describe what Taharqa did to Asiatics. Nonetheless, the text is still sufficiently nebulous that in evaluating its importance we ourselves should probably be restrained.

CHAPTER TWELVE

[1] Shemuel Ahituv, "Economic Factors in the Egyptian Conquest of Canaan," in *Israel Exploration Journal* 28, 1978.

Ahituv's research focuses on Egypt's occupation of Canaan during the reigns of Thutmosis III and Rameses III in the 15th and 12th centuries BC respectively. Much of it is based on lists of booty and tribute rendered to pharaohs. It is hard to think of any reason, however, why the following conclusions by Ahituv would not also apply in a rough way to the seventh century BC:

"Canaan itself had very little to offer to Egypt, for it was not worthwhile to transport agricultural products of great bulk, since Egypt itself was rich and self-sufficient. Even if it was worthwhile to import from Canaan luxury items, such as wine and honey, our sources inform us of their limited importance. The metals taken from Canaan were in small quantities. . . .

"However, the geographical position of Canaan was of great importance as a bridge between Egypt and Mesopotamia, and the Lebanon too" (pp. 104-105).

Why, then, did these New Kingdom pharaohs bother with the region? "The true importance of Canaan for Egypt," says Ahituv, "was the control it allowed over the main commercial road leading to the trading centres in Mesopotamia" (p. 105). He is referring to the "Way of the Sea," the celebrated highway which swerved up from Egypt to Phoenicia and which closely followed the coastline. As well, adds Ahituv, in order to maintain maritime trade to the north with Phoenicia and beyond, Egypt needed "safe nocturnal harbors along the Palestinian-Phoenician coasts."

[2] Layard, *Discoveries among the Ruins*, pp. 132-134.

[3] Breasted, *History of Egypt*, p. 553.

[4] *Ibid.*, p. 552.

[5] In recent years, scholars have speculated that the seal may come from the early years of Shabako's reign. Both T.G.H. James, "Egypt: The Twenty-fifth and Twenty-sixth Dynasties" (pp. 692-693), and Kitchen, *Third Intermediate Period* (p. 583-584), suggest it may date from before 701 — perhaps to the period of warmer Assyria-Kush relations implied by the extradition of Iamani, the anti-Assyrian rebel from Ashdod (see Chapter 6). Yet it is hardly surprising that both these scholars eliminate 701 as the date for the seal: both start from the premise that Shabako was probably dead by then (James, p. 693, n. 82, and Kitchen, p. 171).

NOTES TO PAGES 150-153

In a later revision of the same book, Kitchen allows that Shabako could have died after 701, yet he insists a 701 dating for the seal is "theoretical and uncertain" (p. 584). The same can be said about his continued preference for a date a decade or more earlier.

That the seal was discovered at Nineveh is itself significant. Sennacherib built that city and made it is his capital. His father, Sargon, had had a different capital, Dur-Shar-rukin. (This location is, to be sure, not in itself a smoking gun: Sennacherib could have had the document brought from the old capital. But the document's location at the Nineveh palace adds weight to the identification of the accord with Sennacherib.)

James has an interesting observation. Although he rejects a 701 dating because of his assumption that Shabako was dead, this Egyptologist acknowledges that the image on the seal of Shabako smiting a foe indicates "a seal of some grandeur, which would not have been applied to insignificant documents" (p. 693). I cannot think of *any* other Assyrian-related event during Shabako's reign, including the return of Iamani, a rebel of only second or third magnitude, that would have justified such "grandeur." Nor does James himself propose such an event.

For the record, I should note the contrarian view of Raphael Giveon, *The Impact of Egypt on Canaan: Iconographical and Related Studies* (Freiburg, Switz.: Universitätsverlag; Göttingen, Ger.: Vandenhoeck & Ruprecht, 1978). The Egyptologist at Tel Aviv University says that the artifact in question is not a seal to a document but rather a kind of "sealing" that would have been "applied to stoppers of large storage jars" (p. 123). Giveon says that the sealings "belong doubtlessly to the field of commercial relations between Egypt and Mesopotamia at the time" (emphasis added). No argument or other form of amplification accompanies this self-assured statement.

Two objections: 1) if the seal was indeed but a humdrum jar stopper, one must ask why other seals would not have been found; 2) while one can see how a prized product might bear the ring imprint of one monarch, the donor, it is hard to imagine why it would need that of a second, the recipient.

[6] *ANET,* p. 288.
Sennacherib cannot mean that he "took away" from Judah all 46 of that kingdom's towns and forts that he says he captured.

[7] Sennacherib wrote: "That in days to come the site of that city, and its temples and gods, might not be remembered, I completely blotted it out with floods of water and made it like a meadow" (*ARAB*, vol. 2, p. 152). For the removal of surface soil, see p. 185.

[8] J.A. Brinkman, "Babylonia in the Shadow of Assyria (747-626 B.C.)," in *Cambridge Ancient History, op. cit.,* vol. 3, pt. 2, observes: "The treatment of Babylonia was exceptionally ruthless and vindictive, well beyond the retribution usually exacted of a rebel city and far in excess of the punishment expected for a revered religious centre, no matter what its offences" (p. 39).

[9] Tadmor, "Period of the Second Temple," p. 144.
As well, Cogan, *Imperialism and Religion,* concludes that in the course of Assyria's domination of the region from 740 to 640 "Judah was permitted to retain its national sovereignty in return for loyal submission to Assyrian political will. One is impressed by Assyria's apparent reluctance and/or inability to expend efforts on incorporation of Jerusalem — implying, thereby, the city's insignificance for imperial goals. Accordingly,

as an independent vassal state Judah suffered none of the religious impositions known to Assyrian provinces" (p. 72). See also p. 65.

Also seeing Nineveh as overlord is T.G.H. James, "Egypt: The 25th and 26th Dynasties," who says that in 701 "Sennacherib forcefully confirmed Assyrian supremacy in Palestine" (693). He offers, however, no supporting argument.

More convincingly, Spalinger, "Foreign Policy of Egypt," sees greater margin of maneuver for Judah: ". . . one cannot regard Judah in the 690's as a vassal state of Sennacherib" (p. 35). Again: "From the simple fact that Sennacherib never again returned to Palestine, one must conclude that Judah remained quasi-independent" (p. 40).

[10] Tadmor, "Philistia," is explicit about the insulating effect of this arrangement. Referring to the aftermath of Sennacherib's campaign of 701, he concludes: "Thus, the balance of power between the four cities of Philistia was preserved and Philistia was consolidated as a semi-neutral buffer area between Assyria and Egypt" (p. 97).

Miller & Hayes, *Israel and Judah*, also shrewdly discern the probable logic behind Assyria's demands for the redrawing of Khor's political map: "The redistribution of territory and the possible assignment of portions of Hezekiah's territory to various Philistine rulers restored political equilibrium in the area, so that no ruler had a balance of power in his favor" (p. 362).

[11] Ordinarily, one might suppose that in a militarily oriented empire like Assyria's, a monarch's succession by his son, if that succession were orderly, would bring with it approximate continuity in foreign policy. Here, however, turmoil characterized the passing of the throne from father to son: Esarhaddon succeeded his father Sennacherib in 681 after his own older brothers had assassinated their father. Even though the king had already selected Esarhaddon as his successor, Grayson has not ruled out the possibility that Esarhaddon might have been involved in the regicide ("Assyria: Sennacherib and Esarhaddon," p. 121). Barbara Nevling Porter, *Images, Power, and Politics: Figurative Aspects of Esarhaddon's Babylonian Policy* (Philadelpia: American Philosophical Society, 1993) suggests that Esarhaddon had nothing to do with the murder yet had — for reasons unknown — fallen out of his father's favor (p. 24). Whatever the case, the new monarch felt obliged to demonstrate to a restive empire that Nineveh was to be taken more seriously than ever. Esarhaddon launched the first of several campaigns in Khor about a year and a half after coming to power.

What all this suggests is that a new generation of imperial leadership felt that the postulated agreement of 701 had been too generous to Egypt and its allies.

[12] That is, from the latter half of 701 to early 679 BC.

[13] For this date of 675 BC, I am relying on Spalinger, "Foreign Policy of Egypt," p. 43.

[14] Vernus, "Inscriptions," p. 31. This translation is from Spalinger, "Foreign Policy of Egypt," p. 30.

[15] Yurco, "Shabaka-Shebitku Coregency," differs. He says: "In Egyptian royal inscriptions, tribute can mean anything from diplomatic gifts, to trade goods stemming from foreign trade conducted by the pharaoh, to actual collection of tribute from vassals of the pharaoh. This allows for several options as to what Taharqa meant by loss of tribute. Consistent with the tenor of the document stemming from Taharqa's reign

prior to 674 BC, I would opt for loss of trade as what Taharqa is referring to" (pp. 43-44).

Taharqa might not have considered ordinary trade as something that was due Amon; goods used to build temples to Amon, might, however, qualify. But Yurco may be right to exclude the sort of tribute that a conventional vassal-lord relationship calls for. The tribute of the inscription must refer to goods that lie somewhere between the stuff of a banal commercial transaction and a vassal's show of submission.

[16] Tadmor, "Philistia," p. 91.

[17] *Ibid.*, p. 97.

[18] It is Tadmor, "Philistia," who makes this astute observation (p. 96, n. 40).

[19] The Assyrian king does say that Gaza got back some of the territory that Hezekiah had previously seized from that city-state, but this would not have been a blow to Egypt's interests: a restored Gaza would have helped maintain the balance of power among the Philistine states and helped establish stability in the region.

[20] Spalinger, "Foreign Policy of Egypt," p. 27.

[21] Spalinger, *Ibid.*, pp. 26-27, 42.

[22] Scarabs provide some evidence. Scarabs represent a distinct class of Egyptian artifacts: they are small stone sculptures of beetles, which the Egyptians saw as symbolizing nature's cycles. Scarabs often bore inscribed mottoes, and they were used as seals, ornaments or amulets.

Giveon, *Impact of Egypt on Canaan*, says that a scarab bearing what may be part of Shebitku's name (or prenomen) has been found at Samaria (p. 124). As well, he says two scarab-made sealings with Taharqa's name have been found on ceramic in Palmyra, Syria. Both of these have an identical text: "Amon has caused Taharqa to appear so that he should live eternally." Also, Giveon says that a scarab bearing Taharqa's name has been obtained from a dealer in Jerusalem; he says that "though its exact origin is unknown, it certainly comes from Palestine or Syria and not from Egypt" (p. 124). The archaeologist sees these artifacts as reinforcing Kawa's textual evidence that solid commercial relations existed between Khor and Egypt during the 25th Dynasty (pp. 125-126).

As a further sign of Egyptian influence in Khor, a fragment of a limestone sistrum, a musical instrument that made a jingling sound when shaken, has been discovered at Ekron. Gitin, "Ekron," seems to suggest a 26th-Dynasty origin (p. 41). However, Redford, *Egypt, Canaan, and Israel*, translates the inscription on the fragment as saying, "Amon-Re, Lord of the Thrones of the Two Lands, pre-eminent in the Holy Mountain (*i.e.*, Gebel Barkal) at the Horns of the Earth." Because of the reference to Napata, Redford cogently reassigns the elaborate instrument to the time of the 25th Dynasty (p. 356, n. 179).

[23] Raz Kletter, *Economic Keystones: The Weight System of the Kingdom of Judah* (Sheffield, UK: JSOT, Sheffield Academic Press, 1998), pp. 47-48, 138.

Also dating the period of the weights' introduction to Hezekiah's reign is Yohanan Aharoni, *The Archaeology of the Land of Israel: From the Prehistoric Beginnings to the End of the First Temple Period*, ed. by Miriam Aharoni, trans. from the Hebrew by Anson F. Rainey (Philadelphia: Westminster Press, 1982 {1978}), p. 260.

²⁴ Kletter, *Economic Keystones*, p. 142. Aharoni and many other scholars agree on this Egyptian origin.

That the Kushite Dynasty actively maintained Egypt's long-standing use of this system is beyond doubt: one weight found in Egypt even bears the name of Pharaoh Taharqa (p. 119).

²⁵ Kletter, *Economic Keystones*, p. 140. For most other commodities, he says, it would have been easier to measure by volume.

²⁶ *Ibid*, p. 148.

²⁷ *Ibid.*, pp. 130-131, 143.

²⁸ Tadmor, "Philistia," p. 98.

²⁹ *ANET*, p. 291.

³⁰ A.K. Grayson, *Assyrian and Babylonian Chronicles* (Locust Valley, NY: J.J. Augustin, 1975 (p. 84).

³¹ *ANET*, p. 292.

³² See Tadmor, "Philistia", pp. 99-100.

³³ 2 Chronicles 33:11 (NRSV).

As always with Chronicles, one has to be extra careful about accepting the historical basis for the presentation of events. Cogan & Tadmor say, however, that this incarceration and release are consistent with Assyria's "often lenient policy of pardoning rebellious vassal kings" and call the account "historically credible" (*II Kings*, p. 271). The authors point to Esarhaddon's successor, Assurbanipal, who sent the uncooperative Necho I of Egypt to Assyria for a forced sojourn; Assurbanipal later allowed him to return to Egypt as a malleable vassal (*ANET*, pp. 296-297).

Also regarding Manasseh's deportation as plausible are: Japhet, *I & II Chronicles*, p. 1003; Peter Machinist, "Palestine, Administration of," in *Anchor Bible Dictionary*, vol. 5, p. 74, and T.C. Mitchell, "Judah until the Fall of Jerusalem (c. 700-586 B.C.)," *Cambridge Ancient History, op. cit.*, vol. 3, pt. 2, p. 374.

³⁴ Babylon is not as unlikely a destination as it may sound. The city had rebounded after Sennacherib's obliteration of it. Babylonians during this period recognized Esarhaddon as their king; see Grayson, *Assyrian and Babylonian Chronicles*, p. 30.

³⁵ Cogan, *Imperialism and Religion*, p. 69. The idea receives cautious support from Evans, "Judah's Foreign Policy," pp. 167-168.

Archaeological evidence would seem to be consistent with this idea. Dan Bahat, "The Wall of Manasseh in Jerusalem," in *Israel Exploration Journal* 31 (1981) speculates on the origins of a substantial wall excavated on the City of David's eastern slope. While the wall has been commonly attributed to Hezekiah, Bahat proposes that Manasseh may be responsible for it. While he does not contest the view that Hezekiah built much of Jerusalem's fortifications of that era, Bahat says this eastern wall would correspond to 2 Chronicles 33:14 (p. 236).

If Bahat is right, it may strengthen Second Chronicles' case that for at least part of his reign Manasseh was estranged from Assyria. It is hard to see what other country in the first half of the seventh century would have posed an invasion threat to Judah.

[36] Evans, "Judah's Foreign Policy," has more to say on this. Referring to the reign of Esarhaddon (680-669 BC), he says that "it is clear that Assyria reckoned Manasseh as a loyal vassal from as early as the latter years of Esarhaddon. But since there is nothing that indicates Manasseh's whole-hearted loyalty to Assyria before that time, the intimations of a sometimes rebellious Manasseh suggest that his allegiance to Assyria for the first 20 or 25 years was given out of necessity rather than a pro-Assyrian political alignment. The situation would have changed, however, when the Assyrians returned to him the captive Judahite territory [that Hezekiah had lost in the negotiations following the Assyrian withdrawal of 701], perhaps circa 671 or 670. From that time on, Manasseh could be genuinely pro-Assyrian. . . ." (p. 169).

Evans does not disagree with Cogan's assumption, which he cites, that Manasseh would have been aligned with Taharqa during the early phase of Manasseh's foreign policy (p. 167).

Mitchell, "Judah until the Fall," argues similarly. He says that if Manasseh's captivity took place at all it would have been in the context of 671. "The defeat of Assyria in Egypt in 674," he says, "may have encouraged some of the kingdoms in the area to throw off their vassal status" (p. 375).

[37] Tadmor, "Philistia," assigns this date to it (pp. 99-100).

[38] The translation is from Tadmor, "Philistia," p. 100.

[39] The evidence for this is Esarhaddon's subsequent annal for that campaign. In it, the king describes in unusual detail his successful invasion of Egypt. All the armed clashes he alludes to take place inside the border (*ANET*, p. 293).

[40] Nahum 3:9 (NIV).

[41] KJ. NRSV says that this strength "was without limit."

[42] *Geography of Strabo*, 1.3.21, in vol. 1, pp. 227-229.

[43] Lloyd, *Herodotus, Book II: Commentary 99-182*, pp. 16-17.

[44] For another analysis of the real-life nucleus for this romantic model of a super-king, see Donald B. Redford, "The Relations between Egypt and Israel from El-Amarna to the Babylonian Conquest," in *Biblical Archaeology Today: Proceedings of the International Congress on Biblical Archaeology*, Jerusalem, 1984 (Israel Exploration Society, Israel Academy of Sciences and Humanities, 1985). Redford comes up with a result that is only slightly different from Lloyd: he discerns both Sesostris III and Rameses II, but as a third element he prefers Tuthmosis III (pp. 199-200). That pharaoh's 17 military campaigns took him from Napata to the banks of the Euphrates. Margaret Stefana Drower, "Thutmose III," in *Encyclopaedia Britannica, Macropaedia*, vol. 18, hails Tuthmosis as "perhaps the greatest of the pharaohs" — the "architect of the Egyptian empire" whose "reign marked the beginning of the greatest epoch in the country's history" (pp. 366).

[45] Another possibility has also been offered. J. Leclant, *Recherches sur les monuments thébains*, scoffs at the validity of Taharqa's reputation for military greatness. He says Strabo cited Taharqa as an esteemed conqueror because "under his name was gathered all the glory of Kushite conquest" (p. 351). That is, achievements by other 25th-Dynasty pharaohs were credited to him.

Such a rationale for Strabo's use of Taharqa's name seems unlikely. Why would Strabo's sources have designated Taharqa, of all the Kushite pharaohs, as the composite hero? If, following Leclant, we dismiss the significance of the campaign of 701, the greatest Kushite expeditions of which we are aware would be Piye and Shabako's successive conquests of Lower Egypt. (The only other great military success that we know that the 25th Dynasty registered was Pharaoh Taharqa's defeat of the Assyrians in 674. But that victory took place inside Egypt; it was a defensive success, not the sort of expeditionary conquest that Strabo suggests.)

It therefore seems most peculiar that antiquity would have conferred the generic mantle of conqueror to Taharqa. Piye or Shabako would have been far more deserving choices. Leclant does not address this problem.

[46] Which is not to say there are no possible leads whatsover.

Someone wanting to look for possible post-701 achievements by Taharqa might usefully explore another statement by Strabo.

Much later in his book, he mentions an achievement by Taharqa that is as awesome as it is hard to verify. Strabo affirms that Taharqa and Sesostris "advanced as far as Europe" (Strabo 15.I.6). Strabo says his source for this is an earlier Greek, Megasthenes, a diplomat and historian of the fourth century BC; Megasthenes' text on the matter has not survived. The statement about campaigns by Taharqa and Sesostris is jolting enough to warrant a closer look, but after doing so it is impossible, on the basis of what is now known, to give the statement any credence.

A few lines after his statement that Taharqa and Sesostris "advanced as far as Europe," Strabo specifies that Taharqa's forces went as far as "the Pillars." This may shed some light on what Strabo meant by "Europe."

Strabo is not, evidently, referring to the Pillars of Hercules, near the Strait of Gibraltar. See J.W. McCrindle, *Ancient India as Described by Megasthenês and Arrian*, rev. 2nd ed. by R.C. Majumbar (Calcutta: Chuckervertty, Chatterjee, 1960 {1877}). The 19th-century author says of the other pillars: "Called by Ptolemy the 'Pillars of Alexander,' [they are located] above Albania and Iberia at the commencement of the Asiatic Sarmatia" (note on pp. 109-110). Atlases of the Greek and Roman world show areas labelled "Iberia" and "Albania" to have occupied territory between the Black Sea and Caspian Sea, corresponding approximately to modern Georgia.

Lloyd, *Herodotus, Book II: Commentary 99-182*, addresses the legend of Sesostris. Lloyd does not mention Taharqa, but in light of how Strabo mentions the two in the same breath, Lloyd's comments on Sesostris may be relevant to our understanding of Taharqa.

In the late sixth century BC (well after the Saite 26th Dynasty had left the scene), Lloyd says that "Egyptian propagandists extended Sesostris' conquests into Asia Minor and beyond" (p. 20). Lloyd suggests that the reason for these imaginary conquests may have been rivalry with the Persians, who occupied Egypt in the late sixth century BC and whom the Egyptians "heartily detested" (p. 17). Because the Persian kings had ranged so far afield, Lloyd reasons, the Egyptians went back to their own past, "broadening the range of Sesostris' conquests to keep pace with, and often surpass, those of the [Persians]."

Might the same rationale explain the attribution of European feats to Taharqa?

Meanwhile, Martin Bernal, *Black Athena: The Afroasiatic Roots of Classical Civilization*, vol. 2: *The Archaeological and Documentary Evidence* (London: Free Association Books, 1991), argues that Sesostris I may have invaded the eastern shore of the Black Sea (pp. 228-230, 271-273). Bernal says Sesostris may have wanted to tap minerals in that region which were used in weaponry at that time. The argument is highly speculative. For a critique, see Frank J. Yurco, *"Black Athena:* An Egyptological Review," in *Black Athena Revisited, op. cit.*, pp. 62-100.

In conclusion, Strabo's statement that the two pharaohs "advanced as far as Europe" is supported by no evidence of which I am aware in Taharqa's case and by no sturdy evidence in the case of Sesostris. (This is not to say that the possibility of significant contact between Egyptians/Kushites and the people of Asia Minor and lands beyond is not worthy of investigation.) For the purposes of this book, the 25th Dynasty's sphere of influence will be assumed to have extended no farther than the area controlled by Tyre in modern Lebanon. It is from Esarhaddon's annal described in this chapter that we know Taharqa's influence attained that distance. If his influence extended still farther, my assumption is that what set it in motion was success against Assyria in 701.

It is not clear whether it is these alleged marches to Europe by Taharqa and Sesostris that Strabo had in mind when, earlier in his book, he had alluded to foreign expeditions by these two pharaohs. A French researcher, Godefroy Goossens, "Taharqa le conquérant," in *Chronique d'Égypt* 22 (1947), usefully notes that these widely separated passages' contexts are very different. (In the first passage, the context is princes' undeservedly forgotten campaigns to distant lands; in citing Taharqa as an example of such a prince, Strabo gives no source. In the second passage, the context is India's insularity: in demonstrating how invulnerable India has been to invaders, Strabo cites Megathenes as his source for saying that Sesostris and Taharqa each reached Europe and that Babylon's Nebuchadrezzar and Taharqa each attained "the Pillars," but that "no one of these touched India.") Goossens cautions that it might be a mistake to assume that Strabo is necessarily pinning Taharqa's greatness as an expedition leader on his campaign to Europe. The first allusion to Taharqa, Goossens says, could be based on oral tradition, not on Megasthenes (pp. 239-240).

If a European adventure by Taharqa invites strong skepticism, and if for the sake of this exercise we eliminate the 701 campaign as a vehicle for Taharqa's glory, what other possibilities of foreign campaigns present themselves?

Here is one: on a statuette of Taharqa, found at Thebes, is inscribed a claim that he conquered the Assyrians, as well as the Hittites (of present-day Turkey) and other peoples in present-day Syria as well as in Africa. Such a claim, however, appears to resemble inscriptions on statues of conquering pharaohs of the 18th and 19th dynasties, whom the 25th Dynasty sought to emulate in so many other ways. Accordingly, Redford, *Egypt, Canaan, and Israel,* and others attach no importance to this inscription's high-sounding declaration (p. 355). Goossens, for one, suggests such a list of pharaonic conquests is intended as a divine guarantee of victories rather than as an affirmation of real victories ("Taharqa le conquérant," pp. 243-244). Nonetheless, he notes that Taharqa's inscription includes one victory that does not appear in the lists of the earlier pharaohs: a triumph over the Assyrians. Still, caution is in order: instead of being a reference to success against Sennacherib in Judah, this could be an allusion to Taharqa's defeat of Esarhaddon in 674. That victory would not qualify Taharqa for Strabo's honor roll: as mentioned in an earlier note, it was a defensive exploit and took place inside Egypt, and Strabo says he is speaking only of "expeditions . . . to lands far remote."

Taharqa may also have campaigned in Libya: Redford says, "Taharqa's involvement in Libya is reflected in an unpublished Karnak stela" (*Ibid.*,p. 355, n. 175). This seems, however, like too small potatoes to earn him a spot on Strabo's list.

Is there, then, any reason to believe that, aside from the victory of 674, Taharqa racked up *any* truly major military successes in the post-701 period? On the basis of what we now know, no.

[47] Permit me to anticipate the possible objection that, for Taharqa, Judah would not have qualified as a land "far remote."

Judah may not have been so far from Egypt, but it was from Kush. Indeed, at least one other of Strabo's great expeditions — Psamtik's Delta-to-Napata campaign — would have travelled considerably less far than Taharqa's Napata-to-Judah trek.

[48] As cited in Chapter 1.

CHAPTER THIRTEEN

[1] Erling Hammershaimb, *The Book of Amos: A Commentary*, trans. from the Danish by John Sturdy (New York: Schocken Books, 1970), p. 134. One sign of Hammershaimb's standing in scholarly circles is that until the early 1990s he was a member of the advisory committee of one of the world's top biblical-research journals, *Vetus Testamentum*.

[2] One passage that gives the xenophobic flavor of much of the Hebrew Bible is Deuteronomy 7:1-4. Here, Moses gives his followers these instructions before they enter the promised land:

"When the Lord your God brings you into the land that you are about to enter and occupy, and he clears away many nations before you — the Hittites, the Girgashites, the Amorites, the Canaanites, the Perizzites, the Hivites, and the Jebusites, seven nations mightier and more numerous than you — and when the Lord your God gives them over to you and you defeat them, then you must utterly destroy them. Make no covenant with them and show them no mercy. Do not intermarry with them, . . . for that would turn away your children from following me, to serve other gods" (NRSV).

[3] *Nelson's Complete Concordance of the Revised Standard Version Bible*, 2nd ed., compiled under the supervision of John W. Ellison (New York: Thomas Nelson & Sons, 1957). Kush/Kushite occurs 17 times in the RSV, Ethiopia/Ethiopians 38 times.

Some versions of the Bible, like the TEV, may substitute "Sudan" or "Sudanese."

This total excludes duplicated passages, such as the Book of Isaiah's borrowed mention of Tirhakah's army from Second Kings.

[4] (NIV)

Abraham Malamat, "The Proto-History of Israel: A Study in Method," in *The Word of the Lord Shall Go Forth, op. cit.*, adds clarity. He translates the second sentence: "True, I brought Israel up from the land of Egypt, but also the Philistines from Caphtor and the Arameans from Kir" (p. 306).

Caphtor would refer to Crete, or more generally, the Aegean sphere. According to James Luther Mays, *Amos: A Commentary* (London: SCM Press, 1969), Kir's location is in Mesopotamia (pp. 157-158).

Malamat deduces from the passage that, just as Hebrew society had a tradition of its origins (as having coming from Egypt in the Exodus-wilderness wanderings-conquest epic), so Israel's neighbors, the Philistines and Arameans, "seem to have transmitted traditions, over many generations, concerning their removal from their original homes" (p. 306).

⁵ Soggin, *Introduction*, ascribes it to Deuteronomistic redaction (pp. 285-286). Robert B. Coote, *Amos among the Prophets: Composition and Theology* (Philadelphia: Fortress Press, 1981), also places it the sixth century BC, "near the end of the Babylonian exile or shortly thereafter" (pp. 8, 117).

⁶ H. Wheeler Robinson, "Amos," in *The Abingdon Bible Commentary*, ed. by Frederick Carl Eiselen, Edwin Lewis and David G. Downey (New York, Nashville: Abingdon Press, 1929): "The Ethiopians were known for their dark skin and therefore were despised: "you are no more to me than those Negroes'" (p. 783). Robinson was principal of the Regent's Park (Baptist) College, in London.

In his 1914 book, Buttenwieser, *Prophets of Israel*, takes the same view. He says that in speaking of the Kushites, Amos 9:7 is referring to the "despised negro race" (p. 306). Buttenwieser was professor of biblical exegesis at Hebrew Union College, Cincinnati.

In an earlier book, William Rainey Harper, professor of Semitic languages and literature at the University of Chicago, sees the same contempt. In *A Critical and Exegetical Commentary on Amos and Hosea* (New York: Charles Scribner's Sons, 1910), Harper observes: "Israel, says the prophet, is no more to me than the far-distant, uncivilized, and despised black race of Ethiopians. No reference is made to their Hamitic origin, or their black skin; and yet their color and the fact that slaves were often drawn from them added to the grounds for despising them" (p. 192).

Writing at the turn of the century, a Boston University professor, H.G. Mitchell, takes a slightly different line. Although race is not the reason, he sees Kushites as reputedly being Yahweh's least-loved people. In *Amos: An Essay on Exegesis*, rev. ed. (Boston and New York: Houghton, Mifflin, 1900), Mitchell says: "The Kushites are cited, not because they were Hamites, or because they were black, but because, being outside the circle of civilized nations known to the Hebrews, they were popularly regarded as least favored by Jehovah of all peoples" (pp. 170-171).

⁷ Hammershaimb, *Book of Amos*, p. 134.

⁸ Mays, *Amos: A Commentary*, p. 157.

⁹ Heschel, *Prophets*, p. 33.

¹⁰ Edward Ullendorff, *Ethiopia and the Bible* (London: Oxford University Press, 1968), p. 9.

¹¹ Francis I. Andersen and David Noel Freedman, *Amos: A New Translation with Introduction and Commentary* (Anchor Bible; New York: Doubleday, 1989), p. 869.

¹² John H. Hayes, *Amos the Eighth-Century Prophet: His Times and His Preaching* (Nashville: Abingdon, 1988), p. 219. He also says: "If the text refers to the Ethiopians, then Amos is comparing Israel to a remote, little-known people. In any case, Amos is denying the Israelites any claim of privilege or special status" (p. 219).

See also Shalom M. Paul, *Amos: A Commentary on the Book of Amos*, ed. by Frank Moore Cross (Minneapolis: Fortress, 1991). He says: "The Ethiopians . . . are not referred to disdainfully because of their color or their slave status, but for the remote distance of their land from Israel." Yet Paul nonetheless finds that the passage's "purpose is to contradict the popular belief that Israel, precisely because of its exodus from

Egypt, occupies a privileged place before God. The Lord himself absolutely denies and refutes this assumption of a superior status" (p. 282).

[13] Bernard Lewis, *Race and Slavery in the Middle East: An Historical Enquiry* (New York and Oxford: Oxford University Press, 1990), p. 17.

[14] *Ibid.*, p. 18.

[15] In a book published the same year as Lewis's, another scholar makes the same shrewd point. Cain Hope Felder, "Race, Racism, and the Biblical Narratives" in *Stony the Road We Trod: African American Biblical Interpretation*, ed. by Cain Hope Felder (Minneapolis: Fortress Press, 1991) observes that the "racial values of the Bible are progressive in comparison to later hostile racial attitudes in . . . the modern period" (p. 136).

Frank Snowden, *Before Color Prejudice: The Ancient view of Blacks* (Cambridge: Harvard University Press, 1983), also concludes that "in the Old Testament Kushites were looked upon as one in a family of nations, a people whose color in the eyes of both God and Moses was of no moment" (pp. 45-46). The Howard University historian adds:

"First impressions often have a significant role in the formation of images, sometimes an effect of considerable duration. . . . Warriors were among the first blacks encountered not only by Egyptians but also by Asiatics and Europeans. A majority of the first blacks whom many whites came to know both inside and outside Africa were not 'savages' or slaves but, like the whites themselves, soldiers protecting their own territory against foreign invasion or pursuing their national or personal interests in other lands. Nothing in these initial contacts points to a pejorative view of blacks" (*ibid.*, p. 68).

For a powerfully illustrated discussion of the "varied and often sympathetic treatment" that Greek and Roman artists gave black Africans, see also Snowden's "Iconigraphical Evidence on the Black Populations in Greco-Roman Antiquity," in *The Image of the Black in Western Art*, vol. 1, *From the Pharaohs to the Fall of the Roman Empire* (New York: William Morrow, 1976).

[16] To be sure, the point is debatable.

Some conventional historians contend Numbers' authorship dates from about the same period as the rest of the narrative of Moses' journey from Egypt to Israel — that is, in their opinion, perhaps between the tenth and late eighth centuries BC. Robert B. Coote and David Robert Ord, *The Bible's First History* (Philadelphia: Fortress Press, 1989), assign the authorship to "J", the hypothetical writers whom they suggest lived during the United Monarchy of the 10th century BC, pp. 273 ff., p. 5 ff.). Richard Elliott Friedman, *Who Wrote the Bible?* (Englewood Cliffs, NJ: Prentice Hall, 1987) is adamant that it was written by another writer, the hypothetical "E", whom Friedman places in the separate kingdom of Israel sometime between 922 BC and Israel's fall in 720 BC (pp. 76-87). Soggin, *Introduction*, is of the same opinion (p. 120).

A more recent view comes from John Van Seters, *The Life of Moses: The Yahwist as Historian in Exodus-Numbers* (Louisville, KY: Westminster/John Knox Press, 1994). Van Seters agrees that much of Numbers 12 comes from "J" (pp. 456, 461). But his detailed analysis assigns "J" to the Exile — more specifically, to a period after the writing of Deuteronomy and before the writing of Second Isaiah (pp. 461-468). Also placing Numbers in this exilic time-frame of the sixth century BC is, for example, Akenson in his 1998 book, *Surpassing Wonder*, pp. 23 ff.

Not all such proposals for a post-701 origin are new. Suggesting an even later date for Numbers 12 is George Buchanan Gray, *Numbers: A Critical and Exegetical Commentary* (New York: Charles Scribner's Sons, 1906), pp. 121-122, as cited by Donna Runnalls, "Moses' Ethiopian Campaign" in *Journal for the Study of Judaism* 14, 1983. Gray says the story of Moses' marriage, a late insertion to Numbers, may have been intended to counter the strong sentiment against Jews marrying non-Jews, a view that the priest Ezra promoted vigorously in the fifth century or possibly fourth century BC. As a late returnee to Jerusalem from the Exile, Ezra discovered that Judahites had frequently intermarried with other peoples from Khor; in reaction, he says in the Bible's Book of Ezra, "I tore tunic and cloak, pulled hair from my head and sat down appalled" (Ezra 9:3 ff {NIV}). He later successfully counselled Judahite husbands to divorce their foreign wives.

[17] Martin Noth, *Numbers: A Commentary*, trans. from the German by James D. Martin (London: SCM Press Ltd., 1968), says that Kush is too distant from Lower Egypt and the Sinai, where Moses would have spent most of his life. He says: "The 'Kush' from which the wife mentioned here came can hardly mean, as it does mostly otherwise in the Old Testament, the country on the southern boundary of Egypt, a country far removed from Moses' sphere of activity (as Luther, who has 'negress' [in his translation of the Bible], seems to think) is probably to be identified with 'Cushan' of [the biblical Book of] Habakkuk 3:7 . . ." (p. 94).

Noth does not amplify, and his dismissive treatment barely qualifies as an argument. His skepticism is, nonetheless, quite common in academic circles. See for example, John Marsh, "The Book of Numbers: Introduction and Exegesis," in *The Interpreter's Bible* (New York, Nashville: Abingdon Press, 1953). Marsh, professor of Christian theology at the University, Nottingham, says that Kushite "need not mean Ethiopian, but may refer to a north Arabian people" (p. 201). Similarly, Harvey Guthrie, "The Book of Numbers," in *Interpreter's One-Volume Commentary on the Bible*, ed. by Charles M. Laymon (New York and Nashville: Abingdon Press, 1971), says that Kushite "may mean Midianite" (p. 89). Guthrie is dean of Episcopal Theological Seminary, Cambridge, MA. Astour, in his 1965 article "Sabtah and Sabteca," also sees Moses' wife as being of Arabian origin (p. 422).

[18] For Luther, please see previous note.

[19] Making the same point is Van Seters, *Life of Moses*, pp. 238-239.

[20] In his *Antiquities of the Jews* (chap. 10), Josephus tells a story that is non-historical and that appears nowhere in the Bible: it is about how, long before the Exodus, Moses — the Hebrew whom the Egyptian royal family has adopted — leads an Egyptian army against the Kushites. Just as his army is on the verge of conquering the Kushite capital, a Kushite princess sees Moses fighting courageously and falls "deeply in love with him." A pact is reached: in exchange for her marriage to him, the city will surrender to Moses. As soon as the marriage is consummated, Moses leads his army back to Egypt. McGill University's dean of the faculty of religious studies, Donna Runnalls, "Moses' Ethiopian Campaign," draws the reasonable conclusion that among Josephus' several motives for writing the story was a desire to elucidate the reference to Moses' Kushite wife in Numbers 12 (p. 146).

Why do I discount Josephus' epidemic-theory interpretation of Sennacherib's withdrawal while here I rally to his interpretation of the wife's nationality? The reason is that with Sennacherib's invasion we are trying to understand an historical event; if Josephus was wrong about the facts, then his information is worthless to us. However, the story of Moses' wife, as with many of the Bible's stories of Moses' life, may be an invention; Josephus' perception of what that story is saying is therefore helpful in our attempt to understand the points that the story trying to convey. Writing as he was in the first century AD, Josephus was far closer than we to the climate in which the story was produced.

Indeed, as another sign of prevailing attitudes towards Kush in ancient times, it is also worth noting that Josephus' story itself treats Kush in a not-unflattering light. Moses does not see the Kushites as enemies; the Hebrew hero's true adversaries are the Egyptian priests who want him to go to war so that he will be killed. While Moses does slaughter Kushites in the campaign's early battles, his marriage to the Kushite princess has the effect of sparing a great number of her people from death and enslavement.

[21] The story is in Jeremiah 38-39.

[22] Ullendorff, *Ethiopia and the Bible*, p. 7.

[23] Gene Rice, "Two Black Contemporaries of Jeremiah," in *The Journal of Religious Thought* 33, Spring-Summer 1975, observes that the eunuch had demonstrated "courage, dispatch, compassion, and [an] ability to bring out the best in the king" (p. 97).

[24] Jeremiah 39:18 (TEV).

[25] (NRSV)

[26] Genesis 10:6.

[27] In a study of racial attitudes in the southern United States prior to the Civil War, Thomas Virgil Peterson, *Ham and Japheth: The Mythic World of Whites in the Antebellum South* (Metuchen, NJ, and London: Scarecrow Press and American Theological Library Association, 1978), finds the influence of the Genesis story on those attitudes to have been central. Peterson, of Alfred University in New York, says that "no story was more symbolically persuasive in resolving certain tensions between white Southerners' racial values and their most fundamental religious beliefs than was the myth of Ham. Southern versions of the Ham myth placed the institution of slavery squarely within the context of divine purpose" (p. 5).

[28] For a good example of myth puncturing, see Everett Tilson, *Segregation and the Bible* (New York, Nashville: Abingdon Press, 1958), pp. 23-26.

Also, for discussion of how the curse of Ham evolved in the post-biblical era, see Charles B. Copher, "The Black Presence in the Old Testament," in *Stony the Road We Trod, op. cit.*, pp. 146-153. Copher describes influences that gave impetus to the so-called curse, among them the Babylonian Talmud (pp. 147-148) and the Mormon doctrine (n. 8 on p. 149).

[29] See Genesis 10:15-20.

[30] A.F. Walls, "Africa," in *Baker Encyclopedia of Bible Places, op. cit.*, p. 19.

[31] Some historians have seen this distortion emerging as early as the third to sixth centuries AD with the compilation of the Babylonian Talmud. See Sanhedrin 108b and 70a.

Contesting the view that the Curse of Ham is rabbinic invention is David M. Gold-enberg, "The Curse of Ham: A Case of Rabbinic Racism?" in *Struggles in the Promised Land: Toward a History of Black-Jewish Relations in the United States*, ed. by Jack Salzman and Cornel West (New York, Oxford: Oxford University Press, 1997), pp. 21-51. Gold-enberg says that the Curse of Ham is not an idea found in Judaism but in "those soci-eties that institutionalized Black slavery" (p. 33).

For a broad picture of some Judeo-Christian thinkers' treatment of Africans, see Ivan Hannaford, *Race: The History of an Idea in the West* (Washington, DC: Woodrow Wilson Center Press; Baltimore and London: Johns Hopkins University Press, 1996). Hannaford writes about such developments as these: Maimonides' view in the twelfth century of Kushites and Turks as sub-human because of their religious views (pp. 110-113), the cabalists' elevation of physiognomical criteria in judging peoples (pp. 131-137) and the contribution of the sixteenth-century Christian thinker Agrippa to the estab-lishment of a "theoretical framework in which northern Europeans could understand the 'monstrous,' 'uncivil' peoples they encountered on their hazardous travels to unknown lands" (pp. 139-143). Such opinions, Hannaford argues, foreshadowed the later emergence of racism.

The post-biblical evolution of Western views of Africans is too vast a subject to be treated here. The point that should be emphasized here is that the Hebrew Bible/Old Testament itself is devoid of anti-African sentiment. Those who use biblical texts to jus-tify racism can do so only by reading things into them that are simply not there.

[32] Isaiah 18:1 says the envoys are from a land "beyond" the rivers of Kush. Follow-ing the consensus, I will assume this land to be Kush. If it is a land to the south of Kush, which is possible, it would still be allied with Kush — which, in the context of a diplo-matic mission, means their identities would be quite blended.

[33] Placing the date of this text in the period of Piye's reign are: Childs, *Isaiah and the Assyrian Crisis*, p. 46; Hayes & Irvine, *Isaiah, the Eighth-century Prophet*, p. 253, and Nic-cacci, "Isaiah XVIII-XX," pp. 216-217. At that time the northern kingdom of Israel would have been confronting Assyria.

The passage could also date from the time of the Philistine revolt against Assyria in 713-711. Or — what is most likely — it could date from the anxious time immedi-ately preceding Assyria's invasion of 701. Regarding 713-711 or 705-701, Clements, *Isaiah and the Deliverance*, says that both periods are possible, but that the 713-711 span is "more probable" (p. 31). Gonçalves, *L'expédition de Sennachérib*, prefers the 705-701 period (p. 145).

[34] Isaiah 8:6-8; Isaiah 10:5-6.

[35] For a similar opinion, see Leo H. Honor, *Sennacherib's Invasion of Palestine: A Crit-ical Source Study* (New York: AMS Press Inc., 1966 [1926]). Honor says of Isaiah 18 and those other texts of Isaiah's that deal with Egypt: ". . . there is a marked difference in his attitude towards Ethiopia and Egypt. In the one case, his tone is respectful; in the other, contemptuous" (p. 97).

[36] Klausner, *Messianic Idea in Israel*, pp. 68-69.

[37] Robert A. Bennett, Jr., "Africa and the Biblical Period," in *Harvard Theological Review* 64, October 1971, p. 489.

[38] Clements, *Isaiah 1-39*, p. 254.

[39] Isaiah speaks only of "Egypt" but it is clear he is really referring to Kushite Egypt, for the Kushites took charge of the country as a whole in *c.* 712.

[40] Isaiah 31:2 (NRSV).

[41] Isaiah 20:4 (NRSV).

[42] Isaiah 20:6 (NRSV).

[43] The treatment of what we might call Egyptian Egypt, as distinct from Kushite Egypt, is starkly different in Isaiah 19:1-5. This passage refers to Egypt at a time when the Kushites were not in control: the prophet describes Lower Egypt as a land riven by internal strife. Clements, *Isaiah and the Deliverance*, p. 31, reasonably places Isaiah 19:1-5 in the period of the outbreak of the Ashdodite rebellion, *c.* 713 BC; that would be just prior to Shabako's conquest of northern Egypt in 712.

The prophet says there is no point to this fighting, which pits "neighbor against neighbor, city against city, kingdom against kingdom." In one of the Hebrew Bible's most pungent condemnations, he goes on to say in v. 14 that warring princes "have made Egypt stagger in all its doings as a drunkard staggers around in vomit" (NRSV). He also scorns Egyptians for consulting idols and ghosts (v. 3).

Compare this derogatory treatment with that which Isaiah 31:3 gives to Egypt under the 25th Dynasty: because it is the "helper" of Judah against the imminent Assyrian onslaught, Kushite Egypt will "stumble" and suffer. But this misfortune, according to the prophet, will not represent the wages of its own improper behavior. Rather, defeat will be the consequence of this flaw: "The Egyptians are human, not God." For mortals, that is scarcely a shortcoming.

[44] Isaiah 30:1-2 (NRSV).

[45] Gonçalves, *L'expédition de Sennachérib*, pp. 160, 158.

[46] Isaiah 30:6-7 is another passage that appears to refer to the lead-up to the Assyrian invasion. The prophet's skepticism of Kushite Egypt's ability to turn back Assyria is again clear ("Egypt's help is worthless and empty" {NRSV}), but some biblical commentators see the next line as hostile to Egypt: the prophet says, "Therefore I have called her, 'Rahab who sits still.'" The mythical Rahab is a terrible monster. Commentators have debated this perplexing line this way and that, and I am inclined to accept Clements' view that the line likens Egypt to a "creature that looks fearsome, but is in reality powerless" (*Isaiah 1-39*, p. 245). Gonçalves, *L'expédition de Sennachérib*, says the meaning is probably that although Egypt may seem as redoubtable as Rahab, in fact Yahweh has deprived it of clout (p. 149). This brief passage, then, in no way qualifies as an exception to my statement that the Hebrew Bible is not antagonistic towards Kushite Egypt.

[47] In his list of authentic passages in the Book of Isaiah, Heaton indicates that this seventh verse is a post-Isaiah insertion, unlike the previous six verses which describe the Kushite ambassadors (*Hebrew Kingdoms*, pp. 322-3). Otto Kaiser agrees, finding a clue — Deuteronomic influence — that would place it roughly a century after Sennacherib's invasion (*Isaiah 13-39*, pp. 96-97). Clements (*Isaiah 1-39*, p. 166) and Gonçalves (*L'expédition de Sennachérib*, p. 141) place it even later than that, in the post-exilic period.

My own view is that, since 18:7 describes the Kushites as militarily mighty, the passage may have been written prior to the collapse of the 25th Dynasty at the hands of the Assyrians in the 660s BC. (This suggestion does not rule out the possibility of a later theological touch-up.)

If that suggestion is correct, it would add to the evidence in Chapter 12 showing that Egypt possessed a reputation in Khor for extraordinary military prowess in the years that followed 701.

[48] (TEV)

[49] (AT) The NEB is quite similar: ". . . let Nubia stretch out her hands to God." Exegesis by William R. Taylor, *Interpreter's Bible*, vol. 4, suggests that the verse has a post-exilic origin (p. 354).

[50] Genesis 2:10-14 (NRSV).

[51] See, for example, the discussion by W.W. Müller, "Pishon," in *Anchor Bible Dictionary*, *op. cit.*, vol. 5, p. 374, and B.S. Childs, "Eden, Garden of," *The Interpreter's Dictionary of the Bible*, vol. 2, ed. by Charles M. Laymon (New York, Nashville: Abingdon Press, 1962), p. 23.

[52] E.A. Speiser, "The Rivers of Paradise," originally published in 1959, and republished in *Oriental and Biblical Studies: Collected Writings of E.A. Speiser*, ed. and with an introduction by J.J. Finkelstein and Moshe Greenberg (Philadelphia: University of Pennsylvania Press, 1967), pp. 28-33.

Speiser suggests the Gihon is either the Diyala River, which flows in Iran and Iraq, or the Kerkha (or Karkheh) River of Iran (pp. 26-33). This would place all four rivers flowing into the lowlands at the head of the Persian Gulf, where the biblical Eden is commonly said to have been located.

[53] David M. Rohl, *A Test of Time*, vol. 2, *Legend: The Genesis of Civilization* (London: Century, Random House, 1998), pp. 51-62. Rohl confidently identifies the Gihon as the River Araxes, located in that area. Centuries ago, he claims, the Araxes was known as the Gaihun, which he says is linguistically related to Gihon. The "Kush" of Genesis, he says, would correspond to a mountainous area of the same name just north of the city of Tabriz. The book, however, does not adequately address several problems:

* What would the biblical Eden, a place known for a climate so idyllic that Adam and Eve needed no clothing, be doing at an elevation of about 4,500 feet above sea level in a valley known for harsh winters? Even if one allows for nudity as symbolism, it seems bizarre that Judahites would have deemed paradisaical a climate more severe than their own.

* Why would the biblical writers have departed from their customary usage of the term "Kush" to refer to the African kingdom and employ it here, in a unique instance, to refer to the area near the Caspian Sea? Why would the writers be so confusing?

* Why would the biblical writers, profound believers in the religious importance of Jerusalem, have preferred to use the "Gihon" of Genesis to refer to a river many hundreds of miles away rather than to the stream that nourished their city and that, as we will see, had sacred importance in its own right? The religious and political significance

that this distant river and mountainous area could have had for Jerusalemites is not apparent.

⁵⁴ D.H.K. Amiran, "The Development of Jerusalem, 1860-1970" in *Urban Geography of Jerusalem: A Companion Volume to the Atlas of Jerusalem*, ed. by David H.K. Amiran et al. (Berlin: Walter de Gruyter, 1973), p. 34-35.

⁵⁵ Richard J. Clifford, *The Cosmic Mountain in Canaan and the Old Testament* (Cambridge, MA: Harvard University Press, 1972), p. 3.

⁵⁶ Psalm 46:4 (NRSV).

⁵⁷ Clifford, *Cosmic Mountain*, p. 160, n. 82.

⁵⁸ Levenson, *Sinai and Zion*, p. 131.

⁵⁹ Levenson, *Ibid.*, adds: "In sum, it is reasonable to assume that some in Israel saw in Zion the cosmic mountain which is also the primal paradise called the Garden of Eden. The sacramental spring which is the source of Jerusalem's miraculous waterworks was conceived as the cosmic stream which issues from that mountain and sheds its fertilizing waters upon the surface of the whole earth" (p. 131).

⁶⁰ Several scholars say that in the context of Genesis 2 the term may refer to the land of the Cassites, or Kassites, in western Iran. This identification has the virtue of reinforcing the idea that all four rivers of Paradise were in the area of the Persian Gulf. See: Astour, "Sabtah and Sabteca," p. 422; John H. Marks, "The Book of Genesis," *The Interpreter's One-Volume Commentary, op. cit.*, p. 5, and Speiser, "Rivers of Paradise," pp. 25-26. Rohl, as mentioned earlier, puts "Kush" in northwestern Iran.

⁶¹ Claus Westermann, *Genesis 1-11: A Commentary* (trans. by John J. Scullion (Minneapolis: Augsburg, 1984), notes: "Since the Old Testament for the most part uses Kush to designate the area south of Egypt, this should be its meaning here" (p. 218). As well, Childs, "Eden, Garden of," says: "Kush [in the Bible] signifies almost always Ethiopia, but there are occasional exceptions (Genesis 10:8). Although the meaning in this passage remains uncertain, Ethiopia lends itself as the most probable interpretation" (p. 23).

See also Ullendorff, *Ethiopia and the Bible*, p. 2.

⁶² Many scholars hold that this section of the Book of Genesis was written by a writer or group of writers whom scholars designate as "J". (See note 16.) The dating of "J" is controversial. The traditional view is that "J" was active in the late tenth and early ninth centuries BC; in recent decades, however, an exilic or post-exilic dating has been proposed by such scholars as Van Seters, *In Search of History* (pp. 242, 323 and 361), who favors an exilic dating. This view, which is receiving considerable acceptance, itself predates the emergence of the "minimalist" approach.

The possibility is strong, then, that the Genesis reference to Kush reflects post-Deliverance afterglow. Even if one prefers an origin for "J" in the tenth or ninth centuries, that dating would not exclude the possibility of later editing. (For the possibility of a late reworking of "J", see, for example, Soggin, *Introduction*, p. 117.)

⁶³ M. Görg, "Gihon," *Anchor Bible Dictionary, op. cit.*, vol. 2, p. 1018.

⁶⁴ See, for example, Adams, *Nubia*, p. 248.

[65] (NRSV)

[66] Redford, *Egypt, Canaan, and Israel,* also does not see the order of names as accidental. He says: "The order here is not geographical but political. The precedence of Kush over Egypt is a clear reflection of the political preeminence the kingdom of Kush enjoyed from its conquest of Egypt about 711 BC [by Shabako] down to its defeat by Psammetichus II (*c.* 593 BC). Even after that date Kush continued to hold the first rank in tradition, as Herodotus and Diodorus attest" (pp. 404-405). Psammetichus is another name for Psamtik.

[67] Astour, "Sabtah and Sabteca," pp. 423-425.

I disagree with some of the other points in Astour's article. He says Kush in Genesis 2:13 is the country of the Kassites east of Babylonia and that Moses' bride in Numbers 12:1 is not Kushite (p. 422). He appears to base these opinions on what earlier scholars have said, however, and not on the independent sort of linguistic research that he applies to Genesis 10.

[68] Cain Hope Felder, professor of New Testament language and literature at Howard University's School of Divinity, adds this useful nuance: "By no means are black people excluded from the particularity of Israel's story as long as they claim it, however secondarily, and do not proclaim their own story apart from the activity of Israel's God." (Felder, "Race, Racism, and the Biblical Narratives," p. 136.)

[69] Which is not to say that relations between all Hebrews and Kushites were always necessarily amicable. Assyria's Assurbanipal would have forced Manasseh of Judah, as well as 21 other vassal kings, to help him invade Taharqa's Egypt (*ANET,* p. 294). Also, in the early 6th century BC, the 26th-Dynasty pharaoh Psamtik II may have used Hebrew mercenaries in his invasion of Kush, and subsequently Hebrew mercenaries would have been stationed at the fortresses of Elephantine and Syene, on Egypt's frontier with Kush. See A. Cowley, "Introduction," *Aramaic Papyri of the Fifth Century B.C.,* ed., with trans. and notes, by Cowley (Oxford: Clarendon Press, 1923), p. *xvi.*

CHAPTER FOURTEEN

[1] So named by Diana Craig Patch, "Breasted, James Henry," in *Oxford Encyclopedia of Archaeology in the Near East, op. cit.,* vol. 1, pp. 356-357.

[2] Warren R. Dawson and Eric P. Uphill, *Who Was Who in Egyptology,* 2nd rev. ed. (London: Egypt Exploration Society, 1972), pp. 38-39.

[3] These excerpts are from pp. 553-560 in Breasted, *History of Egypt.*

[4] *Ibid.,* p. 553.

[5] Adams, *Nubia,* p. 246.
Another often-cited book on the region is Arkell's 1955 study, *A History of the Sudan.* It, too, quotes the weak-reed passage approvingly (p. 126).

[6] Grimal, *History of Ancient Egypt,* p. 346.

[7] James, "Egypt: The Twenty-fifth and Twenty-sixth Dynasties," p. 694.

[8] *Ibid.,* p. 703.

[9] Kitchen, "Egypt," pp. 116-117.

[10] The examples I have given — Breasted, Adams, Grimal and James — are all historians specializing in Egypt or Kush/Nubia. But many biblical scholars make the same interpretation of 2 Kings 18:21/Isaiah 36:6. Some of the more recent proponents of this traditional view are Motyer in his 1993 book *Prophecy of Isaiah*, p. 277, and John N. Oswalt, *The Book of Isaiah, Chapters 1-39; The New International Commentary on the Old Testament* (Grand Rapids, MI: William B. Eerdmans Publishing, 1986), p. 635. Oswalt acidly notes of the Rab-shakeh's remark: "[The Hebrews] trusted in Egypt, which had neither strength nor Judah's best interests at heart. Sometimes it is only our enemies who see the true folly of our behavior."

[11] The Kushite-discrediting interpretions that are commonly made of several other biblical texts, such as Isaiah 18:1-6, flow from this passage.

[12] In other translations, the crucial verb may be different but the meaning is identical. Where the NIV says Hezekiah does "depend" on Kushite Egypt and Yahweh, the KJ, the AT and the Cogan & Tadmor versions all employ the verb "trust" while the RSV, the NRSV, the JPS and the NEB use "rely."

[13] See 2 Kings 17:2-23 in conjunction with 18:4-7.

[14] Slotki, *Kings*, pp. 275-276, n. 22.

CHAPTER FIFTEEN

[1] Exceptions: Luckenbill and Redford suggest in passing that the Battle of Eltekeh itself was what drove Sennacherib home. See Chapter 9.

[2] Indeed, Herodotus describes no decisive armed clash: the mice played the key role, with the pharaoh's army inflicting severe losses on the Assyrians only when they were retreating. The four oracles in the Book of Isaiah (14:24-25, 17:12-14, 29:5-7, 31:8-9) that deal with the Assyrian retreat also evoke, implicitly or explicitly, the idea of losses incurred during flight; yet they contain no battle scenes as such. Finally, Second Kings' B[1] version speaks only of the intention of Taharqa's advancing army to do battle with Sennacherib; it does not hint at any realization of that.

Luckenbill, *Annals of Sennacherib*, astutely notes: "That Sennacherib had not met with outright defeat is evidenced, I believe, by the silence of the Babylonian Chronicle, which was not slow to record Assyrian reverses" (p. 13). (Luckenbill is less plausible, as I argued in Chapter 9, when he suggests that Sennacherib instead "may have been fought to a standstill" at Eltekeh.)

[3] Here is one example. In Judges 13, an angel visits a barren woman. He tells her that she will have a child and goes on to give her various instructions, among them that she should see to it that her son's hair is never cut. The story of the son, the invincibly strong Samson, goes on for three pages in a typical double-columned edition of the Bible. The hair seems to have been an irrelevant detail. Only in 16:17 does hair reappear and play a key role in the story. Samson, of course, confides to the temptress Delilah the secret that his hair should never be cut, and his downfall follows.

[4] 2 Kings 18:14,17 and 19:8, as well as the bas-relief from Nineveh, attest to Sennacherib's presence at Lachish; 2 Kings 19:8 indicates his personal participation in the Libnah action. The king's text in Na'aman, "Sennacherib's Letter to God," seems to imply his personal involvement at Azekah (p. 27, line 10), although he could be speaking vicariously.

5 At the end of this chapter there will be discussion of recent discoveries in Judah's road network.

6 2 Kings 18:17 (Cogan & Tadmor).

7 Isaiah 10:28-32. Isaiah's account has been accepted by Aharoni, *Land of the Bible*, pp. 339-340. I see no reason not to accept Isaiah's portrayal, though it is only a detail; my hypothesis in no way depends on a military unit's approach from the north.

8 David Ussishkin, "The 'Camp of the Assyrians' in Jerusalem," in *Israel Exploration Journal* 29 (1979). He says the Northwest Hill would have been an "optimal location" for the camp. It is just out of arrow range, and it is slightly higher than the city itself. As well, he says, it "has a broad summit . . . which could provide spacious grounds for a large camp with all its facilities" (p. 142).

9 The Rab-shakeh begins his speech by saying, "Thus says the great king, the king of Assyria. . . ." (2 Kings 18:19 {NRSV}). Later: "Hear the word of the great king, the king of Assyria! Thus says the king. . . ." (18:28). Again: ". . . for thus says the king of Assyria. . . ." (18:31). Certainly, the reading of a royal text would give added weight to the envoy's message.

10 Norman K. Gottwald, *All the Kingdoms of the Earth: Israelite Prophecy and International Relations in the Near East* (New York: Harper & Row, Publishers, 1964), nuances the authenticity of the Rab-shakeh's declaration: "For the most part there is no difficulty in thinking of the substance of this speech as having been delivered to Hezekiah by Assyrian negotiators. The verisimilitude of historical conditions is impressive, so that it cannot easily have originated much later than Isaiah's time. Nevertheless the form and content of the speech testify against its having been delivered as now written. It is shot through with Yahwistic tendentiousness which we can hardly attribute to an Assyrian mind" (p. 190).

Gonçalves, *L'expédition de Sennachérib*, also presents a nuanced view, but in more detail. As noted in an earlier chapter, he sees 18:32b-35 as having been inserted into the Rab-shakeh's speech at a later time (p. 387) and thus not forming an integral part of the B¹ story. But he says 18:19-32a appears "primitive" (p. 410) — that is, as having been included in the original B¹ version.

See also Cogan & Tadmor, *II Kings:* "It can hardly be denied that the Hebrew text preserves the original argumentation of the Rab-shakeh, whose Hebrew rhetoric so impressed his hearers that it became the focus of the B¹ tradition" (p. 243).

To play it safe, the discussion that follows of the Rab-shakeh's speech will look only at those elements of the speech that, in Gonçalves' conservative view, are part of the original text. To be still safer, I will also omit 2 Kings 18:22, in which the Rab-shakeh alludes to Hezekiah's reliance on Yahweh and to the centralization in Jerusalem of the Yahwist cult. Na'aman, in his 1995 article "Debated Historicity," has suggested that it is a Deuteronomistic insertion (p. 183).

Ehud Ben Zwi, "Who Wrote the Speech of the Rabshakeh and When?" in *Journal of Biblical Literature* 109 (1990), casts doubt on the authenticity of 18:31-32 (pp. 88, 91 n. 36). I also will exclude that.

11 2 Kings 18:17 (NRSV).

12 "When Hezekiah saw that Sennacherib intended to attack Jerusalem also, he and his officials decided to cut off the supply of water outside the city in order to keep the

Assyrians from having any water when they got near Jerusalem. The officials led a large number of people out and stopped all the springs, so that no more water flowed out of them" (2 Chronicles 32:2-4 {TEV}). See also 2 Chronicles 32:30.

Generally speaking, the closer in time that a source is to an event, the more reliable the account. Since Second Chronicles would have been written well after the Second Kings' narrative, one might reasonably ask if I am not being inconsistent in giving credence to its description of the water supply while remaining highly skeptical of the material in the B² account. No. For one thing, there is no contradiction between the two biblical books: 2 Kings 20:20 refers to the waterworks in passing. Also, Second Chronicles' verses on the water supply are free of apparent theologizing. Thirdly, if Hezekiah meant to thwart the immensely resourceful Assyrian army, he must have done quite a job of impeding this supply; stories explaining the original reason for how the blockages came into being could easily have been passed down through the generations. Indeed, the blockages themselves — if done well enough to stymie Assyrian efforts at removing them — may have remained in place for centuries, thereby helping to keep these stories on the blockages' origin alive in the people's memory.

For another example of long-lasting associations that the Assyrian invasion had with some of the Jerusalem area's physical features, it is interesting to consider the Northwest Hill. Ussishkin, "The 'Camp of the Assyrians,'" notes that Flavius Josephus, writing in the first century AD, refers in two places to a site in Jerusalem called 'the camp of the Assyrians.' Ussishkin, who deduces that this site is the Northwest Hill (see note 8), remarks: "The historical impact of the Assyrian campaign and the impression this event left on the populace of Jerusalem was apparently so great that reference to this site still recalled the Assyrian army nearly 800 years later" (p. 142).

[13] Referring to Jerusalemites, Isaiah 22:9 says: "[Y]ou saw that there were many breaches in the city of David, and you collected the waters of the lower pool" (NRSV). Clements, *Isaiah 1-39*, gives a different translation: "The reading should certainly be emended to 'you filled with water the many pools'" (p. 186). The NEB is quite similar: "you filled all the many pools."

[14] Mitchell, "Israel and Judah," p. 361.

[15] Dan Bahat, with Chaim T. Rubinstein, *The Illustrated Atlas of Jerusalem*, trans. from the Hebrew by Shlomo Ketko (New York: Simon & Schuster, 1990), p. 33; see also p. 28.

[16] Yurco, "Sennacherib's Third Campaign," p. 228.

[17] Lon D. Lewis, *Feeding and Care of the Horse* (Philadelphia: Lea & Febiger, 1982), pp. 1, 6.

[18] Mitchell, "Israel and Judah," p. 357.

[19] As well, in order to hinder the besiegers' collection of the overflow, the Jerusalemites could have had the water drain off in multiple locations, thereby avoiding a single centralized stream. Such a plan would also have allowed the earth more easily to absorb run-off and frustrated the besiegers' collection efforts.

The well-known British archaeologist Kathleen M. Kenyon has suggested another possibility. In *Jerusalem: Excavating 3000 Years of History* (London: Thames and Hudson, 1967), Kenyon says the Siloam Pool into which the tunnel poured water was located outside the city's wall; it was, however, covered with solid rock and was a huge, concealed cistern. Besiegers, she says, would have been unaware of this reservoir hewn into the limestone below them. Jerusalemites could have avoided detection of the overflow by building an additional underground channel 100 meters downhill, where the exiting water would have "become visible on the surface, perhaps disguised by filtering out through a pile of rocks, well down the slope of the Kidron Valley" (p. 71). At a later time, says Kenyon, the cistern's roof would have collapsed. A Byzantine church now lies at this spot (p. 77).

20 2 Kings 18:27 (TEV).

21 2 Kings 18:36 (TEV).

22 This assumes that the crucial role that 2 Kings 19:1-7 gives Isaiah is not straight factual information. The passage seems to reflect the B¹ account's likely origin with Isaiah's disciples (see Chapter 10). The passage inflates that prophet's role, presenting him as the conduit for the news (or, rather, the prophecy) that help is coming. It seems unlikely that Hezekiah, implicitly included in many of Isaiah's denunciations of the power structure, would ever have sought the prophet's counsel in the first place (v. 2). The prophecy seems like another of those after-the-fact prophecies that we've seen elsewhere.

23 See, for example, Michael Avi-Yonah, "Building History from Earliest Times to the Nineteenth Century," in *Urban Geography of Jerusalem*, pp. 13-14.

24 2 Kings 18:23 (TEV).
That the Assyrians had a great many chariotry and cavalry horses at Jerusalem is also clear from Isaiah 22:7.

25 The Rab-shakeh, together with the Tartan and the Rab-saris, could have made the decision to remove the horses while all three were at Jerusalem. Or Sennacherib himself could have made it after the Rab-shakeh reported back to him in Libnah, as described in 2 Kings 19:8.

26 Hedging their bets in the event of a Kushite-Egyptian advance, the Assyrians could conceivably have taken the horses to outlying points in the general region of Jerusalem where water was available or even to the hospitable and nearby province of Samarina. But such options seem unlikely: in the event that Sennacherib was indeed not ruling out Kushite-Egyptian intervention and was playing it safe, why would he have let his main forces be so widely dispersed in the first place?

27 Barkay, "Iron Age II-III." "It is reasonable to assume," Barkay writes, "that Hezekiah's Lachish was one of the chief chariot towns of Judah, a place where horse and chariot were mustered in preparation for Hezekiah's rebellion against Assyrian rule" (p. 345).

28 Hezekiah would certainly have emptied or destroyed all cisterns in the region that lay outside Jerusalem's walls, that is, those home reservoirs used to collect rainwater (often from the flat roofs of houses). The closest source of living water would have been the spring of Merneptah, two miles away (Avi-Yonah, "Building History," p. 13). According to the hydrological map in the *Atlas of Jerusalem*, published in 1973, in modern times there were only three springs within a four-mile radius of the Gihon spring; presumably Hezekiah would have seen to it that these were blocked. (See Map 1.2. This 1973 atlas designates all three as having only modest discharges. Two produce

less than one liter of water per second, the third is in the category of those producing 1-9 liters per second. It is hard to know what changes might have occurred to water sources in 27 centuries, but it should have been fairly easy to plug springs of such approximate magnitude.) One has to go beyond a 4.5-mile radius from Gihon before starting to encounter a substantial number of springs, most of them in the hills to the west. Bear in mind these 4.5 miles are as the crow flies; twisting roads would have added considerable distance.

[29] A specialist on horses in the Roman world, Ann Hyland, has calculated the amount of solids required by a Roman army's ala quingenaria, a cavalry unit consisting of over 680 horses (including spares). In her *Equus: The Horse in the Roman World* (New Haven and London: Yale University Press, 1990), Hyland says: "Food consumption per day, at 10 lb (4.5 kg) of hay per beast would be 6,860 lb (3,100 kg) of hay, and 3.5 lb (1.5 kg) of grain [such as barley] per animal would be 2,401 lb (1,000 kg) of grain" (pp. 91-92).

If the Assyrians were willing to give the Jerusalemites 2,000 horses, presumably they would have retained at least that many themselves. Let's assume, then, they had a total of 4,000 battle horses. If we multiply the above sums for an ala by six, we can get a ball-park estimate of the daily food demands of Assyria's cavalry and chariotry horses at Jerusalem: approximately 41,000 lb of hay, plus 14,000 of grain. And that's conservative. The figures do not take into account the additional pack horses, mules and the like.

[30] 2 Kings 19:8-9a, 19:36 (NRSV). I have changed "Ethiopia" to Kush.

[31] Kitchen, "Egypt, the Levant and Assyria," p. 250. Kitchen says Sennacherib's forces were "spread-eagled in four separate locations" — Libnah, Adullam, Jerusalem and Lachish. Adullam (referred to in Micah 1:15) lay some 5-10 miles northeast of Lachish.

[32] But then Kitchen gets thrown off track. He says that scouts or informants would have told Sennacherib, at Libnah, of Taharqa's advance and that the emperor would have quickly called in his far-flung forces, "notably the one at Jerusalem," and unified them; seeing this, Taharqa would have lost heart and "discreetly retreated, first to Gaza, then to Egypt" (*Ibid.*, p. 251). What may have confused Kitchen is the Bible's description in verse 8 of the Rab-shakeh's return to Sennacherib.

Verse 8 says: "The Rab-shakeh *returned*, and found the king of Assyria fighting against Libnah; for he heard that the king had left Lachish" (RSV, emphasis added). Kitchen interprets that to mean that the Rab-shakeh *took his army with him* from Jerusalem to Libnah. He contends that this retreat would have freed Jerusalem, and then all the Assyrians would have left for Nineveh (because, says Kitchen, the "army seems to have fallen victim to some plague.")

The proposition is untenable. The biblical text says nothing about an army accompanying the Rab-shakeh to Libnah. If, as Kitchen says, the besieging army had done so, it is astounding the Bible would not have said so explicitly in this scene that describes the Rab-shakeh's departure. After all, the enemy that had so threatened the city would suddenly have decamped, leaving Jerusalem free. Would not liberation be worth at the very least a mention? In terms of the story's chronology, this would have occurred well before the eventual setback to Sennacherib's forces as whole.

Also, the Bible says nothing about the two important officials, the Tartan and the Rab-saris (whom Sennacherib had sent with the Rab-shakeh to Jerusalem), coming back with the Rab-shakeh; having noted their presence with the Rab-shakeh when they arrive, in 18:17, it would follow that the narrative might allude to their departure. Is there a translation problem that obscures a collective departure? No. In verse 8, the key verb is "returned," or *yahsav*, and it is singular. There is, then, no hint that the Rab-shakeh's departure was a collective one. My assumption is that either the Tartan or Rab-saris, or both, remained at Jerusalem to oversee the maintenance of the siege.

A final observation. Kitchen's scenario implies a swift but orderly march of Assyrian troops from Jerusalem to confront Taharqa. As seen in earlier chapters, Herodotus and various passages in the Book of Isaiah describe the besieging army's departure from Jerusalem as full of tumult and fear.

[33] Although the narrative's terse wording may lead some to infer that Taharqa's reported advance came immediately upon the Rab-shakeh's return to Sennacherib, it is quite possible that days or weeks separated the two events.

[34] Yurco, "Sennacherib's Third Campaign," p. 225.

[35] I differ with Yurco's assertion that the second unit consisted "entirely" of Kushite troops (*Ibid.*, p. 225).

[36] I am not necessarily wedded to Yurco's proposal of a significant time interval between the two armies (he suggests one to three months). If news of Sennacherib's mobilization of his forces early in 701 had reached the pharaoh early (and one assumes he had an intelligence network), he might have mobilized his own forces early enough to dispatch them with little gap in time.

[37] Historically, Egypt also controlled its own border with Khor, maintaining post stations there, as noted by Samuel A. Meier, *The Messenger in the Ancient Semitic World* (Atlanta: Scholars Press, 1988), pp. 95–96. Among other things, these stations could keep close track of travellers capable of carrying late-breaking news of the army's surprise advance toward Khor. Presumably a closure of the border, combined with patrols of potential alternate routes in the Sinai desert, could have impeded spies' movements.

Spies trying to reach Sennacherib might have also had to overcome a further obstacle: remaining members of the Kushite-Egyptian expedition that had fought at Eltekeh could have organized themselves to screen south-to-north traffic from their position in southern Judah or Philistia.

It would have been less easy for the Kushites to close the many Delta ports, especially since they were unloved by many Saite lords in the Delta. However, any messengers or spies embarking by ship from Egypt, would, after reaching Khor's coast, then have to make their way inland to the Assyrians. In short, it is not hard to see how word of the army from Kush could have reached Sennacherib not long before the army itself reached Judah or perhaps only after it was already in the country.

[38] But what about the strangest part of Herodotus's story — the mice who chomp the Assyrians' equipment the eve of the battle with the 25th Dynasty's forces and force the Assyrians to retreat? How do these rodents fit into this scenario?

Let's consider the key passage again. Herodotus says that on the eve of the Kushite-Egyptian army's attack, "thousands of field-mice swarmed over [the Assyrians] during the night, and ate their quivers, their bowstrings, and the leather handles of their shields, so that on the following day, having no arms to fight with, they abandoned their position and suffered severe losses during their retreat."

We've seen that several scholars have cast doubt on the mouse's status in Egypt as a symbol of the plague, but the problems with disease extend beyond that.

To understand Herodotus's account of this folk history, let's hold the mice in abeyance and focus instead on the dilemma in which they place the Assyrians.

Herodotus does not link the mice to any health-related problem. If disease is what had truly caused the Assyrian retreat, then Herodotus might have made that point by having the mice do something related to the Assyrians' *physical well-being*. The rodents, for example, could have consumed the Assyrians' grain, leaving the soldiers too hungry to fight. Or the mice could have done something else, based on the ancients' understanding of hygiene and health, that had some bodily effect on the Assyrians.

But the Assyrians' desperate condition is due, according to Herodotus, to their *lack of weapons and equipment*. The mice could be simply folkloric agents for the Assyrians' lack of arms with which to battle the Kushite-Egyptian forces.

What might have happened when Taharqa's forces arrived at Jerusalem? With no expectation of facing an open battle with the Jerusalemites, and with no other perceptible military threat in the offing, the Assyrian besiegers may have simply sent the bulk of their chariots and other military equipment home with their thirsty, hungry horses. The folk history speaks of a want of functioning quivers, bowstrings and shields, but that may be a way to illustrate a much larger lack of the wherewithal to combat the Kushite-Egyptian army.

The genesis of this folk history was already some 250 years old when Herodotus heard it. Soldiers returning to Egypt might well have said they had expected fierce combat with Assyria's vaunted war machine, but all they had encountered at Jerusalem were forces unequipped for proper battle. Those forces would have been more geared for storming fortifications than for open-field battle. They might have contained many engineers, construction crews, sappers and foot soldiers, but they may have included few if any of those fearsome archers on horseback or on chariots, the backbone of Assyrian strength in open battle.

Another possibility? Since the Jerusalem debacle occurred very late in Sennacherib's campaign, the condition of much of his weaponry and equipment would have been poor. The commander would have seen to it that the units in the prime combat areas received the best stock that could be gleaned from the army as a whole. Units that stood little chance of fighting, such as those at Jerusalem, would have been allocated what was left — the old, tattered gear and weapons.

Either possibility would explain why in Herodotus' story it was so easy for the Kushite-Egyptian army to put the Assyrians to flight. If they seem farfetched, they are no more so than most other explanations others have offered.

Why would would the story ascribe most of the credit to lowly mice rather than to the pharaoh's army?

Consider Herodotus' source for the story: Lower Egyptian. The Greek traveller's account reflects the strong influence of the Saites, whose historical antipathy toward Kushite rule was deep-rooted and intense. (This antipathy is evident early in the account. The story says the Kushite pharaoh's high-handedness threw the local warrior class, presumably Saite, into an immobilizing sulk; according to the story's logic, the pharaoh is thus implicitly to blame for these warriors' refusal to defend Egypt against

Assyria.) By ascribing the Assyrian withdrawal to rodents, not to the Kushite Dynasty's soldiers, the story minimizes this resented regime's military achievement.

39 Isaiah 22:1-2 (NRSV). Clements, *Isaiah and the Deliverance*, confidently assigns this passage to the end of the Assyrian siege (p. 33).

40 *ANET*, pp. 287-288.

41 Breasted's translation of Piye's stela, *Ancient Records*, p. 426.

42 2 Kings 18:13-16 (TEV). Sennacherib's annal essentially corroborates these terms of the bribe, though it speaks of 800 talents of silver (rather than 300) and adds other precious objects (*ANET*, p. 288).

43 2 Kings 18:14.
The more protracted diplomatic negotiations, which would taken place after most of Assyria's forces had departed, could have occurred elsewhere — presumably at a more intact and comfortable venue.

44 Ussishkin, *Conquest of Lachish*, p. 17.

45 *Ibid.*

46 David A. Dorsey, *The Roads and Highways of Ancient Israel* (Baltimore and London: Johns Hopkins University Press, 1991), builds on the earlier work of Yohanan Aharoni and others. Dorsey writes that he used four kinds of clues: names of roads and descriptions of them in the Old Testament and in Egyptian and Assyrian texts; the archaeological evidence of settlements, since towns, villages and forts tended to be strung along routes, and particularly at crossroads; the country's topography, and finally, the locations of roads built by Romans and even modern engineers, since the most direct way between two points seldom varies (new technology, such as bridge-making, aside).

47 *Ibid.*, p. 119 ff. Also, Aharoni, as quoted by Dorsey.

48 *Ibid.*, p. 13.

49 Although they were perhaps not absent from the Beer-sheba area. See below.

50 Dorsey, *Roads and Highways*, p. 129.

51 Dorsey says that between Beer-sheba and Jerusalem there were only four hilly places of any note: these would have required a climb of about 100 meters within one kilometer, a descent of 20 meters within one kilometer, a descent of 75-100 meters within one kilometer and an ascent of 75 meters within two kilometers (*Ibid.*, pp. 121-124).

52 Minimal interference, however, does not necessarily mean no interference at all. It may be significant that archaeological evidence suggests the total destruction in 701 of Beer-sheba and another southern town, Arad. (Yohanan Aharoni, "Excavations at Tel Beer-sheba," in *The Biblical Archaeologist* 25, December 1972, says Sennacherib's army "probably" destroyed the city {p. 114}. His 1982 book, *Archaeology of the Land of Israel*, is more emphatic. Referring to archaeological remains at Beer-sheba and Arad, among other towns, Aharoni concludes: "Today there is no room for doubt that all of these

severe destructions must be assigned to the Sennacherib campaign of 701 . . ." {p. 266}.)

The Assyrians may well have seen the advantage to Taharqa's army of using Beer-sheba as its gateway to Judah (whether specifically to Jerusalem, Lachish or elsewhere). That might help explain an Assyrian foray to Beer-sheba and Arad. With their forces dispersed, the Assyrians lacked the manpower to confront the incoming army successfully and turn it back. Whether they even tried cannot be known. It would have made sense for them, however, to destroy Beer-sheba, as well as nearby Arad, if only to impede the desert-weary army's access to fresh provisions. Another possibility: Assyria could have held the two towns and the Kushite-Egyptian forces could have overcome them.

(There is no way to know exactly who did what to Beer-sheba and Arad in 701. But it seems clear that the conflict of that year did somehow involve these towns, which were far removed from the main theater of war to the north. The destruction of both isolated towns leads one to suspect something worth Assyria's attention was happening in Judah's south-central region, and the presence of Kushite-Egyptian forces would explain it.)

[53] Dorsey, *Roads and Highways*, p. 13.

[54] Hyland, *Equus*, says that, based on Livy's account, a Roman army in 210 BC marched 325 miles in seven days to attack Carthaginian forces in Spain, a daily average of about 46 miles. The baggage train would have been left behind; the rapid strike force, she suggests, would have carried its own rations and lived off the land (pp. 175-176).

CHAPTER SIXTEEN

[1] Soggin, *Introduction*, pp. 15-16. Soggin, an authority on Hebrew literature at the University of Rome, notes that many prophetic, religious and historical texts had a character that was "somewhat fluid" before their consolidation into the Bible.

[2] In fact, the latest trend is to fine-tune the B² text's time of composition from shortly before the Exile to the actual period of the Exile, 586-538. However, given the lack of firm evidence, the consensus could some day change again. For the sake of prudence, I am using this broader, century-sized window.

[3] T.G.H. James, "Egypt: The 25th and 26th Dynasties," goes so far as to say, not unreasonably, that Assyria "in effect founded the Egyptian 26th Dynasty" (p. 701).

[4] Anti-Egyptian resentment may even have preceded Josiah's reign, suggests A. Malamat, "The Twilight of Judah: In the Egyptian-Babylonian Maelstrom," in *Supplements to Vetus Testamentum*, vol. 28 (Leiden: E.J. Brill, 1975). He speculates that the 26th Dynasty may have been behind the mysterious murder in c. 640 BC of Manasseh's son and successor, King Amon, in only the second year of his rule.

The Hebrew University historian writes: "The assassination of Josiah's father, Amon, was undoubtedly of Egyptian instigation, and already then Egypt seems to have been intriguing to install a sympathetic regime in Judah." That kingdom's landed aristocracy, Malamat says, managed to suppress the revolt at court (2 Kings 21:19-26), enthrone the young Josiah and surely also set the deeply anti-Egyptian tone of his policy" (p. 126).

Malamat provides no evidence to support his assertion that Egypt "undoubtedly" lurked behind the regicide. But the possibility of such involvement is worth bearing in mind: it would have given the B² writers all the more reason to resent Egypt.

5 Jeremiah 22:17 (TEV).

6 Tadmor, "Period of the First Temple," p. 155.

7 Personal communication from Ronald Clements, recalling that this information came to him from Rabbi Hugo Gryn.

8 Personal communication. See also Clements, "Central Passage Reconsidered," p. 261. Clements credits Gonçalves with convincing him of this.

9 See 2 Kings 19:34 (NRSV). For Yahweh's original endorsement in perpetuity of the House of David, see 2 Samuel 7:16.

10 Zerubbabel, whom Cyrus appointed governor of Judea. See the Book of Ezra.

11 Deuteronomy 7:6 (NRSV).

12 Stated earlier in Deuteronomy 5:33.

13 See the discussion on Nadav Na'aman's article, "The Conquest of Canaan," in note 35.

14 Deuteronomy 5:33 (NRSV).

15 19:14-16 (Cogan & Tadmor).

16 Childs, for example, asks: "If the message is delivered orally according to the pattern of B¹, why was it necessary for Hezekiah to take the letter(s) from the messengers, read it, and spread it before Yahweh?" (*Isaiah and the Assyrian Crisis*, p. 97).

17 This rigorously literal translation is by Everett Fox in the Schocken Bible.

18 (NRSV)

19 This is true even of the locust swarm. While the devastation that locust swarms can cause is well known, the scale of *this* locust plague is not natural. Exodus 10:14-15 says that "nothing green was left, no tree, no plant in the field, in all the land of Egypt." It describes the insects as "such a dense swarm of locusts as had never been before, nor ever shall be again" (NRSV).

20 See James M. Elfird, "Angel of the Lord," *Harper's Bible Dictionary*, ed. by Paul J. Achtemeier (San Francisco: Harper & Row, 1985), p. 30. Elfird observes: "The angel of the Lord seems to have been understood as distinct from other angels and, in the earlier Old Testament literature, appears to be almost another designation for God."

21 Genesis 22:11-12.

22 Exodus 3:2ff.

23 Exodus 14:19ff. See also Numbers 20:16.

24 Exodus 23:20-23 and 32:34. See also Judges 2:1-4.

[25] Regarding the Bible's use of the angel of the Yahweh, there may be more nuances than my book describes. All biblical writers may not have had a uniform opinion of angels.

Moshe Weinfeld, an expert on Deuteronomic and Deuteronomistic writings, says that Deuteronomy 7 does not take into account the passages on angels that appear in Exodus 23:20-23, 33:2-3 and Judges 2:1-4. "Deuteronomy rejects the view of angels as mediators and denies the role of the angel at the Exodus (cf. Numbers 20:15-16) and at the conquest," says Weinfeld, *Deuteronomy, 1-11: A New Translation with Introduction and Commentary* (Anchor Bible 5; New York: Doubleday, 1991), p. 379.

Clements, *Isaiah 1-39*, also indicates there may be a difference of views among those responsible for the revision of the story of Sennacherib's invasion. Referring to the single verse on the angel (2 Kings 19:35/Isaiah 37:36), he says: "It is very possible that this verse did not belong even in the original B² account, but has been added subsequent to the combining of B¹ with B²" (pp. 287-288).

This kind of analysis about shadings of different points of view and different times of composition is highly conjectural and leaves me skeptical. My own discussion is in broad strokes; following the example of the great majority of scholars, I am lumping the angel verse into B². However, it's worth bearing mind that underlying complexity may exist.

[26] Alfred Edersheim, *The Bible History*, vol. 7, *The History of Israel and Judah from the Decline of the Two Kingdoms to the Assyrian and Babylonian Captivity* (London: Religious Tract Society, 1887), p. 156.

[27] Deuteronomy 34:10.

[28] Not excluding this possibility is, among others, Weinfeld, *Deuteronomy 1-11*, p. 375.

[29] Thus, for example, U. Cassuto, *A Commentary on the Book of Exodus*, trans. from the Hebrew by Israel Abrahams (Jerusalem: Magnes Press, The Hebrew University, 1967). He says: "The hornet . . . is nothing but unreasonable dread, panic, synonomous with the word for terror. . . . This is apparently the correct interpretation of hornet, for the Arabs to this day call panic resulting in mass flight by a word signifying 'hornet' (p. 308). Also translating the term as "panic" are the NEB and TEV.

[30] John Garstang, *Joshua, Judges* (London: Constable, 1931), pp. 258-260. He quotes two zoologists as giving such an identification on the basis of the depiction of the insect in some Theban tombs.

[31] Y. Yadin, "The Transition from a Semi-Nomadic to a Sedentary Society in the Twelth Century B.C.E.," in *Symposia Celebrating the Seventy-fifth Anniversary of the Founding of the American Schools of Oriental Research*, ed. by F. M. Cross (Cambridge: American Schools of Oriental Research, 1979), pp. 57-68, and Oded Borowski, "The Identity of the Biblical sir'â," *The Word of the Lord Shall Go Forth*, op. cit., pp. 315-319. Borowski sees additional wordplay as buttressing the symbolism.

[32] Exodus 23:28 and Joshua 24:12.

[33] Garstang, *Joshua, Judges*, p. 259.

I agree with the thrust of Garstang's statement, but it needs nuancing. Prior to the Deuteronomic/Deuteronomistic period, Isaiah said that Assyria would crush Judah;

and, after that period, biblical writers credited King Cyrus of Persia with liberating the Hebrews. In these cases, human agents were seen as acting on Yahweh's instructions.

[34] Borowski, "Identity of the Biblical sir'â," p. 317.

Borowski continues:

"Israelite ideology recognized that foreign powers could serve as Yahweh's agents, as in, *e.g.*, Isaiah 7: 18; 10:5-12, but in these instances the foreign powers were charged with the mission of punishing Israel and there was no reason to conceal their identity. In the *sir'â [tsir'ah]* references, credit is given to Egypt for its 'help' to Israel, though it is given in a way recognizable only by those familiar with the details of the conquest."

Borowski's proposal has been such a dead letter that when I queried the author 15 years after publication, he expressed surprise that someone should be interested. "I'm glad someone read this," he wrote back, "and even considered my suggestion as plausible."

Giving further plausibility to that suggestion is, in effect, the definition that the latest research attaches to the insect hieroglyph in question. Indicating that the bee and hornet are both acceptable translations of this symbol is James P. Allen, *Middle Egyptian: An Introduction to the Language and Culture of Hieroglyphs* (Cambridge: Cambridge University Press, 2000).

This confirms E.A. Wallis Budge, *An Egyptian Hieroglyphic Dictionary*, vol. 1 (New York : Dover Publications, 1978 {1920}), p. cxx.

[35] In weighing these fascinating questions, here are two additional things to consider.

First, the story of the Conquest may be largely a fabrication. In a 1994 article, Tel Aviv University archaeologist Nadav Na'aman deems the entire story, which he says was written at the earliest in the seventh century BC, to have "only a tenuous contact with historical reality" ("The 'Conquest of Canaan,'" p. 281). Na'aman is addressing the comprehensive Conquest story as presented in the Book of Joshua, one of the three books in which the hornet appears, but his remarks would apply to allusions to the Conquest in the other books, Deuteronomy and Exodus.

Largely on the basis of archaeological evidence, Na'aman concludes: "The comprehensive conquest saga in the Book of Joshua is a fictive literary composition aimed at presenting the occupation of the entire Land of Israel, initiated and guided by the Lord and carried out by the 12 tribes under Joshua." Because writing was all but unknown in both Israel and Judah until the eighth century BC (pp. 219-223), he notes that the authors of this action-filled segment of the Deuteronomistic History could consult no ancient records. Nonetheless, Na'aman notes a "very thin foundation" may underlie the Conquest story: he suggests that the "collective historical memory" of Hebrew society may have "retained the impression of the total destruction of the Canaanite urban system in the late 13th-12th centuries BCE," a destruction that had nothing to do with Hebrew military prowess but which the biblical writers still have credited to Joshua's troops (p. 281; for the migrations of various peoples that may have contributed to this possible downfall of Canaanite cities, see pp. 241 ff.).

That such a "collective historical memory" existed at all, however, is sheer conjecture; Na'aman acknowledges that in the 13th or 12th centuries, the time of this upheaval, it is "inconceivable that at this time [Hebrew society] was already a vast, ethnically unified country" (p. 230).

In short, given the absence at the time of both records and a sense of Hebrew nationhood, it is hard to imagine that 600 or 700 years later the biblical writers would have had much understanding at all of any Egyptian contribution to the emergence of Hebrew rule, especially since that role would have been indirect (the Egyptian departure would simply have left a power vacuum). All this weakens the case for the Garstang-Yadin-Borowski view that the hornet refers to New Kingdom activity.

Second, surprising as it may seem, the Bible's detailed account of the Conquest may itself contain subtle traces of the events of 701 BC. Na'aman's article (which at no point mentions the hornet idea) makes the case that the authors of the Conquest saga modelled some of Joshua's success on Sennacherib's invasion. In Joshua 10:29-39, for example, the Hebrews conquer a series of cities that, he says, happen to be the same cities that Sennacherib destroyed during his invasion of Judah (pp. 254-256, 281); that momentous sequence of events, he suggests, would have remained vivid in Judahites' memory.

If Na'aman is right that the strife of 701 influenced one aspect of the Conquest story, it would strengthen the idea that the same conflict could be at the root of the biblical writers' curious choice of the hornet figure.

[36] So far as available symbols went, there would have been little option: the proper symbol for Upper Egypt, the reed, hardly lent itself to military imagery. The hornet would have been quite suitable.

CHAPTER SEVENTEEN

[1] Among the historians dealing specifically with the political crisis in Khor, the one who from my recollection most clearly differs is Jean Leclant. Remarkably even-handed toward the Kushite Dynasty in many areas, he is also fair to it on this point. Leclant, *In the Steps of the Pharaohs* (New York: Hastings House, 1958), says: "At the request of the sovereigns of Palestine, the Ethiopians intervened in Asia against the Assyrians" (p. 26). The point, however, is made only in passing — and it is made in the introduction to a coffee-table book of photos, not in a text that would attract much scholarly attention. Lacking both argument and sources, Leclant's observation does not represent a rebuttal to the prevailing view.

In Chapter 19, I will point out other writers who are fair to the Kushites generally (but who may not deal with this specific crisis).

[2] Breasted, *History of Egypt*, pp. 550-553, 560.

[3] Sachar, *History of the Jews*, pp. 56-57.

[4] Adams, *Nubia*, pp. 263-4. Here, Adams amplifies on the 25th Dynasty's responsibility in provoking Assyria: "The machinations of Shabako finally convinced the Assyrian emperor Sennacherib that the Egyptian nuisance must be disposed of. In 701 BC, he led a considerable army west, intending to crush Egypt and put an end once and for all to the chronic rebellions in Palestine and Syria."

[5] Miller & Hayes, *Israel and Judah*, p. 358.

[6] Gonçalves, *L'expédition de Sennachérib*, p. 141. See also p. 108.

[7] Motyer, *Prophecy of Isaiah*, pp. 20, 170.

[8] Kuhrt, *Ancient Near East*, vol. 2, p. 499.

[9] Kitchen, "Egypt," p. 117. That assessment develops his 1986 view in *Third Intermediate Period* that the "ambitious" Shebitku, a pharaoh with "nakedly imperialistic pretensions," pursued an "aggressive policy in Western Asia" (pp. 557, 385).

[10] To be fair, I should note that Breasted, *History of Egypt*, and Kitchen, "Egypt," cite the "broken reed" passage of 2 Kings 18:21. That passage, however, does not provide any basis for concluding the 25th Dynasty was involved in the sort of imperialistic meddling that Breasted and Kitchen allege.

[11] Referring to Isaiah 18's description of Kushite envoys in Judah, Gonçalves, *L'expédition de Sennachérib*, says: "Although the text mentions neither the destination nor the goal of the mission, Isaiah's condemnation of it leaves no doubt that the envoys went to Jerusalem in order to foment or organize an anti-Assyrian uprising" (p. 141). Motyer, *Prophecy of Isaiah*, assumes that the envoys "went to all the Palestinian states promising Egyptian aid in an anti-Assyrian uprising" (p. 161).

[12] Isaiah 18:1-2 (RSV).

[13] One of the most astute of analysts, Childs, observes with exasperation that the oracle is "one of the most perplexing" passages in the entire Book of Isaiah (*Isaiah and the Assyrian Crisis*, p. 45).

[14] For the possible dates of the envoys' visit and also for the envoys' imprecise place of origin, please see notes in Chapter 13.

[15] Clements, *Isaiah 1-39*, p. 164.

[16] That in a later verse the gloomy prophet foresees carnage at Jerusalem suggests that Sennacherib may have already made clear he would punish Khor and that the ambassadors' visit is a last-minute affair — not an advance mission to plan insurrection. Also: that the emissaries had to travel by boat, rather than overland as would be normal, could reflect the fact that pro-Assyrian forces had already sealed off road access between Egypt and Khor.

[17] Unlike many commentators, Clements, *Isaiah 1-39*, suggests that a "nation tall and smooth" in v. 2 refers to Assyria; in effect, then, the prophet would be calling on the "messengers' — that is, the Kushite ambassadors — to go to Assyria (pp. 164-165). The problem with that interpretation is that the expression of people "tall and smooth" recurs in v. 7, and this time the reference to Kushites is, as Clements notes (p. 166), quite implicit, evoking as it does Isaiah 45:14. The passage reads better if we assume the prophet is bidding the ambassadors to return to Africa for their own good, afraid as he is that Jerusalem will soon be the scene of carnage (v. 6). That would be consistent with his opinion in Isaiah 31 that Kushite Egypt may perish if it gets drawn into helping Judah against Assyria.

[18] Isaiah 20:6 (NRSV).

[19] Isaiah 31:1 (NRSV).

[20] Isaiah 30:1-6 (NRSV).

[21] Gonçalves, *L'expédition de Sennachérib*, pp. 145, 150.

[22] *Ibid.*, p. 108.

[23] Let me see if I have this right: according to this view, Nation A has helped get Nation B into trouble by inciting it to rebel against Nation C; yet Nation B later has to implore and even offer treasure to Nation A for military protection against Nation C. That would mean A had tried to weasel out of its responsibilities to its ally and leave it in the lurch.

If Nation A did in fact have such a foreign policy, it would be quite perfidious. Surely Nation B would feel betrayed and bitter. Yet none of Nation B's numerous texts on this period make even the slightest allusion to such perfidy.

Indeed, in Isaiah 30, the prophet blames Nation A not for having tried to desert B but rather for what he anticipates will be its insufficient strength — "the help that Egypt gives is useless" (Isaiah 30:7 {TEV}).

[24] Translation by Na'aman, "Sennacherib's 'Letter to God,'" p. 32. For a less fluid translation, see *ANET*, p. 287.

[25] The translations are by Luckenbill (*ANET*) and Ussishkin respectively.

[26] See Herotodus II.139. In this vignette, the pharaoh named "Sabacos" corresponds to Shabako. See also Diodorus, I. 65.

[27] 2 Kings 18:8. See also the Assyrian record in Na'aman, "Sennacherib's 'Letter to God.'"

[28] 2 Kings 20.

[29] The argument here is that those who say the Kushite Dynasty fomented revolt have not made a case for this. My argument is *not* that such a hypothesis is necessarily false. I can't prove that this did not happen. To make a case for Egypt's instigation of outright revolt, however, one would have to show why Egypt might see a departure from its customary don't-rock-the-boat policy to be in its interest. For example, one might want to show that Assyria had choked off Egypt's access to trade routes through Khor. No historians, however, have argued this. And, so far as I am aware, no evidence for it exists.

[30] For all the uncertainty over the identity of "So, King of Egypt," it is clear that the final say on Israel's plea for help would have been up to the only king with any capability of bringing real help, Piye. See Chapter 6.

[31] Nor would Shabako's conquest of Lower Egypt, *c.* 712, represent a reversal of Kushite policy not to offend Sargon. Rather, that action meant that the 25th Dynasty would not countenance Sargon's invasion of Lower Egypt. A show of determination to defend the country against attack is compatible with a policy of non-provocation in Khor.

[32] J. Ki-Zerbo, "General Introduction," *General History of Africa*, vol, 1: *Methodology and African Prehistory* (Heinemann, UNESCO, 1981), p. 2.

CHAPTER EIGHTEEN

[1] A.H.L. Heeren, *Historical Researches into the Politics, Intercourse, and Trade of the Carthaginians, Ethiopians, and Egyptians*, 2nd ed., vol. 1. trans. from the German (Oxford: D.A. Talboys, 1838), pp. 290-291, 471.

2 *Ibid.*, pp. 410-411.

3 *The Holy Bible, according to the authorized version; with notes, explanatory and practical; taken principally from the most eminent writers of the United Church of England and Ireland: together with appropriate introductions, tables, indexes, maps, and plans; prepared and arranged by the Rev. George d'Oyly, B.D., and the Rev. Richard Mant, D.D.*, domestick chaplains to his grace the Lord Archbishop of Canterbury, under the direction of The Society for Promoting Christian Knowledge, vol. 1 (Oxford: Clarendon Press, 1817).

4 *A Dictionary of English Church History*, 3rd ed., rev., by S.L. Ollard, Gordon Crosse and Maurice F. Bond (London and Oxford: Mowbray; New York: Morehouse-Gorham, 1948), p. 461.

5 *A commentary upon the Two Books of Kings*, by the Right Reverend Father in God, Symon Lord Bishop of Ely (London: 1705). The comments cited by d'Oyly and Mant are on p. 541.

6 *Ibid.*, p. 542.

7 *A commentary upon the larger and lesser prophets: being a continuation of Bishop Patrick*, by William Lowth, B.D., Prebendary of Winchester, 3rd ed. (London: Printed for James and John Knapton, *et al.*, 1730), pp. 73, 84-85.

8 *Ibid.*, p. 84.

9 John Calvin, *Commentary on the Book of the Prophet Isaiah*, vol. 3, trans. from the Latin by the Rev. William Pringle (Edinburgh: Calvin Translation Society, 1852).
     The outcome of Sennacherib's invasion, he said, represented the "seal," or "illustrious proofs," of Isaiah's "doctrine" that God would punish his people but in the end be merciful to them. Isaiah's doctrine, Calvin said, "was manifestly sealed when God delivered Jerusalem from the grievous siege of Sennacherib, and when no hope of safety remained, so that believers saw that they had been rescued from the jaws of death by the hand of God alone" (p. 77, with punctuation modified for clarity).

10 *Ibid.*, p. 115. On the details, Calvin may err. He says that the "kings of Egypt and Ethiopia formed a league with each other against Sennacherib." He makes that alliance sound wholly voluntary, when in fact Shabako had to overcome the 24th Dynasty in Lower Egypt in order to respond to Assyria. But Calvin is right in the larger sense: Kush and Egypt were aligned together against Assyria.
     On second thought, perhaps even in the details Calvin has a point: before the Kushites took control of all Egypt in the late eighth century, at least five kings ruled simultaneously in different parts of Egypt north of Theban-controlled territory. Some of these kings, including Osorkon, would have been willing co-participants with Kush in the strategy against Assyria.

11 *Ibid.*, pp. 114-115.

12 *Ibid.*, p. 115.

13 *Ibid.*, p. 145.

14 *Ibid.*, pp. 114, 145.

Despite the significance he gives to Egypt's help, Calvin does not see any irony in the "broken-reed" passage. He says Hezekiah, as a "pious king," truly relied on God and not on Egypt, and that the Rab-shakeh's suggestion that the Hebrews were banking on "receiving aid from the Egyptians is not only false and unfounded, but pernicious" (p. 82).

[15] *Ibid.*, p. 146.

[16] Rev. Henry Constable, "Tirhakah," in *The Imperial Bible-Dictionary, Historical, Biographical, Geographical, and Doctrinal*, vol. 3, ed. by the Rev. Patrick Fairbairn (London: Blackie and Son, 1867), pp. 1042-1043.

After that overthrow, he writes, "It is quite possible that Tirhakah may have led his army in pursuit of the Assyrians. . . ."

[17] Sir J. Gardner Wilkinson, *The Manners and Customs of the Ancient Egyptians*, vol. 1, a new ed., revised and corrected by Samuel Birch (London: John Murray, 1878), pp. 94-95, 97.

In an earlier work, he asserts the same idea. In *A Popular Account of the Ancient Egyptians*, vol. 1, rev. and abridged ed. (New York: Harper & Brothers, 1854), Wilkinson says: "Tirhaka, who with Sabacos [Shabako] composed the 25th Ethiopian dynasty, checked the advance of the Assyrians, and forcing Sennacherib to retire from Judaea, restored the influence of Egypt in Syria" (pp. 308-309).

[18] Brian M. Fagan, *The Rape of the Nile: Tomb Robbers, Tourists, and Archaeologists in Egypt* (New York: Charles Scribner's Sons, 1975) says that this "famous and monumental work" by Wilkinson "is the first study in centuries to look beyond Herodotus and the traditional legends to the Egyptian sources themselves" (p. 264).

[19] Heinrich Ewald, *The History of Israel*, vol. 4, *From the Disruption of the Monarchy to Its Fall*, trans. from the German by J. Estlin Carpenter, 2nd ed. (London: Longmans, Green, 1878), p. 183.

[20] *Ibid.*, p. 179.

[21] *II Kings, a New English Translation: Translation of Text, Rashii and Commentary*, by Rabbi A.J. Rosenberg (New York: Judaica Press, 1980), p. 386 ff.

[22] Radak is the acronym for *Ra*bbi *Da*vid *K*imhi, of France.

[23] Malbim is the acronym for an eastern European rabbi whose full name is Meier Loeb ben Jehiel Michael.

[24] Murray Friedman, with the assistance of Peter Binzen, *What Went Wrong? The Creation and Collapse of the Black-Jewish Alliance* (New York: Free Press, 1995), p. 26.

Max B. May, *Isaac Mayer Wise: The Founder of American Judaism* (New York and London: G.P. Putnam's Sons, 1916), calls Wise "the founder of American Judaism" (p.397). It says: "What Martin Luther was to the Reformation, Samuel Adams to the American Revolution, and William Lloyd Garrison to Abolitionism, Isaac Mayer Wise was to Reform Judaism in America" (p. 395)..

[25] *Ibid.*, p. 26.

[26] Isaac Mayer Wise, *History of the Israelitish Nation, from Abraham to the Present Time*, vol. 1 (Albany, NY: J. Munsell, 1854) proposes this aftermath to the sickness: "When, therefore, the army of Tarhekah approached nearer, and no prospect was left to take Jerusalem, to protect themselves there against the approaching army, Sannacherib was obliged to leave Judah and retrace the Syrian desert" (p. 351).

[27] *Lettres et Journaux de Champollion le Jeune*, vol. 2, ed. by H. Hartleben (Paris: Ernest Leroux, 1909), p. 427-430. The point is not that Champollion was necessarily right on this currently controversial point, but that he was fair-minded.

[28] *Ibid.*, p. 439.

[29] While I will propose below that this great shift in the perception of black Africa occurred in the early 1880s, there would of course have been exceptions. One example is the prominent German Egyptologist Heinrich Brugsch. In his *A History of Egypt under the Pharaohs*, vol. 1 (trans. from the German by Henry Danby Seymour and Philip Smith (London: John Murray, 1879), he disputes the assumption—which Heeren makes—that Egyptian civilization grew out of earlier Kushite civilization. He goes on to say: ". . . much rather it was the Egyptians who first ascended the river, to found in Ethiopia temples, cities, and fortified places, and to diffuse the blessings of a civilized state among the rude dark-coloured population" (p. 4).

[30] Layard, *Discoveries among the Ruins*, p. 123.

[31] I am not suggesting that all scholars who hold that the Kushites were minor players in the 701 conflict are necessarily scornful of the Kushites generally (although a correlation does exist in a majority of cases).

A good example of a turn-of-the-century scholar who is generous in his assessment of Taharqa without believing him to have been important in 701 is the well-known French Egyptologist Gaston Maspero (1846-1916). In his *History of Egypt, Chaldea, Syria, Palestine and Assyria*, vol. 8, ed. by A.H. Sayce, trans. from the French by M.L. McClure (London: Grolier Society, 1903), Maspero has this to say about Taharqa as pharaoh: "What we know to be a fact is that he secured to the valley of the Nile nearly 20 years of prosperity, and he recalled the glories of the great reigns of former days, if not by his victories, at least by the excellence of his administration and his activity" (p. 141). Maspero gives support to the epidemic theory in his book *The Passing of the Empire: 850 B.C. to 330 B.C.*, ed. by A.H. Sayce, trans. by M.L. McClure (London: Society for Promoting Christian Knowledge, 1900), p. 293.

One of Maspero's contemporaries who also gives Kush a fair shake but endorses the epidemic theory is John Kenrick, *Ancient Egypt under the Pharaohs*, vol. 1 (New York: John B Alden, 1883), pp. 306-316.

[32] Cunningham Geikie, *Hours with the Bible, or the Scriptures in the Light of Modern Knowledge*, vol. 4 (New York: James Pott), pp. 472, 475. He is uncertain whether a "fiery" desert wind or a plague played the key role. The unstated source for the fiery wind is presumably Isaiah 10:16-17.

[33] Leopold von Ranke, *Universal History: The Oldest Historical Group of Nations and the Greeks*, ed. by G. W. Prother (New York: Harper & Brothers, 1885, p. 77.)

³⁴ Franz Delitzsch, *Biblical Commentary on the Prophecies of Isaiah*, vol. 2, trans. from the German 4th ed. by the Rev. J.S. Banks (Edinburgh: T. & T. Clark, 1890), pp. 100-101.

³⁵ Edersheim, *Bible History*, vol. 7, p. 155. It was published in 1887.

³⁶ George Adam Smith, *The Historical Geography of the Holy Land*, 3rd ed. (London: Hodder and Stoughton, 1895), p. 158.

³⁷ Additional anglo-American support for the epidemic theory came from: F.J. Foakes-Jackson, *The Biblical History of the Hebrews*, 3rd ed., enl. (Cambridge, UK: W. Heffer & Sons; London: Simpkin Marshall, 1909), p. 292. He was a fellow of Jesus College, Cambridge, honorary canon of Peterborough and later professor of Christian institutions at New York's Union Theological Seminary. Also: Angus M. Mackay, *The Churchman's Introduction to the Old Testament* (London: Methuen, 1901), p. 203. He was rector of Holy Trinity Church, Edinburgh. Also: Robert William Rogers, *A History of Babylonia and Assyria*, vol. 2, 3rd ed. (New York: Eaton & Mains; Cincinnati: Jennings & Pye, 1900), pp. 202-204. Rogers was a professor at Drew Theological Seminary in Madison, NJ. Also: a commentary on 2 Kings 19:35 by the Lord Bishop of Bath and Wells in *The Old Testament according to the Authorised Version* (London: Society for Promoting Christian Knowledge, 1903).

In 1902, one of Breasted's colleagues at the University of Chicago, published a book on Mesopotamia that, in passing, also accepted the epidemic theory. See George Goodspeed, *A History of the Babylonians and Assyrians* (New York: Charles Scribner's Sons, 1902, p. 272. Goodspeed assigns the troubles-elsewhere theory an auxiliary role.

³⁸ *The Two Books of Kings*, with introduction and notes by William Emery Barnes (Cambridge, UK: Cambridge University Press, 1908), p. 286. Barnes is clearly giving his own opinion and not simply presenting Assyria's view of Taharqa.

³⁹ George A. Reisner, *The Archaeological Survery of Nubia, Report for 1907-1908*, vol. 1 (Cairo: National Printing Dept., 1910), p. 348.

⁴⁰ Bernal, *Black Athena*, vol. 1, observes: "All cultures have some degree of prejudice for, or more often against, people whose appearance is unusual. However, the intensity and pervasiveness of Northern European, American and other colonial racism since the 17th century have been so much greater than the norm that they need some explanation.

"It is difficult to say whether or not racism was unusually strong before the 16th century, the first in which Northern Europeans came into frequent contact with peoples from other continents" (p. 201).

Bernal allows that by the 15th century, "clear links were seen between dark skin color and evil and inferiority" in the case of the early Gypsies. But, he adds, "it is generally accepted that a more clear-cut racism grew up after 1650 and that this was greatly intensified by the increased colonization of North America, with its twin policies of extermination of the Native Americans and enslavement of the Africans" (pp. 201-201).

In his 1996 book that represents the first in-depth attempt to track the idea of race in Europe, Hannaford finds that the term "race" entered European languages only during the "period 1200-1500 and did have the same meaning that we attach to it now." The British researcher says that "it was not until the late seventeenth century that the pre-idea began to have a specific connotation different from that of *gens* (Latin, clan) and to be used in conjunction with a new term — 'ethnic group'" (*Race*, pp. 5-6).

[41] Harry Magdoff, "Colonialism: II. European Expansion since 1763," in *Encyclopaedia Britannica, Macropaedia* (1975), vol. 4, p. 899.

[42] Hannaford, *Race*, p. 278.

[43] *Ibid.*, p. 306.

[44] *Ibid.*, pp. 319-324.

[45] *Ibid.*, p. 125.

[46] *Ibid.*, p. 316.
Hannaford also writes: "Between 1870 and 1914, anti-Semitism was invented. The English, searching for their true origins as they engaged in a romantic mission to take their civilization throughout the world, contributed to the ideas of social evolution, hereditarism, and eugenics. In the immediate aftermath of the Franco-Prussian War the Lamarckian-Darwinist, science-based perception of politics and society emerging in France and Germany further derogated the morality of Greco-Roman political life" (p. 323).

[47] This is not to suggest that there was no room for other factors.

For example, Bruce G. Trigger, *A History of Archaeological Thought* (Cambridge: Cambridge University Press, 1989), sees the rise of Marxism as an indirect and inadvertent factor. The 1880s, he notes, were a time when the slums and social cleavages of the Industrial Revolution were creating restiveness in Europe. With their call to workers to show international solidarity, Trigger says, early labor unions caused some worried conservative critics to respond with "a growing emphasis on racial doctrines" (p. 150). These conservatives sought to curb the tendency of workers to identify with their counterparts in other countries by encouraging them to identify with their nation and with their co-citizens of all classes. "It was argued that French, Germans, and English were biologically different from one another and that their behavior was determined, not by economic and political factors, but by essentially immutable racial differences." By this means, he says, conservative intellectuals sought to steer the hostility of workers away from their wealthy fellow citizens and toward rival countries. See also Trigger, "Paradigms in Sudan Archaeology," *The International Journal of African Historical Studies* 27 (1994), p. 326.

Clements also suggests two other trends that, while they had nothing to do with racism, may have contributed to the desire to give more glory to God in the interpretation of the story of the invasion. These are: 1) "the 1870s were rife with a new current of proto-Zionism in Christian as well as Jewish circles, (and) the story of 701 was a suitable focal point for this" and 2) the "triumphalist ideas of divine intervention present in the narrative had a strong appeal to 19th-century religious thinking." (Personal communication.)

CHAPTER NINETEEN

[1] The biography of James Breasted, written by his son Charles, describes Sayce as an "almost legendary figure": "Professor Sayce, James's senior by 20 years, became during the 88 years of his distinguished life not only one of the most eminent Orientalists of his time, but a unique British institution in the Near East, every corner of which he

knew intimately." See Charles Breasted, *Pioneer to the Past: The Story of James Henry Breasted, Archaeologist* (New York: Charles Scribner's Sons, 1943), p. 67.

[2] *The Times*, Feb. 6, 1933.
The generous assessment is not isolated. Also lauding Sayce posthumously for his "very lovable character" is Battiscombe Gunn, "Archibald Henry Sayce," in *The Dictionary of National Biography, 1931-1940*, ed. by L.G. Wickham Legg (London: Oxford University Press, 1949), p. 788.

[3] Descriptions of Sayce's many friendships are scattered throughout his autobiography, *Reminiscences* (London: Macmillan, 1923).
I am relying on that autobiography for much of my description of his personal life; if my information in what follows is not otherwise credited, its source may be assumed to be *Reminiscences*.

[4] John A. Wilson, *Signs and Wonders upon Pharaoh: A History of American Egyptology* (Chicago and London: University of Chicago Press, 1964), p. 100.

[5] "Sayce, Archibald H(enry)," in *Micropaedia*, vol. VIII, *Encyclopaedia Britannica*.

[6] Desmond Bowen, *The Idea of the Victorian Church: A Study of the Church of England, 1833-1889* (Montreal: McGill University Press, 1968), pp. 185-186.

[7] His autobiography makes no mention of such religious work.

[8] C. Breasted, *Pioneer to the Past*, p. 67, and J. Wilson, *Signs and Wonders*, p. 99.

[9] S. Langdon, "Archibald Henry Sayce as Assyriologist," in *The Journal of the Royal Asiatic Society of Great Britain and Ireland*, 1933 (pp. 502-503).

[10] See *The Cambridge Illustrated History of Archaeology*, ed. by Paul G. Bahn (Cambridge: Cambridge University Press, 1996), p. 160.

[11] John David Wortham, *The Genesis of British Egyptology, 1549-1906* (Norman, OK: University of Oklahoma Press, 1971), p. 86.

[12] J. Wilson, *Signs and Wonders*, p. 101.

[13] Sayce, *Reminiscences*, p. 416.

[14] A.H. Sayce, *The Races of the Old Testament* (London: Religious Tract Society, 1891), p. 16.

[15] *Ibid.*, p. 146.

[16] *Ibid.*, pp. 16-17.

[17] *Ibid.*, p. 83.

[18] *Ibid.*, p. 51.

[19] *Ibid.*, p. 144.
Sayce's racial theory, then, calls for three different races to have inhabited Kush in Taharqa's time: "Negroes," "whites" of the royal court and ordinary "Nubians." Of Nubians, whom he also calls Kushites, Sayce says this: "Racially and linguistically they stand apart from the rest of mankind" (p. 145).

[20] The Rev. A.H. Sayce, *The Egypt of the Hebrews and Herodotus* (New York: Macmillan, 1895), p. 113.
The stela in question is the Zinjirli stone.

[21] A.H. Sayce, *Early Israel and the Surrounding Nations* (London: Service & Paton, 1899), p. 174.

[22] *Ibid.*, p. 175. See also *Egypt of the Hebrews*, pp. 113-114.

[23] Ronald Robinson and John Gallagher, with Alice Denny, *Africa and the Victorians: The Climax of Imperialism in the Dark Continent* (New York: St. Martins Press, 1961), p. 468.

[24] For a good account, see *ibid*. Of the initial control of Egypt by the British, Robinson & Gallagher conclude: "Imperialism in the wide sense of empire for empire's sake was not their motive. Their territorial claims were not made for the sake of African empire or commerce as such" (p. 462).

[25] Thomas Pakenham, *The Scramble for Africa: 1876-1912* (New York: Random House, 1991), p. 215.

[26] *Ibid.*, p. 25.

[27] As quoted by Philip Magnus, *Gladstone: A Biography* (London: John Murray, 1954), p. 294.

[28] That official is Sir Reginald Wingate, as cited in David Steele, "Lord Salisbury, the 'False Religion' of Islam, and the Reconquest of the Sudan," in *Sudan: The Reconquest Reappraised*, ed. by Edward M. Spiers (London and Portland, OR: Frank Cass, 1998), p. 21.
Wingate was a leading figure in the war and later the governor general of Sudan. Sayce, who travelled widely in Sudan and knew Wingate, accepts the six-million estimate. See *Reminiscences*, p. 308.
Another contemporary British source gives an even higher figure. Sydney A. Moseley, *With Kitchener in Cairo* (London: Cassell and Co., 1917), estimates seven million deaths out of a total Sudanese population of nine million (p. 226).
Winston S. Churchill, in Sudan as a soldier-journalist, estimates 300,000 dead, but that is for combatants only. See Churchill, *The River War: An Account of the Re-conquest of the Sudan* (London: Eyre & Spottiswoode, 1951 {1899}), p. 360.

[29] Pakenham, *Scramble for Africa*, pp. 263-264.

[30] *Ibid.*, p. 270.

[31] John Hatch, *The History of Britain in Africa; From the Fifteenth Century to the Present* (London: André Deutsch, 1969), p. 205.

[32] Sayce, *Reminiscences*, p. 308.

[33] One may deduce that from Adams, *Nubia*, p. 667. Adams, the historical anthropologist, says that because of only a modest amount of migratory flux, the Nubians of antiquity and the modern period appear to be "the same people." See Chapter 1, note 2.

[34] Steele, "Lord Salisbury," p. 24.

[35] *Ibid.*, p. 21.

[36] Brian Robson, *Fuzzy-Wuzzy, the Campaigns in the Eastern Sudan 1884-85* (Turnbridge Wells, UK: 1993), p. xv. See also p. 71.

[37] *Ibid.*, p. xv.

[38] Owen Chadwick, *The Spirit of the Oxford Movement: Tractarian Essays* (Cambridge: Cambridge University Press, 1990, pp. 247 ff.

[39] Bowen, *The Idea of the Victorian Church*, p. 354.

[40] Magnus, *Gladstone*, p. 227.

As it happens, Sayce's own early career offers a poignant example of such political intrusion. Long before his career as a professor of Assyriology, Sayce was a candidate for the prestigious appointment as the Regius professor of Hebrew; linguistically, he was well qualified, but Gladstone nonetheless rejected his young friend's candidacy. There was nothing personal about this: the problem was that Sayce at that time was sympathetic to a certain theological current within the Church of England (or Anglican church) to which the queen and the prime minister were strongly opposed. The chair of Hebrew at Oxford was an ecclesiastical posting, and the State was insistent upon doctrinal orthodoxy among those charged with educating the next generation. In his autobiography, Sayce expresses no bitterness over his rejection, and he appears to have learned his lesson well. One gathers from his autobiography that never again was he in conflict with the State, either on matters of religious dogma or on matters pertaining to foreign policy. The Bible project (see below) on which he collaborated with Gladstone, often called the foremost British statesman of the 19th century, was a huge personal honor for Sayce; it also represented the State's seal of approval on his intellectual acceptability.

Indeed, the ecclesiastical garb that Sayce so fondly wore on his African adventures may seem like a mere eccentricity, but—as we will see—it is also an apt metaphor for his intellectual fealty to those institutions that defined Britain's place in the world.

[41] *Ibid.*, p. 227.

[42] Oxford at the time had, as Sayce puts it in his autobiography, a tone that was "still highly theological." The university had been the spawning ground of what became known as the Oxford Movement, an attempt by some within the Church of England, itself Protestant, to revive certain Roman Catholic ideas and practices. Gladstone was among those stoutly opposed to the movement and he sought to reaffirm Anglican orthodoxy. In 1882, one of the movement's leaders, the Anglican theologian E.B. Pusey, died. Pusey had held the chair of Hebrew at Oxford. Gladstone's grounds for turning Sayce down as Pusey's successor in that job were that the young man, though qualified on linguistic grounds and a lifelong Anglican, had expressed inappropriate sympathy for certain Roman Catholic dogmas. In his autobiography, Sayce quotes a private letter from Gladstone to a university official who had nominated him for the chair: "I have great respect for Mr. Sayce's talents and learning, but under no circumstances could I give him an ecclesiastical appointment." (*Reminiscences*, p. 34)

The fact that Gladstone intervened in so ostensibly trivial a matter as a faculty appointment was not as unusual as it might appear. Sayce may never have known it, but Gladstone was under extraordinary orders from his own superior, Queen Victoria. In his biography of Gladstone, Sir Philip Magnus reveals that in 1874 (which would have been eight years before the Sayce incident) "the Queen sent Gladstone a hectoring letter on the subject of the appointment to ecclesiastical office of men with leanings toward Rome. She warned Gladstone to be on his guard . . ." (*Gladstone*, p. 227). Oxford's religious mission was of intense interest to Gladstone, who was also MP for Oxford. On his deathbed in 1898, he dictated this reply to a message of sympathy from university officials: "There is no expression of Christian sympathy that I value more than that of the ancient university of Oxford — the God-fearing and God-sustaining university of Oxford. I served her, perhaps mistakenly, but to the best of my ability" (*ibid.*, p. 437).

This kind of intervention by the highest level of government says something about Oxford's intellectual climate.

[43] See *Remiscences*, pp. 113-114.

Sayce was still in his 20s when he caught the attention of Gladstone, then in the first term as prime minister. They also shared an interest in religious matters: when Gladstone had himself been a student at Oxford, he had considered a career as an Anglican cleric.

[44] Exemplifying this politicization of ancient history was France's insistence that, as part of a quid pro quo for a concession on Egypt's debt, a French citizen always serve as the director of Egypt's important Department of Antiquities — even when Britain and nominally Turkey were running the government. The department was the regulatory authority for all excavations.

[45] The term "autocratic" is Sayce's. See *Reminiscences*, p. 286.

[46] Cromer used Sayce for the delicate task of seeing to it that France would bring back the easy-to-work-with Gaston Maspero, a celebrated excavator, from Paris for a second term as the Department of Antiquities' director. *Ibid.*, p. 306.

[47] *Ibid.*, p. 275.

[48] *Ibid.*, p. 230.

[49] *Ibid.*, p. 354.

[50] Such was Kitchener's trust in Sayce that he kept him apprised of heated, top-secret negotiations between himself, Cromer and Salisbury, who was then prime minister, for permission to conquer Sudan (*Reminiscences*, p. 309). In 1898, after winning that policy fight, Kitchener proceeded to crush the rebels, which helped pave the way for his later duties as a successor to Cromer as Egypt's ruler and eventually as Britain's field marshal early in World War I.

[51] Yacoub Pasha Artin, *England in the Sudan*, trans. from the French by George Robb (London: Macmillan, 1911), pp. 3-4.

[52] C. Breasted, *Pioneer to the Past*, p. 145.

[53] Sayce, *Reminiscences*, pp. 235-236.

[54] *Ibid.*, pp. 347-348.

[55] The archaeologist whom Sayce helped put in charge of the excavation was, incidentally, the same John Garstang who proposed the fascinating "hornet" theory described in Chapter 16.

⁵⁶ A. H. Sayce, Introductory Note to Artin, *England in the Sudan*, p. ix.

⁵⁷ *Ibid.*, p. ix.

⁵⁸ That Sayce errs in assigning a decisive role to the Battle of Eltekeh is beside the point.

⁵⁹ See The Rev. A.H. Sayce, "Introductory: The Ethiopian Capital," in *Meroë, the City of the Ethiopians: Being an Account of the First Season's Excavations of the Site, 1909-1910*, by John Garstang, A.H. Sayce and F. Ll. Griffith (Oxford: Clarendon Press, 1911). Here, Sayce says that the Assyrian stela that he had said depicted Taharqa as a captive could not have been of that pharaoh: ". . . as Taharqa was never a prisoner in Assyrian hands, and could never have been seen by the sculptor, it is clear that the representation is taken from one of the Negro soldiers of the Ethiopian king whom the artist assumed to be of the same race as his master" (pp. 3-4). The Kushite kings, he deduces, were therefore not Negro.

This is bizarre. The reason Sayce gives for denying that the Negro captive on the Assyrian stela could have looked like Taharqa (or, for that matter, like other members of his royal line) raises questions about the integrity of his research. As an avid reader of Assyrian texts, Sayce was well placed to know that the Assyrians had captured Taharqa's own son, the crown prince Ushanahuru, in the course of the invasion of Egypt that the stela commemorates. Indeed, the text on the stela itself describes Ushanahuru's capture and his deportation to Assyria *(ANET,* p. 293). That is why today most scholars lean toward an identification of the figure on the stela as Ushanahuru rather than Taharqa. My point is that, regardless of whether the sculpture is intended to represent the father or the son, the Assyrian sculptor would not have had to resort to a Kushite commoner as a model but could have used either the head of the royal family or his intended successor. Sayce should have known that. Given all this, his justification for changing his mind — that the sculptor got his races mixed up — is simply flabbergasting.

Sayce also gives a second puzzling reason for denying the Kushite dynasty's negritude. Archaeological findings at Meroë, he says without expanding, "prove definitely that the Ethiopians had no Negro blood in their veins" (Sayce, "Introductory," *Meroë: The City of the Ethiopians*, p. 4). He does not expand; despite the fact that the book in which he makes this observation is full of photographs and sketches of findings at Meroë, it contains no illustrations to back up Sayce's confident assertion. From Reminiscences, however, one gathers he may be referring to a structure at Meroë called the sun temple built in the sixth century BC; on it, he writes, are depictions of "conquerors" whose heads "were of the Hamitic type, with high foreheads, thin lips and Greek noses; the negroid dynasties had not yet possessed themselves of Meroe" (p. 355). It is widely assumed that racial contininuity characterized the Kushite/Meroitic royal family, so it is hard to know what Sayce is talking about.

⁶⁰ Sayce continues: "Perhaps this means that ethnological science has not advanced so rapidly as some of the other historical sciences; but it may be that the main facts had been already acquired once and for all" ("Preface to the Second Edition," in *Races of the Old Testament*, rev. ed, {London: Religious Tract Society, 1925}, p. *xi*).

⁶¹ A.H. Sayce, *Assyria: Its Princes, Priests, and People* (London: The Religious Tract Society [1926]). In his preface to this new edition, Sayce says he has made minor revi-

sions. One may therefore suppose that he might have made other changes had he so wished.

⁶² In *Reminiscences*, Sayce spends several pages describing Meroitic ruins. This would have been a logical place to speak again of the Kushites in the context of the Assyrian conflict, but he does not do so. Indeed, he seems to imply that most of Meroë's architectural marvels somehow predate the arrival of "the negroid dynasties" (p. 355), an opinion that flies in the face everything I have read elsewhere.

⁶³ Leclant, *In the Steps of the Pharaoh*, pp. 27, 26.

⁶⁴ Keating, *Nubian Rescue:* "The Napatans ruled [Egypt] with varying fortunes. They were able men, Taharqa in particular being an outstanding figure, and they might have restored Egypt to her former greatness had it not been for Assyria, now at her most aggressive and bent on subduing the ancient world" (p. 168).

CHAPTER TWENTY

¹ Psalm 132:13-14 (NEB). In the latter part of the quotation, the speaker is Yahweh. See also Psalm 76:2.

² Psalm 46.4 (NEB), 76:2 (NSRV).

³ Psalm 46.7,5 (NEB).

⁴ Psalm 47:8 (NEB).

⁵ See Psalm 48:1-2. See also Isaiah 2:2.

⁶ Clifford, *Cosmic Mountain*, p. 3, insists on this easternmost hill. So does Levenson, *Sinai and Zion*, who observes: "What is called 'Mount Zion' today is a hill to the southwest of the ancient Zion and across the Tyropoean Valley from it. The identification of this mountain with the Zion in the Hebrew Bible is very late, in fact Byzantine, and generally regarded today as inaccurate" (p. 92). Nahman Avigad, *Discovering Jerusalem* (Nashville: Thomas Nelson Publishers. 1980) traces the popular "misnaming" of the southwestern hill (also called the Western Hill) to a mistake made in the first century AD by the Jewish historian Flavius Josephus (pp. 26-27).
Several subsequent atlases and books on the city still opt, however, for the wrong hill.

⁷ *Yoma* 54b; also, *Tanhuma: Kedoshim* 10.
In the rabbinic texts Jerusalem becomes, as Levenson, *Sinai and Zion*, puts it, "the conduit through which messages pass from earth to heaven, no matter where, in a geographical sense, they originate" (p. 125). For full discussion, see Levenson's pp. 115-125.

⁸ Martin Buber, *On Zion: The History of an Idea*, trans. from the German by Stanley Godman (New York: Schocken Books, 1973), p. xxi. The earlier quotation is also from this page. This was originally published in 1952 as *Israel and Palestine: The History of an Idea*.

⁹ Buber as quoted by Nahum N. Glatzer in his foreword to Buber, *On Zion*, pp. *x-xiv*.

¹⁰ Other names for Shalem were Salim or Shulmanu. For background, see among others: Michael Avi-Yonah, "Jerusalem," *Encyclopaedia Judaica*, Vol. 9, p. 1376-1783;

David Biale, "Zionism," in *Encyclopedia of Religion*, vol. 15, pp. 570 ff; Avraham Holtz, *The Holy City: Jews on Jerusalem* (New York: W.W. Norton Co. Inc., 1971), and John J. Schmitt, "Pre-Israelite Jerusalem," in *Scripture in Context, op. cit.*, pp. 108 ff.

[11] The Hebrew Bible mythologizes the circumstances by which Yahweh made Jerusalem his city. It suggests this happened after David, conqueror of Jerusalem, brought the Ark of the Covenant into the city and kept it in a tent (2 Samuel 6). The Bible says that the Ark, a portable chest, contained the Ten Commandments, which it presents as tangible evidence of the Covenant that Yahweh had made on Mount Sinai. When Solomon succeeded his father David as king, he would have built a true dwelling place for Yahweh and the ark atop the hill, the Temple (2 Samuel 7); the city became the centerpiece of a vast empire. Even if one were to take the Bible at face value, however, one would have to conclude that not for a long time would Jerusalem really become Yahweh's city. For one thing, the Bible says that Solomon himself soon worshipped many other gods and built for them nearby places of worship, too, and that almost all other kings until the time of Hezekiah likewise did little to encourage the worship of Yahweh. For another, the Bible also says that until Hezekiah's reign, two-and-a-half centuries after the construction of Solomon's Temple, places of worship for Yahweh were scattered in many places around the kingdom; Mount Zion was not Yahwism's focal point. Historical research further weakens the idea that Zion was particularly holy so early: many scholars say that both the Covenant and Ten Commandments almost certainly date from the late seventh century BC if not later still (Chapter 3), which raises fundamental questions about the Ark of the Covenant's historicity. As well, the latest archaeological evidence suggests that David, if he lived at all, would have been the head of a modest chiefdom and that Jerusalem would have been a back-country hill town (Introduction), making it unlikely that even Jerusalemites would have seen Mount Zion as having wondrous power.

We need to bear in mind that the Bible's account of Yahweh's early days in Jerusalem is contained in the Deuteronomistic History, written roughly 400-500 years after David's reign in an attempt to glorify Judah's past.

[12] Clifford, *Cosmic Mountain*, pp. 7-8.

[13] For Mount Carmel and Mount Tabor, see Jeremiah 46:18. For Mount Carmel alone, see 1 Kings 18:19 ff.; for Mount Tabor alone, see Psalm 89:12 and Hosea 5:1. For Mount Gerizim, see Deuteronomy 27:12. In the southern kingdom, Mizpah (a few miles north of Jerusalem, near the border with Israel) is described in Judges 20-21 as a place of assembly and worship for all Hebrews; see also 1 Samuel 7:5 ff.

[14] Psalm 48:2 evokes a sense of Judahite pride in being part of a larger mountain tradition when it says, "Like the utmost heights of Zaphon is Mount Zion, the city of the Great King" (NIV). (See also the notation to NEB.) More physically imposing than Zion and located well to the north on what is now the Syrian coast, Mount Zaphon (present-day Mount Casius) was the home of the powerful Baal-Hadad, the Canaanite storm god (Clifford, *Cosmic Mountain*, pp. 4, 131 ff).

Mitchell Dahood, S.J., *Psalms I: 1-50: The Anchor Bible, Introduction, Translation and Notes* (Anchor Bible 16; Garden City, NY: Doubleday, 1966), aptly comments that the verse is in effect saying, "Mount Zion is to Yahwism what Mount Zaphon is to Canaanite religion; namely the dwelling of God and the most hallowed spot of the land" (pp. 289-290).

[15] Clements, *Isaiah and the Deliverance*, pp. 77-78.

See also the 2001 book by two archaeologists, Finkelstein & Silberman, *Bible Unearthed:* "David and Solomon's Jerusalem was only one of a number of religious centers within the land of Israel; it was surely not acknowledged as the spiritual center of the entire people of Israel initially" (p. 238).

[16] Judahites may have also remembered that a generation earlier, in the Syro-Ephraimite war of *c*. 734, Jerusalem had survived another siege, this one mounted by Israel (Chapter 2). The Deuteronomistic school, however, would have regarded that success more as a theological inconsistency than as a welcome precedent for the glory of 701: Judah's king at the time was Ahaz, whom the Deuteronomistic History describes as highly disloyal to Yahweh (2 Kings 16:2-4). Fittingly, it only gives a single and rather staid sentence to Jerusalem's ability to withstand Israel's siege (16:5).

[17] Thus in one of the Book of Isaiah's oracles composed well after 701 but made to appear as if it had preceded it, Yahweh confidently vows, "I will break the Assyrian in my land, and on my mountains trample him under foot" (Isaiah 14:25 {NRSV}).

Taken at face value, several passages in the Book of Isaiah do appear to be prophecies that Yahweh would shelter Jerusalem from Sennacherib. For the likelihood that these ostensible predictions are not authentic to the original Isaiah and are, rather, after-the-fact prophecies inserted after 701, please see Chapter 4.

[18] Clements, *Isaiah 1-39*, p. 162.

[19] Isaiah 17:12-14, 29:5-7.

[20] While that would clash with both Second Kings' and Second Chronicles' accounts of religious development under Hezekiah, it would be consistent with the recent interpretation of archaeological evidence by Nadav Na'aman, as discussed in Chapter 4.

[21] Tadmor, "Period of the First Temple," p. 145.

[22] Japhet, "From the King's Sanctuary to the Chosen City," p. 135.

This idea of an intimate link between Sennacherib's withdrawal and the doctrine of Zion's inviolability is so widely accepted that it would be pointless to list its adherents over the course of the last few centuries. These four serious studies of Jerusalem published in the 1990s attest to scholars' ongoing acceptance of this link: Armstrong, *Jerusalem*, p. 70; Thomas A. Idinopulos, *Jerusalem: A History of the Holiest City as Seen through the Struggles of Jews, Christians and Muslims*, rev. ed. (Chicago: Ivan R. Dee, 1994), p. 48; Philip J. King, "Jerusalem," *Anchor Bible Dictionary*, vol. 3, p. 764, and Mendenhall, "Jerusalem from 1000-63 BC," p. 59.

[23] Psalm 48:3-5 (NRSV)

[24] 2 Kings 19:34 (NRSV).

[25] 2 Samuel 7:16.

[26] Clements, *Isaiah and the Deliverance*, p. 93.

[27] 2 Kings 24:3-4. See also 2 Kings 21.

[28] This explanation for Jerusalem's ruination may date from the mid-sixth century BC, when the Deuteronomistic History was written; key parts of the Book of Deuteronomy, also written then, may have been backdated to Josiah's reign. This is the proposal recently put forward by Akenson, *Surpassing Wonder,* pp. 52, 62-63.

[29] Clements, *Isaiah and the Deliverance,* p. 100.

[30] Zechariah 12:1-13:1(NRSV). See Gonçalves, *L'expédition de Sennachérib,* p. 327. See also 14:3,12-14.

In Zechariah 14:12, note the strong plague imagery, an indication of how rooted had grown the belief that Yahweh can only intervene directly to save his city, and not via human intermediaries (Chapter 16).

[31] Revelation 21:2, 18-27 (NRSV).

[32] Those scholars are a minority who say that prior to the invasion there already existed a core belief about Jerusalem's immunity from harm. One of them is Gonçalves, *L'expédition de Sennachérib,* who says that the doctrine of inviolability preceded the invasion and evolved out of the prior tradition that Jerusalem was especially protected. For evidence, he cites Micah 3:11, which says that Jerusalem's immoral rulers and priests "lean upon the Lord and say, 'Surely the Lord is with us! No harm shall come upon us'" (NRSV). Gonçalves says the invasion's outcome confirmed the correctness of that belief (p. 326). I see the hope to which that passage refers as quite typical of many people's hope that somehow their deity will keep them from great harm ('God is an Englishman'). This is not the same thing as the doctrine of inviolability, which offers much more than hope. Also affirming a pre-invasion ability to resist attack is Childs, *Isaiah and the Assyrian Crisis,* pp. 61-68. The passages from the Book of Isaiah that Childs cites in support of his interpretation are, however, not clearly pre-701.

I strongly doubt that any serious confidence in Jerusalem's impregnability predated the invasion. Such a sense of security does not square with the profound gloom that Sennacherib's approach generated among the population. Indeed, each of the two most ardent Yahwists of the day saw Jerusalem as *certain* to perish: Isaiah predicted that Yahweh would use the Assyrian army to conquer Jerusalemites and "trample them down like mud" (Isaiah 10:6 {NRSV}), while the other great prophet of the day, Micah, was just as pessimistic, predicting that "Zion shall be plowed as a field; Jerusalem shall become a heap of ruins." (Micah 3:12 {NRSV}). As for the king, Hezekiah, so intense was his insecurity that he ordered ambitious engineering work, including new fortifications and extraordinary water-supply arrangements; he was also so desperate for outside human help that he sent a treasure-laden caravan to Egypt to seek it. As for the public, such was its despair over the city's chances of survival that, as we have seen, many people panicked and top military people deserted (Isaiah 22:3). See also note 11.

In other words, in saying that the events of 701 did not initiate the sense of Jerusalem's holiness but gave it a huge impetus I am being quite conservative, perhaps too conservative, but I'd rather err on the side of caution.

Of course, considering that without the rescue there would have been no more Jerusalem, no more Yahwists and therefore no doctrine of inviolability, this debate over the precise degree of influence of the events of 701 in the formulation of the Zion concept might be seen as an exercise in hair-splitting. It comes down to this: the Kushite-

NOTES TO PAGES 278-284

led rescue of Jerusalem is responsible for the Zion idea being alive today, and not perishing 27 centuries ago. No rescue, no concept.

33 Isaiah 2:2-4 (NRSV). See also Micah 4:1-3 and Isaiah 60.

34 This is *not* an argument in support of the Kushite-rescue theory. That harmony should exist between the cause and the effect is philosophically pleasing but is not proof of anything.

In this regard, note that Kush is prominent among the nations called to worship Yahweh at Zion: *e.g.*, Psalm 68:31, Isaiah 18:7.

35 In 720 and c. 716; see Chapter 6.

36 If the army's itinerary had always followed the Nile, it would be greatly in excess of 1,000 miles. A good possibility exists, however, that the force avoided the river's great loop downstream from Napata and took an overland short-cut. More than one commonly used route across the desert existed.

37 *ANET,* p. 293. I have very slightly modified the text for reasons of clarity.

38 *ANET,* p. 295. Again, I have made minor modifications for clarity.

39 James, "Egypt: The Twenty-fifth and Twenty-sixth Dynasties," p. 698.

40 Renan, *History of the People of Israel,* p. 80 n.

41 The original French publication of this book, *Histoire du Peuple d'Israel,* vol. 3 (Paris: Calmann Lévy) was the same year as the English version that I have cited, 1891, when Renan was 68. I should note that the author does not shout this keen observation — it is in a footnote. Elsewhere, the book advances the view that Sennacherib withdrew primarily because of an epidemic but also because of Taharqa (p. 92 of the English version, p. 109 of the French).

Indexes

Author Index

Biblical Citations Index

Subject Index

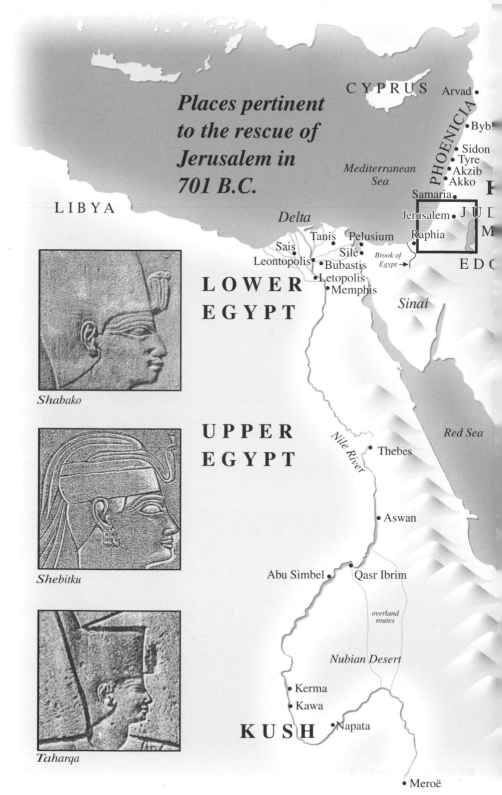

Places pertinent to the rescue of Jerusalem in 701 B.C.

CYPRUS

Arvad

PHOENICIA

Byb[
Sidon
Tyre
Akzib
Akko

Mediterranean
Sea

Samaria

LIBYA

Delta

Jerusalem

JU[

Tanis   Pelusium   Raphia

M

Sais   Silè   Brook of
Leontopolis Bubastis   Egypt →

ED(

Letopolis
Memphis

LOWER
EGYPT

Sinai

Shabako

UPPER
EGYPT

Red Sea

Nile River

Thebes

Aswan

Abu Simbel   Qasr Ibrim

Shebitku

overland
routes

Nubian Desert

Kerma
Kawa

KUSH   Napata

Taharqa

Meroë